A REVISED
SHAPLEY-AMES CATALOG
OF BRIGHT GALAXIES

The Las Campanas ridge in Chile during the last stages of construction of the dome for the du Pont 2.5-meter reflector. The du Pont instrument is at the north end of the long escarpment. The Swope 1-meter reflector is in the left foreground. Photo courtesy of R. J. Brucato (1976).

A Revised Shapley-Ames Catalog of Bright Galaxies

*Containing Data on Magnitudes, Types, and Redshifts
for Galaxies in the Original Harvard Survey,
Updated to Summer 1980. Also Contains
a Selection of Photographs Illustrating
the Luminosity Classification and
a List of Additional Galaxies
that Satisfy the Magnitude
Limit of the Original
Catalog.*

Allan Sandage *and* G. A. Tammann

CARNEGIE INSTITUTION OF WASHINGTON PUBLICATION 635

WASHINGTON, D.C. · 1981

I S B N: 0-87279-652-3

Library of Congress Catalog Card No. 80-68146

Composition, Printing, and Binding by Meriden-Stinehour, Inc.

ACKNOWLEDGMENTS

We are indebted to Miss B. Flach and Mrs. R. C. Kraan-Korteweg for their help in compiling part of the data. We also owe special thanks to Basil Katem for his large effort in determining revised coordinates by measurement of National Geographic–Palomar Sky Survey prints and Uppsala Schmidt plates for most of the listed galaxies, and to John Bedke for his skill in reproducing the photographs. We are especially grateful to R. J. Brucato for his important help in obtaining the most recent plates at Las Campanas.

We greatly appreciate the help of several observers for providing prepublication redshift data. These individuals are listed in the key to the redshift sources (References A at the rear of the volume); we owe special thanks to Drs. H. G. Corwin, J. R. Fisher and R. B. Tully, W. K. Huchtmeier, U. Mebold, V. C. Rubin, R. M. West, and H. van Woerden.

One of us (G.A.T.) thanks with pleasure the Swiss National Science Foundation for partial support.

Finally, it is a pleasure to thank Ray Bowers and Patricia Parratt of the Carnegie Institution editorial office for their meticulous work in transforming a tedious manuscript into a book, Freeman Keith for the book design, and Meriden-Stinehour, Inc. for their care in its production.

A.S.
G.A.T.

Contents

PART I

Description of the Catalog

SINCE THE TIME OF THE HERSCHELS, surveys of bright galaxies have provided the foundations upon which much of observational cosmology rests. A history of the major surveys extends from William and John Herschel in the first half of the 19th century, through William Parsons, the third Earl of Rosse, to Isaac Roberts, Dreyer (1888), Keeler (1900), Perrine (1904), Hardcastle (1914), Fath (1914), Pease (1917), Curtis (1918), Hubble (1922, 1926), and into modern times. The publication of the *New General Catalog* by Dreyer in 1888 and its two *Index Catalog* supplements in 1895 and 1908 marks the beginning of reference works that are still in regular use.

Photographic studies of the brighter Herschel galaxies using large telescopes began with Keeler's survey, employing the Lick 36-inch Crossley reflector, which culminated in the historic *Lick Observatory Publications 13*, 1918, by Curtis. Photographic surveys at Mount Wilson were begun by Ritchey in 1909 and by Pease when the long-focal-length 60-inch reflector (hereafter W60) was completed. In two remarkable summary articles by Pease (1917, 1920), a number of features of famous nearby galaxies were illustrated for the first time.

The Mount Wilson photographic survey was continued by Hubble in the early 1920's using the W60 and the newly completed Hooker 100-inch (W100) reflector, which had been put into routine operation in 1919. The completion of this early work led Hubble (1922, 1926) to the formulation of the system of galaxy morphology that is the foundation of the modern standard method of classification. Hubble's 1926 paper contains the classification of 400 of the brightest NGC galaxies taken from the Hardcastle (1914) listing, which until 1932 was the most homogeneous catalog in existence, based, as it was, on the Franklin-Adams plates taken in the early years of the century and covering the entire sky.

The Harvard survey of 1246 bright galaxies was published by Shapley and Ames in 1932. This catalog (hereafter called the *SA*) has a fair degree of homogeneity within its magnitude limit at $m_{pg} \simeq 13^m2$. Furthermore, the uniform way in which Shapley and Ames compiled the data from both hemispheres using new plate material, produced for the first time an approximation to a magnitude-limited sample. The *SA* became the basic listing of bright galaxies and has played a major role in studies of galaxies in the local region. It has only recently

been supplemented by the first and second editions of the *Reference Catalog of Bright Galaxies* (de Vaucouleurs and de Vaucouleurs, 1964, for *RC1*; de Vaucouleurs, de Vaucouleurs, and Corwin, 1977, for *RC2*).

Following Hubble's initial work, the Mount Wilson photographic survey was continued through the 1930's, principally by Hubble, Baade, and Humason, with a primary aim of obtaining large-scale plates of all galaxies listed in the *SA* north of $\delta = -15°$. The purpose was to classify the galaxies for morphological studies, a process which, as is now known, leads directly to the central problem of galaxy formation and evolution. The survey, stopped between 1940 and 1945 during World War II, resumed in 1946, and was transferred to Palomar when the Hale 5-meter telescope (P200) was put into operation in 1949.

Beginning in 1974, the project was extended to the south using plates taken at the Las Campanas Observatory, Chile, first with the Swope 1-meter reflector (C40), and after 1977 with the du Pont 2.5-meter reflector (C100). Results from the southern survey to 1979 are given elsewhere (Sandage and Brucato, 1979, 1981).

In parallel with Hubble's work to obtain large-scale plates of the bright *SA* galaxies, Humason at Mount Wilson and Mayall at Lick began a program in the 1930's to measure redshifts in the northern sector of the *SA*. By 1956, they had obtained redshifts for all *SA* galaxies brighter than $m_{pg} = 11^m7$ north of $\delta = -30°$, and for many fainter galaxies. The Humason-Mayall redshift catalog (Humason, Mayall, and Sandage, 1956) is 63% complete for all listed *SA* galaxies north of $\delta = -30°$.

Since 1956, a number of radio and optical observers have combined efforts to complete the redshift coverage for nearly the entire Shapley-Ames catalog in both hemispheres. Redshift values now exist for all but six *SA* galaxies; and many of the earlier optical values have been improved through 21-cm observations.

PURPOSE OF THE CATALOG

In the early 1950's, when the first stage of the Mount Wilson and Palomar photographic survey north of $\delta = -15°$ was nearly complete, a plan was set out to compile existing data on types, magnitudes, and redshifts, and to obtain new data where needed for all galaxies in the

Shapley-Ames catalog. From the beginning, it was our intention to restrict the revision of the original *SA* listings and to obtain comparable data for both hemispheres. To this end, we began observations for redshifts, morphological types, and photoelectric magnitudes at the Mount Stromlo and Siding Springs Observatories, Australia, in 1969 at the invitation of the director, O. J. Eggen.

The observations were made by Sandage for redshifts with the Mount Stromlo 1.9-meter reflector, for types with the Uppsala Schmidt, and for photoelectric magnitudes with the Siding Springs 1-meter reflector. Observations of the northern *SA* galaxies still lacking redshift values were begun at Palomar in 1970. The detailed data have been published in the archival literature (Sandage, 1975b, 1978). In the time since the 1969–1970 Australian expedition, galaxy types based on the Uppsala Schmidt plates have been upgraded, in many cases using large-scale reflector plates from the later Las Campanas survey already mentioned.

The present catalog is, then, a compilation of available data on redshifts, morphological types, and magnitudes for Shapley-Ames galaxies, using literature sources to summer 1980. The listed types and luminosity classes are new estimates made by Sandage in a consistent way over the short period 1977–1979. The types are based on plates from Mount Wilson (W60, W100), Palomar (P200, P48), Las Campanas (C40, C100), and in a few remaining cases on the Uppsala Schmidt (UpS) at Mount Stromlo. The types are on the modified Hubble system (de Vaucouleurs, 1959; Sandage, 1961, 1975a). The luminosity classes generally follow van den Bergh's (1960a, b, c) precepts, but are on an internally consistent system defined here by the present listings and illustrated with type examples in the reproductions in part V of this volume.

Redshifts are from the literature sources listed in part VII. The values have been combined and weighted as discussed on pages 10–11.

The magnitudes are on the B_T system of the Second Reference Catalog (*RC2*: de Vaucouleurs *et al.*, 1977), obtained by reducing all new data to this system in the manner described on pages 6–8.

As an aid in using the present catalog, we have binned the 1246 listed galaxies separately into the various morphological types in the tables in part III. We believe that some of these types, and hence this particular binning, will change as better plate material becomes available, but the listing is meant as an aid in planning various observing programs based on knowledge of types as it existed in 1979.

COMPLETENESS OF THE CATALOG

It is known that the *SA* is not complete to its stated magnitude limit of $m_{pg} = 13\overset{m}{.}2$ but becomes progressively more incomplete as this magnitude level is approached. A study of the incompleteness (Sandage, Tammann, and Yahil, 1979) suggests that the fraction $f(m)$ of a complete sample in fact contained in the *SA* is well represented by

$$f(m) = [e^{(m-12.72)/0.19} + 1]^{-1},$$

where m is the magnitude in the B_T system.

In this representation, the progressive incompleteness of the *SA* is a rapid function of m, as shown in figure 6 of the above-stated reference, where the equation is compared with counts of E and S0 galaxies contained in fainter catalogs. Note that at $m = 12^m$, $f(m) = 1$, while at $m \simeq 12\overset{m}{.}7$, $f(m)$ is only 0.5.

As an aid toward the eventual revision of the *SA* to a more complete magnitude-limited catalog, we list in Appendix A those galaxies that should be included to a limit of $B_T \simeq 13\overset{m}{.}2$, obtained by converting the magnitudes in the Nilson and the Zwicky catalogs to the B_T system. In Appendix B, we list particular dwarf galaxies (many of which are well known) that should also be included. These lists are of course incomplete, if only because they are predominantly for the northern hemisphere. It should also be cautioned that the types and magnitudes of these candidate galaxies are more uncertain than those in the main table.

DETAILS OF THE COLUMN ENTRIES

The main catalog (part II of this volume) is composed of 21 columns containing the following data:

Column 1: List of objects

All objects that are galaxies in the original Shapley-Ames Catalog are listed. They are shown in order of Right Ascension (1950). Since the best available positions are used, the sequence has occasionally been changed from the original *SA*.

Three *SA* objects have been omitted because they are not galaxies: NGC 643 is a cluster in SMC, NGC 2149 is a galactic, diffuse nebula, and NGC 6026 is a planetary nebula.

The identification of a few galaxies in the present catalog deserves comment.

NGC 1042: The Shapley-Ames galaxy NGC 1048 is a very faint spiral that clearly does not belong in the catalog. There is, however, a nearby bright spiral, NGC

1042, which should be included. We therefore assume that NGC 1048 in the original *SA* should read NGC 1042.

NGC 2646: It has been proposed (Seyfert, 1937; Hubble, private notes; *RC1*; *RC2*) that the Shapley-Ames galaxy NGC 2646 ($B_T = 12^m95$) should be replaced by the Sa spiral IC 520 ($m_c = 12^m68$). Although the latter galaxy is apparently somewhat brighter, actually both galaxies should have been included. We retain NGC 2646, whose position is correctly given in the original *SA*, and we list IC 520 in Appendix A among the known galaxies that should have been included by Shapley and Ames.

NGC 4183: The *SA* lists NGC 4160, but Seyfert's (1937) suspicion that this object is a star has been confirmed by de Vaucouleurs and de Vaucouleurs (*RC1*). Although the positions leave some discrepancy, the spiral galaxy referred to by Shapley and Ames can only be NGC 4183.

NGC 4342: The nomenclature of NGC 4342 has created considerable confusion in the past (Herzog, 1967). In spite of this, it is possible to relate all relevant observations (position, type, magnitude, velocity) unambiguously to this galaxy. To avoid future confusion, Herzog has proposed that the galaxy be exclusively referred to by its second designation, IC 3256. This has been followed by de Vaucouleurs *et al.* (*RC2*), but other recent authors still use the NGC designation (e.g., Nilson, 1973). For historical reasons we retain the designation NGC 4342 here.

NGC 4889: The Shapley-Ames galaxy listed as NGC 4872 is most likely NGC 4889 (Stebbins and Whitford, 1952), which is the brightest member of the Coma cluster.

IC 5179 = IC 5181: The Shapley-Ames galaxy IC 5186 is actually the galaxy IC 5179, which carries also the designation IC 5181 (*RC2*, p. 337; Corwin, 1977).

New 2: This galaxy is NGC 4517. For historical reasons, we have maintained the designation New 2 of Shapley and Ames.

Two galaxies are designated HA85 (= Harvard Annals, Vol. 85) in the *SA*. To avoid confusion, they are listed here as HA85-1 (= A 0509-14) and HA85-2 (= A 1852-45).

The present catalog contains 1246 entries.

Column 2: Alternative designations for the Shapley-Ames galaxies

These may prove useful for identification purposes, but completeness was not attempted. For the identification of Markarian objects ("Mark"), the Markarian lists

I–X were consulted. We are greatly indebted to Dr. Mira P. Véron for a complete list of certain and probable radio sources (the latter are marked "?"), which are identified with Shapley-Ames galaxies on the basis of the *Catalog of Extragalactic Radio Source Identification* (Véron and Véron, 1974; updated version, 1978). Two radio source identifications (with NGC 3689 and NGC 5444) given in the *RC2* have not been confirmed.

Columns 3 and 4

The 1950 positions of the galaxies as given by Sandage (1978) or, where not given, from de Vaucouleurs *et al.* (*RC2*). For 46 southern galaxies, accurate positions were taken from Holmberg *et al.* (1974, 1975, 1977, 1978a, 1978b, 1979).

The decimals shown correspond to the accuracy with which the positions are known.

Columns 5 and 6

The Galactic Longitude and Galactic Latitude (1950) as given by de Vaucouleurs *et al.* (*RC2*).

Columns 7 and 8

The Supergalactic Longitude and Supergalactic Latitude (1950) as given by de Vaucouleurs *et al.* (*RC2*).

Column 9: The Hubble type and, where applicable, the luminosity class

The classification was made by Sandage independently of previous determinations, but following the precepts set out elsewhere (Sandage, 1961, 1975a). The galaxies are classified in the sequence:

$$E — S0 \Big\langle \begin{array}{l} \text{Sa Sb Sc Sd Sm Im} \\ \text{SBa SBb SBc SBd SBm} \end{array}$$

with intermediate classes (S0/a, etc.) and a new class, "Amorphous," which replaces Irr (Sandage and Brucato, 1979). A few galaxies, mainly spirals, defy a definite classification. At this writing, some of the galaxies have inadequate plate material and may eventually be found to be normal or to have only minor peculiarities. As there are less than 20 such cases, at least 98 percent of the catalog galaxies can be fitted into the revised Hubble system.

Descriptive terms, such as "pec" (= peculiar), "disrupted," "tidal," "ring," "jet," and "edge on," have been added in several cases.

Barred spirals are designated as SB, intermediate types as S/SB.

The presence of an *inner* ring structure is indicated by (r) following the spiral subclass [e.g., SBab(r)]. Those spirals where the arms spring from the ends of the bar or are traced into the center are indicated by (s). Intermediate cases are designated with (rs). Where no information is given on the presence or absence of an inner ring, no decision could be made. *Outer* rings surrounding the galaxy are indicated by R preceding the type (e.g., RSa).

The E *and* S0 galaxies were classified according to their flattening, which, following Hubble, is defined as $10(a-b)/a$. The subdivision of S0 galaxies into S0₁, S0₂, S0₃ according to the absence or the presence of dust is explained in Sandage (1961). Note that the subdivisions SB0₁, SB0₂, and SB0₃ in barred spirals refer to the *character of the bar* and not to the presence of dust, as explained in Sandage (1961).

The spiral and very-late-type galaxies are classified into luminosity classes as originally proposed by van den Bergh (1960a, b, c). The luminosity class of a spiral or Im galaxy is estimated from purely morphological features: the presence of spiral arms, surface brightness, and the degree of order (i.e., the coherence of the pattern and the arm thinness). The earliest class is called "I," the latest class is "V" (not represented in the present catalog, but illustrated in the reproductions). Intermediate classes are given, either as half-class steps (e.g., III–IV) or in decimals (e.g., I.8), as explained by Dressler and Sandage (1978). Although the same symbols I–V are adopted as used by van den Bergh, the present classes cannot be assumed to correspond necessarily to his system. In particular, the calibration in absolute magnitude may not be the same. If a calibration of the present luminosity classes in absolute magnitude is attempted from the listed data, it should be remembered that the present catalog represents a magnitude-limited sample. The bias as a function of redshift in such a sample is of course severe (Sandage, Tammann, and Yahil, 1979) and must be accounted for (Tammann, Yahil, and Sandage, 1979).

The reliability of the classification depends on the angular size of the galaxy, the inclination in the case of spiral and Im galaxies, the quality of the available plate material, and strongly on the scale of the plate. A number of large-scale plates were used here for the first time; hence our classes may differ from those assigned by van den Bergh (1960c).

Our classification is rather conservative in the sense that the given types should be in error by not more than

a subtype, and the luminosity classes in the mean by not more than half a luminosity class. The errors may be somewhat larger in those cases where small-scale plates had to be used or when the sky survey prints were the only source. Larger than average errors are indicated by ":" or "?" following the classification in cases where the galaxy may intrinsically defy a simple classification. In cases where the plate material is clearly insufficient, the types are given in parentheses ( ) or brackets [ ].

Many galaxies were classified independently on plates from different telescopes. A comparison of the types shows that the use of plate material from different telescopes has not introduced systematic errors. The only exceptions are the prints of the Palomar Sky Survey, designated 48 Pr. The classifications from this source could be affected by some systematic errors, especially for galaxies of small angular size. Lower weight should be given to the corresponding types.

The galaxies of the present catalog are separately binned according to type in part III of this volume.

Column 10: The source of the galaxy type

The following codes have been used:

Code	Source	Number of Galaxies
P200	Palomar 200″, glass plate	304
C100	Las Campanas 100″, glass plate	491
W100	Mount Wilson 100″, glass plate	226
W60	Mount Wilson 60″, glass plate	160
P48	Palomar 48″—Schmidt, glass plate	6
48 Pr	Palomar Sky Survey, paper print	37
C40 D	Las Campanas 40″, glass plate	12
C40 IT	Las Campanas 40″, image tube	7
UpS	Uppsala Schmidt, glass plate	0
W10	Mount Wilson 10″, glass plate	2
CTIO 4m	Cerro Tololo 4-meter	1
		Total: 1246

Column 11: List of objects

A repetition of Column 1.

Column 12: The apparent blue magnitude of the galaxy

The magnitudes are given in the B_T system of de Vaucouleurs *et al.* (*RC2*). The magnitudes come from the sources listed below and in Table 1:

(i) The *RC2*.

(ii) Many new source lists have become available that supersede the *RC2*. Examples are Sandage, 1975b; de Vaucouleurs, 1977; de Vaucouleurs and Corwin,

1977; de Vaucouleurs, Corwin, and Bollinger, 1977; de Vaucouleurs and Bollinger, 1977a, 1977b, 1978.

(iii) V_{26} and $(b-V)_{0.5}$ values for E, S0, and a few early-type spiral galaxies, determined photoelectrically by Sandage and Visvanathan (1978), were transformed into the B_T system. From galaxies with known $(b-V)_{0.5}$ and $(B-V)_T$, the relation

$$(B-V)_T = 1.31\,(b-V)_{0.5} + 0^m21$$

was established. The resulting B_{26} magnitudes were compared with de Vaucouleurs' B_T for 291 galaxies in common. The magnitude difference does not depend on galaxy color $(B-V)$, diameter (D_o), or flattening (R_{25}). There is, however, a type-dependent zero-point difference:

$(B_{26}-B_T) = -0^m12$ for E's, and

$(B_{26}-B_T) = -0^m03$ for S0's and early-type spirals.

Therefore the B_{26} magnitudes were corrected by -0^m12, -0^m07, -0^m02, and $+0^m03$ for E, E/S0, S0/E, and S0 galaxies, respectively. For the few spiral galaxies with B_{26}, a correction of $+0.03$ was adopted. The agreement between the corrected B_{26} and B_T magnitudes is very satisfactory, since the mean scatter is

$\sigma(\Delta B) = 0^m19$ for E and E/S0, and

$\sigma(\Delta B) = 0^m16$ for S0 and S0/E.

For galaxies where the corrected B_{26} and B_T magnitudes are available, a straight mean was adopted as the best value.

(iv) Multiaperture UBV measurements of southern galaxies (mainly spirals) were kindly made available by G. Wegner (1979) before publication. We have followed the precepts of the first approximation, as given in the *RC2* (e.g., equation 17a) to derive the logarithmic aperture-diameter ratio ξ, which then leads from de Vaucouleurs (1977, table 1) to B_T magnitudes. These magnitudes were not originally observed with an aim to derive total magnitudes; the measurements were made with relatively small diaphragms. Therefore, a second approximation to obtain B_T is probably not justified. A comparison of these B_T values with those of de Vaucouleurs ($n = 58$) and those derived from Sandage and Visvanathan ($n = 50$) gives a standard deviation of $\sigma = 0^m31$ and 0^m27, respectively. This suggests the standard deviation of a B_T magnitude derived from Wegner's observations to be $\sigma \approx 0^m25$. The error is smaller for galaxies observed with larger apertures ($\xi \geq -0.2$), i.e. $\sigma \lesssim 0.2$, and somewhat larger for cases where $-0.2 > \xi > -0.5$. (No smaller aperture measurements were considered.) Weight 1 was assigned to cases where $\xi \geq -0.2$ and weight 0.5 for smaller values of ξ. The Harvard magnitudes reduced to the B_T system (as given in *RC2*, see item 6) have standard deviations of $\sim 0^m2$ (de Vau-

couleurs and Bollinger, 1977a); they were also assigned weight 1. B_T values from de Vaucouleurs and his collaborators and from Sandage and Visvanathan were assigned weight 2. With these precepts, a total of 113 magnitudes from Wegner have been incorporated into the catalog.

(v) Multiapertive UBV measurements for 39 galaxies from Bucknell and Peach (1976) and Godwin *et al.* (1977) have been reduced to B_T magnitudes the same way as the observations by Wegner (see source iv, above). On the average, they are fainter by $0^m07 \pm 0^m05$ than the weighted mean magnitudes from sources i–iv; this difference was judged to be insignificant and was neglected. The random difference of the magnitudes from source v and the mean from sources i–iv is $\sigma = 0^m29$. If the mean error of the latter is $\sigma \approx 0^m15$ to 0^m20, the magnitudes from source v have mean errors of $\sigma = 0^m2$ to 0^m25. We have assigned errors between 0^m2 and 0^m3 to the magnitudes from source v according to the number of observations, the diaphragm size, and the consistency of the individual measurements. Final mag-

TABLE 1. SOURCES OF MAGNITUDES

Code*	Source	Number of Galaxies
	de Vaucouleurs and collaborators plus Sandage (1975).	552
1)	mean from de Vaucouleurs and collaborators and from Sandage and Visvanathan (1978)	245
2)	Sandage and Visvanathan (1978)	55
3)	weighted mean from de Vaucouleurs and collaborators and from Wegner (1977)	27
4)	weighted mean from Sandage and Visvanathan (1978) and from Wegner (1977)	27
5)	weighted mean from Wegner (1977) and corrected Harvard magnitude (*RC2*)	59
8)	weighted mean from de Vaucouleurs and collaborators and from Bucknell and Peach (1976) or Godwin *et al.* (1977)†	18
( )	Harvard magnitude reduced into the B_T system (*RC2*)	256
[ ]	uncorrected Harvard magnitude as given in the original Shapley-Ames catalog	7

* Refers to superscript entries in column 12 of main tabulation in Part II.

† There are also magnitudes available from Bucknell and Peach (1976) or Godwin *et al.* (1977) for an additional 21 galaxies with superscript 1)–5).

nitudes were computed using the corresponding weights and the weights of the magnitudes from sources i (from *RC2*), ii, iii, and iv.

(vi) For a number of galaxies there are still no magnitudes determined from detailed surface photometry or by photoelectric methods. For these galaxies the magnitudes from the original Shapley-Ames catalog were used, after reduction to the B_T system. The reduced magnitudes were taken from the *RC2*, column 15, upper line (see de Vaucouleurs and Bollinger, 1977a).

(vii) For a few galaxies the original Shapley-Ames magnitudes could not be transformed into the B_T system. In these cases the *uncorrected*, original magnitudes have been used. The uncertainty of these magnitudes is high ($\sim 0^m4$).

No K-correction due to redshift has been applied.

Column 13: Galactic absorption calculated from Sandage (1973)

$$A^o = 0^m132 \, (\text{cosec} \, b - 1) \, (\text{for} \, |b| < 50°)$$
$$A^o = 0^m \, (\text{for} \, |b| \geq 50°).$$

It should be remembered that the cosec law represents an idealized case. The true galactic absorption is very patchy and undoubtedly depends on galactic longitude. Since the control of the absorption dependence on position is judged to be insufficient for $|b| \lesssim 30°$, no attempt has been made to apply absorption corrections beyond the cosec law. For some individual galaxies, particularly at lower latitudes, this could well introduce errors of ~ 0.3 magnitude in the absorption correction. The evidence for essentially absorption-free polar caps is strong, however (Sandage, 1973, 1975a; Colomb, Poppel, and Heiles, 1977; Burstein and Heiles, 1978), and use of the adopted absorptions for $|b| \gtrsim 30°$ should give negligible systematic errors.

Column 14: Total internal absorption

The internal absorption in E, S0, S0/a, and the earliest Sa galaxies was assumed to be zero.

For later-type galaxies the internal absorption was calculated following the principles of Holmberg (1958), who showed that the internal absorption is proportional to cosec i (i = inclination). Approximating cosec i by a/b (where a and b are the major and minor axes of the galaxy), Holmberg expressed the total internal absorption A^i as

$$A^i = \alpha \times a/b.$$

He determined the values of α and the maximum values of A^i for edge-on galaxies of different spiral types. However, there are now indications that his maximum values are too large (see Sandage and Tammann, 1976). Therefore, the maximum values have been tentatively reduced here to the upper limits given below. We have adopted interpolated values so as to obtain a smooth transition between the absorption values from the cosec law at small inclinations and the maximum absorption at high inclination ($a/b \geq 4.7$). Our empirical absorption law can be well represented up to A^i_{max} by

$$A^i = \alpha + \beta \log a/b.$$

This relation has the same form as the one derived by Heidmann *et al.* (1972); but these workers could not determine the value of α (the absorption correction of a face-on spiral), and they found, surprisingly, that β is constant for galaxies of type Sa to Im. Instead, we have adopted the numerical values of α for different types of galaxies as given by Holmberg (1958). The α-value for Im galaxies was chosen to give a mean internal absorption correction of $\sim 0^m3$, as suggested by Holmberg (1964).

For the values of $\log a/b$, we have used the values $\log R_{25}$ as given in the *RC2* (column 11). Our adopted values of α, β, and A^i_{max} are:

Galaxy Type	α	β	A^i_{max}
Sa, Sab, Sb	0^m43	1^m34	1^m33
Sbc, Sc, Scd, Sd	0^m28	0^m88	0^m87
Sdm, Sm, Im	$0^m14.$	0^m44	0^m43

A special problem is posed by the Sa galaxies. Some of them appear to be free of dust, whereas others clearly contain considerable amounts of dust. This makes questionable whether the same internal absorption correction can apply to all Sa galaxies and suggests that Holmberg's high internal absorption corrections apply only to the subsample of Sa galaxies with much dust. For this reason only Sa galaxies with clearly visible dust have been corrected according to the above precepts; for Sa galaxies without any traceable dust, zero internal absorption was adopted, and for the intermediate Sa galaxies only half the correction was applied. In the two latter cases the value of A^i is marked with an asterisk (*).

The uncertainties of the internal absorption corrections are still large. They may well contain systematic errors as large as $\sim 0^m5$ for highly inclined galaxies, and there may be systematic differences between galaxies of different type due to errors in α and β. In addition, nothing is known about the scatter of individual galaxies about the mean relation. However, we believe that, in general, the internal-absorption-corrected magnitudes are closer to the true luminosity than are the uncorrected magnitudes, because it is clear that some correction is necessary. The mean value of A^i is $\sim 0^m5$ for spirals and Im galaxies taken as a whole. Clearly then, the mean error of A^i is less than $\sim 0^m3$.

There are several galaxies, including all those of class Amorphous, for which no correction for internal absorption could be applied.

Column 15: The apparent blue magnitude in the B_T system corrected for galactic and internal absorption

The magnitudes are calculated from the values given in columns 12, 13, and 14.

The magnitudes are shown in brackets [ ] for those galaxies for which no internal absorption correction could be applied.

Column 16: The absolute blue magnitude in the B_T system corrected for galactic and intrinsic absorption

The absolute magnitudes are calculated from the corrected apparent magnitudes (column 15) and the corrected velocities v_0 (column 20), using an adopted Hubble constant of $H_0 = 50$ km s^{-1} Mpc^{-1} (Sandage and Tammann, 1976).

The procedure to derive distances to individual galaxies (and hence absolute magnitudes) from the redshift (corrected to the centroid of the Local Group) using a fixed value of H_0 is justified by the facts that (1) the *random* radial velocities are typically $\lesssim 50$ km s^{-1} (Sandage and Tammann, 1975; Fisher and Tully, 1975; Tammann *et al.*, 1980), and (2) H (local) $\simeq H_0$ (global) (Sandage, Tammann, and Hardy, 1972; Tammann, Yahil, and Sandage, 1981). Even for a field galaxy like NGC 3109 with an exceptionally small radial velocity of $v_0 = 129$ km s^{-1}, the error in the distance introduced by the random component of the radial velocity is $\lesssim 40$ percent, corresponding to an error of only $\lesssim 0^m8$ in M. For galaxies with $v_0 > 500$ km s^{-1}, a random motion of 50 km s^{-1} will cause an error in M of only $< 0^m2$.

The only exceptions where v_0 is not a reliable distance indicator are members of galaxian aggregates in which the velocity dispersion is of the same order as the expansion velocity. The two most noteworthy aggregates of this kind are the Local Group and the Virgo Cluster. That they are exceptional in this respect is shown by the fact that the only galaxies with negative v_0 so far known

are members of these two aggregates. Hence, for galaxies in the Local Group and in the core of the Virgo Cluster (central 6° radius), and for a few additional groups, we have adopted mean distances for the calculation of absolute magnitudes. Table 2 lists those clusters and groups treated in this manner; the member galaxies are identified in the main catalog by capital letters following the M value in column 16.

A special problem is posed by the South Polar (or Sculptor) group. A set of uniform plates taken of the late-type candidate members with the Las Campanas 2.5-meter du Pont telescope shows pronounced differences in resolution and hence in distance: NGC 300 is in the foreground, NGC 7793 and probably NGC 253 lie in the background, while NGC 55 and NGC 247 are between. Preliminary distances of these galaxies are listed in Table 2. They are based on the brightness of the brightest blue and M supergiants in these galaxies (Sandage, 1981). The galaxies NGC 24 and NGC 45, which lie in the field of the South Polar Group and at one time were considered to be members, are definitely much more distant and lie, in agreement with their redshift, at a distance of about 10 Mpc.

The greatest uncertainty in the group and cluster assignments in the main catalog is for galaxies of the Virgo Cluster region (VR) between 6° and 10° away from the cluster center. Some of the galaxies in that region may be foreground or background objects. However, in view of the smaller velocity dispersion [$\sigma(v) = 445$ km s^{-1}] of the external region compared with the central cluster core where $\sigma(v) = 690$ km s^{-1}, and considering that the *mean velocities* of the central core and the outer region are the same to within the errors, most galaxies of the outer region must lie at the same mean distance as the cluster proper.

The distance moduli are given in the preceding table for the two cases where the Hyades modulus is 3.03 and 3.23. The latter value is to be preferred (see van Altena, 1974; Hanson, 1980).

The mean errors of the listed absolute magnitudes for all field galaxies in the catalog are compounded by the mean errors of the apparent magnitudes ($\sim 0^m2$), of the galactic absorption corrections ($\sim 0^m15$), of the intrinsic absorption corrections ($\sim 0^m25$), and of the corrected velocities (~ 50 km s^{-1}, corresponding to $< 0^m1$), and by the random deviations from an ideal Hubble flow ($< 0^m1$). Hence, the compounded mean error in absolute magnitude is $\lesssim 0^m4$.

TABLE 2. CLUSTERS AND GROUPS LACKING A
RELIABLE DISTANCE FROM v_o

Group or Cluster	Designation	$\langle v_o \rangle$	Number of SA Galaxies	$(m-M)°$*	$(m-M)°$†	Source‡
Local Group	L		10			
M31		...				
NGC 147		...				
NGC 185		...		24.12	24.32	1
NGC 205		...				
NGC 221		...				
LMC		...		18.59	18.79	1
SMC		...		19.27	19.47	1
M33		...		24.56	24.76	2
NGC 6822		...		23.95	24.15	2
IC 5152		...			(26.0)	
South Polar Group	S		5			
NGC 300		...		26.7	26.9	3,4,9
NGC 55		...		27.3	27.5	4
NGC 247		...				
NGC 7793		...		27.9	28.1	4
NGC 253		...				
M81/NGC 2403 Group	N	240 ± 22	7	27.56	27.76	5,6
NGC 5128 Group	C	255 ± 25	6	29.0	29.2	7
M101 Group	M	368 ± 23	4	29.2	29.4	8,6,7
Virgo Cluster						
(a) within 6°	V	1026 ± 75	85	31.5	31.7	6
(b) between 6° and 10° from center	VR	1147 ± 93	23			
Fornax Cluster	F	1486 ± 76	19		32.4	from $\langle v_o \rangle$

* $(m-M)°$ corresponding to $(m-M)$ Hyades $= 3.03$.

† $(m-M)°$ corresponding to $(m-M)$ Hyades $= 3.23$.

‡ Sources: 1. Sandage and Tammann, 1971; 2. Sandage and Tammann, 1974a; 3. Graham, 1979; 4. Sandage, 1981; 5. Tammann and Sandage, 1968; 6. Sandage and Tammann, 1976; 7. Tammann, 1977; 8. Sandage and Tammann, 1974b; 9. Melnick, 1978.

Column 17: The weighted mean observed velocity from all available determinations

Optical and 21-cm observations have been used. Only independent determinations were considered: some authors have published the same observations more than one time (occasionally with minor corrections). In these cases we attempted to exclude all values except the latest.

The general agreement between optical and 21-cm redshifts and the absence of any significant systematic difference is now well established (Roberts, 1972; Rubin *et al.*, 1976; de Vaucouleurs *et al.*, *RC2*; Lewis, 1977; Sandage, 1978). The errors in redshifts quoted in the original literature as determined from 21-cm observations are quite consistent with independent 21-cm determinations. Hence, in most cases the errors can be adopted as given in the original source. However, the errors quoted by most optical observers are *internal* errors. (An exception appears to be Humason's estimated errors of the Mount Wilson velocities in Humason *et al.*, 1956.) For the more extensive lists of optical redshifts having sufficient overlap with independent observations (especially 21-cm data), we determined the true external mean errors. Typically these were found to be about twice the quoted errors (see Sandage, 1978). A similar conclusion was reached by de Vaucouleurs *et al.* (*RC2*, table 13), although the mean errors they adopted for different observers are, in some cases, still too small.

For small sets of redshift data where the overlap with independent determinations is insufficient, the true external error was estimated mainly from the spectroscopic dispersion used. The weighted mean velocities were calculated using the adopted mean *external* errors. Clearly deviating values were excluded.

No zero point corrections were applied to the velocities of any source considered. Such zero point corrections may indeed by necessary for some sources. For instance, Roberts (1972) has proposed that optically determined redshifts with $\sim 1200 < v < 2400$ km s^{-1} are systematically too large by ~ 100 km s^{-1} owing to blends of the galaxian and night sky H and K lines, whereas Lewis (1975) has found this effect only in the Lick velocities from Humason *et al.* (1956). Different zero point corrections have also been applied by de Vaucouleurs *et al.* (*RC2*, table 13). In our opinion, this complex problem is not yet settled. Even if one accepts certain zero point corrections, they would be derived accurately only for spiral and late-type galaxies where the precise 21-cm velocities exist. The present 21-cm data for E and S0 galaxies are not sufficient to define a mean correction for these types. In view of this situation and to avoid a different treatment of galaxies of different type, we have neglected any possible correction.

We have used 430 literature sources or private communications for the velocities. These references contain 3437 velocity determinations for galaxies in the present catalog.

More than five independent redshift determinations are available for 134 galaxies of the catalog; from two to five determinations exist for 713 galaxies; and the velocity of 394 galaxies rests on only one determination. No redshift data are known for one galaxy (NGC 3285).

The fact that velocity data are available for ~ 99 percent of the catalog galaxies reflects the increasing number of redshift determinations in the years since the end of the Humason-Mayall program in 1956.

Several observers provided prepublication redshift data, as acknowledged at the front of the volume and listed in References A.

Column 18: The mean error of the observed velocities

The errors are compounded from the assigned errors of the individual velocity determinations, based generally on an estimate of the *external* errors of the various observers (e.g., Sandage, 1978, table XII). The mean errors of the catalog are distributed as:

ε, km s^{-1}	n	ε, km s^{-1}	n
<10	239	100–149	80
10–24	251	150–199	24
25–49	293	200–249	17
50–99	338	250–300	3

The median error of the velocities is 40 km s^{-1}.

Column 19: The velocity corrections Δv to be applied to the observed velocity to obtain the velocity relative to the centroid of the Local Group

The values are calculated from solution number 2 of Yahil, Tammann, and Sandage (1977):

$$\Delta v = -79 \cos l \cos b + 296 \sin l \cos b - 36 \sin b.$$

The listed values Δv differ from this formula by up to ± 3 km s^{-1} because they were computed with a formula in which the coefficients were not rounded off.

Column 20: The corrected recession velocity $v_0 = v + \Delta v$ relative to the centroid of the Local Group

The true errors are generally the same as those of the uncorrected velocities, except that in some directions the value of Δv depends strongly on the exact form of the adopted correction formula. In these cases, the remaining uncertainty due to uncertainties in the adopted apex and velocity of the Yahil *et al.* solution may introduce additional systematic errors of ~ 60 km s^{-1}.

Column 21: The sources for the redshift data

Sources in parentheses have been rejected in the calculation of the mean velocity and its mean error. The key for the references is given in References A at the rear of this volume.

PART II

The Catalog

Galaxy (1)	Other names (2)	RA (1950) (3)	Dec (1950) (4)	l (5)	b (6)	SGL (7)	SGB (8)	Type (9)	Source (10)
NGC 7814		00 00 41	15 52.0	106.42	−45.18	309.1	16.4	S(ab)	P200
NGC 16		00 06 29	27 27.2	111.59	−34.20	321.2	17.2	SB0₁(4)	P200
NGC 23	Mark 545	00 07 19	25 38.8	111.38	−36.01	319.4	16.7	SbI-II	P200
NGC 24		00 07 24	−25 14.6	43.69	−80.44	269.4	3.2	Sc(s)II-III	C100
NGC 45	DDO 223	00 11 32	−23 27.6	55.91	−80.67	271.4	2.9	Scd(s)III	C100
NGC 55		00 12 24	−39 28.0	332.90	−75.74	256.3	−2.4	Sc	W100
NGC 95		00 19 39	10 12.9	111.30	−51.72	304.5	10.6	Sc(s)I.8	P200
NGC 128		00 26 41	02 35.3	111.96	−59.53	297.5	7.0	S0₂(8) pec	P200
NGC 134		00 27 54	−33 31.3	338.25	−82.37	262.9	−3.6	Sbc(s)II-III:	C100
NGC 147	DDO 3	00 30 28	48 13.8	119.82	−14.26	343.3	15.3	dE5	W60
NGC 151		00 31 30	−09 58.9	108.86	−72.10	285.7	2.4	SBbc(rs)II	P200
NGC 148		00 31 48	−32 03.7	340.66	−84.03	264.5	−3.9	S0₂(r)(6)	C100
NGC 150		00 31 49	−28 04.7	21.89	−86.13	268.3	−2.8	Sbc(s)II	C100
NGC 157	MSH 00-07?	00 32 14	−08 40.3	110.28	−70.86	287.0	2.5	Sc(s)I-II	P200
NGC 175		00 34 52	−20 12.3	98.05	−82.12	276.1	−1.3	SBab(r)I-II	P200
NGC 185		00 36 11	48 03.7	120.80	−14.48	343.3	14.3	dE3 pec	P200
NGC 178	IC 39	00 36 37	−14 26.8	109.85	−76.73	281.7	−0.1	ScIV	W100
NGC 205		00 37 38	41 24.9	120.72	−21.13	336.5	13.1	S0/E5 pec	W100
NGC 210		00 38 04	−14 08.8	111.58	−76.50	282.1	−0.4	Sb(rs)I	P200
NGC 214		00 38 49	25 13.5	120.11	−37.32	320.4	9.7	Sc(r)I	W100
NGC 221	M32	00 39 59	40 35.5	121.16	−21.98	335.8	12.5	E2	W100
NGC 224	M31	00 40 00	40 59.7	121.18	−21.57	336.2	12.5	SbI-II	P48
NGC 227		00 40 04	−01 48.3	117.85	−64.32	294.1	2.6	E5	C100
NGC 237		00 40 55	−00 24.0	118.55	−62.93	295.6	2.7	Sc(rs)I-II	W100
NGC 245	Mark 555	00 43 32	−01 59.6	119.83	−64.57	294.2	1.7	SbcII.2:pec	W100
NGC 247		00 44 40	−21 02.0	113.95	−83.56	275.9	−3.7	Sc(s)III-IV	C100
NGC 254		00 45 03	−31 41.7	314.11	−85.62	265.6	−6.6	RS0₁(6)/Sa	C100
NGC 253	PKS 0045-25	00 45 08	−25 33.7	97.57	−87.97	271.6	−5.0	Sc(s)	W100
NGC 255		00 45 16	−11 44.5	119.63	−74.32	284.9	−1.4	SBc(r)II.3	P200
NGC 268		00 47 37	−05 28.1	122.09	−68.06	291.1	−0.2	SBc(r)I-II	48 Pr
NGC 274	VV 81	00 48 30	−07 19.7	122.65	−69.93	289.4	−1.0	S0₁(0)	C100
NGC 275	VV 81	00 48 33	−07 20.1	122.68	−69.93	289.4	−1.0	S pec (tidal)	C100
NGC 278		00 49 15	47 16.8	123.05	−15.32	342.8	12.0	Sbc(s)II.2	P200
NGC 289		00 50 17	−31 28.7	299.15	−85.91	266.1	−7.6	SBbc(rs)I-II	C100
SMC	A0051-73	00 51.0	−73 06	302.80	−44.30	224.2	−14.8	Im IV-V	W10
NGC 300	MSH 00-317?	00 52 31	−37 57.4	299.23	−79.42	259.8	−9.5	ScII.8	W100
NGC 309		00 54 13	−10 11.3	127.32	−72.74	287.0	−3.1	Sc(r)I	P200
NGC 337		00 57 19	−07 50.7	129.14	−70.35	289.5	−3.2	Sc(s)II.2 pec	P200
NGC 357		01 00 50	−06 36.3	131.24	−69.02	290.9	−3.7	SBa	P200
New 1	A0102-06	01 02 33	−06 28.6	132.36	−68.83	291.1	−4.1	SBc(s)II.2	P200
NGC 406		01 05 48	−70 09.0	300.92	−47.19	227.4	−15.8	Sc(s)II	C100
NGC 404		01 06 39	35 27.1	127.04	−27.01	331.9	6.2	S0₃(0)	W100
NGC 434		01 10 13	−58 30.7	297.69	−58.66	239.5	−15.6	Sab (s)	C100
NGC 428		01 10 23	00 42.9	134.24	−61.42	298.6	−4.1	Sc(s)III	P200
NGC 439		01 11 25	−32 00.9	257.79	−83.29	266.5	−12.1	E5	C100

Galaxy (11)	B_T (12)	A^o (13)	A^i (14)	$B_T^{o,i}$ (15)	$M_{B_T}^{o,i}$ (16)	v (17)	ε (18)	Δv (19)	v_o (20)	Sources (21)
NGC 7814	11.35	0.05	0.94	10.36	−21.70	1047	50	242	1289	190
NGC 16	12.98[1]	0.10	0	12.88	−21.27	3110	50	272	3382	190
NGC 23	12.80	0.09	0.64	12.07	−22.86	4568	15	268	4836	190, 385
NGC 24	12.10	0	0.75	11.35	−19.12	560	14	61	621	28, 160, 321
NGC 45	11.10	0	0.41	11.69	−18.45	463	3	70	533	121, 160, 190, 217, 261
NGC 55	8.22	0	0.87	7.35	−20.15 S	129	3	−14	115	501
NGC 95	13.25	0	0.37	12.88	−22.16	4886	96	218	5104	321
NGC 128	12.63[1]	0	0	12.63	−22.11	4253	35	186	4439	58, 190
NGC 134	10.96[3]	0	0.72	10.24	−22.28	1581	14	13	1594	191, 224, 387
NGC 147	10.36[1]	0.40	0	9.96	−14.36 L	−160	50	296	136	19, 332
NGC 151	12.28	0	0.54	11.74	−22.70	3741	10	130	3871	321, 392
NGC 148	13.04[1]	0	0	13.04	−19.88	1897	23	19	1916	284, (321), (332)
NGC 150	11.75	0	0.51	11.24	−21.31	1580	14	40	1620	158, 224, 284, 431
NGC 157	11.04	0	0.43	10.61	−22.19	1678	10	135	1813	46, 77, 190, 319, 400
NGC 175	12.8	0	0.48	12.32	−22.17	3883	49	79	3962	284, (332), 398
NGC 185	10.13[1]	0.40	0	9.73	−14.59 L	−227	22	294	67	19, 190, 191, 229, (332)
NGC 178	13.1	0	0.48	12.62	−19.90	1492	36	107	1599	284, 431
NGC 205	8.83[1]	0.23	0	8.60	−15.72 L	−239	11	288	49	190, 191, 319, (332), 337
NGC 210	11.65	0	0.64	11.01	−21.86	1768	40	107	1875	191
NGC 214	12.95	0.09	0.38	12.48	−22.41	4499	33	258	4757	46, 190, 191
NGC 221	9.01[1]	0.22	0	8.79	−15.53 L	−200	6	286	86	503
NGC 224	4.38	0.64	1.03	2.71	−21.61 L	−297	0.4	287	−10	502
NGC 227	13.35[2]	0	0	13.35	−21.85	5315	65	163	5478	190
NGC 237	13.7	0	0.43	13.27	−21.41	4139	68	169	4308	284
NGC 245	(13.18)	0	0.31	12.87	−21.79	4114	50	161	4275	284
NGC 247	9.51	0	0.63	8.88	−18.62 S	156	4	71	227	604
NGC 254	12.66[1]	0	0	12.66	−19.66	1441	215	17	1458	284
NGC 253	8.13	0	0.75	7.38	−20.72 S	245	5	48	293	504
NGC 255	12.35	0	0.32	12.03	−20.66	1610	10	116	1726	191, 391, 392
NGC 268	(13.28)	0	0.38	12.90	−22.37	5515	83	144	5659	284
NGC 274	12.98[2]	0	0	12.98	−19.91	1759	15	135	1894	229, 247
NGC 275	13.0	0	0.38	12.62	−20.27	1754	6	135	1889	135, 229, 301, 391
NGC 278	11.51	0.37	0.29	10.85	−20.50	642	9	290	932	28, 190, 191, (306), 391
NGC 289	(11.81)	0	0.40	11.41	−21.41	1818	77	16	1834	191, 224
SMC	2.79	0.06	0.25	2.48	−16.99 L	163	5	−182	−19	359
NGC 300	8.70	0	0.39	8.31	−18.59 S	145	2	−17	128	625
NGC 309	12.40	0	0.33	12.07	−23.25	5666	8	120	5786	284, 392, 400
NGC 337	12.08	0	0.40	11.68	−21.07	1647	10	129	1776	321, 392
NGC 357	12.90	0	0.31*	12.59	−21.05	2541	50	133	2674	190
New 1	(12.21)	0	0.32	11.89	−19.85	983	96	133	1116	229
NGC 406	12.51[5]	0.05	0.63	11.83	−20.29	1498	54	−172	1326	284, 438
NGC 404	11.12[1]	0.16	0	10.96	−17.37	−39	24	270	231	58, 190, 229, (306)
NGC 434	12.96[5]	0	0.73	12.23	−22.67	4906	70	−123	4783	104, 224
NGC 428	11.85	0	0.37	11.48	−20.61	1150	9	161	1311	173, 191, 253, 392
NGC 439	[13.0]	0	0	13.0	−22.3	5644	155	6	5650	284

Galaxy (1)	Other names (2)	RA (1950) (3)	Dec (1950) (4)	l (5)	b (6)	SGL (7)	SGB (8)	Type (9)	Source (10)
NGC 450		01 12 57	−01 07.6	136.34	−63.11	297.0	−5.2	Sc(s)II.3	P200
NGC 470		01 17 10	03 09.0	136.63	−58.71	301.4	−5.0	Sbc(s)II.3	P200
NGC 473		01 17 15	16 17.0	132.75	−45.78	314.1	−1.3	Sb(r)	P200
NGC 474		01 17 32	03 09.3	136.81	−58.68	301.5	−5.1	RS0/a	P200
NGC 491		01 19 03	−34 19.4	261.84	−80.54	264.5	−14.1	SBbc(r)II	C100
NGC 488		01 19 11	04 59.8	136.83	−56.79	303.3	−5.0	Sab(rs)I	P200
NGC 514		01 21 25	12 39.5	135.15	−49.18	310.9	−3.3	Sc(s)II	P200
NGC 520	VV 231	01 22 00	03 31.9	138.72	−58.06	302.1	−6.1	Amorphous	P200
NGC 521		01 22 00	01 28.2	139.70	−60.06	300.1	−6.6	SBc(rs) I	P200
NGC 524		01 22 10	09 16.7	136.51	−52.45	307.7	−4.5	S0$_2$/Sa	P200
NGC 533	MSH 01+04?	01 22 56	01 30.3	140.15	−59.97	300.2	−6.9	E3	W100
NGC 578		01 28 05	−22 55.5	188.32	−80.09	276.4	−14.0	Sc(s)I–II	W100
NGC 584	{ IC 1712	01 28 50	−07 07.6	149.82	−67.63	292.2	−10.6	S0$_1$ (3,5)	C100
NGC 596	{ PKS 0129−07	01 30 22	−07 17.3	150.89	−67.63	292.1	−11.0	E0	W60
NGC 598	M 33	01 31 03	30 23.9	133.62	−31.34	328.5	−0.1	Sc(s)II–III	P48
NGC 613	PKS 0131−296	01 31 59	−29 40.3	229.07	−80.30	269.7	−16.0	SBb(rs)II	C100
NGC 615		01 32 35	−07 35.8	152.56	−67.67	292.0	−11.6	Sb(r)I–II	P200
NGC 625		01 32 55	−41 41.4	273.67	−73.13	257.3	−17.7	Amorphous or Im III	C100
NGC 628	M 74	01 34 01	15 31.6	138.63	−45.71	314.5	−5.4	Sc(s)I	P200
NGC 636		01 36 36	−07 45.9	155.07	−67.36	292.1	−12.6	E1	W100
NGC 670		01 44 37	27 38.1	137.77	−33.37	326.8	−3.8	Sb:	P200
NGC 672	VV 338	01 45 05	27 11.1	138.04	−33.78	326.4	−4.1	SBc(s)III	P200
NGC 685		01 45 49	−53 00.6	284.49	−62.28	245.4	−20.4	SBc(r)II	C100
NGC 681		01 46 43	−10 40.5	164.84	−68.46	289.8	−15.7	Sab	P200
NGC 701		01 48 36	−09 57.1	164.67	−67.61	290.6	−16.0	Sc(s)III	C40D
NGC 720	{ VV 175	01 50 34	−13 59.1	173.03	−70.36	286.6	−17.4	E5	W60
NGC 718	{ IIIZw 38	01 50 37	03 57.0	150.75	−55.30	304.6	−12.8	SaI	P200
NGC 741	{ 4C05.10 PKS 0153+05	01 53 44	05 23.1	150.94	−53.68	306.2	−13.1	E0	W100
NGC 750	{ VV 189	01 54 38	32 58.0	138.53	−27.65	332.6	−3.9	E0	W100
NGC 753	{ VIZw 123	01 54 46	35 40.3	137.71	−25.05	335.1	−3.0	Sc(rs) I	P200
NGC 782		01 55 59	−58 02.0	286.62	−57.20	240.0	−21.6	SBb(r)I–II	C40D
NGC 772		01 56 35	18 46.0	144.40	−41.02	319.4	−9.4	Sb(rs)I	P200
NGC 779		01 57 12	−06 12.3	163.50	−63.32	294.9	−17.1	Sb(rs)I–II	P200
NGC 777		01 57 21	31 11.2	139.74	−29.19	331.1	−5.1	E1	W60
NGC 788		01 58 37	−07 03.3	165.26	−63.80	294.2	−17.7	Sa	P200
NGC 821		02 05 41	10 45.5	151.56	−47.56	312.5	−14.2	E6	W60
IC 1783		02 07 57	−33 10.5	236.72	−72.06	266.9	−24.0	Sbc(rs)II	C100
NGC 864		02 12 50	05 46.2	157.56	−51.13	308.1	−17.5	Sbc(r)II–III	P200
IC 1788		02 13 39	−31 26.0	230.45	−71.16	268.9	−25.1	Sbc(s)(II)	C40D
NGC 877		02 15 16	14 18.9	152.33	−43.33	316.7	−15.2	Sc(s)I–II	P200
NGC 890		02 19 02	33 02.3	143.91	−25.89	334.7	−8.6	S0$_1$(5)	P200
NGC 895		02 19 06	−05 45.0	171.78	−59.55	296.9	−22.3	Sc(r)I	W60
NGC 891		02 19 25	42 07.2	140.39	−17.42	343.0	−4.8	Sb on edge	P200
NGC 908		02 20 47	−21 27.7	202.15	−68.32	280.1	−25.8	Sc(s)I–II	W100
NGC 922		02 22 49	−25 01.1	211.87	−68.85	276.2	−26.6	Sc(s)II.2 pec	W100

Galaxy (11)	B_T (12)	A^o (13)	A^i (14)	$B_T^{o,i}$ (15)	$M_{B_T}^{o,i}$ (16)	v (17)	ε (18)	Δv (19)	v_o (20)	Sources (21)
NGC 450	12.50	0	0.36	12.19	−20.72	1759	8	152	1911	158, 284, 301, 431
NGC 470	12.60	0	0.44	12.16	−21.46	2476	(50)	167	2643	158, 263, 284. 321, 385
NGC 473	(13.04)	0.05	0.34*	12.65	−20.71	2129	10	216	2345	160, 284, 402
NGC 474	12.35[1]	0	0	12.35	−21.19	2381	9	167	2548	190, 263
NGC 491	13.17[5,8]	0	0.32	12.85	−21.60	3899	75	−9	3890	284
NGC 488	11.15	0	0.57	10.58	−22.86	2268	9	174	2442	190, 263
NGC 514	12.5	0.04	0.35	12.11	−21.53	2474	12	201	2675	46, 190, 191, 400
NGC 520	12.09	0	—	[12.1]	−21.3	2184	15	166	2350	505
NGC 521	12.5	0	0.31	12.19	−22.88	5065	40	158	5223	160, 284, 407
NGC 524	11.62[1]	0	0	11.62	−21.93	2377	46	189	2566	190, 203
NGC 533	12.75[1]	0	0	12.75	−22.52	5506	53	158	5664	284, (321)
NGC 578	11.48	0	0.44	11.04	−21.59	1632	10	43	1675	46, (191), 224, 398, 400
NGC 584	11.20[1]	0	0	11.20	−21.80	1875	11	117	1992	190, 289, 306, 319
NGC 596	11.88[1]	0	0	11.88	−21.15	1902	15	116	2018	190, 289, 422, 442
NGC 598	6.26	0.12	0.45	5.69	−19.07 L	−180	0.5	249	69	506
NGC 613	10.75[8]	0	0.56	10.19	−22.24	1526	18	8	1534	46, 88, 191
NGC 615	12.3	0	0.91	11.39	−21.59	1858	9	113	1971	229, 263
NGC 625	(12.21)	0	0.30:	11.91	−17.33	403	8	−51	352	158, 160, 284, 438
NGC 628	9.77	0.03	0.31	9.43	−21.75	656	2	205	861	507
NGC 636	12.25[1]	0	0	12.25	−20.74	1868	22	110	1978	190, 442
NGC 670	13.17[1]	0.11	0.87	12.19	−22.34	3788	45	235	4023	190, (332)
NGC 672	11.41	0.10	0.62	10.69	−19.87	413	6	234	647	623
NGC 685	(11.97)	0	0.29	11.68	−20.39	1415	78	−109	1306	284, 438
NGC 681	12.71	0	0.68	12.03	−20.79	1745	9	91	1836	84, 190, 229, 391
NGC 701	12.90	0	0.53	12.37	−20.56	1829	8	94	1923	158, 284, 391, 431
NGC 720	11.15[1]	0	0	11.15	−21.60	1697	22	74	1771	190, 289, 422, 442
NGC 718	12.50	0	0*	12.50	−20.46	1802	40	152	1954	191
NGC 741	12.54[1]	0	0	12.54	−22.75	5567	32	156	5723	190, 289
NGC 750	13.32[1]	0.15	0	13.17	−21.99	5130	40	243	5373	190
NGC 753	12.96	0.18	0.39	12.39	−22.67	4896	14	249	5145	46, 191, 392
NGC 782	12.83[5]	0	0.47	12.36	−22.99	6014	43	−133	5881	284, 399
NGC 772	11.10	0.07	0.70	10.33	−23.29	2443	10	202	2645	596
NGC 779	11.86	0	1.06	10.80	−21.57	1387	9	105	1492	263, 321
NGC 777	(12.37)	0.14	0	12.23	−22.88	5010	54	238	5248	284, (332), 442
NGC 788	13.0	0	0*	13.0	−21.64	4137	65	101	4238	190
NGC 821	11.94[1]	0.05	0	11.89	−21.01	1727	32	170	1897	190, 442
IC 1783	[13.1]	0	0.46	12.64	−21.44	3299	78	−27	3272	284
NGC 864	11.55	0	0.38	11.17	−21.50	1561	9	146	1707	44, 191, 392
IC 1788	13.10	0	0.57	12.53	−21.61	3388	50	−22	3366	284
NGC 877	12.50	0.06	0.38	12.06	−22.50	3911	9	177	4088	191, 391, 385
NGC 890	12.43[2]	0.17	0	12.26	−22.40	4043	65	230	4273	190
NGC 895	12.30	0	0.38	11.92	−21.47	2290	6	93	2383	301, 321, 391
NGC 891	10.95	0.31	1.33	9.31	−21.66	530	4	249	779	(190), 263, 282, 420
NGC 908	10.87	0	0.54	10.33	−22.15	1542	(100)	21	1563	46, 191
NGC 922	12.55	0	0.31	12.24	−21.69	3058	33	3	3061	284, 431

Galaxy (1)	Other names (2)	RA (1950) (3)	Dec (1950) (4)	l (5)	b (6)	SGL (7)	SGB (8)	Type (9)	Source (10)
NGC 925		02 24 18	33 21.1	144.89	−25.17	335.5	−9.5	SBc(s)II–III	P200
NGC 936		02 25 05	−01 22.7	168.58	−55.26	301.9	−22.6	SB0$_{2/3}$/SBa	C100
NGC 941		02 25 55	−01 22.5	168.86	−55.13	301.9	−22.8	ScdIII	W60
NGC 949		02 27 39	36 54.7	144.05	−21.62	339.0	−8.5	Sc(s)III	P200
NGC 955		02 28 00	−01 19.8	169.51	−54.76	302.1	−23.3	Sb	W100
NGC 958		02 28 11	−03 09.8	171.69	−56.11	300.2	−23.8	Sbc(s)II	48 Pr
NGC 976		02 31 11	20 45.4	152.85	−35.87	324.4	−16.2	Sbc(r)I–II	P200
NGC 972		02 31 17	29 05.5	148.40	−28.43	332.2	−12.7	Sb pec	P200
NGC 986		02 31 34	−39 15.9	248.66	−65.64	260.2	−28.8	SBb(rs)I–II	C100
NGC 991		02 33 03	−07 22.0	178.75	−58.24	296.1	−26.1	Sc(rs)II	P200
NGC 1022		02 36 04	−06 53.4	179.02	−57.37	296.8	−26.7	SBa(r) pec	C100
NGC 1035		02 37 01	−08 20.8	181.37	−58.15	295.3	−27.2	Sc:III	W60
NGC 1023		02 37 16	38 50.9	145.03	−19.09	341.6	−9.3	SB0$_1$(5)	P200
NGC 1042		02 37 56	−08 38.8	182.08	−58.17	295.0	−27.5	Sc(rs)I–II	C40D
NGC 1052	PKS 0238−084	02 38 37	−08 28.1	182.03	−57.93	295.2	−27.7	E3/S0	W100
NGC 1055	PKS 0239+002	02 39 11	00 13.7	171.34	−51.75	304.7	−25.5	Sbc(s)II	P200
NGC 1068	{ M 77 3C 71	02 40 07	−00 13.5	172.11	−51.93	304.3	−25.8	Sb(rs)II	P200
NGC 1058		02 40 23	37 07.8	146.41	−20.37	340.4	−10.6	Sc(s)II–III	P200
NGC 1073	PKS 0241+011	02 41 05	01 09.9	170.92	−50.73	305.8	−25.7	SBc(rs)II	P200
NGC 1079		02 41 35	−29 12.9	223.89	−65.21	271.7	−31.1	Sa(s)	C100
NGC 1084	Cul 0243−07	02 43 32	−07 47.1	182.48	−56.55	296.3	−28.7	Sc(s)II.2	W100
NGC 1087		02 43 52	−00 42.5	173.75	−51.65	304.1	−26.9	Sc(s)III.3	W100
NGC 1090		02 44 01	−00 27.4	173.52	−51.44	304.3	−26.8	SBc(s)I–II	W100
NGC 1097	PKS 0244−304	02 44 11	−30 29.1	226.92	−64.68	270.2	−31.6	RSBbc(rs)I–II	W100
NGC 1140		02 52 08	−10 13.9	188.34	−56.34	294.1	−31.3	Sb pec:	W60
NGC 1156		02 56 47	25 02.4	156.32	−29.19	331.2	−19.6	SmIV	P200
NGC 1172		02 59 16	−15 01.8	197.49	−57.35	288.9	−33.9	S0$_1$(0,3)	C100
NGC 1169		03 00 10	46 11.1	145.44	−10.63	350.2	−9.1	SBa(r)I	P200
NGC 1179		03 00 21	−19 05.6	204.68	−58.81	284.1	−34.7	SBc(rs)I–II	W100
NGC 1187		03 00 24	−23 03.8	212.10	−60.06	279.2	−35.0	SBbc(s)I–II	W60
NGC 1175		03 01 16	42 08.7	147.65	−14.05	346.9	−11.5	S0$_2$(8)	P200
NGC 1199		03 01 19	−15 48.6	199.19	−57.26	288.1	−34.5	E2	W60
NGC 1201		03 01 58	−26 15.9	218.55	−60.41	275.3	−35.5	S0$_1$(6)	P200
NGC 1209		03 03 44	−15 48.2	199.65	−56.74	288.2	−35.1	E6	W100
NGC 1232		03 07 30	−20 46.2	208.78	−57.81	282.2	−36.5	Sc(rs)I	C100
NGC 1249		03 08 35	−53 31.4	268.23	−53.41	242.5	−32.4	SBc(s)II	C100
NGC 1241	VV 334	03 08 49	−09 06.6	190.72	−52.31	296.5	−35.1	SBbc(s)I.2	C100
NGC 1255		03 11 23	−25 54.7	218.61	−58.26	275.8	−37.6	Sc(s)II	W100
NGC 1288		03 15 12	−32 45.3	231.71	−58.08	267.1	−38.1	Sab(r)I–II	C40IT
NGC 1291		03 15 29	−41 18.5	247.56	−57.04	256.4	−36.9	SBa	C100
NGC 1292		03 16 08	−27 47.8	222.43	−57.52	273.4	−38.7	Sc(s)II	C100
NGC 1275	3C 84.0	03 16 30	41 19.8	150.59	−13.26	347.9	−14.3	E pec	P200
NGC 1297		03 16 59	−19 17.0	207.60	−55.21	284.3	−38.6	E2	48 Pr
NGC 1300		03 17 25	−19 35.5	208.17	−55.22	283.9	−38.7	SBb(s)I.2	P200
NGC 1313	PKS 0317−666	03 17 39	−66 40.7	283.37	−44.64	228.0	−28.2	SBc(s)III–IV	C100

Galaxy (11)	B_T (12)	A^o (13)	A^i (14)	$B_T^{o,i}$ (15)	$M_{B_T}^{o,i}$ (16)	v (17)	ε (18)	Δv (19)	v_0 (20)	Sources (21)
NGC 925	10.59	0.20	0.46	9.93	−21.07	564	5	228	792	508
NGC 936	11.19[1]	0	0	11.19	−21.21	1404	35	108	1512	26, 190, (306)
NGC 941	12.94	0	0.38	12.56	−20.12	1609	15	108	1717	158, 284
NGC 949	12.55	0.22	0.45	11.88	−19.28	620	19	235	855	135, 284
NGC 955	12.95	0	1.11	11.84	−20.74	1534	43	107	1641	284
NGC 958	12.95	0	0.64	12.31	−23.03	5738	14	99	5837	46, 321, 400
NGC 976	13.21	0.09	0.33	12.79	−22.01	4362	58	188	4550	284
NGC 972	12.10	0.15	0.78	11.17	−21.56	1548	8	213	1761	86, 126, 190, 229, 392
NGC 986	11.8	0	0.59	11.21	−21.81	2073	200	−67	2006	150
NGC 991	(12.42)	0	0.30	12.12	−20.42	1530	15	77	1607	158, 284
NGC 1022	12.20	0	0.54	11.66	−20.83	1498	46	77	1575	321
NGC 1035	(13.07)	0	0.65	12.42	−19.67	1237	10	70	1307	321, 392
NGC 1023	10.36[1]	0.27	0	10.09	−21.17	661	13	234	895	509
NGC 1042	11.49	0	0.35	11.14	−21.15	1368	9	68	1436	(191), 301, 431
NGC 1052	11.53[1]	0	0	11.53	−20.91	1471	11	68	1539	592
NGC 1055	11.42	0	0.63	10.79	−20.92	993	9	105	1098	48, 173, (332), 391
NGC 1068	9.55	0	0.52	9.03	−22.93	1131	6	103	1234	510
NGC 1058	12.15	0.25	0.30	11.60	−19.27	518	1	228	746	605
NGC 1073	11.50	0	0.30	11.20	−20.90	1210	20	108	1318	164, (191)
NGC 1079	12.22[1,8]	0	0*	12.22	−21.02	2252	250	−28	2224	190
NGC 1084	11.25	0	0.52	10.73	−21.62	1410	8	68	1478	46, 81, 190, 391, 392
NGC 1087	11.56	0	0.43	11.13	−21.43	1530	32	98	1628	(190), 319, 391
NGC 1090	12.60	0	0.57	12.03	−21.74	2736	14	99	2835	158, 284, 407
NGC 1097	10.16[8]	0	0.41	9.75	−22.30	1319	16	−35	1284	511
NGC 1140	12.85	0	0.74	12.11	−20.36	1509	7	51	1560	190, 253, 391, 392
NGC 1156	12.25	0.14	0.19	11.92	−18.32	373	10	185	558	618
NGC 1172	13.00[1]	0	0	13.00	−19.48	1542	(50)	24	1566	284, 289
NGC 1169	12.5	0.58	0.32*	11.60	−21.99	2378	15	236	2614	158, 284
NGC 1179	(12.21)	0	0.34	11.87	−20.88	1770	15	6	1776	160
NGC 1187	(10.93)	0	0.36	10.57	−21.70	1436	29	−12	1424	28, 43, 191
NGC 1175	13.81[1]	0.41	0	13.40	−21.88	5458	60	227	5685	284
NGC 1199	12.42[1]	0	0	12.42	−21.23	2666	20	20	2686	190, 442
NGC 1201	11.56[1]	0	0	11.56	−21.09	1722	50	−28	1694	190
NGC 1209	12.26	0	0	12.26	−21.36	2634	37	18	2652	58, 190, 284
NGC 1232	10.50	0	0.32	10.18	−22.57	1782	52	−7	1775	191, 321
NGC 1249	11.80	0	0.54	11.26	−19.98	1031	54	−144	887	284, 438
NGC 1241	(12.66)	0	0.45	12.21	−22.34	4028	(100)	44	4072	284, (332), 431
NGC 1255	11.6	0	0.42	11.18	−21.42	1688	21	−32	1656	321, 398, 400
NGC 1288	12.80	0	0.47	12.33	−22.42	4526	14	−65	4461	284, 345, 398, 400
NGC 1291	9.42	0	0.25*	9.17	−21.68	839	4	−101	738	512
NGC 1292	(12.59)	0	0.53	12.06	−20.16	1434	36	−44	1390	284, 345
NGC 1275	12.35	0.44	0	11.91	−23.27	5216	20	217	5433	619
NGC 1297	(12.61)	0	0	12.61	−19.90	1599	80	−7	1592	284
NGC 1300	11.10	0	0.67	10.43	−21.99	1535	9	−9	1526	43, 46, 191, 399
NGC 1313	9.37	0.06	0.38	8.93	−19.66	452	15	−191	261	1, 225, 331

Galaxy (1)	Other names (2)	RA (1950) (3)	Dec (1950) (4)	l (5)	b (6)	SGL (7)	SGB (8)	Type (9)	Source (10)
NGC 1302		03 17 43	−26 14.4	219.70	−56.92	275.4	−39.0	Sa	C100
NGC 1309		03 19 47	−15 34.7	202.21	−53.16	289.1	−38.9	Sb(rs)II	W60
NGC 1316	Fornax A	03 20 47	−37 23.1	240.17	−56.69	261.0	−38.6	Sa pec (merger?)	C100
NGC 1317		03 20 51	−37 16.9	239.98	−56.69	261.2	−38.7	Sa	C100
NGC 1326		03 22 01	−36 38.4	238.78	−56.52	261.9	−39.0	RSBa	C100
NGC 1325		03 22 13	−21 43.1	212.32	−54.84	281.3	−40.0	Sb	W60
NGC 1332		03 24 04	−21 30.5	212.19	−54.37	281.6	−40.4	$SO_1(6)$	C100
IC 1933		03 24 15	−52 57.5	265.52	−51.63	242.1	−34.9	SBc(s)II-III	C100
NGC 1337		03 25 40	−08 33.7	193.55	−48.52	298.3	−39.0	Sc(s)I-II	P200
NGC 1341		03 26 05	−37 19.3	239.86	−55.65	260.9	−39.7	SBc(s)II-III	C40D
NGC 1339		03 26 06	−32 27.3	231.23	−55.78	267.1	−40.4	E4	48 Pr
NGC 1344		03 26 18	−31 14.4	229.08	−55.68	268.7	−40.6	$SO_1(5)$	W100
NGC 1351		03 28.6	−35 02	235.79	−55.27	263.7	−40.6	$SO_1(6)$/E6	C100
NGC 1350		03 29 10	−33 47.9	233.62	−55.17	265.3	−40.9	Sa(r)	C100
NGC 1353		03 29 49	−20 59.3	212.04	−52.93	282.3	−41.7	Sbc(r)II	C100
IC 1954		03 30 06	−52 04.4	263.66	−51.18	242.7	−36.0	Sc(s)II.2	C100
NGC 1357		03 30 56	−13 50.0	201.79	−50.04	291.7	−41.3	Sa(s)	C100
NGC 1358		03 31 11	−05 15.4	190.60	−45.56	302.9	−39.5	SBa(s)I	C100
IC 1953		03 31 29	−21 38.6	213.27	−52.76	281.5	−42.1	SBbc(rs)II	W60
NGC 1359		03 31 33	−19 39.5	210.19	−52.12	284.1	−42.1	Sc(s)II-III	P200
NGC 1365	PKS 0331−363	03 31 42	−36 18.3	237.96	−54.60	261.9	−41.0	SBb(s)I	W100
NGC 1366		03 31 53	−31 21.6	229.43	−54.50	268.4	−41.8	$SO_1(8)$	P48
NGC 1371		03 32 53	−25 06.0	218.96	−53.35	276.8	−42.5	Sa(s)	C100
NGC 1374		03 33 21	−35 23.5	236.38	−54.28	263.0	−41.5	E0	C100
NGC 1379		03 34 08	−35 36.3	236.75	−54.12	262.7	−41.6	E0	C100
NGC 1380		03 34 31	−35 08.4	235.93	−54.06	263.3	−41.8	$SO_3(7)$/Sa	C100
NGC 1376		03 34 37	−05 12.3	191.23	−44.82	303.3	−40.3	Sc(s)II	W100
NGC 1381		03 34 36	−35 27.5	236.49	−54.02	262.8	−41.7	$SO_1(10)$	C100
NGC 1386		03 34 52	−36 09.9	237.68	−53.94	261.9	−41.7	Sa	C100
NGC 1387		03 35 02	−35 40.2	236.85	−53.93	262.5	−41.8	SBO_2(pec)	C100
NGC 1389		03 35 17	−35 54.5	237.25	−53.89	262.2	−41.8	$SO_1(5)$/SBO_1	C100
NGC 1385		03 35 20	−24 39.9	218.47	−52.71	277.4	−43.0	ScIII:	W100
NGC 1395		03 36 19	−23 11.4	216.22	−52.12	279.4	−43.3	E2	W100
NGC 1399	PKS 0336−35	03 36 35	−35 36.7	236.72	−53.56	262.6	−42.1	E1	C100
NGC 1398		03 36 45	−26 29.9	221.54	−52.79	274.8	−43.3	SBab(r)I	P200
NGC 1404		03 36 57	−35 45.3	236.95	−53.55	262.3	−42.1	E2	C100
NGC 1411		03 37 04	−44 15.9	251.01	−52.52	251.5	−39.9	$SO_2(4)$	C100
NGC 1400		03 37 15	−18 50.9	209.71	−50.57	285.4	−43.4	E1/$SO_1(1)$	W60
NGC 1406		03 37 23	−31 29.1	229.79	−53.34	268.0	−42.9	Sc(II)	C100
NGC 1407		03 37 57	−18 44.4	209.64	−50.38	285.5	−43.5	E0	W60
NGC 1415		03 38 47	−22 43.4	215.74	−51.45	280.0	−43.8	Sa/SBa late	C100
NGC 1417	PKS 0339−04?	03 39 28	−04 51.9	191.77	−43.63	304.2	−41.4	Sb(s)I.3	P200
NGC 1421		03 40 09	−13 38.9	202.81	−47.88	292.6	−43.5	ScIII:	W100
NGC 1425		03 40 10	−30 03.3	227.53	−52.60	269.9	−43.7	Sb(r)II	W100
NGC 1427		03 40 25	−35 33.1	236.63	−52.86	262.4	−42.8	E5	C100

Galaxy (11)	B_T (12)	A^o (13)	A^i (14)	$B_T^{o,i}$ (15)	$M_{B_T}^{o,i}$ (16)	v (17)	ε (18)	Δv (19)	v_0 (20)	Sources (21)
NGC 1302	11.38	0	0*	11.38	−21.23	1703	8	−38	1665	190, 374, 402, 435
NGC 1309	12.00	0	0.45	11.55	−21.61	2136	7	7	2143	321, 391, 392
NGC 1316	9.60[1]	0	0.28*	9.32	−23.08 F	1801	39	−88	1713	58, 150, 190, 327, (345)
NGC 1317	12.04[1]	0	0*	12.04	−20.36 F	1980	70	−87	1893	190, 224
NGC 1326	11.34[1]	0	0*	11.34	−21.06 F	1362	7	−85	1277	513
NGC 1325	12.32	0	0.98	11.34	−21.15	1596	15	−22	1574	158, 284, 345
NGC 1332	11.29[1]	0	0	11.29	−21.03	1477	19	−22	1455	43, 46, 190, 191, 435
IC 1933	(13.01)	0	0.46	12.55	−18.76	1063	98	−149	914	284
NGC 1337	12.28	0.04	0.74	11.50	−20.52	1237	7	33	1270	158, 284, 301, 391
NGC 1341	(13.18)	0	0.29	12.89	−19.51 F	1884	60	−91	1793	284, 345
NGC 1339	12.37[2]	0	0	12.37	−19.56	1287	79	−71	1216	284, 345
NGC 1344	11.28[1]	0	0	11.28	−20.62	1266	36	−66	1200	104, 284, 345
NGC 1351	12.65[2]	0	0	12.65	−19.75 F	1589	120	−83	1506	229
NGC 1350	11.40	0	0.38*	11.02	−21.38 F	1940	82	−78	1862	229
NGC 1353	12.25	0	0.58	11.67	−20.75	1545	91	−24	1521	284, 345
IC 1954	12.05[8]	0	0.53	11.52	−19.77	1054	67	−149	905	284, 438
NGC 1357	12.60	0	0.61	11.99	−21.13	2095	63	6	2101	284, (332)
NGC 1358	13.0	0.05	0*	12.95	−21.63	4071	90	43	4114	284
IC 1953	(12.28)	0	0.36	11.92	−20.93	1884	20	−28	1856	284, 345, 400
NGC 1359	12.6	0	0.34	12.26	−20.72	1992	54	−20	1972	191
NGC 1365	10.21	0	0.76	9.45	−22.95 F	1652	18	−90	1562	514
NGC 1366	(12.81)	0	0	12.81	−18.27	891	118	−70	821	284, (345)
NGC 1371	(11.50)	0	0*	11.50	−20.76	1462	7	−44	1418	158, 284, 345, 402, 439
NGC 1374	12.30[2]	0	0	12.30	−20.10 F	1289	100	−88	1201	229
NGC 1379	12.07[2]	0	0	12.07	−20.33 F	1457	116	−89	1368	229
NGC 1380	11.10[1]	0	0	11.10	−21.30 F	1861	42	−87	1774	190, 229
NGC 1376	(12.79)	0.30	0.06	12.43	−22.19	4157	9	41	4198	284, 301
NGC 1381	12.34[2]	0	0	12.34	−20.06 F	1871	118	−89	1782	229
NGC 1386	12.00[2]	0	0.92	11.08	−21.36 F	918	34	−92	826	284, 345
NGC 1387	11.83[2]	0	0	11.83	−20.57 F	1274	106	−90	1184	229
NGC 1389	12.39[2]	0	0	12.39	−20.01 F	1070	154	−91	979	229
NGC 1385	11.65	0	0.44	11.21	−21.77	2012	180	−44	1968	(46), 191
NGC 1395	11.18[2]	0	0	11.18	−21.43	1702	21	−38	1664	190, 191, 289
NGC 1399	10.79[1]	0	0	10.79	−21.61 F	1465	100	−90	1375	190, 229, (345)
NGC 1398	10.6	0	0.56	10.04	−22.30	1524	40	−53	1471	191
NGC 1404	11.06[1]	0	0	11.06	−21.34 F	1994	100	−91	1903	190, 229
NGC 1411	11.70[2]	0	0	11.70	−19.66	1058	84	−124	934	104, 284, 345
NGC 1400	12.08[1]	0	0	12.08	−17.94	524	31	−20	504	190, 442
NGC 1406	(12.59)	0	0.82	11.77	−19.73	1072	13	−74	998	158, 284, 345
NGC 1407	10.93[1]	0	0	10.93	−21.81	1784	30	−20	1764	190, 442
NGC 1415	12.55[2]	0	0.75	11.80	−20.62	1564	9	−38	1526	190, 402, 435
NGC 1417	12.75	0.06	0.67	12.02	−22.57	4101	50	38	4139	190
NGC 1421	11.95	0.05	0.76	11.14	−21.96	2080	10	−0	2080	321, 392
NGC 1425	(11.60)	0	0.83	10.77	−21.53	1510	15	−70	1440	158, 224, 284, 345
NGC 1427	11.94[2]	0	0	11.94	−20.46 F	1681	92	−93	1588	229

Galaxy (1)	Other names (2)	RA (1950) (3)	Dec (1950) (4)	l (5)	b (6)	SGL (7)	SGB (8)	Type (9)	Source (10)
NGC 1433		03 40 27	−47 22.8	255.70	−51.20	247.4	−39.3	SBb(s)I–II	C100
NGC 1426		03 40 38	−22 16.0	215.23	−50.91	280.7	−44.3	E4	W60
NGC 1437		03 41 42	−36 00.4	237.37	−52.59	261.7	−43.0	Sc(s)II	C100
NGC 1439		03 42 38	−22 04.6	215.16	−50.41	280.9	−44.7	E1	W60
NGC 1440		03 42 48	−18 25.1	209.81	−49.20	286.1	−44.6	S0$_1$(5)/SB0$_1$	W100
NGC 1448		03 42 54	−44 48.1	251.53	−51.39	250.3	−40.7	Sc(II):	C40IT
NGC 1452		03 43 08	−18 47.3	210.38	−49.25	285.6	−44.7	SBa(r)	C100
NGC 1453		03 43 57	−04 07.6	191.79	−42.29	305.5	−42.2	E2	W100
NGC 1461		03 46 11	−16 32.4	207.64	−47.75	288.8	−45.3	S0$_2$(8)	W100
IC 2006		03 52 37	−36 06.9	237.55	−50.47	260.8	−45.0	E1	C100
NGC 1487	VV 78	03 54 03	−42 30.9	247.47	−49.76	252.2	−43.4	S pec (merger)	C100
NGC 1493		03 55 54	−46 21.2	253.20	−48.86	247.2	−42.2	SBc(rs)III	C100
NGC 1494		03 56 15	−49 03.0	257.18	−48.24	244.0	−41.0	Scd(s)II	C100
NGC 1511		03 59.3	−67 46	281.38	−40.74	224.4	−31.0	Sc pec	C100
NGC 1507		04 01 56	−02 19.5	193.07	−37.56	309.9	−45.9	Sc	W100
NGC 1512		04 02 16	−43 29.2	248.67	−48.16	250.2	−44.4	SBb(rs)I pec	C100
NGC 1515		04 02 51	−54 14.0	264.10	−45.85	237.4	−39.3	Sb(s)II	C100
NGC 1518		04 04 38	−21 18.7	216.34	−45.31	282.0	−49.9	ScIII	C100
NGC 1521		04 06 08	−21 11.1	216.32	−44.94	282.2	−50.2	E3	W100
NGC 1527		04 06 55	−48 01.6	255.14	−46.72	244.1	−43.1	S0$_2$(6)	C100
IC 2035		04 07 29	−45 38.8	251.67	−46.96	246.9	−44.3	SB0$_1$(4) pec	C100
NGC 1533		04 08 50	−56 15.0	266.46	−44.43	234.7	−38.9	SB0$_2$(2)/SBa	C100
NGC 1536		04 09 57	−56 36.9	266.87	−44.17	234.2	−38.8	SBc(s) pec	C100
NGC 1531		04 10 04	−32 58.7	233.14	−46.60	263.9	−49.4	Amorphous	C100
NGC 1532		04 10 09	−33 00.0	233.18	−46.58	263.9	−49.4	Sab(s)I (tides?)	C100
NGC 1537		04 11 44	−31 46.3	231.47	−46.10	265.6	−50.1	E6	C100
NGC 1543		04 11 47	−57 52.0	268.41	−43.54	232.7	−38.3	RSB0$_{2/3}$(0)/a	C100
NGC 1546		04 13 33	−56 11.0	266.10	−43.82	234.2	−39.5	Sbc(s)III	C100
NGC 1549		04 14 39	−55 42.9	265.41	−43.80	234.6	−39.9	E2	C100
NGC 1553		04 15 05	−55 54.2	265.64	−43.69	234.3	−39.8	S0$_{1/2}$(5) pec	C100
IC 2056		04 15 39	−60 20.0	271.37	−42.26	229.9	−37.1	Sc(s)II	C100
NGC 1559	PKS 0416−629	04 17 01	−62 54.3	274.52	−41.19	227.3	−35.5	SBc(s)II.8	C100
NGC 1566	PKS 0418−550	04 18 53	−55 03.4	264.32	−43.39	234.8	−40.8	Sc(s)I	C100
NGC 1574		04 20 59	−57 05.4	266.90	−42.58	232.5	−39.7	SB0$_2$(3)	C100
NGC 1569	VII Zw 16	04 26 05	64 44.4	143.69	11.24	11.9	−4.9	SmIV	P200
NGC 1596		04 26 35	−55 08.1	264.08	−42.31	233.8	−41.6	S0$_1$(7)	C100
NGC 1600		04 29 12	−05 11.5	200.42	−33.24	309.3	−53.3	E4	W100
NGC 1617		04 30 37	−54 42.5	263.35	−41.83	233.7	−42.3	Sa(s)	C100
NGC 1625		04 34 35	−03 24.2	199.38	−31.18	312.9	−53.9	Sb/Sc	W100
NGC 1637		04 38 58	−02 57.1	199.57	−30.01	314.4	−54.7	SBc(s)II.3	C100
NGC 1638		04 39 05	−01 54.1	198.54	−29.46	316.0	−54.3	Sa	C100
NGC 1640		04 40 04	−20 31.8	218.88	−37.22	282.9	−58.1	SBbc(r)I–II	P200
NGC 1659		04 44 02	−04 52.7	202.22	−29.86	312.1	−56.6	Sc(s)II–III	P100
NGC 1672	PKS 0444−593	04 44 58	−59 19.6	268.79	−38.99	227.5	−40.4	Sb(rs)II	C100
NGC 1667		04 46 10	−06 24.4	204.06	−30.12	309.8	−57.6	Sc(r):II pec	W60

Galaxy (11)	B_T (12)	A^o (13)	A^i (14)	$B_T^{o,i}$ (15)	$M_{B_T}^{o,i}$ (16)	v (17)	ε (18)	Δv (19)	v_o (20)	Sources (21)
NGC 1433	10.68[8]	0	0.50	10.18	−21.15	1061	14	−138	923	327, 387, 396
NGC 1426	12.37[1]	0	0	12.37	−19.87	1443	6	−38	1405	190, 289
NGC 1437	(12.58)	0	0.40	12.18	−20.22 F	1162	77	−95	1067	284, 345
NGC 1439	12.58[2]	0	0	12.58	−19.99	1670	10	−38	1632	190, 289
NGC 1440	12.69[2]	0.04	0	12.65	−19.75	1534	68	−23	1511	284
NGC 1448	11.30	0	0.85	10.45	−21.14	1168	11	−130	1038	158, 284, 345, 387
NGC 1452	(13.07)	0.04	0*	13.03	−19.85	1904	43	−24	1880	284
NGC 1453	12.65[1]	0.06	0	12.59	−21.91	3941	26	38	3979	58, 190, 191
NGC 1461	12.90[1]	0.05	0	12.85	−19.44	1450	90	−17	1433	284
IC 2006	12.27[2]	0	0	12.27	−20.13 F	1383	86	−103	1280	284, 345
NGC 1487	12.31	0.04	0.42:	11.85	−19.01	871	39	−128	743	284, 345
NGC 1493	11.82	0.04	0.32	11.46	−19.84	1053	10	−143	910	158, 284, 345, 387
NGC 1494	(12.19)	0.04	0.42	11.73	−19.68	1109	122	−152	957	284, 345
NGC 1511	12.05[5,8]	0.07	0.67	11.31	−20.48	1349	55	−207	1142	(240), 284
NGC 1507	12.7	0.08	0.75	11.87	−19.39	867	37	31	898	173, 321
NGC 1512	11.38[1]	0.05	0.56	10.77	−20.14	896	5	−136	760	327, 419, 431
NGC 1515	11.93	0.05	1.23	10.65	−20.76	1131	50	−172	959	284
NGC 1518	12.30	0.03	0.58	11.69	−19.62	966	9	−52	914	43, 46, 191
NGC 1521	12.63[1]	0.05	0	12.58	−22.03	4222	50	−52	4170	190
NGC 1527	11.70[1]	0.05	0	11.65	−19.59	1037	66	−154	883	224, (240), 284
IC 2035	12.18[2]	0.05	0	12.13	−19.96	1458	100	−147	1311	284
NGC 1533	11.71[1]	0.06	0	11.65	−18.59	740	58	−181	559	284, 224
NGC 1536	13.10	0.06	0.34	12.70	−19.14	(1350)	200	−182	1168	240
NGC 1531	12.8	0.05	—	[12.75]	−18.9	1157	76	−104	1053	99, 284
NGC 1532	(11.53)	0.05	1.09	10.39	−21.33	1208	14	−103	1105	626
NGC 1537	11.62[2]	0.05	0	11.57	−20.43	1353	90	−99	1254	284, 345
NGC 1543	11.49[1]	0.06	0	11.43	−20.49	1400	200	−187	1213	297
NGC 1546	12.48[1]	0.06	0.55	11.87	−19.65	1190	93	−183	1007	284
NGC 1549	10.76[1]	0.06	0	10.70	−20.79	1173	53	−182	991	150, 297
NGC 1553	10.42[1]	0.06	0	10.36	−21.26	1236	41	−183	1053	150, 297, 327
IC 2056	12.19[2]	0.06	0.33	11.80	−19.56	1129	103	−195	934	284
NGC 1559	10.97	0.07	0.46	10.44	−21.26	1295	15	−202	1093	99, 104, 387, 438
NGC 1566	10.21	0.06	0.36	9.79	−22.29	1487	14	−182	1305	593
NGC 1574	11.19[1]	0.06	0	11.13	−19.60	890	200	−189	701	297
NGC 1569	11.90	0.55	0.27	11.08	−16.22	−83	10	227	144	160, 190, 191, 253, 261
NGC 1596	12.02[1]	0.06	0	11.96	−20.10	1479	67	−186	1293	224, 284
NGC 1600	12.12[1]	0.11	0	12.01	−22.87	4738	60	−4	4734	190, 422
NGC 1617	11.37[1,8]	0.07	0.82	10.48	−20.68	1040	50	−187	853	284
NGC 1625	13.2	0.12	0.76	12.32	−21.59	3033	96	−1	3032	321
NGC 1637	11.52	0.13	0.33	11.06	−19.72	717	6	−2	715	515
NGC 1638	13.06[1]	0.14	0.28*	12.64	−21.46	3306	85	2	3308	284
NGC 1640	12.45	0.09	0.40	11.96	−20.57	1676	85	−76	1600	191
NGC 1659	13.19	0.13	0.36	12.70	−22.08	4537	74	−15	4522	321
NGC 1672	11.03	0.08	0.55	10.40	−21.37	1335	13	−205	1130	99, 224, 239, 284, 387
NGC 1667	12.75	0.13	0.36	12.26	−22.54	4585	44	−23	4562	284, (332), 431

Galaxy (1)	Other names (2)	RA (1950) (3)	Dec (1950) (4)	l (5)	b (6)	SGL (7)	SGB (8)	Type (9)	Source (10)
NGC 1688		04 47 41	−59 53.3	269.39	−38.54	226.7	−40.3	SBc(s)II–III	C100
NGC 1705		04 53 07	−53 26.5	261.09	−38.74	231.8	−45.5	Amorphous	C100
NGC 1700		04 54 28	−04 56.5	203.71	−27.61	313.8	−59.1	E3	C100
NGC 1726		04 57 18	−07 49.8	206.97	−28.34	308.8	−60.7	E4/S0₂(4)	C100
NGC 1744		04 57 56	−26 05.8	227.00	−35.02	270.6	−61.3	SBcd(s)II–III	C100
NGC 1796		05 02 08	−61 12.4	270.62	−36.56	223.8	−40.3	SBc(s)III	C100
NGC 1784		05 03 07	−11 56.4	211.89	−28.84	301.2	−63.1	SBbc(rs)I–II	P200
NGC 1792	Cul 0503−38	05 03 30	−38 02.7	241.70	−36.46	248.5	−57.1	Sc(s)II	C100
NGC 1800	MSH 05−33?	05 04 33	−32 01.2	234.45	−35.12	258.2	−60.5	Amorphous	C100
NGC 1808	PKS 0505−375	05 05 59	−37 34.7	241.22	−35.90	248.7	−57.8	Sbc pec	C100
HA 85-1	A0509-14	05 09 25	−14 51.0	215.64	−28.63	295.1	−65.1	Sc(s)II	C100
NGC 1832		05 09 48	−15 44.8	216.62	−28.90	292.9	−65.2	SBb(r)I	P200
LMC	A0524-69	05 24.0	−69 48	280.47	−32.89	215.8	−34.1	SBmIII	W10
NGC 1947		05 26 11	−63 48.0	273.33	−33.44	218.9	−39.6	S0₃(0) pec	C100
NGC 1964		05 31 14	−21 58.9	225.28	−26.50	275.4	−69.7	SbI–II	P200
NGC 1961	IC 2133	05 36 34	69 21.3	143.83	19.47	20.1	−3.9	Sb(rs)II pec	P200
NGC 2082		05 41 36	−64 19.2	273.82	−31.75	216.7	−39.8	Sc(s)II–III	C100
NGC 2090		05 45 15	−34 16.4	239.44	−27.43	242.9	−66.0	Sc(s)II	C100
NGC 2139	IC 2154	05 59 04	−23 40.3	229.53	−21.13	262.2	−75.0	SBc(s)II.3	C100
NGC 2179		06 05 47	−21 44.3	228.27	−18.94	266.1	−77.4	Sa	C100
NGC 2188		06 08 21	−34 05.7	240.83	−22.82	233.2	−69.0	ScdIII	C100
NGC 2196		06 10 04	−21 47.8	228.71	−18.08	263.8	−78.2	Sab(s)I	C100
NGC 2146	4C 78.06?	06 10 45	78 22.5	135.66	24.90	24.6	4.2	SbII pec	P200
NGC 2207	Cul 0614−21	06 14 14	−21 21.2	228.69	−17.01	263.2	−79.2	Sc(s)I.2	C100
NGC 2217	MSH 06−25?	06 19 41	−27 12.5	234.86	−18.3	238.9	−76.1	SBa(s)	C100
NGC 2223		06 22 31	−22 48.7	230.88	−15.83	250.4	−79.9	SBbc(r)I.3	C100
NGC 2280		06 42 50	−27 35.2	237.31	−13.55	217.2	−77.8	Sc(s)I.2	C100
NGC 2310		06 52 40	−40 48.0	250.72	−16.90	206.9	−64.8	S0₂/₃(8)	C100
NGC 2325		07 00 42	−28 37.4	239.97	−10.41	199.0	−76.9	E4	C100
NGC 2268		07 00 49	84 27.8	129.25	27.55	26.9	10.1	Sbc(s)II	P200
NGC 2314		07 03 54	75 24.4	139.46	27.38	27.4	1.1	E3	W60
NGC 2339		07 05 25	18 51.7	197.84	12.06	32.0	−55.4	SBc(s)II	C100
NGC 2276	VII Zw 134	07 10 31	85 50.9	127.68	27.71	27.1	11.5	Sc(r)II–III	P200
NGC 2347		07 11 16	64 48.1	151.39	26.94	28.7	−9.5	Sb(r)I–II	P200
NGC 2300		07 15 47	85 48.6	127.71	27.81	27.2	11.5	E3	P200
NGC 2369		07 16 05	−62 15.2	273.33	−21.02	203.0	−43.2	Sbc(s)I pec	C100
NGC 2336		07 18 28	80 16.6	133.97	28.22	27.8	6.0	SBbc(r)I	P200
NGC 2397		07 21 30	−68 54.2	280.30	−22.59	203.5	−36.5	Sc(s)III	C100
NGC 2366	DDO 42	07 23 37	69 19.1	146.43	28.54	29.5	−4.9	SBmIV–V	P200
NGC 2403		07 32 03	65 42.7	150.58	29.19	30.8	−8.3	Sc(s)III	P200
NGC 2434		07 35 00	−69 10.4	281.00	−21.54	202.1	−36.1	E0	C100
NGC 2427		07 35 01	−47 31.4	260.30	−12.70	193.6	−56.9	Sc(s)II–III	C100
NGC 2442		07 36 32	−69 25.0	281.31	−21.50	202.0	−35.8	SBbc(rs)II	C100
NGC 2441		07 46 20	73 09.4	141.98	30.27	30.6	−0.8	Sc(r)I–II	P200
NGC 2460		07 52 36	60 29.0	156.71	31.35	34.2	−12.9	Sab(s)	P200

NGC 1688	12.49[5]	0.08	0.37	12.04	−19.55	1247	30	−207	1040	284, 399
NGC 1705	12.80	0.08	—	[12.7]	−17.0	640	40	−195	445	(240), 284
NGC 1700	11.96[1]	0.15	0	11.81	−22.67	3953	31	−24	3929	190, 422
NGC 1726	12.99[1]	0.15	0	12.84	−21.69	4072	60	−38	4034	284, (332)
NGC 1744	11.7	0.10	0.47	11.13	−19.40	750	8	−111	639	48, 160, 173, 191
NGC 1796	13.06[5]	0.09	0.50	12.47	−18.47	987	40	−216	771	(240), 284
NGC 1784	12.39	0.14	0.43	11.82	−21.45	2314	9	−60	2254	28, 43, 164, 321, 392
NGC 1792	10.85	0.09	0.53	10.23	−21.39	1212	19	−157	1055	43, 46, 269, 321, 438
NGC 1800	13.10	0.10	—	[13.0]	−17.3	723	44	−137	586	284, 431
NGC 1808	10.70[3]	0.09	0.50	10.11	−20.96	977	14	−157	820	23, 27, 61, 99, 229
HA 85-1	(12.69)	0.14	0.35	12.20	−20.88	2140	165	−77	2063	284
NGC 1832	12.1	0.14	0.64	11.32	−21.53	1936	7	−81	1855	46, 62, 190, 392, 400
LMC	0.63	0.11	0.16	0.36	−18.43 L	270	5	−236	34	359
NGC 1947	11.86[3]	0.11	0	11.75	−19.88	1289	115	−229	1060	(240), 284
NGC 1964	11.60	0.16	0.95	10.49	−22.01	1700	32	−121	1579	43, 46, 191, 431
NGC 1961	11.81	0.26	0.64	10.91	−23.68	3935	7	212	4147	46, 191, 392, 401, 423
NGC 2082	(12.96)	0.12	0.37	12.47	−19.12	1273	59	−235	1038	284, 329
NGC 2090	11.85[5]	0.15	0.53	11.17	−19.72	928	15	−173	755	(28), 158, 284, 431
NGC 2139	12.05	0.23	0.33	11.49	−21.15	1836	9	−148	1688	627
NGC 2179	13.40	0.27	0.31*	12.82	−20.77	2761	105	−147	2614	284
NGC 2188	12.31[3]	0.21	0.73	11.37	−18.86	743	12	−188	555	160, 173, 267, 321, (332)
NGC 2196	12.1	0.29	0.56	11.25	−21.95	2334	17	−150	2184	284, 321, 435
NGC 2146	11.24	0.18	0.70	10.36	−21.36	883	8	223	1106	516
NGC 2207	11.35	0.32	0.43	10.60	−22.97	2741	15	−151	2590	190, 401, 431
NGC 2217	11.59[1]	0.29	0.24*	11.06	−21.23	1609	10	−175	1434	629
NGC 2223	12.15	0.35	0.32	11.48	−22.04	2691	15	−162	2529	158, 284, 431
NGC 2280	(11.96)	0.43	0.49	11.04	−21.63	1900	8	−191	1709	43, 46, 158, 284, 431
NGC 2310	12.48[2]	0.32	0	12.16	−19.31	1217	125	−231	986	284, (332)
NGC 2325	12.38[1]	0.60	0	11.78	−21.28	2248	83	−206	2042	284, (332)
NGC 2268	12.23	0.15	0.45	11.63	−21.83	2228	7	230	2458	191, 391, 392
NGC 2314	12.99[1]	0.16	0	12.83	−21.73	3872	26	207	4079	190, 191
NGC 2339	12.30	0.50	0.38	11.42	−21.83	2252	10	−23	2229	(46), 190, 376, 392, 418
NGC 2276	11.98	0.15	0.30	11.53	−22.09	2416	11	232	2648	191, 247, 385, 391
NGC 2347	13.30	0.16	0.60	12.54	−22.32	4521	80	171	4692	191
NGC 2300	12.14[1]	0.15	0	11.99	−21.22	1958	29	232	2190	190, 191
NGC 2369	12.68[5]	0.24	0.67	11.77	−22.13	3282	51	−266	3016	224, 284, 329
NGC 2336	11.12	0.15	0.49	10.48	−22.94	2206	7	218	2424	43, 46, 191, 391, 392
NGC 2397	12.94[5]	0.21	0.53	12.20	−19.40	1311	42	−267	1044	284, 329, 399
NGC 2366	11.46	0.14	0.29	11.03	−16.73 N	98	3	183	281	517
NGC 2403	8.89	0.14	0.46	8.29	−19.47 N	131	2	168	299	518
NGC 2434	12.30	0.23	0	12.07	−19.68	1388	73	−270	1118	224, (240), 284
NGC 2427	12.33	0.47	0.58	11.28	−19.47	970	14	−263	707	(284), 383, 387
NGC 2442	11.16[3]	0.23	0.31	10.62	−21.20	1427	22	−270	1157	(99), 284, 399
NGC 2441	13.0	0.13	0.32	12.55	−21.86	3623	89	192	3815	191
NGC 2460	12.60	0.12	0.58	11.90	−20.62	1451	7	142	1593	190, 385, 391, 435

NGC 2500		07 58 08	50 52.6	168.01	31.57	37.8	−22.0	Sc(s)II.8	P200
NGC 2525		08 03 15	−11 17.1	231.86	10.79	104.7	−72.3	SBc(s)II	C100
NGC 2523	⎰ Mark 86	08 09 15	73 43.8	141.05	31.81	32.0	0.2	SBb(r)I	P200
NGC 2537	⎱ VV138	08 09 43	46 08.7	173.82	32.96	41.4	−25.8	ScIII pec	W100
NGC 2541		08 11 02	49 13.0	170.19	33.48	40.5	−22.9	Sc(s)III	P200
NGC 2545		08 11 20	21 30.4	201.65	27.33	54.7	−48.2	SBc(r)I-II	W100
NGC 2549		08 14 57	57 57.6	159.67	34.24	37.8	−14.5	S0₁/₂(7)	P200
NGC 2552		08 15 42	50 10.1	169.10	34.29	40.9	−21.7	Sc or SdIV	P200
NGC 2551		08 19 13	73 34.6	141.05	32.53	32.7	0.3	Sab(s)I:	P200
NGC 2613		08 31 11	−22 48.0	245.37	10.06	137.7	−65.7	Sb(s)(II)	C100
NGC 2608		08 32 15	28 38.8	195.46	34.05	55.4	−39.6	Sbc(s)II	W100
NGC 2642		08 38 14	−03 56.6	230.05	22.01	95.2	−61.6	SBb(rs)I-II	C100
NGC 2639		08 40 04	50 23.2	168.88	38.19	44.6	−19.9	Sa	P200
NGC 2633		08 42 34	74 17.0	139.69	33.87	33.9	1.6	SBb(s)I.3	P200
NGC 2646		08 45 00	73 38.9	140.34	34.25	34.3	1.1	SB0₂	P200
NGC 2654		08 45 11	60 24.4	156.13	37.81	40.4	−10.7	Sab:	P200
NGC 2672		08 46 31	19 15.6	207.47	34.26	66.4	−45.3	E2	W60
NGC 2655		08 49 08	78 24.8	134.93	32.69	32.4	5.5	Sa pec	P200
NGC 2683		08 49 35	33 36.5	190.47	38.76	55.9	−33.4	Sb(nearly on edge)	P200
NGC 2681		08 49 58	51 30.2	167.33	39.68	45.4	−18.2	Sa	P200
NGC 2685		08 51 41	58 55.5	157.79	38.89	41.9	−11.6	S0₃(7) pec	P200
NGC 2693		08 53 25	51 32.3	167.23	40.21	45.9	−17.9	E2	W60
NGC 2713		08 54 44	03 06.8	225.67	29.17	87.4	−54.5	Sbc(s)I	C100
NGC 2701		08 55 28	53 58.3	164.02	40.23	44.9	−15.6	Sc(s)II-III	P200
NGC 2712		08 56 09	45 06.6	175.65	41.00	49.9	−23.1	SBb(s)I	W100
NGC 2715		09 01 50	78 17.2	134.74	33.32	33.0	5.7	Sc(s)II	P200
NGC 2749		09 02 33	18 30.8	209.99	37.54	71.0	−43.2	E3	W100
NGC 2742		09 03 38	60 40.9	155.13	39.96	42.3	−9.3	Sc(rs)II	P200
NGC 2763		09 04 29	−15 17.9	244.03	20.84	120.6	−58.3	Sc(r)II	C100
NGC 2764		09 05 27	21 38.7	206.51	39.23	68.7	−40.5	Amorphous or Sb pec	P200
NGC 2732		09 06 54	79 23.6	133.43	33.01	32.6	6.7	S0₁(8)	P200
NGC 2775		09 07 41	07 14.5	223.27	33.99	84.8	−49.5	Sa(r)	W100
NGC 2768		09 07 45	60 14.5	155.50	40.56	43.0	−9.4	S0₁/₂(6)	P200
NGC 2748		09 08 01	76 40.9	136.26	34.36	34.1	4.5	Sc(s)II-III	W60
NGC 2776		09 08 56	45 09.6	175.50	43.25	51.9	−21.8	Sc(s)I	W100
NGC 2781		09 09 06	−14 36.7	244.19	22.15	119.6	−57.1	Sa(r)	C100
NGC 2784		09 10 06	−23 57.9	251.98	16.36	136.7	−56.7	S0₁(4)	C100
NGC 2782		09 10 54	40 19.3	182.16	43.68	55.3	−25.5	Sa(s) pec	P200
NGC 2793		09 13 43	34 38.4	190.06	43.85	59.8	−29.6	ScIII pec	W100
NGC 2811		09 13 50	−16 06.2	246.22	22.10	122.5	−56.1	Sa	P200
NGC 2815		09 14 05	−23 25.5	252.18	17.40	135.6	−55.9	Sb(s)I-II	C100
NGC 2798	VV 50	09 14 10	42 12.7	179.53	44.30	54.6	−23.6	SBa(s) (tides)	P200
NGC 2787		09 14 50	69 24.9	144.05	38.05	38.5	−1.3	SB0/a	P200
NGC 2835		09 15 37	−22 08.8	251.42	18.51	133.2	−55.7	SBc(rs)I.2	C100
NGC 2832		09 16 45	33 57.6	191.10	44.39	60.9	−29.7	E3	P48

Galaxy (11)	B_T (12)	A^o (13)	A^i (14)	$B_T^{o,i}$ (15)	$M_{B_T}^{o,i}$ (16)	v (17)	ε (18)	Δv (19)	v_o (20)	Sources (21)
NGC 2500	12.21	0.12	0.30	11.79	-18.66	516	6	99	615	160, 173, 191, 263, 392
NGC 2525	12.29	0.57	0.41	11.31	-20.92	1582	9	-187	1395	46, (191), 392
NGC 2523	12.65	0.12	0.67	11.86	-22.45	3448	140	190	3638	191
NGC 2537	12.35	0.11	0.31	11.93	-18.13	441	6	72	513	519
NGC 2541	12.25	0.10	0.52	11.63	-18.93	560	6	86	646	606
NGC 2545	13.20	0.16	0.47	12.57	-21.54	3361	8	-49	3312	106, 136, 263
NGC 2549	12.16[1]	0.10	0	12.06	-19.85	1082	75	125	1207	190
NGC 2552	12.8	0.10	0.42	12.28	-18.14	518	6	89	607	607
NGC 2551	13.05	0.11	0.63	12.31	-21.17	2296	40	188	2484	191
NGC 2613	11.35	0.62	1.13	9.60	-22.71	1685	30	-239	1446	43, 190, 191
NGC 2608	12.80	0.10	0.45	12.25	-20.88	2135	20	-23	2112	190, 376
NGC 2642	(12.54)	0.22	0.44	11.88	-22.77	4439	40	-177	4262	191
NGC 2639	12.65	0.08	0.67	11.90	-22.18	3187	20	83	3270	190, 424
NGC 2633	(12.85)	0.10	0.66	12.09	-21.33	2228	40	188	2416	191
NGC 2646	12.95	0.10	0	12.85	-21.51	3546	45	185	3731	191
NGC 2654	12.75	0.08	1.32	11.35	-20.99	1339	9	129	1468	190, 391, 402
NGC 2672	12.61[1]	0.10	0	12.51	-21.95	3983	20	-76	3907	190, 376
NGC 2655	10.95	0.11	0.52	10.32	-22.19	1389	13	203	1592	58, 190, 220, 402
NGC 2683	10.61	0.08	1.19	9.34	-20.17	404	(50)	-5	399	520
NGC 2681	11.09	0.07	0.48	10.54	-20.48	715	24	85	800	27, 190, 191
NGC 2685	11.93	0.07	0	11.86	-19.65	881	7	120	1001	521
NGC 2693	12.77[1]	0.07	0	12.70	-22.32	4956	50	85	5041	190
NGC 2713	12.60	0.14	0.59	11.87	-22.47	3845	42	-155	3690	162, 284, 407
NGC 2701	12.80	0.07	0.42	12.31	-21.12	2325	7	96	2421	46, 158, 284, 384, 400
NGC 2712	12.70	0.07	0.74	11.89	-21.00	1840	200	52	1892	190
NGC 2715	11.98	0.11	0.64	11.23	-21.21	1339	4	201	1540	(191), 410
NGC 2749	13.11[1]	0.08	0	13.03	-21.56	4229	31	-86	4143	58, 190
NGC 2742	12.3	0.07	0.50	11.73	-20.54	1296	20	126	1422	321, 391
NGC 2763	12.67	0.24	0.31	12.12	-20.48	1887	8	-229	1658	158, 284, 301, (332), 431
NGC 2764	13.40	0.08	—	[13.32]	-20.29	2707	14	-71	2636	284, 385
NGC 2732	12.83[1]	0.11	0	12.72	-20.62	2120	40	205	2325	191
NGC 2775	11.20	0.10	0*	11.10	-20.79	1336	17	-141	1195	190, 402, 424
NGC 2768	10.99[1]	0.07	0	10.92	-21.51	1408	175	123	1531	190
NGC 2748	12.4	0.10	0.61	11.69	-20.95	1489	48	195	1684	191
NGC 2776	12.20	0.06	0.30	11.84	-21.80	2624	8	49	2673	46, 191, 223, 400
NGC 2781	12.44[1]	0.22	0*	12.22	-20.75	2195	60	-229	1966	284, (332)
NGC 2784	11.21[1]	0.34	0	10.87	-18.91	708	52	-257	451	191
NGC 2782	12.15	0.06	0.59	11.50	-22.06	2551	10	23	2574	597
NGC 2793	(12.95)	0.06	0.35	12.54	-20.08	1681	3	-7	1674	321, 412
NGC 2811	12.25	0.22	0.49*	11.54	-21.75	2514	75	-235	2279	190
NGC 2815	(12.66)	0.31	1.01	11.34	-22.00	2590	115	-257	2333	284
NGC 2798	13.0	0.06	0*	12.94	-19.81	1741	17	32	1773	190, 247, 402, 431
NGC 2787	11.74[1]	0.08	0	11.66	-19.44	664	36	164	828	190, 191
NGC 2835	(10.95)	0.28	0.42	10.25	-20.23	878	12	-254	624	48, 173, 191
NGC 2832	12.45	0.06	0	12.39	-23.32	6946	50	-11	6935	190

Galaxy (1)	Other names (2)	RA (1950) (3)	Dec (1950) (4)	*l* (5)	*b* (6)	SGL (7)	SGB (8)	Type (9)	Source (10)
NGC 2848		09 17 49	−16 18.8	247.05	22.70	123.0	−55.2	Sc(s)II	C100
NGC 2841		09 18 35	51 11.3	166.95	44.15	49.5	−16.0	Sb	P200
NGC 2844		09 18 37	40 22.0	182.13	45.15	56.6	−24.5	Sa:(r)	W100
NGC 2855		09 19 02	−11 41.8	243.33	25.85	115.1	−54.3	Sa(r)	P200
NGC 2865		09 21 14	−22 56.8	252.96	18.94	134.4	−54.3	E4	C100
NGC 2859		09 21 15	34 43.7	190.16	45.40	61.1	−28.5	RSB02(3)	P200
NGC 2888		09 24 09	−27 49.1	257.16	16.09	142.4	−53.0	E2	C100
NGC 2889		09 24 32	−11 25.3	244.08	27.12	115.1	−52.9	Sb(r)II	C100
NGC 2880		09 25 42	62 42.7	151.47	41.77	43.3	−6.2	SB01	W60
NGC 2902		09 28 30	−14 31.0	247.38	25.83	120.3	−52.4	S01(0)	C100
NGC 2903	B 0929+21	09 29 20	21 43.2	208.72	44.54	73.5	−36.4	Sc(s)I-II	P200
NGC 2907		09 29 20	−16 30.9	249.17	24.65	123.6	−52.5	S03(6) pec	C100
NGC 2911		09 31 05	10 22.6	223.18	40.57	85.7	−43.0	S03(2) or S0 pec	P200
NGC 2924		09 32 49	−16 10.6	249.52	25.51	123.2	−51.6	E0	C100
NGC 2935		09 34 27	−20 54.2	253.60	22.57	130.8	−51.4	SBb(s)I.2	C100
NGC 2942		09 36 08	34 14.0	191.26	48.41	64.0	−26.8	Sc(s)I.3	P200
NGC 2955		09 38 15	36 06.6	188.45	48.94	62.9	−25.1	Sc(s)I	W100
NGC 2962		09 38 17	05 23.6	230.00	39.67	92.8	−43.9	RSB02	W100
NGC 2950		09 38 59	59 04.8	155.20	44.66	46.9	−8.0	RSB02/3	P200
NGC 2967		09 39 29	00 33.9	235.38	37.28	99.1	−45.8	Sc(rs)I-II	C100
NGC 2964	Mark 404 / B2 0939+32B	09 39 56	32 04.6	194.62	49.02	66.4	−27.7	Sc(s)II.2	P200
NGC 2974		09 40 02	−03 28.1	239.52	35.01	104.7	−47.1	E4	C100
NGC 2968		09 40 15	32 09.6	194.51	49.09	66.4	−27.6	Amorphous or S03 pec	P200
NGC 2983		09 41 22	−20 14.8	254.32	24.19	129.8	−49.7	SBa	C100
NGC 2986		09 41 57	−21 02.9	255.05	23.72	131.0	−49.6	E2	C100
NGC 2989		09 43 04	−18 08.6	252.98	25.95	126.6	−49.3	Sc(s)I	C100
NGC 2976		09 43 10	68 08.9	143.92	40.90	41.3	−0.8	SdIII-IV	P200
NGC 2992		09 43 18	−14 05.7	249.71	28.78	120.4	−48.8	Sa (tides)	C100
NGC 2993		09 43 23	−14 08.1	249.77	28.77	120.5	−48.8	Sab (tides)	C100
NGC 2997		09 43 27	−30 57.7	262.59	16.76	146.0	−48.2	Sc(s)I.3	C100
NGC 2990		09 43 40	05 56.6	230.31	41.10	93.0	−42.5	ScII:	W60
NGC 3001		09 44 07	−30 12.4	262.17	17.42	144.8	−48.2	SBbc(s)I-II	C100
NGC 2998		09 45 35	44 19.0	175.72	49.81	57.8	−18.3	Sc(rs)I	W100
NGC 3003		09 45 37	33 39.2	192.35	50.34	66.0	−25.8	Sc:III:	W60
NGC 2985		09 45 54	72 30.7	139.02	38.68	38.6	2.7	Sab(s)	P200
NGC 3021		09 47 59	33 47.1	192.19	50.84	66.3	−25.3	Sbc(s)II	W100
NGC 3038		09 49 05	−32 31.1	264.60	16.39	147.9	−46.7	Sb(s)II	C100
NGC 3032		09 49 14	29 28.3	199.02	50.67	70.1	−28.0	S03(2)/Sa	P200
NGC 3059		09 49 41	−73 41.2	291.16	−15.36	194.0	−26.9	SBc(s)III	C100
NGC 3041		09 50 23	16 54.8	217.67	47.57	82.0	−35.4	Sc(rs)II	W60
NGC 3044		09 51 06	01 49.0	236.20	40.37	99.1	−42.6	Scd (on edge)	C100
NGC 3031	M 81	09 51 30	69 18.3	142.09	40.90	41.1	0.6	Sb(r)I-II	P200
NGC 3034	M 82 / 3C 281	09 51 41	69 54.9	141.42	40.56	40.7	1.0	Amorphous	P200
NGC 3052		09 52 07	−18 24.3	254.88	27.28	127.1	−47.1	Sc(r)II	C100
NGC 3054		09 52 12	−25 28.0	260.20	22.13	137.5	−47.1	SBbc(s)I	C100

Galaxy (11)	B_T (12)	A^o (13)	A^i (14)	$B_T^{o,i}$ (15)	$M_{B_T}^{o,i}$ (16)	v (17)	ε (18)	Δv (19)	v_o (20)	Sources (21)
NGC 2848	12.65	0.21	0.44	12.00	−20.78	2032	15	−237	1795	158, 284, 431
NGC 2841	10.17	0.06	0.87	9.24	−21.53	637	4	77	714	522
NGC 2844	13.65	0.05	0.82	12.78	−19.62	1486	9	21	1507	284, 402
NGC 2855	12.45	0.17	0.49	11.79	−20.85	1911	35	−222	1689	58, 190
NGC 2865	12.36[1]	0.27	0	12.09	−21.37	2714	75	−257	2457	190
NGC 2859	11.80[1]	0.05	0	11.75	−20.76	1599	20	−9	1590	190, 376
NGC 2888	13.5	0.34	0	13.16	−19.81	2233	168	−270	1963	284
NGC 2889	12.50	0.16	0.50	11.84	−22.19	3417	190	−223	3194	284
NGC 2880	12.61[1]	0.07	0	12.54	−20.05	1514	50	132	1646	190
NGC 2902	13.42[2]	0.17	0	13.25	−19.57	2065	98	−234	1831	284
NGC 2903	9.50[8]	0.06	0.53	8.91	−20.96	550	(50)	−78	472	523
NGC 2907	(13.01)	0.18	0	12.83	−19.98	2065	83	−241	1824	284
NGC 2911	12.60	0.07	0	12.53	−21.36	3131	32	−134	2997	58, 139, 190
NGC 2924	13.28[2]	0.17	0	13.11	−21.60	4615	35	−241	4374	284
NGC 2935	(12.00)	0.21	0.54	11.25	−21.76	2258	15	−255	2003	158, 284
NGC 2942	(12.79)	0.04	0.36	12.39	−22.33	4414	20	−15	4399	275, 284
NGC 2955	13.45	0.04	0.51	12.90	−22.85	7056	85	−5	7051	284, (332)
NGC 2962	12.78[1]	0.07	0	12.71	−20.25	2117	20	−159	1958	106, 284, 376
NGC 2950	11.82[1]	0.06	0	11.76	−20.61	1375	31	113	1488	190, 191
NGC 2967	12.30	0.09	0.30	11.91	−21.17	2245	60	−180	2065	191
NGC 2964	12.06	0.04	0.49	11.53	−20.53	1319	18	−27	1292	134, 190, 385
NGC 2974	11.78[1]	0.10	0	11.68	−21.12	2011	35	−197	1814	58, 190
NGC 2968	12.80	0.04	—	[12.76]	−19.73	1603	93	−27	1576	284, 321, (402)
NGC 2983	12.57[1]	0.19	0*	12.38	−20.35	2015	100	−255	1760	190
NGC 2986	12.04[1]	0.20	0	11.84	−21.32	2397	100	−258	2139	190
NGC 2989	(13.42)	0.17	0.38	12.87	−21.60	4166	55	−250	3916	284
NGC 2976	10.85	0.07	0.53	10.25	−17.51 N	13	14	155	168	160, 191
NGC 2992	12.8	0.14	1.05	11.61	−21.36	2200	36	−237	1963	92, 284
NGC 2993	13.1	0.14	0.56	12.40	−20.46	2105	46	−237	1868	92, 284
NGC 2997	10.32	0.33	0.37	9.62	−21.40	1081	7	−282	799	524
NGC 2990	13.2	0.07	0.49	12.64	−21.26	3164	58	−158	3006	284, 431
NGC 3001	12.72[5]	0.31	0.42	11.99	−21.20	2451	15	−280	2171	158, 284
NGC 2998	(12.65)	0.04	0.53	12.08	−22.84	4777	8	36	4813	284, 384, 400, 429
NGC 3003	12.17	0	0.75	11.42	−20.91	1481	7	−20	1461	190, 385, 391, 392
NGC 2985	11.21	0.08	0.56	10.57	−21.74	1277	50	174	1451	190
NGC 3021	(13.07)	0	0.46	12.61	−19.80	1540	15	−20	1520	284, 321, 385
NGC 3038	12.65[5]	0.34	0.33*	11.98	−21.44	2698	80	−286	2412	224, 284
NGC 3032	12.55[1]	0	0	12.55	−19.82	1535	14	−43	1492	190, 376, 385
NGC 3059	12.03[5]	0.37	0.31	11.35	−20.14	1274	33	−283	991	630
NGC 3041	12.25	0.05	0.44	11.76	−20.31	1403	12	−107	1296	46, 158, 284, 341
NGC 3044	12.55	0.07	0.87	11.61	−20.30	1384	29	−178	1206	321, 324
NGC 3031	7.86	0.07	0.78	7.01	−20.75 N	−36	5	160	124	525
NGC 3034	9.28	0.07	—	[9.2]	−18.6 N	247	2	162	409	526
NGC 3052	(12.84)	0.16	0.39	12.29	−21.85	3616	113	−252	3364	284
NGC 3054	(12.13)	0.22	0.44	11.47	−21.46	2194	84	−271	1923	321

Galaxy (1)	Other names (2)	RA (1950) (3)	Dec (1950) (4)	l (5)	b (6)	SGL (7)	SGB (8)	Type (9)	Source (10)
NGC 3056		09 52 18	−28 03.8	262.07	20.21	141.3	−46.8	S0$_{1/2}$(5)	C100
NGC 3055		09 52 41	04 30.4	233.55	42.22	96.1	−41.1	Sc(s)II	W100
NGC 3043		09 52 42	59 32.7	153.54	46.05	47.9	−6.5	?	48 Pr
IC 2522		09 52 59	−32 54.0	265.51	16.63	148.2	−45.9	Sc/SBc(s)I-II	C100
NGC 3067		09 55 26	32 36.5	194.23	52.32	68.4	−24.9	Sb(s)III	W100
NGC 3078		09 56 08	−26 41.2	261.79	21.80	139.2	−46.1	E3	C100
NGC 3087		09 56 59	−33 59.0	266.90	16.33	149.4	−44.8	E2	C100
NGC 3081		09 57 11	−22 35.1	259.03	25.03	133.2	−46.1	SBa(s)	C100
NGC 3089		09 57 22	−28 05.1	262.99	20.91	141.1	−45.7	Sc(s)II	C100
NGC 3065	VII Zw 303	09 57 35	72 24.6	138.44	39.45	39.4	3.2	S0$_2$(0)	P200
NGC 3091		09 57 53	−19 23.8	256.76	27.50	128.7	−45.8	E3	C100
NGC 3095	PKS 0958−314	09 57 53	−31 18.8	265.28	18.51	145.7	−45.1	Sc(s)I-II pec	C100
NGC 3079	4C 55.19?	09 58 35	55 55.4	157.82	48.36	51.0	−8.5	Sc pec:	W60
NGC 3077		09 59 22	68 58.5	141.91	41.66	41.9	0.8	Amorphous	P200
NGC 3098		09 59 27	24 57.2	206.81	52.07	75.7	−29.0	S0$_1$(9)	W100
NGC 3109	DDO 236	10 00 47	−25 54.8	262.10	23.07	138.0	−45.1	SmIV	P200
IC 2537		10 01 35	−27 19.5	263.23	22.10	139.9	−44.8	Sc(s)I-II	C100
NGC 3115		10 02 44	−07 28.5	247.79	36.78	112.4	−42.9	S0$_1$(7)	P200
NGC 3124		10 04 17	−18 58.3	257.71	28.83	128.2	−44.3	SBbc(r)I	W100
NGC 3125		10 04 18	−29 41.5	265.33	20.64	143.1	−44.0	Amorphous	C100
NGC 3136		10 04 30	−67 07.8	287.99	−9.45	187.3	−29.9	E4	C100
NGC 3145		10 07 43	−12 11.3	252.99	34.37	119.0	−42.7	SBbc(rs)I	C100
NGC 3156	MSH 10+04?	10 10 06	03 22.7	238.27	45.13	99.7	−37.6	E5:	W60
NGC 3162		10 10 45	22 59.2	211.04	54.08	79.2	−28.1	Sbc(s)I.8	W100
NGC 3158		10 10 53	39 00.7	183.22	55.26	65.3	−18.4	E3	W100
NGC 3166		10 11 10	03 40.5	238.15	45.52	99.5	−37.3	Sa(s)	C100
NGC 3169		10 11 38	03 43.2	238.20	45.64	99.5	−37.1	Sb(r)I-II (tides)	C100
NGC 3175		10 12 24	−28 37.2	266.13	22.58	141.4	−42.3	Sc(s)III: pec	C100
NGC 3147		10 12 40	73 39.0	136.30	39.46	39.2	4.8	Sb(s)I.8	W60
NGC 3177		10 13 49	21 22.4	214.03	54.30	81.2	−28.4	Sb(s)II	W100
NGC 3185		10 14 54	21 56.3	213.23	54.70	80.8	−27.8	SBa(s)	P200
NGC 3184		10 15 17	41 40.0	178.36	55.64	63.7	−16.1	Sc(r)II.2	W100
NGC 3190	{ NGC 3189	10 15 21	22 05.1	213.04	54.85	80.7	−27.7	Sa	P200
NGC 3193	{ VV 307	10 15 40	22 08.8	212.97	54.94	80.7	−27.6	E2	P200
NGC 3200		10 16 12	−17 43.9	259.24	31.62	126.8	−41.4	Sb(r)I	C100
NGC 3198		10 16 53	45 48.0	171.23	54.83	60.6	−13.2	Sc(rs)I-II	W60
NGC 3203		10 17 14	−26 26.9	265.62	24.96	138.4	−41.4	S0$_2$(7)	C100
NGC 3223	IC 2571	10 19 21	−34 01.0	270.80	19.09	148.3	−40.2	Sb(s)I-II	C100
NGC 3226	VV 209	10 20 43	20 09.2	216.93	55.44	83.3	−27.6	S0$_1$(1)	W100
NGC 3227	VV 209	10 20 47	20 07.1	217.00	55.45	83.4	−27.6	Sb(s)III	W100
NGC 3241		10 22 01	−32 13.7	270.21	20.88	145.9	−39.9	Sb(r)II	C100
NGC 3250		10 24 21	−39 41.4	274.98	14.93	155.3	−38.3	E3	C100
NGC 3245		10 24 30	28 45.8	201.91	58.22	75.8	−22.3	S0$_1$(5)	W100
NGC 3256	{ VV65	10 25 42	−43 38.9	277.38	11.73	160.1	−37.1	Sb(s) pec	C100
NGC 3254	{ PKS 1025−436	10 26 32	29 44.9	200.12	58.76	75.2	−21.4	Sb(s)II	P200

Galaxy (11)	B_T (12)	A^o (13)	A^i (14)	$B_T^{o,i}$ (15)	$M_{B_T}^{o,i}$ (16)	v (17)	ε (18)	Δv (19)	v_0 (20)	Sources (21)
NGC 3056	12.83[2]	0.25	0	12.58	−18.36	1047	120	−277	770	284
NGC 3055	12.7	0.06	0.46	12.18	−20.54	1913	139	−166	1747	191
NGC 3043	(12.46)	0.05	—	[12.4]	−21.5	2935	128	113	3048	284
IC 2522	(12.72)	0.33	0.47	11.92	−21.74	2988	15	−287	2701	160
NGC 3067	12.70	0	0.94	11.76	−20.52	1456	25	−27	1429	89, 118, 190, 431
NGC 3078	12.14[1]	0.22	0	11.92	−21.31	2492	29	−275	2217	130, 139, 190
NGC 3087	(12.87)	0.34	0	12.53	−20.85	2662	65	−290	2372	284
NGC 3081	12.68[2]	0.18	0*	12.50	−20.67	2413	33	−265	2148	284
NGC 3089	(13.09)	0.24	0.41	12.44	−20.94	2653	58	−278	2375	284
NGC 3065	12.89[1]	0.08	0	12.81	−20.39	2008	40	173	2181	58, 191
NGC 3091	12.50[2]	0.16	0	12.34	−21.96	3882	93	−256	3626	284
NGC 3095	12.52[5]	0.28	0.42	11.82	−21.73	2849	22	−285	2564	441
NGC 3079	11.20	0.04	0.85	10.31	−21.64	1130	9	95	1225	48, 173, 191, 392, 431
NGC 3077	10.64	0.07	—	[10.6]	−17.2 N	7	3	158	165	527
NGC 3098	12.85	0	0	12.85	−19.18	1340	75	−68	1272	284
NGC 3109	(10.39)	0.20	0.41	9.78	−17.28	403	1	−274	129	528
IC 2537	12.9	0.22	0.40	12.28	−21.23	2800	50	−277	2523	383
NGC 3115	9.98[1]	0.09	0	9.89	−19.82	655	8	−218	437	529
NGC 3124	(12.35)	0.14	0.34	11.87	−22.23	3563	11	−256	3307	284, 384, 400
NGC 3125	(13.12)	0.24	—	[12.9]	−18.2	1110	50	−283	827	386
NGC 3136	12.09[1]	0.67	0	11.42	−20.82	1696	93	−295	1401	153, (240), 284
NGC 3145	(12.35)	0.10	0.52	11.73	−22.44	3651	11	−235	3416	191, 400, 401, 429
NGC 3156	13.05[2]	0.05	0	13.00	−18.50	1174	58	−175	999	284
NGC 3162	12.15	0	0.33	11.82	−20.12	1303	9	−80	1223	190, 391, 418
NGC 3158	12.90[1]	0	0	12.90	−22.84	7024	50	5	7029	190
NGC 3166	11.52	0.05	0.82	10.65	−21.19	1339	22	−173	1166	190, 402
NGC 3169	11.28	0.05	0.67	10.56	−21.09	1240	18	−173	1067	43, 190, 191, 435
NGC 3175	12.2	0.21	0.38	11.61	−19.52	1125	75	−282	843	284
NGC 3147	11.45	0.07	0.50	10.88	−22.94	2721	80	178	2899	190
NGC 3177	13.00	0	0.55	12.45	−19.49	1309	19	−89	1220	190, 418
NGC 3185	12.95	0	0.32*	12.63	−19.18	1237	19	−86	1151	190, 402
NGC 3184	10.43[8]	0	0.29	10.14	−20.28	589	6	18	607	530
NGC 3190	11.99	0	0.97	11.02	−21.19	1469	(22)	−85	1384	181, 190, 191, 402
NGC 3193	11.83[1]	0	0	11.83	−20.26	1392	24	−85	1307	190, 442
NGC 3200	(12.29)	0.12	1.01	11.16	−22.95	3567	48	−254	3313	284
NGC 3198	10.94	0	0.59	10.35	−20.39	662	4	40	702	531
NGC 3203	12.83[2]	0.18	0	12.65	−20.51	2424	38	−277	2147	284
NGC 3223	11.88[5]	0.27	0.70	10.91	−22.69	2911	138	−292	2619	(240), 284
NGC 3226	12.3	0	0	12.3	−19.71	1356	13	−96	1260	58, 190, 273, 313
NGC 3227	11.55	0	0.63	10.92	−20.80	1198	6	−96	1102	532
NGC 3241	13.6	0.24	0.59	12.77	−20.80	2874	148	−290	2584	284
NGC 3250	12.17[1]	0.38	0	11.79	−21.76	2871	123	−301	2570	284
NGC 3245	11.69[1]	0	0	11.69	−20.23	1261	30	−51	1210	190
NGC 3256	11.98[3]	0.52	0.75	10.71	−22.80	2821	100	−304	2517	(99), 327
NGC 3254	12.2	0	1.02	11.18	−20.75	1265	51	−46	1219	190, 391

Galaxy (1)	Other names (2)	RA (1950) (3)	Dec (1950) (4)	*l* (5)	*b* (6)	SGL (7)	SGB (8)	Type (9)	Source (10)
NGC 3258		10 26 38	−35 21.0	272.91	18.82	149.8	−38.6	E1	C100
NGC 3261		10 26 54	−44 24.0	277.97	11.20	161.0	—36.7	SBbc(rs)I-II	C100
NGC 3268		10 27 46	−35 04.2	272.95	19.18	149.4	—38.4	E2	C100
NGC 3271	IC 2585	10 28 12	−35 06.2	273.05	19.20	149.4	−38.3	Sa	C100
NGC 3275		10 28 39	−36 29.0	273.92	18.09	151.1	−38.0	SBab(r)I	C100
NGC 3259		10 29 05	65 18.1	143.27	46.22	46.5	0.5	SbIII	W60
NGC 3274		10 29 30	27 55.6	203.76	59.21	77.2	−21.8	SIV	P48
NGC 3281		10 29 36	−34 36.0	273.02	19.78	148.7	−38.1	Sa	C100
NGC 3277		10 30 08	28 46.2	202.15	59.45	76.6	−21.2	Sa(r)I-II	W100
NGC 3285		10 31 15	−27 11.8	268.92	26.16	139.3	−38.2	Sab(s)	C100
NGC 3287		10 32 04	21 54.5	215.39	58.51	83.2	−24.5	SBcd(s)III	W100
NGC 3294		10 33 24	37 35.1	184.62	59.84	69.2	−15.8	Sc(s)I.3	W100
NGC 3300		10 33 58	14 25.8	228.51	56.05	90.7	−27.6	SB0₁	P48
NGC 3301		10 34 13	22 08.4	215.24	59.05	83.2	−23.9	Sa	P200
NGC 3309		10 34 15	−27 15.8	269.58	26.48	139.4	−37.6	E1	C100
NGC 3312	IC 629	10 34 42	−27 18.3	269.70	26.49	139.4	−37.5	Sab(r)	C100
NGC 3318		10 35 03	−41 22.1	277.68	14.57	156.9	−35.9	SBbc(rs)II.2	C100
NGC 3310		10 35 39	53 45.9	156.61	54.06	56.1	−5.9	Sbc(r) pec	W60
NGC 3319		10 36 14	41 56.8	175.99	59.34	65.9	−12.8	SBc(s)II.4	P200
NGC 3320		10 36 37	47 39.4	165.86	57.26	61.2	−9.4	Sc(s)II-III	C100
NGC 3338		10 39 29	14 00.6	230.34	57.02	91.8	−26.6	Sbc(s)I-II	W100
NGC 3347		10 40 30	−36 05.3	275.86	19.66	150.3	−35.7	SBb(r)I	C100
NGC 3329	NGC 3397	10 40 31	77 04.3	131.70	38.08	37.7	8.3	Sab	P200
NGC 3344		10 40 47	25 11.1	210.05	61.25	81.2	−21.1	SBbc(rs)I	W100
NGC 3346		10 40 59	15 08.1	228.82	57.88	90.9	−25.8	SBc(rs)II.2	W100
NGC 3358		10 41 16	−36 08.8	276.02	19.72	150.3	−35.5	Sa(r)I	C100
NGC 3351	M 95	10 41 19	11 58.1	233.96	56.37	94.1	−27.1	SBb(r)II	P200
NGC 3353	Haro 3 / Mark 35	10 42 17	56 13.6	152.31	53.37	54.7	−3.7	?	48 Pr
NGC 3359		10 43 21	63 29.2	143.60	48.59	48.9	0.6	SBc(s)I.8 pec	P200
NGC 3348		10 43 28	73 06.2	134.64	41.35	41.0	6.2	E0	W60
NGC 3367	4C 14.37	10 43 56	14 00.8	231.32	57.96	92.3	−25.6	SBc(s)II	W100
NGC 3368	M 96	10 44 08	12 05.1	234.44	57.01	94.3	−26.4	Sab(s)II	P200
NGC 3370		10 44 23	17 32.3	225.36	59.67	88.9	−24.0	Sc(s)I-II	W60
NGC 3377		10 45 03	14 15.0	231.18	58.32	92.2	−25.3	E6	P200
NGC 3379	M 105	10 45 11	12 50.8	233.50	57.63	93.6	−25.9	E0	P200
NGC 3384		10 45 38	12 53.7	233.53	57.75	93.6	−25.7	SB0₁(5)	P200
NGC 3390		10 45 44	−31 16.2	274.27	24.38	144.2	−35.0	S0₃(8) or (Sb)	C100
NGC 3389		10 45 50	12 47.9	233.73	57.74	93.8	−25.7	Sc(s)II.2	P200
NGC 3395	VV 246	10 47 02	33 14.7	192.93	63.14	74.6	−15.8	Sc(s)II-III	W60
NGC 3396	VV 246	10 47 08	33 15.3	192.91	63.16	74.6	−15.8	Sc	W60
NGC 3412		10 48 15	13 40.5	232.88	58.70	93.2	−24.8	SB0₁/₂(5)	W100
NGC 3414		10 48 32	28 14.5	204.08	63.42	79.3	−18.1	S0₁	P200
NGC 3423		10 48 38	06 06.3	244.17	54.37	101.0	−27.7	Sc(s)II-III	W100
NGC 3415		10 48 52	43 59.0	170.53	60.76	65.5	−9.8	E5	48 Pr
NGC 3430	IC 2613	10 49 25	33 12.9	192.91	63.64	74.9	−15.4	Sbc(r)I-II	W100

Galaxy (11)	B_T (12)	A^o (13)	A^i (14)	$B_T^{o,i}$ (15)	$M_{B_T}^{o,i}$ (16)	v (17)	ε (18)	Δv (19)	v_0 (20)	Sources (21)
NGC 3258	12.76[1]	0.28	0	12.48	−21.06	2848	78	−295	2553	284
NGC 3261	(12.16)	0.55	0.38	11.23	−22.09	2612	125	−305	2307	284
NGC 3268	12.84[1,8]	0.27	0	12.57	−20.93	2801	110	−295	2506	284
NGC 3271	12.85[1]	0.27	0.86	11.72	−22.52	3824	53	−295	3529	284
NGC 3275	12.40[5]	0.29	0.54	11.57	−22.28	3241	100	−297	2944	284
NGC 3259	(12.91)	0.05	0.74	12.12	−20.90	1866	77	139	2005	191
NGC 3274	13.15	0	0.26	12.89	−17.05	542	10	−56	486	158, 160, 284, 431
NGC 3281	12.62	0.26	0.40*	11.96	−22.11	3549	55	−294	3255	224, 284
NGC 3277	12.55	0	0.24*	12.31	−19.87	1417	15	−52	1365	190, 402
NGC 3285	(12.98)	0.17	0.66	12.15	—	—	—	−280	—	—
NGC 3287	(12.86)	0	0.54	12.32	−19.62	1307	15	−88	1219	284, (332), 385
NGC 3294	12.2	0	0.51	11.69	−20.79	1571	21	−5	1566	46, 191, 392
NGC 3300	13.29[2]	0	0	13.29	−20.50	2992	78	−126	2866	284
NGC 3301	12.24	0	0*	12.24	−19.74	1333	75	−87	1246	190
NGC 3309	12.81[1,8]	0.16	0	12.65	−21.76	4093	43	−281	3812	245, 284, 334
NGC 3312	(12.73)	0.16	0.93	11.64	−21.85	2775	54	−281	2494	229, 284
NGC 3318	12.70[5]	0.39	0.48	11.83	−21.49	2609	95	−303	2306	240, 438
NGC 3310	11.2	0	0.36	10.84	−20.82	992	4	81	1073	533
NGC 3319	11.78	0	0.49	11.29	−19.66	758	5	18	776	534
NGC 3320	(12.93)	0	0.52	12.41	−20.98	2331	9	49	2380	301
NGC 3338	11.32	0	0.43	10.89	−20.96	1299	7	−128	1171	46, 191, 391, 392
NGC 3347	12.27[3]	0.26	0.72	11.29	−22.31	2923	63	−297	2626	284
NGC 3329	(12.99)	0.08	0.71	12.20	−20.92	1910	57	192	2102	106, 284
NGC 3344	10.48	0	0.30	10.18	−20.31	698	4	−71	627	173, 190, 220, 253
NGC 3346	(12.18)	0	0.32	11.86	−19.93	1260	11	−122	1138	158, 284, 400
NGC 3358	12.52[3]	0.26	0.36*	11.90	−21.69	2910	212	−297	2613	284
NGC 3351	10.52	0	0.64	9.88	−20.66	779	4	−138	641	535
NGC 3353	13.2	0	—	[13.2]	−18.5	995	21	94	1089	284, 344
NGC 3359	10.99	0.04	0.46	10.49	−21.30	1008	4	130	1138	105, 191, 253, 261, 302
NGC 3348	12.15[1]	0.07	0	12.08	−21.83	2855	75	175	3030	190
NGC 3367	12.05	0	0.31	11.74	−22.08	3034	20	−128	2906	46, 190
NGC 3368	10.11	0	0.62	9.49	−21.41	895	8	−137	758	536
NGC 3370	(12.28)	0	0.47	11.81	−20.25	1400	78	−111	1289	191
NGC 3377	11.10[1]	0	0	11.10	−19.26	718	40	−127	591	190
NGC 3379	10.33[1]	0	0	10.33	−20.58	893	19	−134	759	190, 229, (306), (332), 442
NGC 3384	10.70[1]	0	0	10.70	−19.83	771	28	−133	638	190, 229
NGC 3390	13.09[3]	0.19	0:	12.90	−20.65	2850	100	−289	2561	284
NGC 3389	12.35	0	0.5	11.85	−19.91	1261	12	−134	1127	191, 272
NGC 3395	12.4	0	0.46	11.94	−20.58	1628	6	−29	1599	537
NGC 3396	12.6	0	0.61	11.99	−20.56	1648	15	−29	1619	140, 164, 191, 241
NGC 3412	11.47[1]	0	0	11.47	−19.35	861	75	−130	731	190
NGC 3414	11.74[1]	0	0	11.74	−20.44	1419	20	−55	1364	190, 376
NGC 3423	11.62	0	0.32	11.30	−19.84	1010	8	−165	845	158, 284, 301
NGC 3415	12.84[2]	0	0	12.84	−21.28	3301	15	29	3330	284, 385
NGC 3430	12.15	0	0.47	11.68	−20.78	1584	7	−29	1555	164, 191, 263, 400, 431

Galaxy (1)	Other names (2)	RA (1950) (3)	Dec (1950) (4)	l (5)	b (6)	SGL (7)	SGB (8)	Type (9)	Source (10)
NGC 3433		10 49 27	10 24.7	238.33	57.16	96.6	−25.9	Sc(r)I.3	W100
NGC 3432	VV 11	10 49 43	36 53.1	184.78	63.16	71.7	−13.4	Sc(II–III:)	W60
NGC 3437		10 49 54	23 12.0	215.19	62.82	84.1	−20.2	Sc(s)(III)	W60
NGC 3403		10 50 14	73 57.4	133.45	40.95	40.6	7.1	SbcIII:	W60
NGC 3449		10 50 34	−32 39.7	275.99	23.67	145.9	−33.9	Sa	C100
NGC 3445	VV 14	10 51 34	57 15.3	149.60	53.67	54.6	−2.1	Sc(s)III	W60
NGC 3448		10 51 40	54 34.5	153.06	55.45	56.8	−3.5	Amorphous?	W60
NGC 3455		10 51 52	17 33.1	226.86	61.29	89.7	−22.4	Sc(s)II:	W100
NGC 3464		10 52 15	−20 48.1	269.58	34.13	131.7	−33.2	Sc(rs)I	C100
NGC 3458		10 52 58	57 23.0	149.22	53.72	54.6	−1.8	SB0₁	P200
NGC 3478		10 56 35	46 23.4	164.85	60.85	64.2	−7.3	Sc(s)?	48 Pr
NGC 3485		10 57 24	15 06.6	232.65	61.34	92.7	−22.2	SBbc(s)II	W60
NGC 3489		10 57 41	14 10.2	234.39	60.91	93.7	−22.5	S0₃/Sa	W100
NGC 3486		10 57 42	29 14.6	202.09	65.49	79.4	−15.8	Sc(r)I–II	W100
NGC 3495		10 58 41	03 53.8	249.89	54.72	104.3	−26.1	Sc(s)III	W100
NGC 3504	B2 1100+28	11 00 29	28 14.5	204.61	66.04	80.6	−15.8	Sb(s)/SBb(s)I–II	P200
NGC 3506		11 00 35	11 20.3	239.95	59.93	96.8	−23.0	Sb(s)I–II	W100
NGC 3511		11 00 57	−22 49.0	272.91	33.41	134.2	−31.4	Sc(s)II.8	C100
NGC 3510	Haro 26	11 01 01	29 09.3	202.38	66.21	79.8	−15.2	SBc(s)	W100
NGC 3512		11 01 20	28 18.3	204.49	66.23	80.6	−15.6	Sc(rs)I–II	W100
NGC 3513		11 01 20	−22 58.6	273.09	33.31	134.4	−31.3	SBc(s)II.2	C100
NGC 3521	PKS 1103+002	11 03 15	00 14.2	255.54	52.83	108.5	−26.2	Sb(s)II–III	W100
NGC 3516		11 03 23	72 50.4	133.24	42.40	42.1	7.3	RSB0₂	P200
NGC 3547		11 07 19	10 59.5	242.54	61.03	97.8	−21.6	ScIII	W100
IC 2627		11 07 26	−23 27.3	274.85	33.55	135.1	−29.9	Sc(r)I–II	W60
NGC 3557	PKS 1107−372	11 07 36	−37 16.0	281.59	21.09	151.1	−30.2	E3	C100
NGC 3549		11 08 03	53 39.6	151.35	57.84	58.9	−2.0	Sbc(s)II	W60
NGC 3556		11 08 37	55 56.7	148.32	56.25	56.9	−0.8	Sc(s)III	W60
NGC 3571		11 09 02	−18 01.0	272.10	38.52	129.0	−28.9	Sa	C100
NGC 3585		11 10 50	−26 28.8	277.25	31.18	138.7	−29.4	E7/S0₁(7)	C100
NGC 3583	5C 2.203	11 11 24	48 35.4	158.12	61.63	63.5	−4.0	Sb(s)II	W60
NGC 3593		11 12 00	13 05.4	240.44	63.21	96.2	−19.8	Sa pec	C100
NGC 3596		11 12 29	15 03.5	236.90	64.42	94.3	−18.9	Sc(r)II.2	W60
NGC 3605		11 14 08	18 17.6	230.64	66.38	91.4	−17.3	E5	P200
NGC 3607		11 14 17	18 19.7	230.60	66.42	91.4	−17.2	S0₃(3)	P200
NGC 3608		11 14 21	18 25.6	230.40	66.48	91.3	−17.2	E1	P200
NGC 3611		11 14 55	04 49.7	254.01	58.20	104.8	−22.0	Sa	P200
NGC 3610		11 15 31	59 03.6	143.55	54.46	54.7	1.6	E5	W60
NGC 3614		11 15 34	46 01.2	161.56	63.78	66.2	−4.7	Sc(r)I	W60
NGC 3613		11 15 42	58 16.3	144.35	55.10	55.4	1.2	E6	W60
NGC 3621	PKS 1115−325	11 15 50	−32 32.4	281.22	26.10	145.7	−28.6	Sc(s)II.8	C100
NGC 3623	M 65	11 16 19	13 21.9	241.34	64.22	96.4	−18.7	Sa(s)II	W100
NGC 3619		11 16 28	58 02.0	144.47	55.35	55.6	1.2	Sa	P200
NGC 3626		11 17 26	18 37.8	230.78	67.23	91.4	−16.4	Sa	P200
NGC 3627	{ M 66 / Cul 1117+132	11 17 38	13 15.8	241.97	64.42	96.6	−18.4	Sb(s)II.2	W100

Galaxy (11)	B_T (12)	A^o (13)	A^i (14)	$B_T^{o,i}$ (15)	$M_{B_T}^{o,i}$ (16)	v (17)	ε (18)	Δv (19)	v_o (20)	Sources (21)
NGC 3433	(12.28)	0	0.31	(11.97)	−21.58	2711	7	−145	2566	158, 284, 385, 400, 406
NGC 3432	11.73	0	0.81	10.92	−19.50	616	7	−9	607	34, 160, 191, 253, 263
NGC 3437	(12.83)	0	0.67	12.16	−19.74	1283	15	−82	1201	158, 284
NGC 3403	(12.74)	0.07	0.60	12.07	−20.20	1244	55	178	1422	191
NGC 3449	12.95[5])	0.20	0.43*	12.32	−21.55	3267	120	−292	2975	284
NGC 3445	12.8	0	0.31	12.49	−20.61	1984	128	99	2083	321
NGC 3448	12.15	0	—	[12.1]	−20.2	1357	9	85	1442	187, 220, 321, 324
NGC 3455	(12.81)	0	0.44	12.37	−19.12	1102	10	−111	991	241
NGC 3464	(12.82)	0.10	0.41	12.31	−21.96	3836	165	−265	3571	284
NGC 3458	(13.15)	0	0	13.15	−19.75	1800	80	99	1899	284
NGC 3478	(12.95)	0	0.57	12.38	−23.27	6688	105	42	6730	284
NGC 3485	(12.57)	0	0.32	12.25	−19.98	1518	93	−123	1395	284
NGC 3489	11.13[1])	0	0	11.13	−19.00	659	31	−127	532	58, 190, (306), 376
NGC 3486	10.85	0	0.38	10.47	−20.05	686	9	−50	636	28, (190), 392
NGC 3495	(12.42)	0	0.76	11.66	−19.78	1145	10	−175	970	321, 392
NGC 3504	11.8	0	0.55	11.25	−21.11	1535	19	−55	1480	73, 190
NGC 3506	(13.44)	0	0.47	12.97	−22.55	6489	53	−141	6348	284
NGC 3511	11.56	0.11	0.61	10.84	−20.56	1221	62	−270	951	321
NGC 3510	13.3	0	0.82	12.48	−18.12	710	19	−50	660	42, 191
NGC 3512	13.0	0	0.31	12.69	−19.45	1395	19	−55	1340	191, 391
NGC 3513	(11.99)	0.11	0.35	11.53	−19.61	1116	14	−271	845	158, 284, 431
NGC 3521	9.64[8])	0	0.80	8.84	−21.65	818	11	−191	627	48, 65, 173, 190, (306)
NGC 3516	12.40[1])	0.06	0	12.34	−21.43	2664	22	174	2838	538
NGC 3547	13.2	0	0.53	12.67	−19.57	1543	70	−142	1401	284
IC 2627	12.6	0.11	0.30	12.19	−20.60	2076	15	−272	1804	160
NGC 3557	11.46[1])	0.23	0	11.23	−22.55	3151	80	−298	2853	284
NGC 3549	(12.67)	0	0.63	12.04	−21.79	2840	15	81	2921	158, 284
NGC 3556	10.71	0	0.74	9.97	−21.02	698	3	92	790	539
NGC 3571	(12.81)	0.08	0.95	11.78	−22.46	3777	60	−257	3520	284
NGC 3585	10.93[1])	0.12	0	10.81	−21.11	1491	75	−279	1212	190
NGC 3583	(12.18)	0	0.63	11.55	−21.65	2130	8	54	2184	284, 311, (313), 384, 400
NGC 3593	11.7	0	0.92	10.78	−19.19	625	4	−132	493	608
NGC 3596	(11.64)	0	0.29	11.35	−20.30	1194	9	−122	1072	28, 284, 391
NGC 3605	(13.06)	0	0	13.06	−17.29	693	65	−106	587	190
NGC 3607	11.08[1])	0	0	11.08	−20.02	934	36	−106	828	190, 191
NGC 3608	11.88[1])	0	0	11.88	−19.84	1210	50	−105	1105	190
NGC 3611	12.8	0	0.52	12.28	−20.03	1620	15	−170	1450	190, 402, 409
NGC 3610	11.54[1])	0	0	11.54	−21.33	1765	50	108	1873	190
NGC 3614	(12.21)	0	0.46	11.75	−21.62	2321	15	41	2362	156, 284
NGC 3613	11.65[1])	0	0	11.65	−21.53	2054	75	104	2158	190
NGC 3621	(10.03)	0.17	0.45	9.41	−20.29	726	7	−291	435	631
NGC 3623	10.24	0	1.07	9.17	−21.48	805	5	−130	675	609
NGC 3619	12.55[1])	0	0.53	12.02	−20.59	1559	15	103	1662	190, 402
NGC 3626	11.74[1])	0	0.31*	11.43	−20.81	1507	6	−104	1403	190, 263, 402, 409
NGC 3627	9.74	0	0.83	8.89	−21.48	723	8	−130	593	540

Galaxy (1)	Other names (2)	RA (1950) (3)	Dec (1950) (4)	*l* (5)	*b* (6)	SGL (7)	SGB (8)	Type (9)	Source (10)
NGC 3628	{ VV 308 { Cul 1117+138	11 17 40	13 52.1	240.85	64.78	96.0	−18.2	Sbc	W100
NGC 3630		11 17 42	03 14.3	256.96	57.46	106.6	−21.8	S0$_1$(9)	W60
NGC 3629		11 17 52	27 14.4	208.18	69.79	83.3	−12.8	Sc(s)II–III	W100
NGC 3637		11 18 08	−09 59.0	269.39	46.61	120.6	−25.3	RSB0$_2$/3/SBa	C100
NGC 3631		11 18 13	53 26.7	149.54	59.04	59.8	−0.8	Sc(s)I–II	W60
NGC 3640		11 18 33	03 30.6	256.93	57.80	106.4	−21.6	E2	W60
NGC 3646		11 19 05	20 26.7	226.86	68.35	89.8	−15.3	Sbc(r)II	W100
NGC 3642		11 19 25	59 21.0	142.56	54.53	54.7	2.1	Sb(r)I	P200
NGC 3655		11 20 17	16 51.7	235.60	66.97	93.3	−16.5	Sc(s)III pec	W60
NGC 3659		11 21 08	18 05.4	233.09	67.75	92.2	−15.8	Sc(s)III	W60
NGC 3666		11 21 50	11 37.1	246.41	64.18	98.6	−18.1	ScII–III	W100
NGC 3664	{ DDO 95 { VV 251	11 21 51	03 36.3	258.03	58.40	106.6	−20.8	SBmIII–IV	W100
NGC 3665	B2 1122+39	11 22 01	39 02.2	174.72	68.49	72.9	−6.8	S0$_3$(3)	P200
NGC 3672		11 22 31	−09 31.2	270.43	47.55	120.3	−24.1	Sc(s)I–II	W100
NGC 3673		11 22 44	−26 27.8	280.10	32.28	138.9	−26.7	SBbII	W100
NGC 3675		11 23 25	43 51.7	163.67	66.19	68.7	−4.4	Sb(r)II	P200
NGC 3681		11 23 54	17 08.3	236.14	67.85	93.4	−15.6	SBb(r)I–II	W100
NGC 3684		11 24 35	17 18.3	235.99	68.07	93.3	−15.4	Sc(s)II	W100
NGC 3683		11 24 52	57 09.2	143.82	56.72	56.9	1.8	Sc(III)	W60
NGC 3686		11 25 07	17 30.0	235.72	68.28	93.2	−15.2	SBbc(s)I–II	W100
NGC 3687	Mark 736	11 25 23	29 47.0	200.63	71.51	81.7	−10.2	SBbc(r)I.2	P200
NGC 3689		11 25 35	25 56.2	212.72	71.32	85.3	−11.8	Sc(r)II	W60
NGC 3691	{ VV 118	11 25 35	17 11.8	236.56	68.21	93.5	−15.2	S	48 Pr
NGC 3690	{ Mark 171	11 25 42	58 50.0	141.92	55.41	55.5	2.6	S pec	W60
NGC 3706	{ DA 302	11 27 17	−36 06.7	285.09	23.62	149.7	−26.2	E4	C100
NGC 3705		11 27 33	09 33.2	252.03	63.79	101.1	−17.5	Sab(r)I–II	W100
NGC 3717		11 29 04	−30 01.9	283.14	29.47	143.0	−25.6	Sb(s)	C100
NGC 3720		11 29 48	01 04.8	263.87	57.55	109.8	−19.6	Sbc(s)I	C100
NGC 3718		11 29 50	53 20.7	147.02	60.22	60.7	0.7	Sa pec?	W60
NGC 3726		11 30 38	47 18.4	155.39	64.88	66.2	−1.8	Sc(r)I–II	W100
NGC 3729	1131+53W1	11 31 04	53 24.0	146.65	60.28	60.7	0.9	SB(ring) pec	W60
NGC 3732		11 31 41	−09 34.2	273.46	48.56	120.9	−21.9	Sc(r) pec	C100
NGC 3738		11 33 04	54 47.9	144.56	59.32	59.6	1.8	SdIII	P200
NGC 3735	1133+70W1	11 33 06	70 48.6	131.75	45.28	44.9	8.4	Sc(II–III)	W60
NGC 3756		11 34 05	54 34.3	144.58	59.58	59.8	1.8	Sc(s)I–II	P200
NGC 3769		11 35 02	48 10.3	152.73	64.76	65.7	−0.7	SBc(s)II	P200
NGC 3773	Mark 743	11 35 38	12 23.4	250.54	67.19	99.1	−14.6	pec jet	W100
NGC 3783		11 36 33	−37 27.7	287.46	22.94	151.2	−24.4	SBa(r)I	C100
NGC 3780		11 36 38	56 33.0	141.92	58.12	58.2	3.0	Sc(r)II.3	P200
NGC 3782		11 36 41	46 47.4	154.45	65.96	67.1	−1.1	SBmIV	W60
NGC 3810	MC 1138+117	11 38 24	11 44.9	252.95	67.22	99.9	−14.2	Sc(s)II	W100
NGC 3813	B 1138+36	11 38 40	36 49.4	176.20	72.42	76.3	−4.8	Sc(s)II.8	W60
NGC 3818		11 39 24	−05 52.7	273.60	52.71	117.6	−19.2	E5	W60
NGC 3865		11 42 19	−08 57.5	276.72	50.22	120.9	−19.3	Sab(rs)	C100
NGC 3872		11 43 14	14 02.7	250.78	69.68	98.1	−12.3	E4	W60

Galaxy (11)	B_T (12)	A^o (13)	A^i (14)	$B_T^{o,i}$ (15)	$M_{B_T}^{o,i}$ (16)	v (17)	ε (18)	Δv (19)	v_0 (20)	Sources (21)
NGC 3628	10.31	0	0.82	9.49	−21.30	847	9	−128	719	191, 253, 263
NGC 3630	12.65[2]	0	0	12.65	−19.49	1517	52	−177	1340	106, 284
NGC 3629	(12.80)	0	0.38	12.42	−19.89	1510	8	−59	1451	158, 284, 301
NGC 3637	(12.85)	0.05	0	12.80	−19.76	1855	90	−230	1625	284
NGC 3631	11.03	0	0.32	10.71	−21.26	1158	17	80	1238	164, 191, 253
NGC 3640	11.26[1]	0	0	11.26	−20.60	1354	40	−176	1178	190
NGC 3646	11.88	0	0.44	11.44	−23.13	4195	24	−95	4100	76, 191, 194
NGC 3642	11.53	0	0.52	11.01	−21.69	1623	50	110	1733	190
NGC 3655	12.30	0	0.43	11.87	−20.33	1490	15	−112	1378	158, 284
NGC 3659	(12.81)	0	0.50	12.31	−19.42	1215	75	−106	1109	284, 431
NGC 3666	(12.36)	0	0.70	11.66	−19.68	1064	15	−138	926	158, 284
NGC 3664	(12.72)	0	0.15	12.57	−19.39	1406	56	−175	1231	321
NGC 3665	11.75[1]	0	0	11.75	−21.27	2002	50	4	2006	190
NGC 3672	(11.66)	0.05	0.53	11.08	−21.49	1861	8	−228	1633	191, 391, 400, 401, 429
NGC 3673	(12.41)	0.12	0.64	11.65	−20.96	1940	15	−278	1662	160, 284
NGC 3675	10.9	0	0.78	10.12	−20.88	762	9	30	792	190, 209, 229, 391
NGC 3681	12.40	0	0.46	11.94	−19.84	1246	10	−111	1135	190, 392
NGC 3684	12.3	0	0.40	11.90	−19.74	1175	9	−110	1065	190, 391, 392
NGC 3683	(13.40)	0	0.61	12.79	−19.97	1686	45	99	1785	284
NGC 3686	12.0	0	0.37	11.63	−19.95	1143	16	−109	1034	190, 391, 392
NGC 3687	(12.85)	0	0.28	12.57	−20.89	2501	10	−45	2456	284, 402
NGC 3689	13.0	0	0.40	12.60	−21.01	2706	27	−65	2641	284, 357
NGC 3691	(13.53)	0	0.37:	13.16	−18.23	1057	20	−110	947	411
NGC 3690	(12.02)	0	0.36:	11.66	−22.30	2988	20	108	3096	198, 288, 315, 321
NGC 3706	12.13[5]	0.20	0	11.93	−21.77	3045	108	−295	2750	284
NGC 3705	(11.77)	0	0.89	10.88	−20.32	1017	15	−147	870	156, 284
NGC 3717	(12.12)	0.14	1.25	10.73	−21.57	1728	8	−285	1443	158, 284, 402
NGC 3720	13.70[1]	0	0.31	13.39	−21.94	6016	70	−185	5831	284
NGC 3718	11.26	0	0.82	10.44	−21.24	1002	5	80	1082	541
NGC 3726	10.95	0	0.39	10.56	−20.74	860	9	49	909	190, 253, 391, 392
NGC 3729	12.00	0	0.42:	11.58	−20.16	1035	28	81	1116	284
NGC 3732	12.69[2]	0.04	0.30	12.35	−20.03	1719	5	−226	1493	284, 402
NGC 3738	12.14	0	0.37	11.77	−17.21	224	10	88	312	158, 160, 284, 431
NGC 3735	(12.50)	0.05	0.83	11.62	−22.15	2673	15	165	2838	158, 284, 431
NGC 3756	12.15	0	0.51	11.64	−20.55	1285	15	87	1372	158, 284
NGC 3769	12.52	0	0.67	11.85	−19.15	737	69	54	791	241
NGC 3773	(13.08)	0	—	[13.0]	−18.2	983	19	−132	851	284, 433
NGC 3783	(12.89)	0.21	0*	12.68	−20.81	2790	(100)	−296	2494	199, 224, 238, (240), 386
NGC 3780	(12.27)	0	0.35	11.92	−21.56	2384	11	97	2481	158, 284, 385
NGC 3782	(13.08)	0	0.21	12.87	−18.11	738	15	47	785	159, 431
NGC 3810	11.36	0	0.40	10.96	−20.22	995	10	−135	860	190, 191, 391
NGC 3813	12.30	0	0.52	11.78	−20.55	1465	7	−6	1459	594
NGC 3818	12.79[1]	0	0	12.79	−19.26	1498	65	−212	1286	190
NGC 3865	(12.86)	0	0.60	12.26	−22.94	5714	175	−223	5491	284
NGC 3872	12.80[1]	0	0	12.80	−21.08	3109	75	−123	2986	190

Galaxy (1)	Other names (2)	RA (1950) (3)	Dec (1950) (4)	l (5)	b (6)	SGL (7)	SGB (8)	Type (9)	Source (10)
NGC 3877		11 43 29	47 46.2	150.72	65.96	66.6	0.4	ScII.2	W60
NGC 3885		11 44 15	−27 38.7	285.92	32.80	140.7	−22.1	Sa	C100
NGC 3887	⎰ Mark 188	11 44 33	−16 34.6	281.56	43.33	129.0	−20.3	Sb(r)I−II	W100
NGC 3888	⎱ 1144+56W1	11 44 55	56 14.9	140.31	58.96	58.9	3.9	Sc(s)I−II	P200
NGC 3892		11 45 28	−10 41.0	278.85	48.92	122.9	−18.9	SB0₃	W60
NGC 3893		11 46 01	48 59.4	148.16	65.23	65.7	1.3	Sc(s)I.2	P200
NGC 3900		11 46 34	27 18.1	209.81	76.15	85.8	−6.9	Sa(r)	P200
NGC 3898		11 46 36	56 21.8	139.80	58.96	58.9	4.2	SaI	P200
NGC 3904		11 46 42	−28 59.9	286.99	31.66	142.2	−21.7	E2	W100
NGC 3912		11 47 30	26 45.3	212.16	76.30	86.4	−6.9	SB (late) pec	P200
NGC 3917		11 48 08	52 06.2	143.66	62.79	62.9	2.8	Sc(s)III	W60
NGC 3923		11 48 30	−28 31.7	287.29	32.22	141.8	−21.3	E4/S0₁(4)	C100
NGC 3936		11 49 48	−26 37.6	286.99	34.13	139.8	−20.7	Sc(s)I−II	C100
NGC 3938		11 50 13	44 24.0	153.88	69.32	70.2	0.2	Sc(s)I	P200
NGC 3941		11 50 20	37 15.9	170.72	74.19	76.8	−2.5	SB0₁/₂/a	P200
NGC 3945		11 50 36	60 57.3	135.34	55.03	54.8	6.3	RSB0₂	W60
NGC 3949		11 51 05	48 08.3	147.64	66.40	66.8	1.7	Sc(s)III	W60
NGC 3952		11 51 07	−03 43.1	276.60	55.89	116.2	−15.8	S or Sm	48 Pr
NGC 3953		11 51 13	52 36.5	142.22	62.59	62.6	3.4	SBbc(r)I−II	P200
NGC 3955		11 51 25	−22 53.2	286.15	37.83	135.9	−19.8	S pec	W100
NGC 3956		11 51 28	−20 17.3	285.21	40.32	133.2	−19.4	Sc(s)II	W100
NGC 3957		11 51 33	−19 17.3	284.83	41.27	132.1	−19.2	S0₃(9)	W100
NGC 3962		11 52 07	−13 41.8	282.66	46.65	126.4	−18.0	E1	W60
NGC 3963		11 52 22	58 46.3	136.51	57.12	56.9	5.8	SBc(rs)I−II	W60
NGC 3976		11 53 23	07 01.7	267.54	65.73	105.7	−12.2	Sc(s)I−II	W60
NGC 3981	VV 8	11 53 35	−19 36.9	285.58	41.10	132.6	−18.8	Sb:(I)	W60
NGC 3982		11 53 53	55 24.0	138.83	60.27	60.2	4.8	Sbc(r)II−III	W60
NGC 3985		11 54 06	48 36.9	145.95	66.28	66.5	2.4	S	W60
NGC 3992		11 55 01	53 39.3	140.10	61.92	61.9	4.3	SBb(rs)I	P200
NGC 3995	VV 249	11 55 10	32 34.3	185.81	77.26	81.6	−3.2	ScIII	W100
NGC 3998		11 55 20	55 44.1	138.18	60.06	59.9	5.1	S0₁(3)	P200
NGC 4008		11 55 43	28 28.2	204.70	78.19	85.5	−4.6	S0₁(3)	W100
NGC 4013		11 55 58	44 13.4	151.86	70.09	70.7	1.1	Sbc:	W100
NGC 4024		11 55 59	−18 04.2	285.74	42.75	131.1	−17.9	E4	W60
IC 749		11 56 00	43 00.8	154.09	71.05	71.9	0.6	SBc(rs)II−III	P200
IC 750		11 56 17	43 00.1	153.98	71.10	71.9	0.7	S(b)	P200
NGC 4026		11 56 50	51 14.4	141.95	64.20	64.2	3.7	S0₁/₂(9)	P200
NGC 4027	VV 66	11 56 56	−18 59.4	286.38	41.93	132.1	−17.9	Sc(s)III	W100
NGC 4030	PKS 1157−008	11 57 50	−00 49.4	277.38	59.21	113.8	−13.4	Sbc(r)I	W100
NGC 4032		11 58 00	20 21.1	241.44	76.39	93.3	−6.9	S(b):	48 Pr
NGC 4033		11 58 01	−17 34.0	286.19	43.37	130.7	−17.4	E6/S0₁(6)	W100
NGC 4037		11 58 50	13 40.7	260.04	71.97	99.7	−8.9	SBc(s)II.3:	W60
NGC 4036		11 58 54	62 10.5	132.99	54.25	54.0	7.7	S0₃(8)/Sa	P200
NGC 4038	⎰ VV 245	11 59 19	−18 35.1	286.96	42.47	131.8	−17.3	Sc pec	P200
NGC 4041	⎱ PKS 1159−185	11 59 39	62 25.0	132.71	54.05	53.8	7.8	Sc(s)II−III	W60

Galaxy (11)	B_T (12)	A^o (13)	A^i (14)	$B_T^{o,i}$ (15)	$M_{B_T}^{o,i}$ (16)	v (17)	ε (18)	Δv (19)	v_o (20)	Sources (21)
NGC 3877	(11.78)	0	0.76	11.02	−20.35	886	13	53	939	159, 284
NGC 3885	(13.27)	0.11	0.83	12.33	−20.10	1807	15	−277	1530	284, 402
NGC 3887	11.6	0.06	0.55	10.99	−20.32	1163	42	−248	915	191
NGC 3888	(13.09)	0	0.37	12.72	−20.73	2358	15	96	2454	12, 158, 284, 288
NGC 3892	(12.50)	0.04	0	12.46	−19.92	1727	80	−228	1499	284
NGC 3893	11.1	0	0.45	10.65	−20.91	967	7	59	1026	598
NGC 3900	12.20	0	0.76	11.44	−21.27	1799	10	−55	1744	190, 402
NGC 3898	11.7	0	0.74	10.96	−21.04	1161	12	97	1258	190, 391, 402, 424
NGC 3904	11.95[1]	0.12	0	11.83	−20.30	1613	75	−280	1333	190
NGC 3912	(13.27)	0	0.72	12.55	−20.15	1791	19	−58	1733	284, 402
NGC 3917	(12.40)	0	0.75	11.65	−19.94	965	8	76	1041	159, 301
NGC 3923	10.91[1]	0.12	0	10.79	−21.61	1788	65	−279	1509	190, (307)
NGC 3936	(12.83)	0.10	0.87	11.86	−20.85	2012	15	−274	1738	160
NGC 3938	10.91	0	0.31	10.60	−20.54	808	7	36	844	164, 191, 253, 391, 392
NGC 3941	11.28[2]	0	0	11.28	−20.10	944	18	−2	942	190, 191, 376
NGC 3945	11.49[1]	0	0	11.49	−20.65	1220	75	120	1340	191
NGC 3949	11.4	0	0.46	10.94	−20.23	801	15	56	857	159, 190
NGC 3952	(13.46)	0	0.49:	12.97	−19.30	1625	68	−201	1424	284
NGC 3953	10.79	0	0.51	10.28	−21.30	957	43	79	1036	190, 191
NGC 3955	12.55	0.08	0.79:	11.68	−19.95	1325	45	−265	1060	112
NGC 3956	(12.54)	0.07	0.68	11.79	−20.44	1651	15	−257	1394	160
NGC 3957	12.98[2]	0.07	0	12.91	−19.59	1838	98	−255	1583	284
NGC 3962	11.66[1]	0.05	0	11.61	−20.89	1821	31	−237	1584	58, 190, 416
NGC 3963	(12.38)	0	0.31	12.07	−22.02	3185	15	110	3295	(159), 284, 385
NGC 3976	(12.24)	0	0.67	11.57	−21.77	2487	14	−154	2333	158, 284
NGC 3981	(12.44)	0.07	0.98	11.39	−21.07	1809	227	−255	1554	284
NGC 3982	(11.91)	0	0.32	11.59	−20.30	1102	15	93	1195	159, 284
NGC 3985	(13.02)	0	0.55:	12.47	−19.04	946	38	58	1004	284, 431
NGC 3992	10.64	0	0.69	9.95	−21.83	1049	6	85	1134	159, 190, 391, 392
NGC 3995	12.8	0	0.61	12.19	−21.93	3353	32	−26	3327	191, 241
NGC 3998	11.50[1]	0	0	11.50	−20.43	1119	21	95	1214	58, 130, 139, 190, 191
NGC 4008	12.9	0	0	12.9	−21.34	3571	95	−47	3524	107, 284
NGC 4013	(12.00)	0	0.83	11.17	−20.02	830	15	36	866	159, 284, 431
NGC 4024	12.67[2]	0.06	0	12.61	−19.69	1694	140	−250	1444	284
IC 749	12.80	0	0.36	12.44	−18.65	798	15	29	827	158
IC 750	12.80	0	0.71:	12.09	−18.77	713	75	29	742	284
NGC 4026	11.47[1]	0	0	11.47	−19.93	878	75	73	951	190
NGC 4027	11.65	0.07	0.37	11.21	−21.06	1672	10	−253	1419	229, (307), 333
NGC 4030	(11.07)	0	0.38	10.69	−21.42	1509	47	−187	1322	191
NGC 4032	(12.76)	0	0.44	12.32	−19.38 VR	1267	20	−89	1178	370, 431
NGC 4033	12.47[2]	0.06	0	12.41	−19.62	1521	75	−248	1273	284
NGC 4037	(12.52)	0	0.33	12.19	−19.51 VR	933	15	−122	811	158, 284
NGC 4036	11.56[1]	0	0	11.56	−20.84	1382	50	127	1509	190
NGC 4038	11.3	0.06	0.42	10.82	−21.40	1642	12	−251	1391	542
NGC 4041	11.64	0	0.30	11.34	−20.83	1233	10	128	1361	321, 392

Galaxy (1)	Other names (2)	RA (1950) (3)	Dec (1950) (4)	l (5)	b (6)	SGL (7)	SGB (8)	Type (9)	Source (10)
NGC 4045		12 00 09	02 15.5	275.99	62.27	110.9	−12.0	Sbc(s)I-II	W60
NGC 4047		12 00 18	48 55.2	143.36	66.52	66.6	3.4	Sc(s)I-II	P200
NGC 4050		12 00 20	−16 05.4	286.39	44.93	129.3	−16.5	SBb(rs)I-II	W100
NGC 4051		12 00 37	44 48.7	148.89	70.08	70.5	2.1	Sbc(s)II	W100
NGC 4062		12 01 31	32 10.4	185.26	78.65	82.4	−2.1	Sc(s)II-III	W100
NGC 4064		12 01 38	18 43.3	249.08	76.09	95.1	−6.6	SBc(s):	W100
NGC 4073		12 01 54	02 10.6	276.92	62.37	111.1	−11.6	E5	C100
NGC 4085	1202+50W3	12 02 51	50 38.0	140.59	65.17	65.1	4.4	ScIII:	W60
NGC 4088		12 03 02	50 49.1	140.33	65.01	65.0	4.5	Sc(s)II-III/SBc	W60
IC 2995		12 03 13	−27 39.7	290.79	33.85	141.3	−17.9	Sc(s)III	C100
NGC 4094		12 03 18	−14 15.1	286.70	46.90	127.6	−15.4	Sbc(s)II	C100
NGC 4096		12 03 29	47 45.7	143.55	67.79	67.9	3.5	Sc(s)II-III	W60
NGC 4100		12 03 37	49 51.4	141.11	65.92	65.9	4.2	Sc(s)I-II	W60
NGC 4102		12 03 52	52 59.3	138.09	63.07	63.0	5.3	Sb(r)II	W60
NGC 4105		12 04 06	−29 28.9	291.47	32.11	143.2	−18.0	S0$_{1/2}$(3)	C100
NGC 4106		12 04 11	−29 29.4	291.49	32.11	143.3	−18.0	SB0/a (tides)	C100
NGC 4111		12 04 32	43 20.7	149.53	71.70	72.1	2.2	S0$_1$(9)	P200
NGC 4116		12 05 04	02 58.2	277.85	63.41	110.6	−10.6	SBc(r)III	W60
NGC 4125		12 05 35	65 27.3	130.20	51.34	51.1	9.6	E6	W60
NGC 4124	IC 3011	12 05 36	10 39.5	269.55	70.39	103.2	−8.2	S0$_3$(6)	P200
NGC 4123		12 05 38	03 09.3	277.99	63.64	110.4	−10.5	SBbc(rs)	W60
NGC 4128		12 06 04	69 02.8	128.71	47.88	47.6	10.5	S0$_1$(6)	W60
NGC 4129		12 06 19	−08 45.7	285.56	52.39	122.2	−13.4	ScIII:	W100
NGC 4136		12 06 46	30 12.3	193.64	80.34	84.6	−1.7	Sc(r)I-II	W60
NGC 4138		12 06 59	43 57.8	147.31	71.40	71.7	2.8	Sab(r)	P200
NGC 4143		12 07 05	42 48.8	149.19	72.40	72.8	2.5	S0$_1$(5)/Sa	P200
NGC 4144		12 07 28	46 44.1	143.18	69.01	69.1	3.8	ScdIII	P200
NGC 4145		12 07 30	40 09.7	154.28	74.62	75.3	1.7	SBc(r)II	W60
IC 764		12 07 39	−29 27.5	292.36	32.29	143.3	−17.2	Sb(r)I-II	W100
NGC 4151	B2 1208+39	12 08 00	39 40.9	155.10	75.06	75.8	1.6	Sab	P200
NGC 4150		12 08 01	30 40.9	190.44	80.47	84.3	−1.3	S0$_3$(4)/Sa	P200
NGC 4152		12 08 05	16 18.7	260.40	75.42	97.9	−5.9	Sc(r)I.4	W100
NGC 4157		12 08 35	50 45.8	138.48	65.41	65.3	5.3	Sbc	W60
NGC 4158		12 08 37	20 27.2	247.84	78.46	94.0	−4.5	Sa:	W100
NGC 4162		12 09 20	24 24.0	229.38	80.59	90.3	−3.1	Sc(s)I-II	W100
NGC 4168		12 09 44	13 29.0	267.69	73.34	100.8	−6.4	E2	W60
NGC 4178	IC 3042	12 10 14	11 08.8	271.87	71.37	103.0	−7.0	SBc(s)II	W100
NGC 4179		12 10 19	01 34.7	281.63	62.57	112.3	−9.8	S0$_1$(9)	W60
NGC 4183		12 10 47	43 58.6	145.40	71.73	71.9	3.5	Scd (on edge)	W100
NGC 4190	VV 104	12 11 13	36 54.6	160.64	77.59	78.6	1.3	SmIV	P200
NGC 4189	IC 3050	12 11 14	13 42.2	268.38	73.72	100.7	−6.0	SBc(sr)II.2	48 Pr
NGC 4192	M 98	12 11 15	15 10.8	265.44	74.96	99.2	−5.6	SbII:	W100
NGC 4203		12 12 34	33 28.7	173.02	80.08	82.0	0.5	S0$_2$(1)	P200
NGC 4212		12 13 07	14 10.8	268.90	74.36	100.3	−5.4	Sc(s)II-III	C100
NGC 4214		12 13 08	36 36.5	160.25	78.07	79.0	1.6	SBmIII	P200

Galaxy (11)	B_T (12)	A^o (13)	A^i (14)	$B_T^{o,i}$ (15)	$M_{B_T}^{o,i}$ (16)	v (17)	ε (18)	Δv (19)	v_o (20)	Sources (21)
NGC 4045	12.65	0	0.39	12.26	−20.48	1939	80	−174	1765	284, (332), 380
NGC 4047	13.10	0	0.33	12.77	−21.40	3355	43	61	3416	284
NGC 4050	12.25	0.05	0.62	11.58	−21.03	1904	110	−243	1661	284
NGC 4051	10.93	0	0.37	10.56	−20.31	706	5	40	746	543
NGC 4062	12.0	0	0.57	11.43	−19.44	772	7	−27	745	544
NGC 4064	12.30	0	0.60	11.70	−20.00 VR	1033	47	−96	937	191
NGC 4073	(12.74)	0	0	12.74	−22.53	5844	97	−174	5670	284, 380
NGC 4085	12.91	0	0.70	12.21	−18.87	753	14	70	823	159, 284, 431
NGC 4088	11.14	0	0.60	10.54	−20.53	750	12	70	820	159, 191, 229, 284, 403
IC 2995	(12.68)	0.10	0.65	11.93	−20.55	1840	15	−274	1566	160
NGC 4094	(12.54)	0.05	0.61	11.88	−19.99	1420	15	−236	1184	160, 284
NGC 4096	11.02	0	0.72	10.30	−20.15	560	11	56	616	599
NGC 4100	(11.62)	0	0.66	10.96	−20.82	1069	15	66	1135	159, 284, 431
NGC 4102	12.3	0	0.71	11.59	−19.80	865	14	83	948	159, 190, 191
NGC 4105	11.88[5]	0.12	0	11.76	−20.80	1900	33	−277	1623	190, 224, 372a
NGC 4106	12.36[3]	0.12	0	12.24	−20.66	2182	45	−277	1905	190, 224
NGC 4111	11.75[1]	0	0	11.75	−19.33	791	14	33	824	190, 191, (306)
NGC 4116	12.37	0	0.46	11.91	−19.88	1309	10	−169	1140	191, 385
NGC 4125	10.76[1]	0	0	10.76	−21.65	1375	29	143	1518	58, 190, 191, 201, 313
NGC 4124	12.35[2]	0	0	12.35	−19.35 V	1635	64	−134	1501	284, 380
NGC 4123	11.84	0	0.37	11.47	−20.35	1325	10	−168	1157	158, 284, 380, 385, 431
NGC 4128	12.78	0.05	0	12.73	−20.81	2395	62	160	2555	191
NGC 4129	13.2	0	0.74	12.46	−19.03	1210	172	−216	994	284
NGC 4136	(11.58)	0	0.30	11.28	−18.28	445	50	−36	409	190
NGC 4138	12.13[1]	0	0.68	11.45	−20.21	1039	100	36	1075	190
NGC 4143	12.07[1]	0	0	12.07	−18.99	784	100	30	814	190
NGC 4144	(12.01)	0	0.79	11.22	−17.78	265	11	51	316	160, (173), 301
NGC 4145	11.50	0	0.38	11.12	−20.45	1013	7	17	1030	545
IC 764	(12.35)	0.12	0.99	11.24	−21.60	2127	15	−276	1851	160
NGC 4151	11.13	0	0.60	10.53	−20.93	964	2	14	978	546
NGC 4150	12.40[1]	0	0	12.40	−15.73	244	50	−33	211	190
NGC 4152	12.5	0	0.36	12.14	−20.93	2161	10	−106	2055	188, 284, 431
NGC 4157	(11.56)	0	0.83	10.73	−20.43	780	8	72	852	547
NGC 4158	(12.84)	0	0.49	12.35	−21.04	2463	21	−86	2377	284, 380, 402
NGC 4162	12.25	0	0.46	11.79	−21.69	2546	135	−65	2481	191
NGC 4168	12.21	0	0	12.21	−19.49 V	2389	60	−120	2269	284, 380
NGC 4178	11.89	0	0.63	11.26	−20.44 V	355	12	−131	224	120, 160, 191
NGC 4179	11.84[1]	0	0	11.84	−19.88	1279	50	−174	1105	190
NGC 4183	(12.40)	0	0.87	11.53	−19.90	931	9	37	968	301
NGC 4190	(13.00)	0	0.16	12.84	−15.48	231	15	+0	231	160, 431
NGC 4189	12.53	0	0.33	12.20	−19.50 V	2098	9	−118	1980	204, 284, 301, 330, 431
NGC 4192	10.92	0	1.07	9.85	−21.85 V	−140	14	−111	−251	120, 160, 190
NGC 4203	11.62[1]	0	0	11.62	−20.04	1089	14	−17	1072	190, 374, 376
NGC 4212	11.86	0	0.42	11.44	−20.26 V	−50	100	−115	−165	(191), 440
NGC 4214	10.22	0	0.19	10.03	−18.79	291	3	−1	290	548

Galaxy (1)	Other names (2)	RA (1950) (3)	Dec (1950) (4)	*l* (5)	*b* (6)	SGL (7)	SGB (8)	Type (9)	Source (10)
NGC 4216		12 13 21	13 25.4	270.46	73.73	101.1	−5.6	Sb(s)	C100
NGC 4217		12 13 21	47 22.3	139.91	68.84	68.8	5.0	Sb:	W60
NGC 4215		12 13 22	06 41.0	279.18	67.62	107.6	−7.6	S0₁(9)	C100
NGC 4220		12 13 43	48 09.5	138.95	68.14	68.0	5.3	Sa(r)	P200
NGC 4219		12 13 50	−43 02.8	296.21	19.09	157.6	−17.6	Sbc(s)(II–III)	C100
NGC 4224		12 14 01	07 44.4	278.54	68.67	106.6	−7.1	Sa	C100
NGC 4236		12 14 22	69 45.0	127.42	47.35	47.1	11.4	SBdIV	P200
NGC 4233		12 14 35	07 54.1	278.74	68.87	106.5	−7.0	SB0₁(6)	C100
NGC 4234	Haro 7	12 14 36	03 57.7	282.20	65.17	110.3	−8.1	SBcIII.4	48 Pr
NGC 4235	IC 3098	12 14 37	07 28.1	279.19	68.47	106.9	−7.1	Sa	C100
NGC 4237		12 14 39	15 36.1	267.22	75.76	99.1	−4.6	Sc(r)II.8	W100
NGC 4244		12 15 00	38 05.2	154.57	77.16	77.7	2.4	Scd	P200
NGC 4242		12 15 01	45 53.8	140.78	70.32	70.3	4.8	SBdIII	P200
NGC 4245		12 15 05	29 52.9	192.56	82.16	85.5	−0.1	SBa(s)	P200
NGC 4251		12 15 36	28 27.1	202.95	82.55	86.9	−0.5	S0₁(8)	P200
NGC 4254	M 99	12 16 17	14 41.7	270.44	75.19	100.1	−4.5	Sc(s)I.3	C100
NGC 4256		12 16 21	66 10.6	128.22	50.89	50.7	10.7	Sb(s)	W60
NGC 4258	{ M 106 ON 427	12 16 29	47 35.0	138.33	68.84	68.7	5.5	Sb(s)II	P200
NGC 4260		12 16 49	06 22.6	281.57	67.63	108.1	−6.9	SBa(s)	C100
NGC 4261	3C 270.0	12 16 50	06 06.1	281.82	67.37	108.4	−6.9	E3	C100
NGC 4262		12 16 59	15 09.3	270.10	75.67	99.7	−4.2	SB0₂/₃	P200
NGC 4267		12 17 13	13 04.6	274.02	73.86	101.7	−4.8	SB0₁	C100
NGC 4270		12 17 17	05 44.5	282.38	67.07	108.8	−6.9	S0₁(6)	C100
NGC 4274		12 17 20	29 53.3	191.43	82.62	85.7	0.3	Sa(s)	P200
NGC 4273		12 17 23	05 37.3	282.54	66.96	108.9	−6.9	SBc(s)II	C100
NGC 4278	B2 1217+29	12 17 36	29 33.6	193.78	82.77	86.0	0.3	E1	P200
NGC 4281		12 17 49	05 39.9	282.76	67.03	108.9	−6.8	S0₃(6)	C100
NGC 4283		12 17 50	29 35.2	193.47	82.81	86.0	0.3	E0	P200
NGC 4291		12 18 07	75 38.8	125.56	41.60	41.3	13.0	E3	W60
NGC 4290		12 18 23	58 22.3	130.71	58.57	58.4	8.9	SBb	W60
NGC 4293		12 18 42	18 39.7	262.86	78.83	96.5	−2.8	Sa pec	W100
NGC 4294		12 18 45	11 47.4	277.10	72.85	103.0	−4.8	SBc(s)II–III	C100
NGC 4298		12 19 00	14 53.1	272.37	75.67	100.1	−3.9	Sc(s)III	C100
NGC 4299		12 19 08	11 46.8	277.41	72.88	103.1	−4.7	Sd(s)III	C100
NGC 4302		12 19 10	14 52.5	272.52	75.68	100.1	−3.8	Sc (on edge)	C100
NGC 4303	M 61	12 19 22	04 45.1	284.38	66.28	109.9	−6.7	Sc(s)I.2	P200
NGC 4307		12 19 33	09 19.1	280.60	70.63	105.5	−5.4	Sb?	C100
NGC 4304		12 19 35	−33 12.4	295.97	28.99	147.6	−15.3	SBbc(s)II	C100
NGC 4314		12 20 03	30 10.1	187.72	83.08	85.6	1.0	SBa(rs) pec	P200
NGC 4321	M 100	12 20 23	16 06.0	271.14	76.90	99.0	−3.2	Sc(s)I	C100
NGC 4324		12 20 34	05 31.7	284.55	67.11	109.2	−6.2	Sa(r) ring	C100
NGC 4346		12 21 01	47 16.2	136.58	69.39	69.3	6.2	SB0₁(9)	W100
NGC 4339		12 21 02	06 21.6	284.22	67.94	108.4	−5.9	S0₁/₂(0)	C100
NGC 4340		12 21 04	17 00.0	269.73	77.76	98.2	−2.8	SB0₂(r)	P200
IC 3253		12 21 07	−34 20.7	296.49	27.90	148.8	−15.2	Sc(s)II–III	C100

Galaxy (11)	B_T (12)	A^o (13)	A^i (14)	$B_T^{o,i}$ (15)	$M_{B_T}^{o,i}$ (16)	v (17)	ε (18)	Δv (19)	v_o (20)	Sources (21)
NGC 4216	10.97	0	1.21	9.76	−21.94 V	111	13	−119	−8	120, 160, 190, 191
NGC 4217	(11.30)	0	1.08	10.22	−21.46	1029	8	55	1084	28, 43, 159, 385
NGC 4215	13.04	0	0	13.04	−19.91	2093	43	−151	1942	284
NGC 4220	12.23[1]	0	1.00	11.23	−20.36	979	50	60	1039	190
NGC 4219	12.30[5]	0.27	0.65	11.38	−21.26	1980	19	−296	1684	284, (438), 439
NGC 4224	12.95	0	0.91	12.04	−21.40	2588	74	−146	2442	284, 380
NGC 4236	10.06	0.05	0.66	9.35	−18.41 N	−7	4	164	157	610
NGC 4233	12.97[1]	0	0	12.97	−18.73 V	2224	188	−145	2079	284
NGC 4234	13.43	0	0.30	13.13	−19.86	2143	90	−162	1981	229
NGC 4235	12.62	0	0.62*	12.00	−21.39	2527	41	−147	2380	284, 380, 431
NGC 4237	12.53	0	0.42	12.11	−19.59 V	922	40	−108	814	284, 380, 431
NGC 4244	10.60	0	0.87	9.73	−18.76	242	2	7	249	611
NGC 4242	11.54	0	0.37	11.17	−19.09	516	15	48	564	160, 229
NGC 4245	12.25	0	0*	12.25	−18.91	890	65	−35	855	190
NGC 4251	11.62[1]	0	0	11.62	−19.82	1014	75	−43	971	190
NGC 4254	10.43	0	0.32	10.11	−21.59 V	2413	10	−112	2301	120, 190, 191, 256
NGC 4256	(12.67)	0	1.33	11.34	−22.34	2577	51	148	2725	191, 201
NGC 4258	8.95	0	0.91	8.04	−22.05	463	5	57	520	549
NGC 4260	12.70	0	0.40*	12.30	−20.49	1957	19	−151	1806	229, 402
NGC 4261	11.38[1]	0	0	11.38	−21.71	2227	34	−152	2075	190, 442
NGC 4262	12.38)	0	0	12.38	−19.32 V	1364	8	−110	1254	212, 321, 376, 409
NGC 4267	11.78[1]	0	0	11.78	−19.92 V	1260	75	−120	1140	190
NGC 4270	13.17[1]	0	0	13.17	−20.04	2347	50	−154	2193	190
NGC 4274	11.30	0	0.95	10.35	−20.87	913	4	−35	878	190, 212, 220, 402, 409
NGC 4273	12.37	0	0.43	11.94	−21.31	2386	9	−154	2232	190, 300, 392
NGC 4278	11.13[1]	0	0	11.13	−19.24	630	14	−36	594	620
NGC 4281	12.26[1]	0	0	12.26	−21.19	2602	50	−154	2448	190
NGC 4283	13.12[1]	0	0	13.12	−18.50	1089	58	−36	1053	190, 241
NGC 4291	12.33[1]	0.07	0	12.28	−20.75	1827	40	189	2016	190, 191
NGC 4290	(12.59)	0	0.60	11.99	−21.81	2766	102	112	2878	284
NGC 4293	11.20	0	0.84	10.36	−21.34 V	933	38	−92	841	120, 191
NGC 4294	12.62	0	0.60	12.02	−19.68 V	352	15	−125	227	(120), 229, (301), 385
NGC 4298	12.08	0	0.47	11.61	−20.09 V	1114	24	−110	1004	164, 284
NGC 4299	12.86	0	0.30	12.56	−19.14 V	232	11	−125	107	(120), 160, 229, 385
NGC 4302	12.55	0	0.86	11.69	−20.01 V	1114	15	−110	1004	158, 284, 380, 431
NGC 4303	10.17	0	0.31	9.86	−21.84 VR	1561	3	−157	1404	550
NGC 4307	(12.82)	0	0.62*	12.20	−19.50 V	1305	202	−137	1168	284
NGC 4304	12.79[3]	0.14	0.28	12.37	−20.97	2608	15	−281	2327	158, 284
NGC 4314	11.35	0	0*	11.35	−19.80	883	85	−33	850	190
NGC 4321	10.11	0	0.32	9.79	−21.91 V	1568	4	−104	1464	551
NGC 4324	12.34[2]	0	0.43*	11.91	−19.79 VR	1662	9	−154	1508	190, 212, 402, 409
NGC 4346	12.19	0	0	12.19	−19.10	849	95	57	906	284
NGC 4339	12.32	0	0	12.32	−19.38 VR	1278	100	−150	1128	190
NGC 4340	11.93[1,8]	0	0	11.93	−19.77 V	874	53	−99	775	284, 380
IC 3253	12.42[5]	0.15	0.55	11.72	−21.84	2864	59	−282	2582	441

Galaxy (1)	Other names (2)	RA (1950) (3)	Dec (1950) (4)	l (5)	b (6)	SGL (7)	SGB (8)	Type (9)	Source (10)
NGC 4342	IC 3256	12 21 07	07 20.0	283.49	68.87	107.5	−5.6	E7	C100
NGC 4348		12 21 20	−03 10.0	289.62	58.71	117.7	−8.4	S on edge	48 Pr
NGC 4350		12 21 26	16 58.3	270.18	77.78	98.3	−2.7	S0₁(8)	P200
NGC 4365		12 21 56	07 35.7	283.82	69.18	107.3	−5.3	E3	C100
NGC 4369	{ Mark 439 { 4C 39.36?	12 22 09	39 39.7	145.75	76.53	76.6	4.2	Sc(s)III–IV	W100
NGC 4386		12 22 22	75 48.3	125.18	41.48	41.2	13.3	S0₁(5)	W60
NGC 4371	{ M 84	12 22 23	11 58.8	279.68	73.37	103.1	−3.9	SB0₂/₃(r)(3)	C100
NGC 4374	{ 3C 272.1	12 22 31	13 09.8	278.21	74.48	102.0	−3.5	E1	C100
NGC 4373		12 22 40	−39 28.7	297.50	22.84	154.1	−15.6	E(4, 2)	C100
NGC 4377	III Zw 65	12 22 40	15 02.4	275.35	76.21	100.2	−3.0	S0₁(3)	W60
NGC 4379		12 22 43	15 53.0	273.79	76.97	99.4	−2.7	S0₁(2)	C100
NGC 4378		12 22 45	05 12.1	286.12	66.94	109.7	−5.8	Sa(s)	C100
NGC 4380		12 22 50	10 17.6	281.95	71.82	104.8	−4.3	Sab(s)	C100
NGC 4382	M 85	12 22 53	18 28.0	267.73	79.24	96.9	−1.9	S0₁(3) pec	P200
NGC 4383	Mark 769	12 22 54	16 44.8	272.13	77.76	98.6	−2.4	S0:	W60
NGC 4389		12 23 10	45 57.7	136.74	70.74	70.6	6.2	SB pec	P200
NGC 4385	Mark 52	12 23 12	00 50.9	288.79	62.74	113.9	−6.9	SBbc(s)II	C100
NGC 4388		12 23 14	12 56.3	279.13	74.33	102.3	−3.4	Sab	C100
NGC 4395		12 23 20	33 49.5	162.10	81.53	82.3	2.7	SdIII–IV	P200
NGC 4394		12 23 25	18 29.4	268.23	79.32	97.0	−1.8	SBb(sr)I–II	P200
NGC 4406	M 86	12 23 40	13 13.4	279.09	74.64	102.0	−3.3	S0₁(3)/E3	C100
NGC 4414	B2 1223+31	12 23 57	31 29.9	174.57	83.18	84.6	2.2	Sc(sr)II.2	W100
NGC 4412		12 24 02	04 14.3	287.50	66.09	110.7	−5.7	SBbc(s)II	W100
NGC 4417		12 24 18	09 51.7	283.47	71.52	105.3	−4.1	S0₁(7)	C100
NGC 4419		12 24 25	15 19.4	276.46	76.64	100.1	−2.5	SBab:	W60
NGC 4420		12 24 25	02 46.3	288.53	64.68	112.1	−6.1	Sc(s)III	W100
NGC 4424		12 24 40	09 41.8	283.90	71.39	105.5	−4.0	S(a?) pec	C100
NGC 4425		12 24 42	13 00.7	280.26	74.53	102.3	−3.1	SB0 pec or Sa pec	C100
NGC 4428		12 24 53	−07 53.9	292.76	54.23	122.5	−8.8	Sc(s)II.3	P200
NGC 4429		12 24 54	11 23.1	282.38	73.02	103.9	−3.5	S0₃(6)/Sa pec	C100
IC 3370		12 24 59	−39 03.7	297.93	23.30	153.8	−15.1	E2 pec	C100
NGC 4433		12 25 03	−08 00.3	292.86	54.13	122.7	−8.8	SbcIII	W100
NGC 4435	VV 188	12 25 08	13 21.4	280.18	74.89	102.0	−2.9	SB0₁(7)	C100
NGC 4438	VV 188	12 25 14	13 17.1	280.36	74.83	102.1	−2.9	Sb (tides)	C100
NGC 4442		12 25 32	10 04.7	284.19	71.82	105.2	−3.7	SB0₁(6)	C100
NGC 4448		12 25 46	28 53.8	195.36	84.66	87.2	1.8	Sb(r)I–II	W100
NGC 4449		12 25 47	44 22.3	136.84	72.40	72.3	6.2	SmIV	W100
NGC 4450		12 25 59	17 21.7	273.92	78.64	98.2	−1.5	Sab pec	W100
NGC 4452		12 26 12	12 02.0	282.71	73.73	103.3	−3.0	S0₁(10)	C100
NGC 4455		12 26 13	23 05.5	251.63	83.29	92.8	0.2	Sc on edge	48 Pr
NGC 4454		12 26 16	−01 39.7	291.44	60.43	116.6	−6.8	Sa	C100
NGC 4460		12 26 19	45 08.6	135.82	71.70	71.6	6.5	Sbc	W60
NGC 4457		12 26 26	03 50.8	289.14	65.84	111.2	−5.3	RSb(rs)II	W100
NGC 4459		12 26 29	14 15.3	280.12	75.85	101.2	−2.3	S0₃(3)	C100
NGC 4461		12 26 31	13 27.7	281.26	75.11	102.0	−2.5	Sa	C100

Galaxy (11)	B_T (12)	A^o (13)	A^i (14)	$B_T^{o,i}$ (15)	$M_{B_T}^{o,i}$ (16)	v (17)	ε (18)	Δv (19)	v_0 (20)	Sources (21)
NGC 4342	13.54	0	0	13.54	−18.16 V	714	50	−145	569	190
NGC 4348	(12.89)	0	0.93	11.96	−21.01	2154	57	−190	1964	284, 380
NGC 4350	11.88[1,8]	0	0	11.88	−19.82 V	1184	60	−99	1085	190
NGC 4365	10.60[1]	0	0	10.60	−21.10 V	1230	10	−144	1086	190, 191, 442
NGC 4369	(12.28)	0	0.29	11.99	−19.66	1052	8	17	1069	552
NGC 4386	12.60[2]	0.07	0	12.53	−20.48	1811	61	190	2001	191
NGC 4371	11.74[1]	0	0	11.74	−19.96 V	977	76	−123	854	321
NGC 4374	10.23[1]	0	0	10.23	−21.47 V	952	13	−117	835	58, 120, 139, 190
NGC 4373	12.07[3]	0.21	0	11.86	−22.14	3444	47	−290	3155	224, 284
NGC 4377	12.67[1]	0	0	12.67	−19.03 V	1335	43	−108	1227	284, 287, 330
NGC 4379	12.30[1]	0	0	12.30	−19.40 V	1030	49	−104	926	284, 380
NGC 4378	(12.28)	0	0*	12.28	−21.12	2545	8	−154	2391	212, 284, 406, 409, 429
NGC 4380	(12.38)	0	0.72	11.66	−20.04 V	963	7	−131	832	284, 380, 409
NGC 4382	10.10[1]	0	0	10.10	−21.60 V	739	20	−91	648	190, (306), 442
NGC 4383	12.98	0	0	12.98	−18.72 V	1609	90	−100	1509	284
NGC 4389	(12.69)	0	0*	12.69	−18.24	717	11	50	767	160, 284, 402
NGC 4385	13.05	0	0.45	12.60	−20.38	2142	7	−173	1969	(15), 212, 284, 343, 409
NGC 4388	11.83	0	1.18	10.65	−21.05 V	2487	36	−118	2369	164, 188, 284, 431
NGC 4395	10.69	0	0.34	10.35	−18.57	317	9	−13	304	108, 160, 191, 391
NGC 4394	11.76	0	0.48	11.28	−20.42 V	944	10	−91	853	188, 190
NGC 4406	10.02[1]	0	0	10.02	−21.68 V	−250	17	−117	−367	190, 191, 229, 442
NGC 4414	10.95	0	0.47	10.48	−20.26	727	45	−25	702	190, 388
NGC 4412	(13.07)	0	0.31	12.76	−19.73	1735	10	−158	1577	(284), 400
NGC 4417	12.07[1]	0	0	12.07	−19.63 V	843	57	−133	710	284, 380
NGC 4419	12.13	0	1.01	11.12	−20.58 V	−229	18	−106	−335	284, 380, 409, 424
NGC 4420	(12.71)	0	0.53	12.18	−20.23	1680	10	−165	1515	188, 284, 380
NGC 4424	12.32	0	0.82	11.50	−20.20 V	456	79	−133	323	30, 284
NGC 4425	12.79[1]	0	0	12.79	−18.91 V	1883	50	−118	1765	190
NGC 4428	(13.32)	0	0.56	12.76	−21.00	3036	40	−208	2828	284
NGC 4429	11.15	0	0	11.15	−20.55 V	1114	65	−125	989	190
IC 3370	12.11[1]	0.20	0	11.91	−21.74	2973	83	−289	2684	284
NGC 4433	(13.01)	0	0.56	12.45	−21.27	2979	40	−208	2771	112, 197, 284
NGC 4435	11.72[1]	0	0	11.72	−19.98 V	869	100	−116	753	190
NGC 4438	10.91	0	0.94	9.97	−21.73 V	1	19	−116	−115	(58), (66), 187, 190
NGC 4442	11.31[1]	0	0	11.31	−20.39 V	580	100	−131	449	190
NGC 4448	12.0	0	0.95	11.05	−19.54	693	65	−38	655	190
NGC 4449	9.85	0	0.20	9.65	−18.84	207	5	43	250	553
NGC 4450	10.93	0	0.62	10.31	−21.39 V	1958	12	−96	1862	190, 409
NGC 4452	13.30	0	0	13.30	−18.40 V	152	82	−122	30	284, 380
NGC 4455	(12.93)	0	0.66	12.27	−19.43 VR	630	12	−67	563	158, 284, 370, 382
NGC 4454	13.0	0	0*	13.0	−20.25	2414	103	−183	2231	284, 380
NGC 4460	(12.11)	0	0.72	11.39	−19.02	558	28	47	605	284
NGC 4457	11.66	0	0.54	11.12	−20.58 VR	868	21	−159	709	321, 409
NGC 4459	11.49[1]	0	0	11.49	−20.21 V	1111	75	−111	1000	190
NGC 4461	12.09	0	0*	12.09	−19.61 V	1887	40	−115	1772	190

Galaxy (1)	Other names (2)	RA (1950) (3)	Dec (1950) (4)	l (5)	b (6)	SGL (7)	SGB (8)	Type (9)	Source (10)
NGC 4462		12 26 44	−22 53.6	296.36	39.42	137.5	−11.8	SBab(s)I–II	W100
NGC 4469		12 26 56	09 01.5	286.14	70.90	106.3	−3.7	Sab (on edge)	C100
NGC 4472	M 49	12 27 14	08 16.7	286.93	70.20	107.0	−3.8	E1/S0$_1$(1)	C100
NGC 4473		12 27 17	13 42.4	281.62	75.40	101.8	−2.3	E5	C100
NGC 4474		12 27 22	14 20.7	280.82	76.01	101.2	−2.1	S0$_1$(8)	C100
NGC 4476		12 27 28	12 37.5	283.11	74.39	102.9	−2.6	E5 pec (dust)	C100
NGC 4477		12 27 31	13 54.7	281.56	75.61	101.6	−2.2	SB0$_{1/2}$/SBa	C100
NGC 4478		12 27 46	12 36.3	283.39	74.39	102.9	−2.5	E2	C100
NGC 4485	VV 30	12 28 05	41 58.5	138.00	74.81	74.7	5.9	S (tidal)	W100
NGC 4483		12 28 08	09 17.1	286.82	71.23	106.1	−3.3	SB0$_1$(5)	C100
NGC 4490	VV 30	12 28 10	41 54.9	138.02	74.87	74.8	5.9	ScdIII pec	W100
NGC 4486	M 87 Virgo A 3C 274.0	12 28 17	12 40.1	283.78	74.49	102.9	−2.3	E0	C100
NGC 4487		12 28 30	−07 46.5	294.24	54.47	122.6	−7.9	SBc(s)II.2	W100
NGC 4494		12 28 55	26 03.1	228.60	85.32	90.1	1.6	E1	P200
NGC 4496	VV 76	12 29 07	04 12.9	290.57	66.33	111.1	−4.5	SBcIII–IV	W60
NGC 4501	M 88	12 29 28	14 41.7	282.34	76.51	101.0	−1.5	Sbc(s)II	C100
NGC 4503		12 29 34	11 27.2	286.10	73.41	104.1	−2.4	Sa	C100
NGC 4504		12 29 42	−07 17.3	294.64	55.00	122.2	−7.5	Sc(s)II	W100
R80	NGC 4517A	12 29 55	00 39.9	292.49	62.88	114.5	−5.3	SdIV	W60
NGC 4517		12 30 12	00 23.3	292.75	62.61	114.8	−5.3	Sc	W60
NGC 4519		12 30 58	08 55.8	289.17	71.04	106.7	−2.8	SBc(rs)II.2	C100
NGC 4522		12 31 08	09 27.0	288.95	71.56	106.2	−2.6	Sc/Sb:	C100
NGC 4526		12 31 31	07 58.5	290.17	70.14	107.6	−2.9	S0$_3$(6)	C100
NGC 4527		12 31 35	02 55.7	292.61	65.18	112.5	−4.3	Sb(s)II	W100
NGC 4532		12 31 47	06 44.7	291.03	68.94	108.8	−3.2	SmIII–IV	W100
NGC 4535		12 31 48	08 28.6	290.08	70.64	107.1	−2.7	SBc(s)I.3	C100
NGC 4536		12 31 54	02 27.7	292.96	64.73	112.9	−4.3	Sc(s)I	W60
NGC 4540		12 32 20	15 49.6	283.69	77.80	100.1	−0.5	Scd(s)III–IV	W100
New 2	NGC 4507	12 32 55	−39 38.0	299.64	22.86	154.6	−13.7	SBab(rs)I	C100
NGC 4546		12 32 55	−03 31.1	295.24	58.84	118.8	−5.7	SB0$_1$/Sa	W100
NGC 4548		12 32 55	14 46.4	285.70	76.83	101.2	−0.7	SBb(rs)I–II	C100
NGC 4550		12 32 59	12 29.8	288.10	74.63	103.4	−1.3	E7/S0$_1$(7)	C100
NGC 4552	M 89	12 33 08	12.50.0	287.94	74.97	103.1	−1.2	S0$_1$(0)	C100
NGC 4559		12 33 29	28 14.1	198.42	86.47	88.3	3.2	Sc(s)II–III	W100
NGC 4561	IC 3569	12 33 38	19 36.1	277.91	81.45	96.6	0.9	SBcIV	W100
NGC 4565		12 33 52	26 15.6	230.80	86.44	90.2	2.8	Sb	P200
NGC 4564		12 33 55	11 42.9	289.57	73.92	104.2	−1.3	E6	C100
NGC 4567	VV 219	12 34 01	11 32.0	289.79	73.75	104.4	−1.3	Sc(s)II–III	C100
NGC 4568	VV 219	12 34 02	11 30.9	289.82	73.73	104.4	−1.3	Sc(s)II–III	C100
NGC 4569	M 90	12 34 19	13 26.4	288.47	75.62	102.6	−0.7	Sab(s)I–II	C100
NGC 4570		12 34 21	07 31.4	292.43	69.82	108.2	−2.4	S0$_1$(7)/E7	W100
NGC 4571	IC 3588	12 34 25	14 29.6	287.54	76.65	101.6	−0.4	Sc(s)II–III	C100
NGC 4578		12 34 59	09 49.8	291.69	72.12	106.1	−1.6	S0$_{1/2}$(4)	C100
NGC 4579	M 58	12 35 12	12 05.6	290.40	74.36	103.9	−0.9	Sab(s)II	C100
NGC 4580		12 35 16	05 38.6	293.85	68.00	110.1	−2.7	Sbc(r)II	W100

Galaxy (11)	B_T (12)	A^o (13)	A^i (14)	$B_T^{o,i}$ (15)	$M_{B_T}^{o,i}$ (16)	v (17)	ε (18)	Δv (19)	v_0 (20)	Sources (21)
NGC 4462	12.56[5]	0.08	0.91	11.57	−20.97	(1866)	127	−255	1611	(275), 284
NGC 4469	(12.28)	0	0.99	11.29	−20.41 V	508	25	−136	372	284, 380
NGC 4472	9.32[1]	0	0	9.32	−22.38 V	961	13	−139	822	554
NGC 4473	11.07[1]	0	0	11.07	−20.63 V	2275	28	−113	2162	190, 263
NGC 4474	12.70	0	0	12.70	−19.00 V	1526	50	−110	1416	190
NGC 4476	13.08[1]	0	0	13.08	−18.62 V	1978	70	−118	1860	284
NGC 4477	11.24[1]	0	0	11.24	−20.46 V	1263	75	−112	1151	190
NGC 4478	12.15	0	0	12.15	−19.55 V	1482	75	−118	1364	190
NGC 4485	12.36	0	0.51	11.85	−19.22	786	104	31	817	241
NGC 4483	(13.41)	0	0	13.41	−18.29 V	875	80	−134	741	284
NGC 4490	10.23	0	0.53	9.70	−20.70	570	2	31	601	555
NGC 4486	9.62[1,8]	0	0	9.62	−22.08 V	1254	14	−118	1136	556
NGC 4487	(11.66)	0	0.39	11.27	−19.83	1037	8	−206	831	158, 284, 301
NGC 4494	10.74[1]	0	0	10.74	−21.27	1310	28	−51	1259	190, 191, 236
NGC 4496	(11.71)	0	0.37	11.34	−20.36 VR	1725	5	−157	1568	188, 229, 321
NGC 4501	10.27	0	0.50	9.77	−21.93 V	2269	5	−108	2161	120, 188, 190, 430
NGC 4503	12.22	0	0*	12.22	−19.48 V	1392	76	−123	1269	284, 380
NGC 4504	(11.92)	0	0.42	11.50	−19.50	998	9	−204	794	301
R 80	12.65	0	0.40	12.25	−19.91	1521	28	−172	1349	160, 431
NGC 4517	11.20	0	0.87	10.33	−21.08	1129	6	−173	956	191, 256, 306, 385, 430
NGC 4519	12.34	0	0.40	11.94	−19.76 V	1229	5	−135	1094	188, 191
NGC 4522	(12.70)	0	0.73	11.97	−19.73 V	2318	10	−132	2186	188, 284, 380, 431
NGC 4526	10.59[1]	0	0	10.59	−21.11 V	448	22	−139	309	120, 190, (306)
NGC 4527	11.32	0	1.02	10.30	−22.19	1738	8	−161	1577	190, 385, 430
NGC 4532	12.30	0	0.30	12.00	−19.70 VR	2002	4	−144	1858	188, 300, 321, 392
NGC 4535	10.51	0	0.39	10.12	−21.58 V	1953	6	−135	1818	557
NGC 4536	11.01	0	0.57	10.44	−22.15	1809	6	−163	1646	191, 256, 385, 391, 430
NGC 4540	(12.87)	0	0.36	12.51	−19.19 V	1285	10	−101	1184	188, 380, 431
New 2	12.81[5]	0.21	0.51	12.09	−21.96	3513	25	−287	3226	224, 284, 386
NGC 4546	11.30	0	0	11.30	−19.85	1037	24	−188	849	190, 389
NGC 4548	10.98	0	0.55	10.43	−21.27 V	472	9	−106	366	120, 188, 190
NGC 4550	12.33[1]	0	0	12.33	−19.37 V	378	14	−117	261	190, 385
NGC 4552	10.80[1]	0	0	10.80	−20.90 V	319	26	−116	203	139, 190, 191, 442
NGC 4559	10.36	0	0.57	9.79	−21.15	810	6	−39	771	624
NGC 4561	(12.96)	0	0.35	12.61	−19.09 VR	1407	20	−82	1325	284, 370, 431
NGC 4565	10.39	0	1.33	9.06	−22.79	1220	14	−49	1171	190, 191, 264, (306), 430
NGC 4564	11.87[1]	0	0	11.87	−19.83 V	1015	68	−121	894	321
NGC 4567	12.08	0	0.41	11.67	−20.03 V	2257	9	−121	2136	120, 141, 191, 392
NGC 4568	11.70	0	0.57	11.13	−20.57 V	2320	42	−121	2199	120, 141, 190
NGC 4569	10.23	0	0.84	9.39	−22.31 V	−261	(50)	−112	−373	558
NGC 4570	11.68[1]	0	0	11.68	−20.02 V	1730	75	−140	1590	190
NGC 4571	11.81	0	0.32	11.49	−20.21 V	343	6	−107	236	188, 160, 380, 402
NGC 4578	12.04[1]	0	0	12.04	−19.66 V	2282	50	−129	2153	188
NGC 4579	10.56	0	0.55	10.01	−21.69 V	1805	36	−118	1687	120, 190
NGC 4580	(12.69)	0	0.38	12.31	−19.39 VR	1253	64	−148	1105	284, 380

Galaxy (1)	Other names (2)	RA (1950) (3)	Dec (1950) (4)	*l* (5)	*b* (6)	SGL (7)	SGB (8)	Type (9)	Source (10)
NGC 4589		12 35 28	74 28.0	124.24	42.90	42.7	13.9	E2	W60
NGC 4586		12 35 55	04 35.6	294.65	66.98	111.2	−2.8	Sa	C100
NGC 4592	MSH 12−011?	12 36 45	−00 15.4	296.43	62.19	115.9	−3.9	ScdIII	C100
NGC 4593		12 37 05	−05 04.2	297.49	57.40	120.6	−5.1	SBb(rs)I–II	C100
NGC 4595		12 37 21	15 34.3	289.54	77.87	100.7	0.6	Sc(s)II.8	W100
NGC 4594	{ M 104 Cul 1237−11	12 37 23	−11 21.0	298.46	51.15	126.7	−6.7	Sa$^+$/Sb$^-$	P200
NGC 4596		12 37 24	10 27.0	293.31	72.83	105.6	−0.8	SBa (very early)	C100
NGC 4597		12 37 38	−05 31.5	297.81	56.96	121.1	−5.1	SBc(r)III:	C100
NGC 4605		12 37 47	61 53.1	125.34	55.46	55.5	12.0	Sc(s)III	W60
NGC 4602		12 38 03	−04 52.0	297.90	57.63	120.4	−4.8	Sc(s)I–II	C100
NGC 4603		12 38 11	−40 42.1	300.80	21.85	155.8	−12.8	Sc(s)I–II	C40IT
NGC 4608		12 38 42	10 25.7	294.39	72.86	105.7	−0.5	SB0$_3$/a	C100
NGC 4612		12 39 00	07 35.3	295.74	70.05	108.5	−1.2	RSB0$_{1/2}$	P200
NGC 4618	VV 73	12 39 08	41 25.6	130.58	75.83	75.8	7.8	SBbc(rs)II.2 pec	P200
NGC 4621	M 59	12 39 31	11 55.2	294.38	74.36	104.4	0.1	E5	C100
NGC 4623		12 39 38	07 57.0	296.08	70.43	108.2	−1.0	E7	P200
NGC 4631	B2 1239+32	12 39 41	32 48.8	142.86	84.22	84.2	5.7	Sc on edge	P200
NGC 4630		12 39 58	04 13.9	297.30	66.73	111.8	−1.9	S	48 Pr
NGC 4632		12 39 59	00 11.4	298.08	62.70	115.7	−3.0	Sc(s)II.3	C100
NGC 4635		12 40 09	20 13.2	286.82	82.54	96.4	2.5	ScII–III	48 Pr
NGC 4638		12 40 16	11 42.9	295.15	74.18	104.6	0.2	S0$_1$(7)	C100
NGC 4636		12 40 17	02 57.7	297.76	65.47	113.0	−2.2	E0/S0$_1$(6)	P200
NGC 4639		12 40 21	13 31.9	294.30	75.99	102.9	0.7	SBb(r)II	C100
NGC 4643		12 40 48	02 15.1	298.19	64.78	113.8	−2.3	SB0$_3$/SBa	P200
NGC 4647	{ VV 206 1241+11W1	12 41 01	11 51.2	295.76	74.34	104.5	0.4	Sc(rs)III	C100
NGC 4649	{ M 60 VV 206 1241+11W2	12 41 09	11 49.5	295.88	74.32	104.6	0.4	S0$_1$(2)	C100
NGC 4651	VV 66	12 41 13	16 40.1	293.08	79.12	99.9	1.8	Sc(r)I–II	W100
NGC 4653		12 41 17	−00 17.2	298.87	62.25	116.2	−2.8	Sc(rs)I.3	C100
NGC 4645		12 41 25	−41 28.7	301.49	21.10	156.7	−12.4	E5	C100
NGC 4654	IC 3708	12 41 26	13 24.0	295.45	75.89	103.1	0.9	SBc(rs)II	W100
NGC 4656	NGC 4657	12 41 32	32 26.5	140.35	84.71	84.7	6.0	Im	W100
NGC 4660		12 42 01	11 27.6	296.80	73.98	105.0	0.5	E5	C100
NGC 4658		12 42 02	−09 48.7	300.17	52.74	125.5	−5.2	SBc(s)I–II	W60
NGC 4665		12 42 33	03 19.8	299.07	65.88	112.8	−1.6	SB0$_{1/3}$/SBa:	W100
NGC 4666		12 42 35	−00 11.2	299.55	62.37	116.2	−2.5	SbcII.3	C100
NGC 4670	Haro 9	12 42 50	27 24.0	212.65	88.63	89.7	5.0	SB pec	P200
NGC 4668		12 42 58	−00 15.7	299.76	62.30	116.3	−2.4	SBc(s)III	C100
NGC 4682		12 44 40	−09 47.4	301.24	52.80	125.6	−4.5	Sc(s)II.4	48 Pr
NGC 4684		12 44 43	−02 27.1	300.86	60.13	118.6	−2.6	S0$_{2/3}$(7)	W100
NGC 4679		12 44 46	−39 17.9	302.12	23.29	154.7	−11.3	Sb(s)I–II	C40IT
NGC 4688		12 45 14	04 36.6	300.58	67.19	111.8	−0.6	SBc(s)II	48 Pr
NGC 4689		12 45 15	14 02.1	299.08	76.61	102.7	2.0	Sc(s)II.3	W100
NGC 4691		12 45 39	−03 03.6	301.36	59.53	119.2	−2.5	SBb pec	P200
NGC 4694		12 45 44	11 15.4	300.13	73.84	105.4	1.4	Amorphous	C100
NGC 4698		12 45 52	08 45.6	300.58	71.35	107.8	0.7	Sa	W100

Galaxy (11)	B_T (12)	A^o (13)	A^i (14)	$B_T^{o,i}$ (15)	$M_{B_T}^{o,i}$ (16)	v (17)	ε (18)	Δv (19)	v_0 (20)	Sources (21)
NGC 4589	11.87[1]	0.06	0	11.81	−21.36	1971	32	186	2157	190, 442
NGC 4586	12.54	0	1.01	11.53	−20.17 VR	823	57	−163	660	284, 380, 402
NGC 4592	(12.16)	0	0.70	11.46	−19.82	1076	15	−173	903	160, 284, 380
NGC 4593	(11.72)	0	0.57	11.15	−22.35	2698	38	−193	2505	321
NGC 4595	(13.22)	0	0.43	12.79	−18.91 V	660	85	−101	559	284
NGC 4594	9.28	0	0.88	8.40	−22.81	1089	6	−216	873	591
NGC 4596	11.45[1]	0	0	11.45	−20.25 V	1959	86	−125	1834	284, 380
NGC 4597	(12.58)	0	0.53	12.05	−19.10	1045	15	−194	851	160
NGC 4605	10.96	0	0.61	10.35	−18.34	141	15	132	273	36, 160, 191
NGC 4602	(12.28)	0	0.63	11.65	−21.71	2538	15	−191	2347	158, 284, 380
NGC 4603	(12.09)	0.22	0.44	11.43	−21.66	2360	200	−287	2073	379
NGC 4608	12.05	0	0	12.05	−19.65 V	1863	43	−125	1738	284, 380
NGC 4612	12.04	0	0	12.04	−19.66 VR	1883	53	−138	1745	284, (376), 380
NGC 4618	11.20	0	0.33	10.87	−19.39	532	31	31	563	191, 194, 321, (332)
NGC 4621	10.67[1]	0	0	10.67	−21.03 V	438	29	−118	320	190, 442
NGC 4623	13.09[2]	0	0	13.09	−18.61 VR	1963	105	−136	1827	284
NGC 4631	9.84	0	0.86	8.98	−21.44	619	3	−13	606	559
NGC 4630	(12.97)	0	0.50:	12.47	−19.23 VR	686	49	−153	533	284, 431
NGC 4632	(12.22)	0	0.61	11.61	−20.86	1727	50	−170	1557	321, 407
NGC 4635	(12.92)	0	0.38	12.54	−19.16 VR	979	15	−77	902	160, 284
NGC 4638	12.05[1]	0	0	12.05	−19.65 V	1080	150	−118	962	190
NGC 4636	10.50[1]	0	0	10.50	−20.58	979	20	−158	821	621
NGC 4639	12.19	0	0.62	11.57	−20.13 V	970	8	−110	860	158, 164, 188, 284
NGC 4643	11.55	0	0	11.55	−20.48	1432	40	−161	1271	191
NGC 4647	12.02[1,8]	0	0.36	11.66	−20.04 V	1448	130	−117	1331	(141), 191
NGC 4649	9.83[1,8]	0	0	9.83	−21.87 V	1259	26	−117	1142	633
NGC 4651	11.36	0	0.41	10.95	−20.75 V	817	4	−94	723	560
NGC 4653	12.82	0	0.31	12.51	−20.93	2605	15	−172	2433	160, 284
NGC 4645	12.79[4]	0.23	0	12.56	−20.75	2588	80	−287	2301	284, 379
NGC 4654	11.14	0	0.46	10.68	−21.02 V	1036	6	−110	926	120, 164, 253, 301, 321
NGC 4656	10.86	0	0.41	10.45	−20.03	638	4	−14	624	561
NGC 4660	11.87[1]	0	0	11.87	−19.83 V	1017	30	−119	898	190
NGC 4658	(12.74)	0	0.57	12.17	−21.05	2407	43	−209	2198	284
NGC 4665	(11.43)	0	0	11.43	−19.07	785	50	−156	629	190
NGC 4666	11.56	0	0.70	10.86	−21.49	1645	40	−171	1474	191
NGC 4670	13.05	0	0.48:	12.57	−19.01	1076	6	−40	1036	562
NGC 4668	13.59	0	0.47	13.12	−19.31	1701	125	−171	1530	284
NGC 4682	(12.87)	0	0.49	12.38	−20.74	2306	10	−207	2099	424
NGC 4684	(12.27)	0	0	12.27	−19.98	1590	51	−179	1411	284, 380
NGC 4679	(12.95)	0.20	0.52	12.23	−22.55	4792	63	−283	4509	441
NGC 4688	(12.45)	0	0.30	12.15	−18.96	981	9	−149	832	165, 301
NGC 4689	11.55	0	0.33	11.22	−20.48 V	1554	15	−105	1449	158, 284, 380, 431
NGC 4691	11.7	0	0.54	11.16	−20.22	1123	13	−181	942	113, 284, 321, 384
NGC 4694	12.21	0	—	[12.21]	−19.49 V	1177	14	−118	1059	212, 284, 380, 409, 418
NGC 4698	11.53	0	0.38*	11.15	−20.55 VR	986	5	−130	856	612

Galaxy (1)	Other names (2)	RA (1950) (3)	Dec (1950) (4)	l (5)	b (6)	SGL (7)	SGB (8)	Type (9)	Source (10)
NGC 4697		12 46 01	−05 31.7	301.64	57.06	121.6	−3.1	E6	P200
NGC 4696	PKS 1245−41	12 46 04	−41 02.3	302.41	21.56	156.4	−11.4	(E3)	48 Pr
NGC 4699		12 46 26	−08 23.6	301.93	54.20	124.4	−3.8	Sab(sr)	W100
NGC 4700		12 46 32	−11 08.2	302.03	51.46	127.1	−4.5	Sc or Sm	C100
NGC 4701		12 46 39	03 39.7	301.55	66.26	112.8	−0.5	Sbc(s)II	W100
New 3	A1246−09	12 46 47	−09 50.8	302.10	52.75	125.8	−4.1	SBcd(s)III	W100
NGC 4712		12 47 08	25 44.5	288.75	88.29	91.5	5.5	Sc(s)II	W100
NGC 4710		12 47 09	15 26.3	300.86	78.03	101.5	2.8	S0₃(9)	W100
NGC 4713		12 47 25	05 35.0	301.95	68.18	111.0	0.2	SBc(s)II−III	W100
NGC 4725		12 48 00	25 46.5	295.12	88.36	91.5	5.7	Sb/SBb(r)II	W100
NGC 4750		12 48 20	73 08.8	123.08	44.25	44.2	14.6	Sb(r)II pec	W60
NGC 4731		12 48 26	−06 07.3	302.75	56.48	122.3	−2.7	SBc(s)III:	W60
NGC 4736	M 94	12 48 32	41 23.6	123.37	76.01	76.2	9.5	RSab(s)	P200
NGC 4742		12 49 12	−10 11.0	303.09	52.42	126.3	−3.6	E4	W60
NGC 4747		12 49 19	26 02.8	305.95	88.64	91.3	6.1	SBc:	W100
NGC 4754		12 49 47	11 35.1	303.71	74.18	105.4	2.4	SB0₁(5)	P200
NGC 4753		12 49 48	−00 55.7	303.43	61.67	117.4	−1.0	S0 pec	P200
NGC 4756		12 50 15	−15 08.6	303.45	47.46	131.2	−4.6	E3	48 Pr
NGC 4762		12 50 25	11 30.1	304.28	74.10	105.5	2.5	S0₁(10)	P200
NGC 4760	PKS 1250−10	12 50 31	−10 13.3	303.62	52.37	126.4	−3.3	E0	W100
NGC 4763		12 50 35	−16 44.1	303.63	45.86	132.8	−4.9	SBbc(r)II	C100
NGC 4765		12 50 42	04 44.1	304.11	67.33	112.0	0.8	SdIII:	W60
NGC 4771		12 50 48	01 32.4	304.04	64.16	115.1	−0.1	ScII−III:	W100
NGC 4772		12 50 56	02 26.4	304.15	65.04	114.3	0.2	Sa:	P200
NGC 4767		12 51 08	−39 27.0	303.45	23.15	155.1	−10.2	S0/a	C100
NGC 4775		12 51 11	−06 21.2	303.98	56.24	122.7	−2.1	Sc(s)II.8	W60
NGC 4781		12 51 47	−10 15.9	304.13	52.33	126.6	−3.0	Sc(s)II.8	W60
NGC 4786		12 51 57	−06 35.3	304.32	56.00	123.0	−2.0	E3	W60
NGC 4782	{ VV 201, 3C 278	12 51 59	−12 18.1	304.15	50.29	128.5	−3.5	E0 (tides)	W100
NGC 4783	VV 201	12 52 00	−12 17.4	304.15	50.30	128.5	−3.5	E1 (tides)	W100
NGC 4790		12 52 16	−09 58.6	304.33	52.61	126.3	−2.8	SdII	W100
NGC 4793	5C 4.022	12 52 16	29 12.5	101.74	88.06	88.4	7.4	Sc(s)II.2	W100
NGC 4800		12 52 20	46 48.0	121.29	70.59	71.0	11.3	Sb(rs)II−III	W60
NGC 4795		12 52 31	08 20.2	305.67	70.92	108.7	2.2	SBa(s) (tides?)	P200
New 4	A1252+00	12 52 39	00 23.2	305.02	62.97	116.4	0.1	Sc(s)III	W100
NGC 4814		12 53 14	58 36.9	121.94	58.78	59.1	13.4	Sb(s)I	W60
NGC 4808		12 53 17	04 34.4	305.76	67.15	112.4	1.4	Sc(s)III	W100
IC 3896		12 53 51	−05 04.6	303.78	12.54	165.7	−11.8	E1	C100
NGC 4818		12 54 13	−08 15.1	305.22	54.32	124.8	−1.9	Sab:	W100
NGC 4826	{ M 64, B 1254+21	12 54 17	21 57.1	315.70	84.42	95.6	6.1	Sab(s)II	W60
NGC 4825		12 54 36	−13 23.9	305.08	49.18	129.8	−3.2	S0₁/₂(3)	C100
NGC 4835		12 55 17	−45 59.6	304.15	16.60	161.7	−10.7	Sc(s)(I−II)	C40D
NGC 4845		12 55 28	01 50.8	306.75	64.40	115.1	1.2	Sa	P200
NGC 4861	{ I Zw 49, Mark 59	12 56 40	35 07.9	111.54	82.10	82.8	9.7	SBmIV−V:	W60
NGC 4856		12 56 42	−14 46.3	305.78	47.79	131.2	−3.0	S0₁(6)/Sa	C100

Galaxy (11)	B_T (12)	A^o (13)	A^i (14)	$B_T^{o,i}$ (15)	$M_{B_T}^{o,i}$ (16)	v (17)	ε (18)	Δv (19)	v_0 (20)	Sources (21)
NGC 4697	10.11[1]	0	0	10.11	−21.47	1224	10	−191	1033	38, 190, 442
NGC 4696	11.59[1]	0.23	0	11.36	−22.30	2983	27	−281	2702	63, 284, 297, 379
NGC 4699	10.44[1]	0	0.59	9.85	−22.24	1511	49	−202	1309	191
NGC 4700	(12.57)	0	0.63	11.94	−19.95	1405	14	−212	1193	158, 284
NGC 4701	12.75	0	0.35	11.40	−18.89	724	15	−152	572	160, 380, 431
New 3	(12.10)	0	0.36	11.74	−19.98	1312	15	−207	1105	160
NGC 4712	13.59	0	0.56	13.03	−21.66	4379	8	−47	4332	106, 107, 136, 263, 400
NGC 4710	11.85	0	0	11.85	−19.85 V	1117	45	−98	1019	200, 321
NGC 4713	12.21	0	0.43	11.78	−19.92 VR	656	8	−144	512	160, 191, 392
NGC 4725	9.99	0	0.62	9.37	−22.47	1213	9	−46	1167	106, 136, 190, 263, 264
NGC 4750	(12.26)	0.06	0.48	11.72	−21.10	1647	89	182	1829	191
NGC 4731	(11.55)	0	0.53	11.02	−21.06	1495	9	−192	1303	229, 301
NGC 4736	8.92	0	0.54	8.38	−20.81	311	3	34	345	563
NGC 4742	12.11[1]	0	0	12.11	−19.63	1321	50	−207	1114	190
NGC 4747	13.01	0	0.63	12.38	−19.44	1198	7	−44	1154	106, 136, 247, 263
NGC 4754	11.41[1]	0	0	11.41	−20.29 VR	1461	75	−115	1346	190
NGC 4753	10.85	0	0	10.85	−20.90	1288	(50)	−171	1117	111, 191, 321, (332)
NGC 4756	13.33[4]	0.05	0	13.28	−21.20	4164	90	−224	3940	284
NGC 4762	11.26[1]	0	0	11.26	−20.44 VR	937	19	−115	822	190, 191, 212, 229
NGC 4760	13.04[2]	0	0	13.04	−21.71	4658	95	−207	4451	284, 380
NGC 4763	13.32[5]	0.05	0.49:	12.78	−21.71	4190	58	−229	3961	284
NGC 4765	(13.27)	0	0.38	12.89	−17.60	772	48	−146	626	284
NGC 4771	(12.70)	0	0.80	11.90	−19.69	1202	130	−160	1042	380
NGC 4772	(12.40)	0	0.82	11.58	−19.66	1042	10	−156	886	284, 380, 402
NGC 4767	12.65[4]	0.20	0	12.45	−21.29	3075	36	−281	2794	284, 379
NGC 4775	(11.74)	0	0.30	11.44	−20.76	1567	10	−192	1375	191, 392
NGC 4781	(11.69)	0	0.54	11.15	−19.55	895	67	−206	689	191
NGC 4786	12.82[2]	0	0	12.82	−21.93	4647	70	−193	4454	284
NGC 4782	12.75	0	0	12.75	−21.64	3986	38	−213	3773	174, 193, 241
NGC 4783	12.80	0	0	12.80	−21.94	4642	38	−213	4429	174, 193, 241
NGC 4790	(12.81)	0	0.42	12.39	−19.43	1359	15	−205	1154	158, 284, 380
NGC 4793	12.3	0	0.49	11.81	−21.65	2487	17	−27	2460	564
NGC 4800	12.3	0	0.58	11.72	−19.32	746	50	62	808	190
NGC 4795	(13.18)	0	0.51	12.67	−21.03	2879	105	−129	2750	284, 380
New 4	(12.55)	0	0.45	12.10	−19.73	1324	15	−164	1160	158
NGC 4814	12.8	0	0.59	12.21	−21.41	2531	65	119	2650	190
NGC 4808	(12.56)	0	0.57	11.99	−18.51	776	9	−146	630	301, 321
IC 3896	12.85[4]	0.48	0	12.37	−20.62	2274	110	−291	1983	284
NGC 4818	(11.89)	0	0.98	10.91	−20.24	1046	94	−198	848	284, 380
NGC 4826	9.37	0	0.75	8.62	−20.61	413	8	−63	350	565
NGC 4825	12.92[1]	0.04	0	12.88	−21.76	4452	45	−216	4236	284
NGC 4835	12.54[5]	0.33	0.75	11.46	−21.52	2261	82	−288	1973	240, 284, 438
NGC 4845	(12.17)	0	1.10	11.07	−20.22	1061	72	−157	904	284, 380, 431
NGC 4861	12.8	0	0.32	12.48	−18.64	831	6	5	836	66, 98, 191, 194
NGC 4856	11.4	0.05	0	11.35	−20.22	1251	75	−220	1031	190

Galaxy (1)	Other names (2)	RA (1950) (3)	Dec (1950) (4)	l (5)	b (6)	SGL (7)	SGB (8)	Type (9)	Source (10)
NGC 4868		12 56 49	37 34.7	114.34	79.69	80.4	10.2	Sc: or Sb:	48 Pr
NGC 4866		12 56 58	14 26.5	311.55	76.91	103.1	4.8	Sa	W100
NGC 4880		12 57 40	12 45.1	311.32	75.21	104.8	4.6	E4/S0$_1$(4)	48 Pr
NGC 4889		12 57 43	28 14.7	57.18	87.90	89.6	8.4	E4	P200
NGC 4900		12 58 06	02 46.1	308.45	65.27	114.4	2.0	ScIII–IV	W60
NGC 4891		12 58 15	−13 10.9	306.49	49.37	129.8	−2.2	SBbc(r)I–II	C100
NGC 4899		12 58 19	−13 40.6	306.45	48.86	130.3	−2.3	Sc(s)II.2	W100
NGC 4902		12 58 22	−14 14.7	306.42	48.29	130.8	−2.5	SBb(s)I–II	W60
NGC 4914		12 58 23	37 35.0	112.65	79.63	80.4	10.6	[S0$_1$(5)]	48 Pr
NGC 4904		12 58 25	00 14.5	308.15	62.75	116.9	1.4	SBbc(rs)II–III	W100
NGC 4915		12 58 53	−04 16.6	307.69	58.23	121.3	0.3	E0	W60
NGC 4928		13 00 26	−07 49.0	307.90	54.68	124.8	−0.3	Sbc(s)III.3	W100
NGC 4933		13 01 20	−11 13.8	307.84	51.25	128.1	−1.0	S0$_3$ pec (tides?)	W100
NGC 4936		13 01 34	−30 15.4	306.21	32.26	146.5	−6.0	E2	C100
NGC 4941		13 01 37	−05 17.0	308.81	57.17	122.4	0.7	Sab(s)II	C100
NGC 4939		13 01 38	−10 04.4	308.11	52.40	127.0	−0.6	Sbc(rs)I	W100
NGC 4951		13 02 31	−06 13.7	309.06	56.21	123.4	0.7	Sc(s)II:	W60
NGC 4945	PKS 1302-49	13 02 32	−49 12.0	305.28	13.34	165.2	−10.2	Sc	C100
NGC 4947		13 02 34	−35 04.2	306.14	27.45	151.3	−6.9	Sbc(s)I–II pec	C100
NGC 4958		13 03 12	−07 45.1	309.10	54.68	124.9	0.4	S0$_1$(7)	W60
NGC 4961	5C 4.175	13 03 24	28 00.1	44.53	86.76	90.2	9.6	SBbc(s)III	W60
NGC 4976		13 05 42	−49 14.5	305.81	13.27	165.3	−9.7	S0$_1$(4)	C100
NGC 4981		13 06 13	−06 30.8	310.64	55.83	123.9	1.5	SBbc(sr)II	W60
NGC 4984		13 06 23	−15 15.0	309.15	47.14	132.3	−0.9	Sa(s)	C100
NGC 4999		13 07 00	01 56.4	313.38	64.18	115.8	4.0	SBb(r)	W60
NGC 4995		13 07 04	−07 34.0	310.78	54.76	125.0	1.4	Sbc(s)II	W100
NGC 5005	B2 1308+37	13 08 37	37 19.4	101.63	79.25	81.1	12.5	Sb(s)II	W100
NGC 5012		13 09 12	23 10.9	351.39	83.79	95.2	9.8	Sc(rs)I–II	W100
NGC 5016		13 09 42	24 21.7	1.03	84.44	94.1	10.1	Sc(r)II	W100
NGC 5011		13 10 00	−42 50.1	307.09	19.60	159.2	−7.5	E2	48 Pr
NGC 5017		13 10 15	−16 30.1	310.33	45.80	133.8	−0.3	E2	C100
NGC 5018		13 10 20	−19 15.2	309.90	43.06	136.4	−1.1	E4	W60
NGC 5033	B2 1311+36	13 11 08	36 51.8	98.09	79.44	81.6	12.9	Sbc(s)I–II	W100
NGC 5037		13 12 22	−16 19.6	311.06	45.91	133.8	0.2	Sab(s)	C100
NGC 5044		13 12 44	−16 07.3	311.24	46.10	133.6	0.3	E0	C100
NGC 5055	M 63	13 13 35	42 17.8	106.00	74.28	76.2	14.2	Sbc(s)II–III	W100
NGC 5054		13 14 19	−16 22.1	311.73	45.80	133.9	0.6	Sb(s)I–II	C100
NGC 5061		13 15 20	−26 34.4	310.26	35.66	143.8	−2.1	E0	W100
NGC 5064		13 16 04	−47 38.8	307.70	14.70	164.2	−7.7	Sa	C100
NGC 5074		13 16 05	31 44.0	70.99	82.69	87.0	13.0	S	48 Pr
NGC 5068		13 16 13	−20 46.6	311.49	41.38	138.3	−0.2	SBc(s)II–III	P200
NGC 5077		13 16 53	−12 23.7	313.55	49.63	130.3	2.4	E3	W100
NGC 5085		13 17 33	−24 10.7	311.28	37.96	141.6	−0.9	Sc(r)I–II	W100
NGC 5084		13 17 34	−21 33.9	311.76	40.55	139.1	−0.1	S0$_1$(8)	W100
NGC 5088		13 17 42	−12 18.8	313.88	49.69	130.3	2.6	ScIII	W100

Galaxy (11)	B_T (12)	A^o (13)	A^i (14)	$B_T^{o,i}$ (15)	$M_{B_T}^{o,i}$ (16)	v (17)	ε (18)	Δv (19)	v_0 (20)	Sources (21)
NGC 4868	(13.14)	0	0.38	12.76	−22.15	4731	43	17	4748	284
NGC 4866	11.84	0	1.25	10.59	−21.11 VR	1980	11	−99	1881	190, 374, 402
NGC 4880	(12.57)	0	0	12.57	−19.13 VR	1498	57	−106	1392	284, 380
NGC 4889	12.57[1]	0	0	12.57	−22.99	6512	23	−30	6482	190, 191, 228, 308, 309
NGC 4900	12.06	0	0.30	11.76	−19.32	975	10	−152	823	191, 392
NGC 4891	12.61[5]	0.04	0.32	12.25	−21.17	2632	85	−214	2418	284
NGC 4899	(12.61)	0.04	0.47	12.10	−21.34	2653	133	−216	2437	284
NGC 4902	11.90	0.04	0.47	11.39	−22.04	2643	15	−217	2426	191, 400
NGC 4914	(12.30)	0	0	12.30	−22.61	4778	58	18	4796	284
NGC 4904	12.7	0	0.41	12.29	−19.47	1285	(60)	−162	1123	284, 431
NGC 4915	12.88[1]	0	0	12.88	−20.99	3152	40	−181	2971	190
NGC 4928	(13.36)	0	0.38	12.98	−19.31	1628	73	−194	1434	284, 431
NGC 4933	13.18[2]	0	0	13.18	−20.76	3276	34	−206	3070	284
NGC 4936	12.40	0.12	0	12.28	−21.65	3309	83	−261	3048	284
NGC 4941	11.9	0	0.75	11.15	−20.07	1061	(50)	−183	878	(27), 190, 402
NGC 4939	(11.56)	0	0.51	11.05	−22.77	3104	5	−201	2903	613
NGC 4951	(12.56)	0	0.61	11.95	−19.54	1180	9	−187	993	284, 301
NGC 4945	9.60	0.44	0.86	8.30	−20.90 C	563	14	−288	275	615
NGC 4947	12.74[5]	0.15	0.48	12.11	−21.13	2492	71	−270	2222	224, 284, 438
NGC 4958	11.48[1]	0	0	11.48	−20.63	1515	75	−192	1323	190, (374)
NGC 4961	13.9	0	0.40	13.50	−20.00	2537	9	−29	2508	228, 301, 309, 310
NGC 4976	11.17[1]	0.44	0	10.73	−20.95	1369	57	−287	1082	150, 297
NGC 4981	11.83	0	0.37	11.46	−20.91	1678	14	−186	1492	158, 284, 407
NGC 4984	11.71[4]	0.05	0.56	11.10	−20.49	1259	30	−217	1042	284
NGC 4999	12.64[5]	0	0.52	12.12	−21.74	3105	240	−151	2954	284
NGC 4995	11.90	0	0.41	11.49	−21.10	1835	66	−190	1645	191
NGC 5005	10.64	0	0.83	9.81	−21.78	1022	16	20	1042	74, 190, 191, 220, (306)
NGC 5012	(12.47)	0	0.46	12.01	−21.63	2728	49	−51	2677	284, 309, 431
NGC 5016	(12.94)	0	0.37	12.57	−20.97	2603	33	−45	2558	284, 309
NGC 5011	12.40[4]	0.26	0	12.14	−21.58	3055	78	−280	2775	224, 284
NGC 5017	13.24[4]	0.05	0	13.19	−20.15	2543	68	−220	2323	284
NGC 5018	11.71[1]	0.06	0	11.65	−21.99	2897	75	−228	2669	190
NGC 5033	10.63	0	0.52	10.11	−21.16	878	3	19	897	600
NGC 5037	13.00[5]	0.05	1.05	11.90	−20.73	1897	43	−218	1679	284, 380
NGC 5044	11.92[1]	0.05	0	11.87	−21.61	2704	69	−217	2487	284, 380
NGC 5055	9.33	0	0.46	8.87	−21.34	503	3	47	550	566
NGC 5054	11.51[5]	0.05	0.71	10.75	−21.67	1741	8	−217	1524	158, 284, 380, 392
NGC 5061	11.35[2]	0.09	0	11.26	−21.54	2065	46	−247	1818	191
NGC 5064	12.69[5]	0.39	0.91	11.39	−22.27	2982	25	−282	2700	284
NGC 5074	14.4	0	0.40:	14.0	−21.27	5680	100	−5	5675	309
NGC 5068	(10.53)	0.07	0.31	10.15	−19.05 C	673	11	−230	443	160, 191, 387
NGC 5077	12.56[1]	0.04	0	12.52	−21.03	2764	58	−203	2561	58, 139, 190
NGC 5085	12.04[5]	0.08	0.32	11.64	−21.04	1959	14	−239	1720	284, 387
NGC 5084	12.02	0.07	0	11.95	−20.45	1739	75	−232	1507	284
NGC 5088	(13.17)	0.04	0.68	12.45	−19.51	1432	14	−202	1230	284, 384

Galaxy (1)	Other names (2)	RA (1950) (3)	Dec (1950) (4)	*l* (5)	*b* (6)	SGL (7)	SGB (8)	Type (9)	Source (10)
NGC 5087		13 17 43	−20 20.9	312.04	41.75	138.0	0.3	S0₃(5)	C100
NGC 5090		13 18 17	−43 26.5	308.60	18.82	160.2	−6.2	E2	48 Pr
NGC 5101		13 19 01	−27 10.1	311.16	34.96	144.6	−1.4	SBa	C100
NGC 5102		13 19 07	−36 22.1	309.74	25.84	153.4	−4.1	S0₁(5)	C40D
NGC 5112		13 19 41	38 59.8	96.08	76.76	79.7	14.9	Sc(rs)II	W60
NGC 5116		13 20 34	27 14.5	33.53	82.99	91.7	13.1	Sc(s)II	W60
NGC 5121		13 21 53	−37 25.3	310.19	24.72	154.6	−3.8	S0₁(4)/Sa	C100
NGC 5128	Cen A	13 22 32	−42 45.5	309.52	19.42	159.8	−5.2	S0+S pec	P200
NGC 5134		13 22 36	−20 52.6	313.43	41.05	138.8	1.2	Sb(s)(II-III)	C100
NGC 5135		13 22 56	−29 34.3	311.76	32.45	147.1	−1.3	SBb:	W100
NGC 5147		13 23 47	02 21.7	322.88	63.62	116.5	8.1	Sc(s)III-IV	W60
NGC 5150		13 24 50	−29 18.2	312.28	32.65	147.0	−0.8	Sb(r)I-II	C100
NGC 5156		13 25 43	−48 39.4	309.23	13.51	165.6	−6.4	SBbc(rs)I	C40D
NGC 5161		13 26 25	−32 54.9	311.98	29.03	150.6	−1.6	Sc(s)I	C100
NGC 5172		13 26 53	17 18.6	345.89	76.65	102.0	12.5	SbI	W60
NGC 5170		13 27 05	−17 42.3	315.66	43.96	136.1	3.2	Sb:	W100
NGC 5204	⎰M 51, VV 1	13 27 44	58 40.7	113.51	58.00	59.4	17.8	SdIV	P200
NGC 5194	⎱4C 47.36.1?	13 27 46	47 27.3	104.87	68.56	71.2	17.3	Sbc(s)I-II	P200
NGC 5195	VV 1	13 27 53	47 31.8	104.90	68.48	71.1	17.3	SB0₁ pec	P200
NGC 5198	I Zw 59	13 28 04	46 55.7	104.13	69.02	71.7	17.3	E1	W60
NGC 5188		13 28 37	−34 32.0	312.19	27.36	152.2	−1.7	SBbc(s)II-III pec	C100
NGC 5193		13 29 04	−32 58.6	312.60	28.88	150.8	−1.1	S0₁(0)	C100
NGC 5230	⎧PKS 1332−33	13 33 05	13 55.8	342.55	73.06	105.7	13.2	Sc(s)I	W60
IC 4296	⎨PKS 1333−33, PKS 1334−33	13 33 47	−33 42.4	313.54	27.97	151.8	−0.4	E0	W100
NGC 5236	⎰M 83, PKS 1334−29	13 34 10	−29 36.8	314.58	31.97	147.9	1.0	SBc(s)II	C100
NGC 5248		13 35 03	09 08.5	335.94	68.75	110.6	12.6	Sbc(s)I-II	P200
NGC 5247		13 35 21	−17 38.1	318.33	43.59	136.6	5.0	Sc(s)I-II	C100
NGC 5253	Haro 10	13 37 05	−31 23.4	314.87	30.10	149.8	1.0	Amorphous	C100
NGC 5273		13 39 55	35 54.5	74.37	76.24	83.5	18.5	S0/a	P200
NGC 5266		13 39 56	−47 55.0	311.75	13.80	165.6	−3.9	S0₃(5) pec (prolate)	C100
NGC 5297		13 44 19	44 07.4	93.02	69.92	74.9	20.0	Sc(s)II	W60
NGC 5301		13 44 22	46 21.4	96.71	68.12	72.5	20.1	Sc(s)	P200
NGC 5308		13 45 21	61 13.3	111.26	54.88	56.7	20.0	S0₁(8)	P200
NGC 5300		13 45 44	04 11.9	335.76	63.14	116.2	13.9	Sc(s)II	W60
IC 4329		13 46 14	−30 02.8	317.45	30.94	149.2	3.3	S0₁(5)	C100
NGC 5322		13 47 35	60 26.4	110.29	55.49	57.5	20.3	E4	W60
NGC 5313		13 47 37	40 14.0	83.42	72.36	79.0	20.4	S:	48 Pr
NGC 5326		13 48 42	39 49.2	81.93	72.47	79.5	20.6	?	48 Pr
NGC 5324	MSH13−016?	13 49 30	−05 48.4	329.02	53.71	126.3	12.0	Sbc(r)I.3	W100
NGC 5328		13 50 03	−28 14.7	318.96	32.46	147.8	4.7	E4	C100
NGC 5334	IC 4338	13 50 20	−00 52.1	333.05	58.12	121.5	13.6	SB:	W60
NGC 5347		13 51 04	33 44.2	62.19	75.23	86.0	20.6	SBb(s)I-II	48 Pr
NGC 5350		13 51 14	40 36.7	82.84	71.59	78.7	21.1	SBbc(rs)I-II	P200
NGC 5351		13 51 19	38 09.5	76.45	73.09	81.3	21.0	SBb(rs)I	48 Pr
NGC 5353		13 51 21	40 31.5	82.60	71.63	78.8	21.1	S0₁(7)/E7	P200

Galaxy (11)	B_T (12)	A^o (13)	A^i (14)	$B_T^{o,i}$ (15)	$M_{B_T}^{o,i}$ (16)	v (17)	ε (18)	Δv (19)	v_0 (20)	Sources (21)
NGC 5087	12.0[1]	0.07	0	11.93	−20.60	1832	150	−228	1604	190
NGC 5090	12.64[4]	0.28	0	12.36	−21.37	3067	69	−277	2790	284, 396
NGC 5101	(11.58)	0.10	0	11.48	−21.06	1857	15	−246	1611	158, 284
NGC 5102	10.64[1]	0.17	0	10.47	−18.73 C	420	9	−266	154	43, 48, 150, 321
NGC 5112	(11.82)	0	0.39	11.43	−20.07	965	7	33	998	301, 385, 431
NGC 5116	(13.15)	0	0.64	12.51	−21.26	2862	20	−25	2837	309, 370
NGC 5121	12.40[5]	0.18	0	12.22	−19.80	1532	125	−267	1265	284
NGC 5128	7.89	0.27	1.0:	[6.6]	−22.6 C	526	8	−275	251	567
NGC 5134	(12.39)	0.07	0.72	11.60	−20.82	1754	10	−227	1027	284, 402
NGC 5135	(12.94)	0.11	0.92	11.91	−22.55	4157	35	−251	3906	284
NGC 5147	12.29	0	0.34	11.95	−19.47	1104	9	−141	963	321, 391, 392
NGC 5150	(13.26)	0.11	0.43	12.72	−21.86	4376	80	−249	4127	284
NGC 5156	12.87[5]	0.43	0.29	12.15	−21.49	2950	43	−280	2670	224, 284, 399
NGC 5161	11.98[5]	0.14	0.60	11.24	−21.89	2370	15	−257	2113	158, 284
NGC 5172	12.60	0	0.75	11.85	−22.64	4031	8	−71	3960	284, 385, 400
NGC 5170	11.88[5]	0.06	1.33	10.49	−21.56	1500	14	−215	1285	158, 284, 380
NGC 5204	11.75	0	0.46	11.29	−18.11 M	201	2	128	329	570
NGC 5194	8.98	0	0.41	8.57	−21.60	464	2	77	541	568
NGC 5195	10.51	0	−	[10.5]	−19.7	475	8	77	552	569
NGC 5198	(12.9)	0	0	12.9	−20.68	2531	31	74	2605	190, 191
NGC 5188	[12.7]	0.16	0.6:	11.94	−21.18	2366	43	−259	2107	284
NGC 5193	12.88[4]	0.14	0	12.74	−21.44	3684	133	−255	3429	284
NGC 5230	(12.75)	0	0.32	12.43	−23.22	6839	15	−84	6755	284, 392
IC 4296	11.58[1]	0.15	0	11.43	−22.72	3633	66	−255	3378	150, 284, 321
NGC 5236	8.51	0.12	0.31	8.08	−21.12 C	520	6	−245	275	571
NGC 5248	10.80	0	0.38	10.42	−21.19	1154	5	−105	1049	601
NGC 5247	11.1	0.06	0.33	10.71	−21.09	1354	8	−211	1143	(28), 158, 284, 392
NGC 5253	11.11	0.13	−	[10.98]	−18.2 C	395	3	−248	147	572
NGC 5273	12.42[1]	0	0	12.42	−19.23	1044	12	26	1070	190, 313, 376
NGC 5266	12.27[4]	0.42	0	11.85	−21.92	3110	73	−274	2836	224, 284
NGC 5297	12.23[8]	0	0.80	11.43	−22.19	2587	71	67	2654	22, 313
NGC 5301	(12.66)	0	0.82	11.84	−20.83	1631	42	78	1709	43, 46, 191
NGC 5308	12.20	0	0	12.20	−21.00	2038	35	144	2182	190, 191
NGC 5300	(11.93)	0	0.42	11.51	−20.09	1168	9	−121	1047	160, 370, 400
IC 4329	12.60[1,8]	0.12	0	12.48	−22.10	4356	56	−241	4115	199, 284
NGC 5322	10.91[1]	0	0	10.91	−22.04	1804	60	142	1946	190, 201
NGC 5313	(13.15)	0	0.46:	12.69	−20.88	2538	15	50	2588	284, 385
NGC 5326	12.94[8]	0	−	[12.9]	−20.7	2554	55	49	2603	284
NGC 5324	(12.43)	0	0.29	12.14	−21.64	3013	15	−160	2853	158, 284
NGC 5328	12.89[1,8]	0.11	0	12.78	−22.03	4816	125	−234	4582	284
NGC 5334	(11.90)	0	0.48:	11.42	−20.55	1377	15	−140	1237	160
NGC 5347	(13.40)	0	0.54	12.86	−20.54	2373	12	21	2394	284, 370, 385
NGC 5350	12.2	0	0.36	11.84	−21.48	2251	70	54	2305	284
NGC 5351	13.00	0	0.75	12.25	−22.07	3621	11	42	3663	284, 385, 400
NGC 5353	12.05	0	0	12.05	−21.19	2171	48	53	2224	190, 201, 241

Galaxy (1)	Other names (2)	RA (1950) (3)	Dec (1950) (4)	l (5)	b (6)	SGL (7)	SGB (8)	Type (9)	Source (10)
NGC 5362		13 52 48	41 33.7	84.44	70.74	77.7	21.4	S(b or c)	48 Pr
NGC 5357		13 53 06	−30 05.8	319.10	30.50	149.8	4.7	E3	C100
NGC 5371		13 53 33	40 42.4	82.19	71.20	78.6	21.5	Sb(rs)I/SBb(rs)I	W100
NGC 5363		13 53 37	05 30.0	340.97	63.25	115.4	16.1	[S0$_3$(5)]	W100
NGC 5376		13 53 39	59 45.0	108.57	55.80	58.1	21.1	Sbc(s)II	P200
NGC 5364		13 53 42	05 15.6	340.72	63.03	115.7	16.1	Sc(r)I	P200
NGC 5377		13 54 17	47 28.9	94.92	66.21	71.3	21.8	SBa or Sa	P200
NGC 5365		13 54 45	−43 41.3	315.39	17.32	162.6	−0.0	RSB0$_1$/3	C100
NGC 5380		13 54 49	37 51.1	74.30	72.69	81.7	21.6	S0$_1$(0)	P200
NGC 5383	Mark 281	13 55 01	42 05.6	84.79	70.08	77.1	21.9	SBb(s)I–II	W60
IC 4351	VV 48 I Zw 77 B1356+37	13 55 03	−29 04.3	319.92	31.36	149.0	5.5	Sb	W100
NGC 5395		13 56 30	37 38.2	73.17	72.50	81.9	22.0	SbII	W100
HA 72	A 1357-45	13 57 39	−45 10.6	315.50	15.76	164.1	−0.1	Sc(s)II–III	C40D
NGC 5406		13 58 14	39 09.2	76.64	71.41	80.3	22.4	Sc(s)I.2	48 Pr
NGC 5398	MSH 13-35?	13 58 27	−32 49.3	319.44	27.56	152.7	4.7	SBc(s)II–III	C100
NGC 5422		13 58 57	55 24.3	103.50	59.27	62.7	22.2	Sa or S0$_3$(8)	W60
NGC 5430	Mark 799	13 59 09	59 34.1	107.32	55.65	58.3	21.8	SBb(r)II	W60
NGC 5419	PKS 1400-33	14 00 44	−33 44.5	319.63	26.54	153.8	4.8	S0$_1$(2)	C100
NGC 5426	VV 21	14 00 48	−05 49.8	333.26	52.51	127.2	14.7	Sbc(rs)I.2	C100
NGC 5427	VV 21	14 00 49	−05 47.5	333.29	52.55	127.2	14.7	Sbc(s)I	C100
NGC 5448		14 00 56	49 24.8	95.73	64.01	69.2	22.9	Sa(s)	P200
NGC 5444	M 101	14 01 13	35 22.5	64.88	72.68	84.4	22.8	E3	48 Pr
NGC 5457	VV 344	14 01 28	54 35.6	102.05	59.77	63.6	22.6	Sc(s)I	P200
NGC 5473	4C 54.30.1	14 02 59	55 07.9	102.27	59.20	63.0	22.8	SB0$_1$(3)	P200
NGC 5474	VV 344	14 03 15	53 54.0	100.84	60.19	64.3	22.9	Scd(s)IV pec	P200
NGC 5468		14 03 58	−05 12.8	334.87	52.70	126.9	15.6	Sc(s)II	W100
NGC 5464		14 04 11	−29 46.8	321.86	30.06	150.4	7.0	IBmIII	C100
NGC 5480		14 04 31	50 57.7	96.87	62.44	67.5	23.3	Sc(s)III	W60
NGC 5485		14 05 27	55 14.2	101.81	58.91	62.8	23.1	S0$_3$(2) pec (prolate)	P200
NGC 5483		14 07 17	−43 05.3	317.86	17.25	162.9	2.3	SBbc(s)II	C40IT
NGC 5493		14 08 53	−04 48.5	336.96	52.46	126.9	16.9	E7/S0$_2$(7)	W100
NGC 5496		14 09 04	−00 55.4	340.47	55.76	123.0	18.1	Sc(s)	W60
NGC 5494		14 09 29	−30 24.8	322.85	29.08	151.4	7.8	Sc(s)I–II	C40D
NGC 5523		14 12 35	25 33.0	32.12	71.23	95.3	24.4	Sc(s)II–III	W100
NGC 5533		14 14 00	35 34.5	62.63	70.18	84.3	25.4	Sb(s)I	P200
NGC 5534		14 15 01	−07 11.2	337.17	49.64	129.7	17.6	SBbc(s)II (merger?)	C100
NGC 5530		14 15 18	−43 09.7	319.27	16.70	163.6	3.6	Sc(s)II.8	C100
NGC 5548		14 15 43	25 22.0	31.97	70.50	95.6	25.1	Sa	P200
NGC 5557		14 16 20	36 43.4	65.31	69.35	83.1	25.9	E2	W60
NGC 5556	DDO 243	14 17 38	−29 01.1	325.33	29.72	150.9	10.0	SBc(sr)II–III	C100
NGC 5566		14 17 49	04 09.7	349.28	58.56	118.4	21.6	SBa(r)II	P200
NGC 5585		14 18 12	56 57.5	101.01	56.48	60.7	24.7	Sd(s)IV	P200
NGC 5574		14 18 25	03 28.0	348.65	57.93	119.2	21.5	S0$_1$(8)	W100
NGC 5576		14 18 33	03 29.9	348.74	57.94	119.2	21.6	E4	W100
NGC 5584		14 19 50	−00 09.6	345.12	54.86	123.0	20.9	Sc(s)I–II	W100

Galaxy (11)	B_T (12)	A^o (13)	A^i (14)	$B_T^{o,i}$ (15)	$M_{B_T}^{o,i}$ (16)	v (17)	ε (18)	Δv (19)	v_0 (20)	Sources (21)
NGC 5362	(13.14)	0	0.71:	12.43	−20.90	2262	143	59	2321	284
NGC 5357	[13.2]	0.13	0	13.07	−21.83	5019	115	−237	4782	284
NGC 5371	11.40	0	0.59	10.81	−22.78	2561	9	55	2616	190, 191, 392
NGC 5363	11.06	0	0	11.06	−20.50	1138	41	−111	1027	190, 191
NGC 5376	(13.00)	0	0.44	12.56	−20.67	2069	64	141	2210	201, 284
NGC 5364	11.05	0	0.41	10.64	−21.15	1252	20	−112	1140	190, 418, 431
NGC 5377	12.0	0	0.74	11.26	−21.62	1796	10	87	1883	190, 402
NGC 5365	12.21⁵⁾	0.31	0	11.90	−21.33	2472	45	−263	2209	224, 284
NGC 5380	(12.75)	0	0	12.75	−21.18	3017	70	42	3059	201, 284
NGC 5383	12.05	0	0.51	11.54	−21.79	2260	3	62	2322	616
IC 4351	(12.30)	0.12	1.32	10.86	−22.52	2601	37	−234	2367	151, 284
NGC 5395	12.35	0	0.76	11.59	−22.69	3542	30	42	3584	284
HA 72	(12.83)	0.35	0.38	12.10	−19.79	1456	50	−264	1192	383
NGC 5406	(12.96)	0	0.38	12.58	−22.52	5191	83	50	5241	201, 284
NGC 5398	12.74⁵⁾	0.15	0.28	12.31	−19.16	1225	14	−241	984	158, 284
NGC 5422	12.71²⁾	0	0*	12.71	−20.26	1837	43	124	1961	284
NGC 5430	(12.78)	0	0.68	12.10	−21.80	2875	90	141	3016	201, 284
NGC 5419	[12.4]	0.16	0	12.2	−22.3	4254	82	−242	4012	63, 284
NGC 5426	12.78	0	0.50	12.28	−21.18	2609	8	−154	2455	241, 247, 392, 401
NGC 5427	12.07	0	0.31	11.76	−21.79	2719	20	−154	2565	241, 401
NGC 5448	12.2	0	0.85	11.35	−21.79	2023	10	98	2121	190, 402
NGC 5444	(12.51)	0	0	12.51	−22.01	3974	41	34	4008	139, 284
NGC 5457	8.18	0	0.29	7.89	−21.51 M	251	2	121	372	573
NGC 5473	12.36¹⁾	0	0	12.36	−20.80	2023	42	124	2147	190, 191
NGC 5474	11.31	0	0.30	11.01	−18.39 M	275	2	119	394	574
NGC 5468	(12.24)	0	0.29	11.95	−21.71	2845	9	−149	2696	191, 301
NGC 5464	(13.15)	0.13	0.21	12.81	−20.65	2686	38	−231	2455	284
NGC 5480	(12.89)	0	0.42	12.47	−20.50	1856	18	107	1963	241, (313), 385, 392
NGC 5485	12.44¹⁾	0	0	12.44	−20.69	1985	50	125	2110	190
NGC 5483	12.09⁵⁾	0.31	0.31	11.47	−20.94	1773	8	−256	1517	284, 387, 400, 438
NGC 5493	12.30¹⁾	0	0	12.30	−21.18	2627	75	−145	2482	190
NGC 5496	(12.59)	0	0.84	11.75	−20.48	1527	20	−129	1398	28
NGC 5494	12.71⁵⁾	0.14	0.32	12.25	−21.21	2690	(50)	−229	2461	441
NGC 5523	(12.47)	0	0.71	11.76	−19.83	1047	8	−7	1040	(173), 301, 370
NGC 5533	(12.65)	0	0.67	11.98	−22.48	3862	10	41	3903	190, 400
NGC 5534	(13.50)	0.04	0.49	12.97	−20.51	2633	10	−150	2483	284, 402
NGC 5530	(11.98)	0.33	0.51	11.14	−20.24	1196	15	−253	943	(151), (224), 387
NGC 5548	13.15	0	0.25*	12.90	−22.08	4970	29	−6	4964	614
NGC 5557	12.01¹⁾	0	0	12.01	−22.08	3195	60	48	3243	190
NGC 5556	(11.88)	0.13	0.33	11.42	−20.41	1384	10	−221	1163	156
NGC 5566	11.35	0	1.00	10.35	−21.99	1569	24	−101	1468	190, 229, 402
NGC 5585	11.37	0	0.43	10.94	−18.46 M	304	2	137	441	575
NGC 5574	13.25¹⁾	0	0	13.25	−19.29	1716	50	−104	1612	190
NGC 5576	11.76¹⁾	0	0	11.76	−20.51	1528	100	−104	1424	190
NGC 5584	(11.95)	0	0.38	11.57	−20.84	1636	9	−118	1518	301, 319

Galaxy (1)	Other names (2)	RA (1950) (3)	Dec (1950) (4)	*l* (5)	*b* (6)	SGL (7)	SGB (8)	Type (9)	Source (10)
NGC 5592		14 21 02	−28 27.9	326.36	29.94	150.7	10.9	Sbc(s)I–II	C100
NGC 5600		14 21 26	14 51.8	7.46	65.14	107.3	24.9	Sb pec	W60
NGC 5595		14 21 27	−16 30.0	332.78	40.71	139.4	15.8	Sc(s)II	W100
NGC 5597		14 21 42	−16 32.2	332.82	40.65	139.5	15.8	SBc(s)II	W100
NGC 5614	VV 77	14 22 01	35 05.1	59.97	68.75	84.9	27.0	Sa(s) (tides)	P200
NGC 5605		14 22 25	−12 56.3	335.33	43.74	136.0	17.3	Sbc(s)II	48 Pr
NGC 5631		14 25.0	56 48	99.53	56.02	60.7	25.6	S0₃(2)/Sa	P200
NGC 5633	I Zw 89	14 25 37	46 22.1	84.34	63.13	72.2	27.2	Sbc(s)II	W100
NGC 5641		14 27 05	29 02.6	43.16	68.37	91.8	27.9	S(B)abI	48 Pr
NGC 5638		14 27 09	03 27.3	351.69	56.50	119.8	23.6	E1	W60
NGC 5653		14 28 01	31 26.3	49.61	68.11	89.1	28.2	Sc(s)III pec	W100
NGC 5660		14 28 04	49 50.8	89.57	60.64	68.3	27.2	Sc(s)I.8	W100
NGC 5645		14 28 10	07 29.8	357.35	59.22	115.6	24.9	ScIII pec	W60
NGC 5612		14 28 12	−78 09.8	308.15	−16.58	195.7	−10.6	Sb(s)II	C100
IC 4444		14 28 27	−43 11.9	321.59	15.79	164.7	5.8	Sc(s)II	C40D
NGC 5643		14 29 28	−43 57.2	321.45	15.03	165.4	5.6	SBc(s)II–III	C100
NGC 5665		14 29 58	08 18.0	359.09	59.44	114.9	25.5	Sc(s)IV pec	W60
NGC 5669		14 30 17	10 06.6	1.94	60.56	112.9	26.0	Sc/SBc(r)I–II	W60
NGC 5678		14 30 38	58 08.4	100.05	54.50	59.1	26.1	Sc(s)II–III	P200
NGC 5668		14 30 54	04 40.2	354.44	56.75	118.8	24.9	Sc(s)II–III	W100
NGC 5676		14 31 02	49 40.8	88.69	60.38	68.4	27.7	Sc(s)II	W100
NGC 5687		14 33 16	54 41.6	95.39	56.77	62.7	27.2	E3	W60
NGC 5689		14 33 44	48 57.6	86.99	60.48	69.1	28.2	Sa	P200
NGC 5690		14 35 09	02 30.4	353.16	54.45	121.4	25.3	ScII:	W60
NGC 5691		14 35 20	−00 10.9	350.21	52.42	124.3	24.6	S(B)b pec III	C100
NGC 5701		14 36 41	05 34.8	357.46	56.37	118.3	26.5	(PR)SBa	C100
NGC 5713		14 37 38	−00 04.5	351.03	52.12	124.4	25.2	Sbc(s) pec	C100
NGC 5728		14 39 37	−17 02.3	337.33	38.10	141.7	19.6	SBb(s)II	C100
NGC 5739		14 40 34	42 03.3	73.12	62.99	76.8	30.3	Sa(s)	P200
NGC 5740		14 41 52	01 53.4	354.50	52.85	122.6	26.7	Sb(r)I	W60
NGC 5746		14 42 23	02 09.9	354.97	52.96	122.4	26.9	Sb(s)	P200
NGC 5750		14 43 37	−00 00.8	352.89	51.17	124.8	26.6	SBa(s)	C100
NGC 5756		14 44 48	−14 38.4	340.34	39.44	139.9	21.7	Sc(s)II	C100
NGC 5757		14 44 57	−18 52.1	337.47	35.87	144.1	20.0	SBb(rs)II	C100
NGC 5768		14 49 33	−02 19.7	352.16	48.46	127.8	27.3	Sc(s)III	W100
NGC 5775		14 51 27	03 44.8	359.44	52.42	121.4	29.6	Sc (on edge)	W60
NGC 5792	MSH 14-019?	14 55 48	−00 53.4	355.36	48.43	126.8	29.2	SBb(s)I.3	C100
NGC 5791		14 55 50	−19 03.9	339.99	34.29	145.5	22.2	S0₁(4)	C100
NGC 5796		14 56 36	−16 25.4	342.02	36.36	143.0	23.5	E1 pec	C100
NGC 5820		14 57 11	54 05.1	90.60	54.50	62.5	30.7	S0₂(4)	P200
NGC 5806		14 57 28	02 05.4	359.10	50.19	123.7	30.5	Sb(s)II.8	W100
NGC 5812		14 58 17	−07 15.5	349.82	43.32	133.9	27.6	E0	W100
NGC 5813		14 58 39	01 53.9	359.19	49.85	124.0	30.8	E1	W100
NGC 5831		15 01 34	01 24.9	359.40	48.98	124.8	31.3	E4	W60
NGC 5838		15 02 54	02 17.6	0.74	49.32	123.9	31.9	S0₂(5)	P200

Galaxy (11)	B_T (12)	A^o (13)	A^i (14)	$B_T^{o,i}$ (15)	$M_{B_T}^{o,i}$ (16)	v (17)	ε (18)	Δv (19)	v_o (20)	Sources (21)
NGC 5592	(13.27)	0.13	0.40	12.74	−21.88	4408	45	−218	4190	(284), 425
NGC 5600	13.2	0	0.44	12.76	−20.55	2348	23	−51	2297	284, 431
NGC 5595	12.69	0.07	0.47	12.15	−21.35	2681	40	−180	2501	284, 431
NGC 5597	12.6	0.07	0.33	12.20	−21.25	2624	66	−180	2444	284, 431
NGC 5614	12.54	0	0.52	12.02	−22.45	3872	75	43	3915	190
NGC 5605	(13.15)	0.06	0.35	12.74	−21.29	3363	15	−167	3196	400
NGC 5631	12.46[1]	0	0	12.46	−20.67	1979	60	139	2118	190
NGC 5633	12.90	0	0.46	12.44	−21.00	2341	41	96	2437	190, 191
NGC 5641	(12.90)	0	0.74	12.16	−22.60	4467	95	18	4485	284
NGC 5638	12.20	0	0	12.20	−20.31	1690	39	−98	1592	190, 313
NGC 5653	12.90	0	0.34	12.56	−21.72	3557	118	30	3587	191
NGC 5660	12.3	0	0.31	11.99	−21.45	2321	8	112	2433	158, 201, 284, 391, 431
NGC 5645	12.8	0	0.45	12.35	−19.85	1455	222	−80	1375	284
NGC 5612	13.14[5]	0.33	0.96	11.85	−21.65	2764	148	−259	2505	284
IC 4444	12.19[5]	0.35	0.33	11.51	−21.22	2006	13	−246	1760	284, 400, 425, 438
NGC 5643	10.89[3]	0.38	0.32	10.19	−21.20	1194	10	−247	947	632
NGC 5665	(12.79)	0	0.41	12.38	−20.84	2281	24	−75	2206	20, 321
NGC 5669	(12.00)	0	0.38	11.62	−20.46	1371	7	−67	1304	301, 385, 400, 431
NGC 5678	(12.08)	0	0.53	11.55	−21.90	2300	89	146	2446	191
NGC 5668	12.15	0	0.30	11.85	−20.52	1581	6	−90	1491	576
NGC 5676	11.68[8]	0	0.53	11.15	−22.11	2127	9	112	2239	602
NGC 5687	12.6	0	0	12.6	−20.67	2119	75	134	2253	190
NGC 5689	12.8	0	0.36*	12.44	−20.85	2163	22	111	2274	190, 201, 402
NGC 5690	12.5	0	0.69	11.81	−20.79	1750	15	−97	1653	158, (332)
NGC 5691	(12.95)	0	0.55	12.40	−20.34	1876	50	−108	1768	284
NGC 5701	11.8	0	0*	11.8	−20.47	1506	4	−82	1424	284, 384, 391, 402
NGC 5713	12.00	0	0.32	11.68	−21.07	1883	6	−106	1777	577
NGC 5728	12.1	0.08	0.75	11.27	−22.47	2970	40	−170	2800	284
NGC 5739	13.3[2]	0	0.47	12.8	−22.5	5608	118	84	5692	284
NGC 5740	12.62	0	0.76	11.86	−20.51	1585	9	−95	1490	160, 284, 370, 385
NGC 5746	11.55	0	1.31	10.24	−22.34	1731	10	−93	1638	190, 191, 229, 385
NGC 5750	12.5	0	0.72	11.78	−21.14	2023	173	−101	1922	284
NGC 5756	(13.23)	0.08	0.54	12.61	−20.43	2183	75	−158	2025	284
NGC 5757	(12.62)	0.09	0.50	12.03	−21.55	2771	58	−173	2598	284
NGC 5768	(12.94)	0.04	0.37	12.53	−20.44	2067	20	−107	1960	402
NGC 5775	12.24	0	0.76	11.48	−20.91	1582	99	−80	1502	241
NGC 5792	(11.72)	0.04	1.14	10.54	−22.35	1985	68	−96	1889	321
NGC 5791	12.86[2]	0.10	0	12.76	−21.25	3339	73	−166	3173	284
NGC 5796	12.65[2]	0.09	0	12.56	−21.17	2946	30	−156	2790	284
NGC 5820	12.99[1]	0	0	12.99	−21.18	3269	60	141	3410	190
NGC 5806	12.3	0	0.51	11.79	−20.23	1352	10	−82	1270	190, 385
NGC 5812	12.33[1]	0.06	0	12.27	−20.68	2066	50	−120	1946	190
NGC 5813	11.61[1]	0.04	0	11.57	−21.21	1882	65	−82	1800	190
NGC 5831	12.50[1]	0.04	0	12.46	−20.07	1684	50	−82	1602	190
NGC 5838	11.76[1]	0.04	0	11.72	−20.44	1427	50	−78	1349	190

Galaxy (1)	Other names (2)	RA (1950) (3)	Dec (1950) (4)	l (5)	b (6)	SGL (7)	SGB (8)	Type (9)	Source (10)
NGC 5846		15 03 56	01 47.8	0.43	48.80	124.6	32.0	$S0_1(0)$	C100
NGC 5850		15 04 35	01 44.2	0.52	48.64	124.7	32.1	SBb(sr)I–II	C100
NGC 5866	M 102	15 05 07	55 57.3	92.04	52.49	60.0	31.2	$S0_3(8)$	P200
NGC 5854		15 05 16	02 45.6	1.87	49.18	123.6	32.6	Sa	P200
NGC 5861		15 06 33	−11 07.9	348.53	39.05	138.8	28.0	Sc(s)II	C100
NGC 5864		15 07 02	03 14.6	2.87	49.15	123.2	33.2	SBa	P200
NGC 5879		15 08 29	57 11.4	93.24	51.39	58.4	31.2	Sb(s)II	P200
NGC 5878		15 11 00	−14 05.1	347.19	36.09	142.3	27.7	Sb(s)I.2	C100
F 703	A1511–15	15 11 00	−15 16.7	346.27	35.17	143.5	27.1	Sc(s)II.2	C100
NGC 5885		15 12 22	−09 54.0	350.96	39.04	138.2	29.8	SBc(s)II	C100
NGC 5899		15 13 14	42 14.0	69.41	57.22	75.4	36.3	Sc(s)II	P200
NGC 5905		15 14 02	55 42.1	90.57	51.59	59.7	32.4	SBb(rs)I	W60
NGC 5907		15 14 37	56 30.4	91.58	51.09	58.8	32.2	Sc (on edge)	P200
NGC 5898		15 15 17	−23 55.0	340.98	27.72	152.4	23.8	$S0_2/3(0)$	C100
NGC 5908		15 15 24	55 35.4	90.26	51.49	59.8	32.7	Sb (on edge)	P200
NGC 5903		15 15 40	−23 53.1	341.08	27.70	152.5	23.9	$E3/S0_1(3)$	C100
NGC 5915		15 18 48	−12 54.9	349.91	35.74	142.1	29.9	SBbc(s) pec	C100
NGC 5921		15 19 28	05 14.9	8.13	47.94	121.9	36.7	SBbc(s)I–II	W100
NGC 5949		15 27 19	64 56.0	100.58	44.97	49.2	29.9	Sc	P200
NGC 5936		15 27 39	13 09.6	20.07	50.38	112.6	40.4	Sc(r)I–II	W60
NGC 5962		15 34 14	16 46.4	26.26	50.47	108.1	42.5	Sc(r)II.3	P200
NGC 5970		15 36 08	12 21.0	20.42	48.17	114.1	42.3	SBbc(r)II	W60
NGC 5982		15 37 38	59 31.1	93.11	46.92	54.0	33.7	E3	P200
NGC 5985		15 38 36	59 29.6	92.99	46.83	54.0	33.8	SBb(r)I	P200
NGC 5984		15 40 34	14 23.4	23.88	48.11	111.6	43.7	SBcdIII:	W60
NGC 5967		15 42 10	−75 31.2	313.30	−16.49	196.0	−5.7	Sc(rs)II.2	C100
NGC 6015		15 50 39	62 27.5	95.70	44.13	50.0	33.4	Sc(s)II–III	P200
NGC 6052	VV 86	16 03 01	20 40.5	35.31	45.47	103.0	49.5	S pec	P200
NGC 6070	Mark 297	16 07 26	00 50.4	12.48	35.59	132.6	46.6	Sc(s)I	P200
NGC 6106		16 16 22	07 32.0	21.02	37.17	124.1	50.9	Sc(rs)II.3	C100
NGC 6118		16 19 13	−02 10.1	11.46	31.47	138.5	48.1	Sc(s)I.3	C100
NGC 6181		16 30 10	19 55.9	37.17	39.21	104.1	55.8	Sc(s)II	P200
NGC 6217		16 35 03	78 18.0	111.32	33.37	34.0	25.2	RSBbc(s)II	P200
NGC 6207		16 41 18	36 55.7	59.55	40.68	74.2	54.0	Sc(s)III	P200
NGC 6215		16 46 48	−58 54.3	329.79	−9.27	190.8	11.1	Sc(s)II	C100
NGC 6221		16 48 25	−59 08.0	329.75	−9.57	191.1	11.1	Sbc(s)II–III	C100
NGC 6239		16 48 31	42 49.4	67.39	39.76	64.7	52.0	SBcIII pec	P200
NGC 6340		17 11 16	72 21.9	103.73	33.35	35.5	31.4	Sa(r)I	P200
NGC 6300		17 12 18	−62 45.8	328.50	−14.05	195.4	9.2	SBb(s)II pec	C100
NGC 6384		17 29 59	07 05.8	30.27	20.77	137.3	68.0	Sb(r)I	P200
NGC 6412		17 31 22	75 44.3	107.24	31.24	32.3	28.9	SBc(s)/Sc(s)I–II	P200
IC 4662		17 42 12	−64 37.3	328.56	−17.85	199.2	8.6	ImIII	C100
NGC 6482		17 49 44	23 05.0	48.10	22.91	87.7	73.4	E2	W100
NGC 6503		17 49 58	70 09.5	100.58	30.64	33.1	34.6	Sc(s)II.8	P200
NGC 6574		18 09 35	14 58.2	42.15	15.40	119.0	79.6	Sbc(s)II.3	W100

Galaxy (11)	B_T (12)	A^o (13)	A^i (14)	$B_T^{o,i}$ (15)	$M_{B_T}^{o,i}$ (16)	v (17)	ε (18)	Δv (19)	v_0 (20)	Sources (21)
NGC 5846	11.17[1]	0.04	0	11.13	−21.49	1753	18	−79	1674	190, 191, 313, 372a, 442
NGC 5850	11.71	0.04	0.47	11.20	−22.23	2509	18	−79	2430	190, 191, 391
NGC 5866	10.86[1]	0	0	10.86	−20.22	672	9	152	824	578
NGC 5854	12.64[1]	0.04	0*	12.60	−20.00	1728	27	−74	1654	190, 402
NGC 5861	12.31	0.08	0.48	11.75	−20.94	1855	7	−130	1725	628
NGC 5864	12.63[2]	0.04	0*	12.59	−19.86	1618	66	−70	1548	321
NGC 5879	12.1	0	0.99	11.11	−20.24	772	7	157	929	28, 190, 391, 392
NGC 5878	12.3	0.09	0.86	11.35	−21.63	2111	65	−137	1974	190
F 703	(12.41)	0.10	0.34	11.97	−21.18	2270	15	−142	2128	160
NGC 5885	12.2	0.08	0.32	11.80	−21.07	1999	8	−120	1879	160, 392
NGC 5899	12.6	0	0.59	12.01	−21.62	2554	14	103	2657	190, 385
NGC 5905	(12.33)	0	0.56	11.77	−22.48	3389	14	155	3544	30, 284, 385, 431
NGC 5907	11.15	0	0.87	10.28	−20.68	621	19	158	779	48, 173, 190, 191, 391
NGC 5898	12.56[1]	0.15	0	12.41	−20.70	2267	111	−169	2098	190, 284
NGC 5908	12.9	0	0.98	11.92	−22.28	3312	15	155	3467	284, 385, 431
NGC 5903	12.50[1]	0.15	0	12.35	−21.04	2547	97	−169	2378	190, 284
NGC 5915	(12.89)	0.09	0.39	12.41	−20.75	2273	14	−127	2146	321, 402
NGC 5921	11.53[8]	0.05	0.34	11.14	−21.14	1480	10	−52	1428	173, 190, 392
NGC 5949	(12.94)	0.05	0.54	12.35	−18.13	435	10	189	624	191, 284, 392
NGC 5936	13.00	0	0.30	12.70	−21.81	4007	(60)	−12	3995	284, 431
NGC 5962	12.10[8]	0	0.40	11.70	−21.28	1963	10	9	1972	43, 46, 190, 392
NGC 5970	12.15	0.05	0.41	11.69	−21.37	2056	26	−9	2047	46, 190, 191, 391
NGC 5982	12.08[1]	0.05	0	12.03	−21.89	2869	10	177	3046	190, 191
NGC 5985	11.80	0.05	0.74	11.01	−22.65	2517	7	177	2694	190, 385, 391
NGC 5984	(12.94)	0.05	0.73	12.16	−19.60	1118	9	4	1122	370, 392, 431
NGC 5967	12.76[5]	0.33	0.46	11.97	−21.66	2904	90	−247	2657	284
NGC 6015	11.73	0.06	0.61	11.06	−20.48	828	5	190	1018	579
NGC 6052	13.45	0.05	0.19	13.21	−21.69	4729	16	48	4777	580
NGC 6070	12.35	0.09	0.49	11.77	−21.22	2012	7	−33	1979	46, 190, 191, 301, 400
NGC 6106	12.80	0.09	0.48	12.23	−20.10	1456	10	3	1459	321, 392
NGC 6118	(11.91)	0.12	0.55	11.24	−21.20	1571	9	−36	1535	301, 431
NGC 6181	12.50	0.08	0.54	11.88	−21.56	2372	8	66	2438	46, 85, 190, 392
NGC 6217	11.86	0.11	0.34	11.41	−21.11	1365	5	233	1598	581
NGC 6207	12.15	0.07	0.57	11.51	−19.96	846	7	138	984	43, 46, 97, 190, 392
NGC 6215	11.89[5]	0.69	0.37	10.83	−21.33	1563	15	−208	1355	150, 224, 387
NGC 6221	11.52[5]	0.66	0.39	10.47	−21.55	1478	15	−208	1270	150, 224, 387
NGC 6239	12.80	0.07	0.55	12.18	−19.53	938	12	162	1100	43, 46, 191
NGC 6340	11.90	0.11	0.50	11.29	−21.05	1234	11	235	1469	26, 43, 46, 190, 402
NGC 6300	11.04	0.41	0.67	9.96	−21.32	1107	14	−206	901	153, 284, 387
NGC 6384	11.29	0.24	0.63	10.42	−22.28	1673	9	62	1735	46, 190, 191, 229, 392
NGC 6412	12.32	0.12	0.32	11.88	−20.60	1326	6	242	1568	191, 263, 385, 392
IC 4662	11.76[3]	0.30	0.23	11.23	−17.18	439	24	−199	240	99, 150, 163, (214), 242
NGC 6482	12.10[1]	0.21	0	11.89	−22.66	3922	60	139	4061	190
NGC 6503	10.93	0.13	0.65	10.15	−18.76	60	7	243	303	582
NGC 6574	12.85	0.37	0.37	12.11	−21.31	2290	16	125	2415	132, 190, 191, 385

Galaxy (1)	Other names (2)	RA (1950) (3)	Dec (1950) (4)	l (5)	b (6)	SGL (7)	SGB (8)	Type (9)	Source (10)
NGC 6643		18 21 14	74 32.7	105.55	28.17	29.2	30.9	Sc(s)II	P200
IC 4710	PKS 1822–670	18 23 28	−67 00.8	327.87	−22.65	203.9	7.2	SBd(s)IV	C100
IC 4721		18 30 03	−58 32.2	336.81	−20.75	203.7	15.7	Sc(s)II	C100
NGC 6684		18 44 02	−65 13.8	330.34	−24.19	205.8	9.1	SBa(s)	C100
NGC 6699		18 47 48	−57 22.7	338.74	−22.65	206.0	17.0	Sbc(s)I.2	C100
IC 4797		18 52 28	−54 22.3	342.07	−22.45	206.7	20.0	E5/S0₁(5)	C100
HA 85–2	A1852–54	18 52 53	−54 36.9	341.84	−22.58	206.8	19.7	E3	C100
NGC 6721		18 56 34	−57 49.6	338.58	−23.90	207.3	16.5	E1	C100
NGC 6744		19 05 02	−63 56.3	332.23	−26.15	208.1	10.4	Sbc(r)II	C100
NGC 6753		19 07 13	−57 07.7	339.70	−25.14	208.8	17.2	Sb(r)I	C100
NGC 6754		19 07 34	−50 43.4	346.55	−23.68	209.3	23.6	Sbc(s)II–III	C100
NGC 6758		19 09 44	−56 23.7	340.58	−25.32	209.2	17.9	E2	C100
IC 4837		19 11 12	−54 45.1	342.41	−25.17	209.6	19.5	Sc(s)II–III	C100
NGC 6769	VV 304	19 13 57	−60 36.2	336.09	−26.63	209.4	13.6	Sb(r)II	C100
NGC 6780		19 18 46	−55 52.4	341.42	−26.45	210.6	18.3	Sbc(rs)I–II	C100
NGC 6782		19 19 38	−60 01.1	336.86	−27.24	210.2	14.1	SBab(s)	C100
NGC 6776		19 20 43	−63 57.9	332.46	−27.86	209.8	10.2	E1 pec (merger?)	C100
NGC 6808		19 38 30	−70 45.2	324.78	−29.81	210.5	3.2	Sc(s)II	C100
NGC 6810		19 39 21	−58 46.5	338.58	−29.60	213.0	15.0	Sb	C100
NGC 6814		19 39 55	−10 26.6	29.36	−16.01	231.6	61.4	Sbc(rs)I–II	P200
IC 4889		19 41 19	−54 27.6	343.55	−29.42	214.2	19.1	S0₁/₂(5)	C100
NGC 6822	IC 4895 DDO 209	19 42 07	−14 55.7	25.34	−18.40	229.1	57.1	ImIV–V	P200
NGC 6835		19 51 47	−12 42.0	28.52	−19.60	234.8	58.1	Amorphous?	C100
NGC 6851		19 59 55	−48 25.0	350.92	−31.58	218.9	24.2	E4	C100
NGC 6854		20 01 46	−54 31.0	343.76	−32.39	217.2	18.3	E1+E0	C100
NGC 6861	IC 4949	20 03 42	−48 30.8	350.89	−32.21	219.5	23.9	S0₃(6)	C100
NGC 6868		20 06 19	−48 31.4	350.93	−32.64	219.9	23.8	E3/S0₂/₃(3)	C100
NGC 6875		20 09 41	−46 18.5	353.62	−32.97	221.4	25.7	S0/a (merger)	C100
NGC 6878		20 10 25	−44 40.4	355.57	−32.90	222.1	27.1	Sc(r)I.3	C100
NGC 6876		20 13 05	−71 01.0	324.13	−32.60	213.2	2.3	E3	C100
NGC 6887		20 13 30	−52 57.1	345.75	−34.05	219.4	19.3	Sab(s)I–II	C100
NGC 6890		20 14 50	−44 57.4	355.35	−33.71	222.8	26.6	Sab(s)II–III	C100
NGC 6893		20 17 14	−48 23.7	351.27	−34.44	221.8	23.3	S0₃(4)	C100
New 5	A2020–44	20 20 33	−44 09.4	356.45	−34.63	224.2	26.9	SBa	C100
NGC 6902		20 21 04	−43 49.0	356.88	−34.69	224.5	27.2	Sa(r)	C100
NGC 6907		20 22 07	−24 58.3	18.86	−30.82	235.3	43.9	SBbc(s)II	C100
NGC 6909		20 24 09	−47 11.6	352.82	−35.52	223.5	23.9	E5	C100
IC 5020		20 27 29	−33 39.2	9.26	−34.33	231.1	35.7	Sab(r)	C100
NGC 6923		20 28 34	−31 00.1	12.47	−33.87	232.9	38.0	SBbc(s)II	C100
NGC 6925		20 31 14	−32 09.2	11.28	−34.70	232.8	36.7	Sbc(r)I	C100
NGC 6946	4C 59.31.1?	20 33 48	59 59.0	95.73	11.68	10.0	42.0	Sc(s)II	P200
NGC 6935		20 34 41	−52 17.2	346.52	−37.28	222.9	18.6	Sa(r)	C100
NGC 6951		20 36 37	65 55.9	100.91	14.85	13.8	36.8	Sb/SBb(rs)I.3	P200
NGC 6942		20 36 53	−54 28.8	343.71	−37.50	222.2	16.4	SBa(s)	C100
NGC 6943		20 39 52	−68 55.6	325.96	−35.30	216.1	3.3	Sbc(rs)I	C100

Galaxy (11)	B_T (12)	A^o (13)	A^i (14)	$B_T^{o,i}$ (15)	$M_{B_T}^{o,i}$ (16)	v (17)	ε (18)	Δv (19)	v_0 (20)	Sources (21)
NGC 6643	11.74	0.15	0.52	11.07	−21.64	1491	5	252	1743	583
IC 4710	(12.35)	0.21	0.39	11.75	−18.28	700	50	−192	508	383
IC 4721	12.63[5]	0.24	0.66	11.73	−21.21	2095	45	−163	1932	425
NGC 6684	11.34[1]	0.19	0.31*	10.84	−19.91	886	54	−181	705	150, 224, 284
NGC 6699	12.73[5]	0.21	0.30	12.22	−21.91	3509	21	−152	3357	(99), 163, 224, 284, 438
IC 4797	12.29[1]	0.21	0	12.08	−21.41	2632	76	−139	2493	150, 284
HA 85-2	12.65[1]	0.21	0	12.44	−21.16	2761	113	−140	2621	284
NGC 6721	13.12[1]	0.19	0	12.93	−21.75	4467	78	−151	4316	224, 284
NGC 6744	9.24	0.17	0.44	8.63	−21.98	833	15	−170	663	150, 224, 387
NGC 6753	11.93[3]	0.18	0.50	11.25	−22.64	3145	65	−144	3001	150, 224, 284
NGC 6754	(13.16)	0.20	0.54	12.42	−21.62	3325	24	−118	3207	163, 284
NGC 6758	12.61[4]	0.18	0	12.43	−21.62	3367	108	−140	3227	284
IC 4837	12.75[5]	0.18	0.53	12.04	−21.52	2708	60	−133	2575	284
NGC 6769	12.58[3]	0.16	0.64	11.78	−22.57	3858	81	−155	3703	(154), 224, 284, 352
NGC 6780	(13.15)	0.16	0.35	12.64	−21.51	3516	80	−135	3381	284
NGC 6782	12.71[4]	0.16	0.74	11.81	−22.57	3903	78	−151	3752	224, 284
NGC 6776	12.91[3]	0.15	0	12.76	−22.38	5488	78	−165	5323	224, 284
NGC 6808	13.39[5]	0.13	0.61	12.65	−21.44	3466	47	−185	3281	224, 284
NGC 6810	12.21[5]	0.14	1.12	10.95	−21.87	1975	87	−139	1836	150, 224
NGC 6814	12.02	0.35	0.30	11.37	−21.21	1560	9	83	1643	603
IC 4889	(12.20)	0.14	0	12.06	−21.36	2531	68	−120	2411	284
NGC 6822	9.35	0.29	0.16	8.90	−15.25 L	−49	5	64	15	584
NGC 6835	13.13[1]	0.26	—	[12.87]	−19.8	1631	14	80	1711	634
NGC 6851	12.61[4]	0.12	0	12.49	−21.35	3020	23	−87	2933	163, 224, 284
NGC 6854	13.27[4]	0.11	0	13.16	−22.08	5692	78	−114	5578	224, 284
NGC 6861	12.07[1]	0.12	0	11.95	−21.77	2859	80	−86	2773	284
NGC 6868	11.83[4]	0.11	0	11.72	−21.92	2764	39	−85	2679	150, 297
NGC 6875	12.77[4]	0.11	0	12.66	−21.25	3103	48	−73	3030	297
NGC 6878	14.07[3]	0.11	0.38	13.58	−21.74	5856	29	−65	5791	275, 284
NGC 6876	12.56[4,8]	0.11	0	12.45	−21.95	3971	148	−180	3791	284, 396
NGC 6887	12.46[5]	0.10	0.93	11.43	−22.42	3041	107	−103	2938	441
NGC 6890	13.02[3]	0.11	0.56	12.35	−21.06	2466	65	−65	2401	224, 284
NGC 6893	12.54[2]	0.10	0	12.44	−21.52	3175	95	−80	3095	284
New 5	12.66[2]	0.10	0*	12.56	−21.24	2942	63	−59	2883	284
NGC 6902	12.65[3]	0.10	0.28*	12.27	−21.41	2781	11	−57	2724	26, 284, 434
NGC 6907	12.00	0.13	0.33	11.54	−22.49	3155	80	37	3192	284
NGC 6909	12.78[2]	0.10	0	12.68	−20.91	2680	200	−72	2608	284
IC 5020	[13.1]	0.10	0.70	12.3	−21.6	3050	50	−4	3046	383
NGC 6923	12.85	0.10	0.50	12.25	−21.61	2948	34	10	2958	441
NGC 6925	12.10	0.10	0.64	11.36	−22.37	2775	11	5	2780	150, 387, 400
NGC 6946	9.68	0.52	0.32	8.84	−20.30	48	2	288	336	585
NGC 6935	13.01[5]	0.09	0.51	12.41	−22.46	4794	200	−93	4701	284
NGC 6951	12.2	0.38	0.51	11.31	−21.36	1425	10	285	1710	28, 43, 191, 392
NGC 6942	13.10[4]	0.08	0*	13.02	−21.42	3964	250	−103	3861	284
NGC 6943	12.16[5]	0.10	0.54	11.52	−22.33	3114	248	−167	2947	284

Galaxy (1)	Other names (2)	RA (1950) (3)	Dec (1950) (4)	*l* (5)	*b* (6)	SGL (7)	SGB (8)	Type (9)	Source (10)
IC 5039		20 40 11	−30 02.1	14.35	−36.07	236.3	37.5	Sc(sIII)	C40D
NGC 6958		20 45 30	−38 10.9	4.51	−38.60	232.1	30.0	R?S0$_1$(3)	C100
IC 5052		20 47 26	−69 23.6	325.18	−35.81	216.5	2.6	Sd (on edge)	C100
IC 5063	PKS 2048−57	20 48 12	−57 15.2	339.99	−38.73	222.3	13.3	S0$_3$(3) pec/Sa	C100
NGC 6970		20 48 40	−48 57.8	350.62	−39.62	226.6	20.5	Sc(s)II	C100
NGC 6984		20 54 19	−52 03.8	346.52	−40.29	225.7	17.3	SBbc(r)I.8	C100
NGC 7007		21 01 53	−52 45.1	345.43	−41.36	226.4	16.2	(S0$_2$/a)	C100
NGC 7014		21 04 29	−47 22.8	352.54	−42.35	229.9	20.4	E5	C100
NGC 7020		21 07 16	−64 14.0	330.54	−39.30	220.7	6.1	RS0$_2$(5)/RSa	C100
NGC 7029		21 08 27	−49 29.6	349.60	−42.81	229.2	18.3	S0$_1$(5)	C100
NGC 7038		21 11 48	−47 25.4	352.34	−43.58	230.9	19.7	Sbc(s)I.8	C100
NGC 7041		21 13 09	−48 34.2	350.73	−43.68	230.4	18.6	S0$_1$(7)/E7	C100
NGC 7049		21 15 38	−48 46.4	350.38	−44.06	230.6	18.2	S0$_3$(4)/Sa	C100
New 6	A2120−46	21 19 56	−45 59.2	354.12	−45.12	233.0	20.0	Sc(s)I	C40D
IC 5105		21 21 12	−40 45.1	1.45	−45.64	236.7	23.9	E5	C100
NGC 7059		21 23 34	−60 14.0	334.70	−42.43	224.6	8.3	Sc(s)II	C100
NGC 7064		21 25 34	−52 59.0	344.17	−44.82	229.3	13.9	Scd (on edge)	C100
NGC 7070		21 27 13	−43 18.4	357.80	−46.66	235.9	21.2	SBc(s)II.8	C100
NGC 7079		21 29 22	−44 17.3	356.32	−46.93	235.5	20.3	SBa	C100
NGC 7083		21 31 52	−64 07.6	329.37	−41.82	223.0	4.6	Sb(s)I−II	C100
NGC 7090		21 32 59	−54 46.9	341.30	−45.38	229.0	11.8	SBc: (on edge)	C100
NGC 7097		21 37 04	−42 46.1	358.38	−48.49	237.7	20.5	E4	C100
NGC 7096		21 37 28	−64 08.2	328.99	−42.36	223.5	4.2	Sa(r)I	C100
NGC 7107		21 39 15	−45 01.3	354.91	−48.58	236.4	18.5	SBc(s)/SBmIII−IV	C100
NGC 7119		21 43 03	−46 44.8	352.16	−48.95	235.7	16.8	Sc(s)II	C100
NGC 7124		21 44 48	−50 48.0	346.11	−48.25	233.1	13.7	SbcI	C100
IC 5135		21 45 21	−35 11.2	9.95	−50.35	244.7	24.8	Sa pec	C100
NGC 7125		21 45 38	−60 56.8	332.33	−44.64	226.3	6.0	Sc(rs)I	C100
NGC 7126		21 45 41	−60 50.4	332.46	−44.69	226.3	6.1	Sa(r):	C100
NGC 7137		21 45 54	21 55.6	76.44	−23.74	312.3	48.7	Sc(rs)II.8	P200
NGC 7135		21 46.8	−35 07	10.07	−50.65	245.0	24.6	S0$_1$ pec	C100
NGC 7144		21 49 30	−48 29.4	349.19	−49.60	235.3	14.8	E0	C100
NGC 7145		21 50 08	−48 07.1	349.71	−49.80	235.6	15.0	E0	C100
NGC 7155		21 52 56	−49 45.8	347.06	−49.79	234.8	13.5	SB0	C100
NGC 7162		21 56 33	−43 32.7	356.37	−51.92	239.8	17.4	Sbc(rs)II	C100
NGC 7166		21 57 27	−43 37.7	356.17	−52.06	239.9	17.2	S0$_1$(6)	C100
NGC 7177		21 58 18	17 29.9	75.37	−28.96	306.0	45.6	Sab(r)II.2	P200
NGC 7171	MSH 21−125?	21 58 20	−13 30.6	43.47	−47.93	266.8	35.6	Sb(r)I	P200
NGC 7168		21 58 53	−51 59.0	343.33	−49.95	233.8	11.3	E3/S0$_1$(3)	C100
IC 5152		21 59.6	−51 32	343.92	−50.22	234.3	11.5	SdmIV−V	C100
NGC 7184		21 59 54	−21 03.3	32.90	−51.11	259.4	31.2	Sb(r)II	W100
IC 5156		22 00 20	−34 05.0	11.95	−53.42	247.9	23.2	Sb(s)II−III	C100
NGC 7196		22 02 47	−50 22.0	345.37	−51.09	235.5	12.0	E3/S0$_3$(3)	C100
NGC 7192		22 03 08	−64 33.4	326.53	−44.54	225.2	2.0	S0$_2$(0)	C100
NGC 7205		22 05.1	−57 40	334.87	−48.36	230.4	6.7	Sb(r)II.8	C100

Galaxy (11)	B_T (12)	A^o (13)	A^i (14)	$B_T^{o,i}$ (15)	$M_{B_T}^{o,i}$ (16)	v (17)	ε (18)	Δv (19)	v_o (20)	Sources (21)
IC 5039	13.25	0.09	0.75	12.41	−21.27	2700	50	19	2719	383
NGC 6958	12.21[2,8]	0.08	0	12.13	−21.56	2757	175	−20	2737	150
IC 5052	(12.12)	0.09	0.87	11.16	−16.08	307	(70)	−167	140	(99), 284, 438
IC 5063	13.22	0.08	0	13.14	−20.95	3402	15	−113	3289	224, 284
NGC 6970	13.27[3]	0.07	0.32	12.88	−22.21	5280	42	−73	5207	99, (153), 224, 284, 396
NGC 6984	13.33[5]	0.07	0.42	12.84	−21.90	4522	113	−87	4435	284
NGC 7007	12.99[4]	0.07	0	12.92	−20.87	2954	60	−88	2866	284
NGC 7014	13.34[1]	0.06	0	13.28	−21.60	4790	63	−61	4729	284
NGC 7020	12.49[4]	0.08	0	12.41	−21.40	3029	160	−142	2887	284
NGC 7029	12.59[1]	0.06	0	12.53	−21.20	2863	75	−71	2792	150, 284
NGC 7038	(12.36)	0.06	0.46	11.84	−23.06	4844	168	−59	4785	284
NGC 7041	12.05[1]	0.06	0	11.99	−20.86	1920	90	−65	1855	150, 284
NGC 7049	11.64[1]	0.06	0	11.58	−21.57	2193	92	−65	2128	150, 284
New 6	(12.56)	0.05	0.73	11.78	−21.80	2650	50	−50	2600	383
IC 5105	12.66[1]	0.05	0	12.61	−22.53	5363	160	−23	5340	284
NGC 7059	12.92[3,8]	0.06	0.50	12.36	−20.25	1781	76	−121	1660	284, 352
NGC 7064	13.08	0.06	0.87	12.15	−18.65	807	24	−85	722	284, 438
NGC 7070	12.86[3]	0.05	0.33	12.48	−20.89	2400	50	−35	2365	(332), 383
NGC 7079	12.54[1]	0.05	0*	12.49	−21.23	2819	124	−39	2780	104, 151
NGC 7083	11.80[5]	0.07	0.69	11.04	−22.81	3089	125	−138	2951	284
NGC 7090	11.1	0.05	0.87	10.18	−20.71	846	15	−92	754	150, 387
NGC 7097	12.52[5]	0.04	0	12.48	−20.90	2404	80	−30	2374	284
NGC 7096	12.59[5]	0.06	0*	12.53	−21.23	2958	35	−137	2821	284
NGC 7107	(12.93)	0.04	0.24	12.65	−20.80	2487	144	−41	2446	441
NGC 7119	(13.82)	0.04	0.52	13.26	−23.21	9875	49	−50	9825	441
NGC 7124	13.10[3]	0.04	0.58	12.48	−22.50	5027	153	−70	4957	284
IC 5135	12.92[3]	0	0.28*	12.64	−22.27	4796	71	12	4808	224, 284
NGC 7125	12.89[8]	0.06	0.43	12.40	−21.42	3031	50	−121	2910	284
NGC 7126	13.10[8]	0.06	0.84	12.20	−21.61	3009	65	−121	2888	284
NGC 7137	13.05	0.20	0.31	12.54	−20.42	1690	4	261	1951	617
NGC 7135	12.61[1]	0	0	12.61	−22.34	4877	46	12	4889	321
NGC 7144	11.79[1]	0.04	0	11.75	−21.32	2113	175	−58	2055	150, (332)
NGC 7145	12.17[1]	0.04	0	12.13	−20.73	1921	57	−56	1865	153, 284
NGC 7155	12.83[4]	0.04	0	12.79	−20.03	1893	110	−64	1829	284
NGC 7162	13.29	0	0.64	12.65	−20.54	2200	50	−31	2169	383
NGC 7166	12.71[1,8]	0	0	12.71	−20.67	2407	73	−31	2376	284
NGC 7177	11.95	0.14	0.64	11.17	−21.10	1168	8	251	1419	43, 46, 190, 400
NGC 7171	13.00	0.05	0.70	12.25	−21.46	2632	50	126	2758	190
NGC 7168	12.85[4]	0.04	0	12.81	−20.91	2842	90	−75	2767	153, 284
IC 5152	(11.68)	0	0.24	11.44	−14.6 L	119	14	−72	47	150, 154, 387, 437
NGC 7184	(11.67)	0	1.10	10.57	−23.10	2617	15	88	2705	158, 431
IC 5156	[13.2]	0	—	[13.2]	−20.4	2584	193	21	2605	284
NGC 7196	12.46[1]	0	0	12.46	−21.37	2981	70	−66	2915	150, 417
NGC 7192	12.21[4]	0.06	0	12.15	−21.55	2879	43	−137	2742	284
NGC 7205	(11.57)	0.04	0.81	10.72	−21.48	1482	175	−103	1379	150

Galaxy (1)	Other names (2)	RA (1950) (3)	Dec (1950) (4)	*l* (5)	*b* (6)	SGL (7)	SGB (8)	Type (9)	Source (10)
NGC 7217		22 05 36	31 07.0	86.51	−19.70	325.0	43.5	Sb(r)II–III	P200
NGC 7213	PKS 2206−474	22 06 12	−47 25.0	349.58	−52.59	238.1	13.6	Sa(rs)	C100
NGC 7218		22 07 29	−16 54.6	40.11	−51.35	264.7	32.0	Sc(s)II.8	W60
IC 5181		22 10 18	−46 16.4	351.05	−53.60	239.4	13.8	S0$_1$(7)	C100
NGC 7232		22 12 35	−46 06.0	351.13	−54.03	239.8	13.6	S0$_3$(7) or Sb	C100
IC 5179	IC5184	22 13 14	−37 05.7	6.50	−56.44	247.5	18.9	Sc(s)II–III	C100
IC 5201		22 17 55	−46 17.0	350.24	−54.90	240.3	12.7	SBcd II	C100
NGC 7252		22 17 58	−24 55.9	28.44	−56.15	258.4	25.6	merger	CTIO4m
NGC 7300		22 28 21	−14 15.7	47.65	−54.76	270.2	28.9	Sc(s)I–II	P200
NGC 7302	IC 5228	22 29 44	−14 22.7	47.75	−55.12	270.2	28.6	S0$_1$(3)	P200
NGC 7307		22 30 59	−41 11.7	357.92	−58.59	245.9	14.1	SBc(s)II	C100
NGC 7309		22 31 42	−10 37.0	53.76	−53.65	274.4	29.8	Sc(rs)I–II	P200
NGC 7314		22 33 00	−26 18.5	27.14	−59.74	259.2	22.0	Sc(s)III	P200
NGC 7331	B2 2234+34	22 34 47	34 09.5	93.73	−20.72	328.0	37.1	Sb(rs)I–II	P200
NGC 7332		22 35 01	23 32.3	87.40	−29.67	314.7	37.4	S0$_{2/3}$(8)	P200
NGC 7329		22 36 56	−66 44.6	320.98	−45.80	225.9	−2.0	SBbc(r)I–II	C100
IC 5240		22 38 53	−45 02.0	349.97	−58.72	243.6	10.6	SBa(r)	C100
NGC 7361		22 39 31	−30 19.2	19.31	−61.60	256.3	18.7	ScII–III:	W100
NGC 7371		22 43 25	−11 16.0	55.52	−56.42	275.0	26.9	SBa(r)II	C100
NGC 7377		22 45 05	−22 34.6	35.83	−61.58	264.1	21.5	S0$_{2/3}$/Sa pec	C100
NGC 7392		22 49 07	−20 52.3	39.87	−61.96	266.2	21.5	Sbc(s)I–II	C100
NGC 7410		22 52 11	−39 55.7	358.03	−62.83	249.3	11.4	SBa	C100
NGC 7412		22 52 55	−42 54.6	351.93	−61.88	246.8	9.7	Sc(rs)I–II	C40IT
NGC 7418		22 53 49	−37 17.6	3.47	−63.87	251.8	12.5	Sc(rs)I.8	C100
NGC 7421		22 54 06	−37 37.0	2.73	−63.84	251.5	12.3	SBbc(rs)II–III	C100
IC 5267		22 54 22	−43 39.9	350.24	−61.80	246.3	9.1	Sa(r)	C100
IC 1459		22 54 23	−36 43.8	4.67	−64.11	252.3	12.7	E4	C100
NGC 7424		22 54 28	−41 20.4	354.80	−62.75	248.3	10.3	Sc(s)II.3	C40IT
IC 5269		22 54 57	−36 17.7	5.59	−64.31	252.8	12.8	S0$_1$(7)	C100
IC 5271		22 55 16	−34 00.6	10.78	−64.77	254.8	13.9	Sb(rs)II	C100
IC 5273		22 56 40	−37 58.4	1.64	−64.24	251.5	11.7	SBc(s)II–III	C100
NGC 7448		22 57 35	15 42.8	87.57	−39.12	305.9	31.3	Sc(r)II.2	P200
NGC 7457		22 58 37	29 52.7	96.23	−26.93	322.5	32.2	S0$_1$(5)	P200
NGC 7456		22 59 22	−39 50.3	357.18	−64.14	250.1	10.3	Sc(s)II–III	C100
NGC 7462		22 59 58	−41 06.2	354.42	−63.81	249.1	9.5	SBc(s)	C100
NGC 7469		23 00 44	08 36.3	83.11	−45.47	298.0	29.2	Sab pec	W100
NGC 7479		23 02 26	12 03.1	86.28	−42.84	301.9	29.5	SBbc(s)I–II	P200
NGC 7496		23 06 59	−43 42.0	347.84	−63.80	247.5	7.1	SBc(s)II.8	C100
NGC 7507		23 09 26	−28 48.8	23.45	−68.04	261.0	13.7	E0	C100
NGC 7531		23 12 03	−43 52.4	346.42	−64.49	247.7	6.2	Sbc(r)I–II	C100
NGC 7541	IC 5294	23 12 11	04 15.6	82.85	−50.65	294.0	25.3	Sc(s)II	W100
NGC 7552	PKS 2313−428	23 13 25	−42 51.5	348.15	−65.24	248.8	6.5	SBbc(s)I–II	C100
NGC 7585		23 15 28	−04 55.3	74.08	−58.36	284.7	21.8	S0$_1$(3)/Sa	P200
NGC 7582	PKS 2315−426	23 15 38	−42 38.7	348.08	−65.70	249.1	6.2	SBab(rs)	C100
NGC 7590		23 16 11	−42 30.7	348.24	−65.85	249.3	6.2	Sc(s)II	C100

Galaxy (11)	B_T (12)	A^o (13)	A^i (14)	$B_T^{o,i}$ (15)	$M_{B_T}^{o,i}$ (16)	v (17)	ε (18)	Δv (19)	v_o (20)	Sources (21)
NGC 7217	11.08	0.26	0.52	10.30	−21.66	948	4	286	1234	622
NGC 7213	11.18[1]	0	0.46	10.72	−21.96	1770	60	−50	1720	150, 297
NGC 7218	12.55	0	0.53	12.02	−20.74	1671	8	110	1781	43, 46, 191, 301
IC 5181	12.36[1,8]	0	0	12.36	−20.62	2017	76	−43	1974	224, 284
NGC 7232	12.83[5]	0	0	12.83	−19.79	1710	62	−42	1668	224, 284, 396
IC 5179	12.70[8]	0	0.52	12.18	−22.02	3447	25	6	3453	284
IC 5201	11.54	0	0.54	11.00	−19.82	771	(70)	−43	728	284, 438
NGC 7252	12.87	0	0	12.87	−22.02	4688	15	71	4759	26, 190
NGC 7300	13.7	0	0.52	13.18	−21.83	4895	90	126	5021	(284), 431
NGC 7302	13.21[1]	0	0	13.21	−20.46	2586	65	125	2711	190
NGC 7307	(12.84)	0	0.83	12.01	−20.85	1880	60	−15	1865	284
NGC 7309	13.05	0	0.30	12.75	−21.81	3938	66	144	4082	321
NGC 7314	11.65[8]	0	0.54	11.11	−21.26	1426	47	65	1491	43, 46, (190), 431
NGC 7331	10.39	0.24	1.01	9.14	−22.60	820	4	294	1114	586
NGC 7332	11.71[1]	0.13	0	11.58	−20.78	1211	19	272	1483	190, 235, (321), 376, 415
NGC 7329	12.32[5]	0.05	0.43	11.84	−22.08	3189	63	−146	3043	284
IC 5240	(12.26)	0	0.59	11.67	−21.04	1773	19	−35	1738	104, 224, 284, 439
NGC 7361	12.95	0	0.74	12.21	−19.82	1232	28	44	1276	173, 321
NGC 7371	12.8	0	0.22*	12.58	−21.18	2685	15	141	2826	(321), 402
NGC 7377	12.61[1,8]	0	0	12.61	−21.62	3416	65	85	3501	190
NGC 7392	12.65	0	0.46	12.19	−21.73	2941	40	94	3035	191
NGC 7410	11.3	0	1.01	10.29	−22.40	1731	66	−7	1724	297
NGC 7412	12.05[3,8]	0	0.38	11.67	−20.98	1714	12	−23	1691	160, 398, 400
NGC 7418	12.0	0	0.35	11.65	−20.66	1444	14	7	1451	28, 158, 224, 284
NGC 7421	12.68	0	0.30	12.38	−20.45	1833	56	5	1838	441
IC 5267	11.39[1,8]	0	0.27*	11.12	−21.53	1719	19	−27	1692	297, 439
IC 1459	10.96[1]	0	0	10.96	−21.61	1628	36	10	1638	150, 297
NGC 7424	10.99	0	0.32	10.67	−20.67	940	14	−15	925	158, 284, 431, 438
IC 5269	13.57[2]	0	0	13.57	−19.62	2162	38	12	2174	284
IC 5271	[12.6]	0	0.6:	[12.0]	−20.73	1735	10	24	1759	441
IC 5273	11.90	0	0.39	11.51	−20.56	1293	15	3	1296	158, 284, 438
NGC 7448	12.15	0.08	0.56	11.51	−21.97	2235	26	250	2485	43, 46, 190
NGC 7457	11.84[1]	0.16	0	11.68	−19.81	(705)	200	286	991	190, (332)
NGC 7456	(12.06)	0	0.73	11.33	−20.57	1206	15	−7	1199	160
NGC 7462	(12.79)	0	0.87	11.92	−19.63	1036	41	−14	1022	160, 431
NGC 7469	12.60	0.05	0.60	11.95	−23.10	4889	12	226	5115	587
NGC 7479	11.7	0.06	0.37	11.27	−22.34	2392	9	238	2630	46, 72, 190, 191, 392
NGC 7496	11.78[8]	0	0.37	11.41	−20.89	1472	16	−28	1444	224, 297
NGC 7507	11.43[1]	0	0	11.43	−21.10	1548	12	52	1600	190, 289
NGC 7531	12.14	0	0.60	11.54	−21.00	1636	95	−29	1607	153, (332), 431
NGC 7541	12.45	0	0.63	11.82	−21.99	2678	6	209	2887	190, 313, 392, 401, 429
NGC 7552	11.40	0	0.41	10.99	−21.49	1589	14	−24	1565	99, 153, 224, 297, 387
NGC 7585	12.57[1]	0	0.18	12.39	−21.85	3356	49	170	3526	190, 191
NGC 7582	11.46	0	0.86	10.60	−21.75	1498	61	−23	1475	99, 224, 297
NGC 7590	12.20[3]	0	0.61	11.59	−20.78	1509	33	−22	1487	99, 150, 224, 297

Galaxy (1)	Other names (2)	RA (1950) (3)	Dec (1950) (4)	l (5)	b (6)	SGL (7)	SGB (8)	Type (9)	Source (10)
NGC 7600		23 16 18	−07 51.2	70.38	−60.62	281.8	20.7	$SO_1(5)$	P200
NGC 7606		23 16 29	−08 45.6	69.11	−61.29	280.9	20.3	Sb(r)I	W100
NGC 7599		23 16 36	−42 31.8	348.10	−65.91	249.3	6.1	Sc(s)II	C100
NGC 7619	2317+C7W2	23 17 43	07 56.0	87.71	−48.33	298.3	24.9	E3	W100
NGC 7625	VV 280 III Zw 102	23 18 00	16 57.2	93.91	−40.46	308.2	26.7	S pec	P200
NGC 7626	PKS 2318+07	23 18 10	07 56.6	87.87	−48.38	298.4	24.8	E1	C100
NGC 7640		23 19 43	40 34.2	105.25	−18.94	334.7	27.7	SBc(s)II:	P200
NGC 7678		23 25 59	22 08.7	98.89	−36.55	314.2	25.6	SBbc(s)I–II	P200
IC 5325	VV 329 Mark 534	23 26 02	−41 36.7	347.72	−67.88	251.0	5.0	Sc(s)II–III	C100
NGC 7679		23 26 14	03 14.2	86.69	−53.44	294.0	21.7	Sc(s)/Sa (tides?)	P200
NGC 7690		23 30 20	−51 58.6	328.67	−61.34	241.9	−0.2	Sab(s)	C100
NGC 7689		23 30 34	−54 22.4	325.79	−59.40	239.8	−1.2	Sc(rs)II	C100
IC 5328		23 30 36	−45 17.4	338.89	−66.24	248.0	2.6	$SO_1(3)$	C100
IC 5332		23 31 48	−36 22.6	359.40	−71.37	256.2	6.2	Sc(s)II–III	C100
NGC 7702		23 32 46	−56 17.4	323.06	−58.05	238.2	−2.4	RSa(r)	C100
NGC 7713		23 33 35	−38 13.0	353.75	−70.91	254.7	5.1	Sc(s)II–III	C100
NGC 7716	MSH 23-014?	23 33 58	00 01.3	86.60	−57.19	291.2	18.9	Sab(r)I	P200
NGC 7721		23 36 14	−06 47.7	79.72	−63.12	284.6	16.3	Sbc(s)II.2	P200
NGC 7723		23 36 22	−13 14.2	69.25	−67.90	278.3	14.2	SBb(rs)I–II	P200
NGC 7727	VV 67	23 37 19	−12 34.2	70.95	−67.62	279.0	14.2	Sa pec	P200
NGC 7741		23 41 23	25 47.9	104.52	−34.37	318.6	22.5	SBc(s)II.2	P200
NGC 7742		23 41 43	10 29.3	97.44	−48.75	302.5	19.7	Sa(r!)	P200
NGC 7743		23 41 49	09 39.3	96.97	−49.53	301.6	19.5	SBa	P200
NGC 7744		23 42 26	−43 11.4	339.12	−69.24	250.8	1.6	$SBO_1(3)$	C100
NGC 7755		23 45 15	−30 47.9	15.48	−75.68	262.5	5.9	SBbc(r)/Sbc(r)I–II	C100
NGC 7764		23 48 17	−41 00.5	341.62	−71.54	253.2	1.4	SBmIII	C100
NGC 7769		23 48 31	19 52.3	104.18	−40.51	312.6	20.0	Sbc(s)II (tides?)	P200
NGC 7782		23 51 21	07 41.5	99.25	−52.24	300.2	16.8	Sb(s)I–II	P200
NGC 7785		23 52 46	05 38.3	98.55	−54.28	298.2	15.9	E5	W100
NGC 7793		23 55 15	−32 52.1	4.53	−77.17	261.3	3.1	Sd(s)IV	C100
NGC 7796		23 56 27	−55 44.4	317.90	−60.12	240.0	−5.2	E1	C100

Galaxy (11)	B_T (12)	A^o (13)	A^i (14)	$B_T^{o,i}$ (15)	$M_{B_T}^{o,i}$ (16)	v (17)	ε (18)	Δv (19)	v_0 (20)	Sources (21)
NGC 7600	12.99[2]	0	0	12.99	−21.26	3391	60	156	3547	190
NGC 7606	11.55	0	0.90	10.65	−22.69	2171	42	152	2323	30, 190
NGC 7599	12.04	0	0.68	11.36	−21.26	1692	15	−22	1670	99, 158, 284
NGC 7619	12.21[1]	0.04	0	12.17	−22.36	3798	34	222	4020	190, 353, 422
NGC 7625	12.80	0.07	0.24:	12.49	−20.38	1622	7	253	1875	588
NGC 7626	12.21[1]	0.04	0	12.17	−22.13	3403	14	222	3625	139, 190, 289, 422, 442
NGC 7640	11.44	0.27	0.84	10.33	−20.30	368	7	301	669	589
NGC 7678	12.8	0.09	0.38	12.33	−22.05	3489	10	267	3756	46, 190, 392
IC 5325	(12.31)	0	0.28	12.03	−20.30	1477	22	−18	1459	284, 398
NGC 7679	13.23[1]	0	0.44:	12.79	−22.38	5194	13	203	5397	590
NGC 7690	12.69[5]	0	0.87	11.82	−20.24	1364	66	−73	1291	224, 284
NGC 7689	12.18	0	0.41	11.77	−20.86	1766	(125)	−85	1681	284, 438
IC 5328	11.95[1]	0	0	11.95	−21.95	3049	120	−38	3011	284
IC 5332	11.25	0	0.38	10.87	−19.90	704	11	9	713	160, 387
NGC 7702	13.02[1]	0	0.75	12.27	−21.66	3152	85	−96	3056	(150), 284
NGC 7713	(11.65)	0	0.57	11.08	−19.60	685	15	−1	684	(99), 321, 387, (438)
NGC 7716	12.95	0	0.52	12.43	−21.26	2546	150	189	2735	190
NGC 7721	12.30	0	0.58	11.72	−21.50	2039	54	159	2198	321
NGC 7723	11.85	0	0.62	11.23	−21.75	1848	32	128	1976	191, 407
NGC 7727	11.55	0	0.55	11.00	−21.98	1842	29	131	1973	190, 191
NGC 7741	11.88	0.10	0.41	11.37	−20.20	756	8	274	1030	190, 253, 301, 321, (332)
NGC 7742	12.25	0.04	0.22*	11.99	−20.91	1673	17	228	1901	190, 191, 415
NGC 7743	12.08[1]	0.04	0*	12.04	−21.00	1802	65	225	2027	190
NGC 7744	12.35[4]	0	0	12.35	−21.51	2990	128	−28	2962	284
NGC 7755	12.10[8]	0	0.37	11.73	−22.14	2932	54	37	2969	104, 224, 321
NGC 7764	12.7	0	0.22	12.48	−20.14	1692	17	−18	1674	160, 393, 431, 438
NGC 7769	12.8	0.07	0.29	12.44	−22.38	4349	187	257	4606	191
NGC 7782	13.1	0	0.74	12.36	−22.88	5368	50	216	5584	284, (332)
NGC 7785	12.67[1]	0	0	12.67	−21.87	3830	40	208	4038	190, 422
NGC 7793	9.65	0	0.40	9.25	−18.85 S	217	8	24	241	595
NGC 7796	12.32[4]	0	0	12.32	−21.75	3358	82	−95	3263	(48), 150, 224, 284

III

Binning According to Type

For convenience in organizing observing programs on galaxies of any
given Hubble type, the 1246 entries in The Catalog are binned separately in the tables that follow. The declination is listed in the second
column of each table as an aid in designing programs for the northern
and southern hemispheres. The absolute magnitudes, fully corrected,
are also listed as an aid in choosing galaxies with particular luminosities.
The ordinary and the barred spirals of given Hubble types are listed in
separate tables.

NGC IC*	δ	TYPE	$M_{B_T}^{o,i}$
		Ellipticals	
147	+48	dE5	−14.36
185	+48	dE3 pec	−14.59
221	+40	E2	−15.53
227	−1	E5	−21.85
439	−32	E5	−22.3
533	+1	E3	−22.52
596	−7	E0	−21.15
636	−7	E1	−20.74
720	−13	E5	−21.59
741	+5	E0	−22.75
750	+32	E0	−21.99
777	+31	E1	−22.88
821	+10	E6	−21.01
1199	−15	E2	−21.23
1209	−15	E6	−21.36
1275	+41	E pec	−23.27
1297	−19	E2	−19.90
1339	−32	E4	−19.56
1374	−35	E0	−20.10
1379	−35	E0	−20.33
1395	−23	E2	−21.43
1399	−35	E1	−21.61
1404	−35	E2	−21.34
1407	−18	E0	−21.81
1427	−35	E5	−20.46
1426	−22	E4	−19.87
1439	−22	E1	−19.99
1453	−4	E2	−21.91
2006*	−36	E1	−20.13
1521	−21	E3	−22.03
1537	−31	E6	−20.43
1549	−55	E2	−20.79
1600	−5	E4	−22.87
1700	−4	E3	−22.67
2325	−28	E4	−21.28
2314	+75	E3	−21.73
2300	+85	E3	−21.22
2434	−69	E0	−19.68
2672	+19	E2	−21.95
2693	+51	E2	−22.32
2749	+18	E3	−21.56
2832	+33	E3	−23.32
2865	−22	E4	−21.37
2888	−27	E2	−19.81
2924	−16	E0	−21.60

NGC IC*	δ	TYPE	$M_{B_T}^{o,i}$
		(Ellipticals *continued*)	
2974	−3	E4	−21.12
2986	−21	E2	−21.32
3078	−26	E3	−21.31
3087	−33	E2	−20.85
3091	−19	E3	−21.96
3136	−67	E4	−20.82
3156	+3	E5:	−18.50
3158	+39	E3	−22.84
3193	+22	E2	−20.26
3250	−39	E3	−21.76
3258	−35	E1	−21.06
3268	−35	E2	−20.93
3309	−27	E1	−21.76
3348	+73	E0	−21.83
3377	+14	E6	−19.26
3379	+12	E0	−20.58
3415	+43	E5	−21.28
3557	−37	E3	−22.55
3605	+18	E5	−17.29
3608	+18	E1	−19.84
3610	+59	E5	−21.33
3613	+58	E6	−21.53
3640	+3	E2	−20.60
3706	−36	E4	−21.77
3818	−5	E5	−19.26
3872	+14	E4	−21.08
3904	−28	E2	−20.30
3962	−13	E1	−20.89
4024	−18	E4	−19.69
4073	+2	E5	−22.53
4125	+65	E6	−21.65
4168	+13	E2	−19.49
4261	+6	E3	−21.71
4278	+29	E1	−19.24
4283	+29	E0	−18.50
4291	+75	E3	−20.75
4342	+7	E7	−18.16
4365	+7	E3	−21.10
4374	+13	E1	−21.47
4373	−39	E(4,2)	−22.14
3370*	−39	E2 pec	−21.74
4473	−13	E5	−20.63
4476	+12	E5 pec (dust)	−18.62
4478	+12	E2	−19.55
4486	+12	E0	−22.08

NGC IC*	δ	TYPE	$M_{B_T}^{o,i}$
		(Ellipticals *continued***)**	
4494	+26	E1	−21.27
4564	+11	E6	−19.83
4589	+74	E2	−21.36
4621	+11	E5	−21.03
4623	+7	E7	−18.61
4645	−41	E5	−20.75
4660	+11	E5	−19.83
4697	−5	E6	−21.47
4696	−41	(E3)	−22.30
4742	−10	E4	−19.63
4756	−15	E3	−21.20
4760	−10	E0	−21.71
4786	−6	E3	−21.93
4782	−12	E0 (tides)	−21.64
4783	−12	E1 (tides)	−21.94
3896*	−50	E1	−20.62
4889	+28	E4	−22.99
4915	−4	E0	−20.99
4936	−30	E2	−21.65
5011	−42	E2	−21.58
5017	−16	E2	−20.15
5018	−19	E4	−21.99
5044	−16	E0	−21.61
5061	−26	E0	−21.54
5077	−12	E3	−21.03
5090	−43	E2	−21.37
5198	+46	E1	−20.68
4296*	−33	E0	−22.72
5322	+60	E4	−22.04
5328	−28	E4	−22.03
5357	−30	E3	−21.83
5444	+35	E3	−22.01
5557	+36	E2	−22.08
5576	+3	E4	−20.51
5638	+3	E1	−20.31
5687	+54	E3	−20.67
5796	−16	E1 pec	−21.17
5812	−7	E0	−20.68
5813	+1	E1	−21.21
5831	+1	E4	−20.07
5982	+59	E3	−21.89
6482	+23	E2	−22.66
HA85−2	−54	E3	−21.16
6721	−57	E1	−21.75
6758	−56	E2	−21.62

NGC IC*	δ	TYPE	$M_{B_T}^{o,i}$
		(Ellipticals *continued***)**	
6776	−63	E1 pec (merger?)	−22.38
6851	−48	E4	−21.35
6854	−54	E1+E0	−22.08
6876	−71	E3	−21.95
6909	−47	E5	−20.91
7014	−47	E5	−21.60
5105*	−40	E5	−22.53
7097	−42	E4	−20.90
7144	−48	E0	−21.32
7145	−48	E0	−20.73
1459*	−36	E4	−21.61
7507	−28	E0	−21.10
7619	+7	E3	−22.36
7626	+7	E1	−22.13
7785	+5	E5	−21.87
7796	−55	E1	−21.75

E/S0 and S0/E

NGC IC*	δ	TYPE	$M_{B_T}^{o,i}$
205	+41	S0/E5 pec	−15.72
1052	−8	E3/S0	−20.91
1351	−35	S0₁(6)/E6	−19.75
1400	−18	E1/S0₁(1)	−17.94
1726	−7	E4/S0₂(4)	−21.69
3585	−26	E7/S0₁(7)	−21.11
3923	−28	E4/S0₁(4)	−21.61
4033	−17	E6/S0₁(6)	−19.62
4406	+13	S0₁(3)/E3	−21.68
4472	+8	E1/S0₁(1)	−22.38
4550	+12	E7/S0₁(7)	−19.37
4570	+7	S0₁(7)/E7	−20.02
4636	+2	E0/S0₁(6)	−20.58
4880	+12	E4/S0₁(4)	−19.13
5353	+40	S0₁(7)/E7	−21.19
5493	−4	E7/S0₂(7)	−21.18
5903	−23	E3/S0₁(3)	−21.04
4797*	−54	E5/S0₁(5)	−21.41
6868	−48	E3/S0₂/₃(3)	−21.92
7041	−48	S0₁(7)/E7	−20.86
7168	−51	E3/S0₁(3)	−20.91
7196	−50	E3/S0₃(3)	−21.37

NGC IC*	δ	TYPE	$M_{B_T}^{o,i}$

S0

NGC IC*	δ	TYPE	$M_{B_T}^{o,i}$
128	+2	$S0_2(8)$ pec	−22.11
148	−32	$S0_2(r)(6)$	−19.88
274	−7	$S0_1(0)$	−19.91
404	+35	$S0_3(0)$	−17.37
584	−7	$S0_1(3,5)$	−21.80
890	+33	$S0_1(5)$	−22.40
1172	−15	$S0_1(0,3)$	−19.48
1175	+42	$S0_2(8)$	−21.88
1201	−26	$S0_1(6)$	−21.09
1332	−21	$S0_1(6)$	−21.03
1344	−31	$S0_1(5)$	−20.62
1366	−31	$S0_1(8)$	−18.27
1381	−35	$S0_1(10)$	−20.06
1389	−35	$S0_1(5)/SB0_1$	−20.01
1411	−44	$S0_2(4)$	−19.66
1440	−18	$S0_1(5)/SB0_1$	−19.75
1461	−16	$S0_2(8)$	−19.44
1527	−48	$S0_2(6)$	−19.59
1553	−55	$S0_{1/2}(5)$ pec	−21.26
1596	−55	$S0_1(7)$	−20.10
1947	−63	$S0_3(0)$ pec	−19.88
2310	−40	$S0_{2/3}(8)$	−19.31
2549	+57	$S0_{1/2}(7)$	−19.85
2685	+58	$S0_3(7)$ pec	−19.65
2732	+79	$S0_1(8)$	−20.62
2768	+60	$S0_{1/2}(6)$	−21.51
2784	−23	$S0_1(4)$	−18.91
2902	−14	$S0_1(0)$	−19.57
2907	−16	$S0_3(6)$ pec	−19.98
2911	+10	$S0_3(2)$ or S0 pec	−21.36
2968	+32	Amorphous or $S0_3$ pec	−19.73
3056	−28	$S0_{1/2}(5)$	−18.36
3065	+72	$S0_2(0)$	−20.39
3098	+24	$S0_1(9)$	−19.18
3115	−7	$S0_1(7)$	−19.82
3203	−26	$S0_2(7)$	−20.51
3226	+20	$S0_1(1)$	−19.71
3245	+28	$S0_1(5)$	−20.23
3390	−31	$S0_3(8)$ or (Sb)	−20.65
3414	+28	$S0_1$	−20.44
3607	+18	$S0_3(3)$	−20.02
3630	+3	$S0_1(9)$	−19.49
3665	+39	$S0_3(3)$	−21.27
3957	−19	$S0_3(9)$	−19.59
3998	+55	$S0_1(3)$	−20.43

(S0 continued)

NGC IC*	δ	TYPE	$M_{B_T}^{o,i}$
4008	+28	$S0_1(3)$	−21.34
4026	+51	$S0_{1/2}(9)$	−19.93
4105	−29	$S0_{1/2}(3)$	−20.80
4111	+43	$S0_1(9)$	−19.33
4124	+10	$S0_3(6)$	−19.35
4128	+69	$S0_1(6)$	−20.81
4179	+1	$S0_1(9)$	−19.88
4203	+33	$S0_2(1)$	−20.04
4215	+6	$S0_1(9)$	−19.91
4251	+28	$S0_1(8)$	−19.82
4270	+5	$S0_1(6)$	−20.04
4281	+5	$S0_3(6)$	−21.19
4339	+6	$S0_{1/2}(0)$	−19.38
4350	+16	$S0_1(8)$	−19.82
4377	+15	$S0_1(3)$	−19.03
4379	+15	$S0_1(2)$	−19.40
4382	+18	$S0_1(3)$ pec	−21.60
4383	+16	S0:	−18.72
4386	+75	$S0_1(5)$	−20.48
4417	+9	$S0_1(7)$	−19.63
4452	+12	$S0_1(10)$	−18.40
4459	+14	$S0_3(3)$	−20.21
4474	+14	$S0_1(8)$	−19.00
4526	+7	$S0_3(6)$	−21.11
4552	+12	$S0_1(0)$	−20.90
4578	+9	$S0_{1/2}(4)$	−19.66
4638	+11	$S0_1(7)$	−19.65
4649	+11	$S0_1(2)$	−21.87
4684	−2	$S0_{2/3}(7)$	−19.98
4710	+15	$S0_3(9)$	−19.85
4753	−0	S0 pec	−20.90
4762	+11	$S0_1(10)$	−20.44
4825	−13	$S0_{1/2}(3)$	−21.76
4914	+37	$(S0_1(5))$	−22.61
4933	−11	$S0_3$ pec (tides?)	−20.76
4958	−7	$S0_1(7)$	−20.63
4976	−49	$S0_1(4)$	−20.95
5084	−21	$S0_1(8)$	−20.45
5087	−20	$S0_3(5)$	−20.60
5102	−36	$S0_1(5)$	−18.73
5128	−42	S0+S pec	−22.6
5193	−32	$S0_1(0)$	−21.44
5266	−47	$S0_3(5)$ pec (prolate)	−21.92
5308	+61	$S0_1(8)$	−21.00
4329*	−30	$S0_1(5)$	−22.10

NGC IC*	δ	TYPE	$M_{B_T}^{o,i}$
		(S0 *continued*)	
5363	+5	[S0₃(5)]	−20.50
5380	+37	S0₁(0)	−21.18
5419	−33	S0₁(2)	−22.3
5422	+55	Sa or S0₃(8)	−20.26
5485	+55	S0₃(2) pec (prolate)	−20.69
5574	+3	S0₁(8)	−19.29
5791	−19	S0₁(4)	−21.25
5820	+54	S0₂(4)	−21.18
5838	+2	S0₂(5)	−20.44
5846	+1	S0₁(0)	−21.49
5866	+55	S0₃(8)	−20.22
5898	−23	S0₂/₃(0)	−20.70
4889*	−54	S0₁/₂(5)	−21.36
6861	−48	S0₃(6)	−21.77
6893	−48	S0₃(4)	−21.52
6958	−38	R?S0₁(3)	−21.56
7029	−49	S0₁(5)	−21.20
7135	−35	S0₁ pec	−22.34
7166	−43	S0₁(6)	−20.67
7192	−64	S0₂(0)	−21.55
5181*	−46	S0₁(7)	−20.62
7232	−46	S0₃(7) or Sb	−19.79
7302	−14	S0₁(3)	−20.46
7332	+23	S0₂/₃(8)	−20.78
5269*	−36	S0₁(7)	−19.62
7457	+29	S0₁(5)	−19.81
7600	−7	S0₁(5)	−21.26
5328*	−45	S0₁(3)	−21.95

SB0

NGC IC*	δ	TYPE	$M_{B_T}^{o,i}$
16	+27	SB0₁(4)	−21.27
1023	+38	SB0₁(5)	−21.17
1387	−35	SB0₂ (pec)	−20.57
1389	−35	S0₁(5)/SB0₁	−20.01
1440	−18	S0₁(5)/SB0₁	−19.75
2035*	−45	SB0₁(4) pec	−19.96
1574	−57	SB0₂(3)	−19.60
2646	+73	SB0₂	−21.51
2859	+34	RSB0₂(3)	−20.76
2880	+62	SB0₁	−20.05

NGC IC*	δ	TYPE	$M_{B_T}^{o,i}$
		(SB0 *continued*)	
2962	+5	RSB0₂	−20.25
2950	+59	RSB0₂/₃	−20.61
3300	+14	SB0₁	−20.50
3384	+12	SB0₁(5)	−19.83
3412	+13	SB0₁/₂(5)	−19.35
3458	+57	SB0₁	−19.75
3516	+72	RSB0₂	−21.43
3892	−10	SB0₃	−19.92
3945	+60	RSB0₂	−20.65
4233	+7	SB0₁(6)	−18.73
4262	+15	SB0₂/₃	−19.32
4267	+13	SB0₁	−19.92
4346	+47	SB0₁(9)	−19.10
4340	+17	SB0₂(r)	−19.77
4371	+11	SB0₂/₃(r)(3)	−19.96
4425	+13	SB0 pec or Sa pec	−18.91
4435	+13	SB0₁(7)	−19.98
4442	+10	SB0₁(6)	−20.39
4483	+9	SB0₁(5)	−18.29
4612	+7	RSB0₁/₂	−19.66
4754	+11	SB0₁(5)	−20.29
5195	+47	SB0₁ pec	−19.7
5365	−43	RSB0₁/₃	−21.33
5473	+55	SB0₁(3)	−20.80
7155	−49	SB0	−20.03
7744	−43	SB0₁(3)	−21.51

S0/Sa, SB0/Sa, and SB0/SBa

NGC IC*	δ	TYPE	$M_{B_T}^{o,i}$
254	−31	RS0₁(6)/Sa	−19.66
474	+3	RS0/a	−21.19
524	+9	S0₂/Sa	−21.93
936	−1	SB0₂/₃/SBa	−21.21
1380	−35	S0₃(7)/Sa	−21.30
1533	−56	SB0₂(2)/SBa	−18.59
1543	−57	RSB0₂/₃(0)/a	−20.49
2787	+69	SB0/a	−19.44
3032	+29	S0₃(2)/Sa	−19.82
3489	+14	S0₃/Sa	−19.00
3637	−9	RSB0₂/₃/SBa	−19.76
3941	+37	SB0₁/₂/a	−20.10
4036	+62	S0₃(8)/Sa	−20.84
4106	−29	SB0/a (tides)	−20.66
4143	+42	S0₁(5)Sa	−18.99

NGC IC*	δ	TYPE	$M^{o,i}_{B_T}$
		(S0Sa/, SB0/Sa, and SB0/SBa *continued***)**	
4150	+30	S0₃(4)/Sa	−15.73
4429	+11	S0₃(6)/Sa pec	−20.55
4477	+13	SB0₁/₂/SBa	−20.46
4546	−3	SB0₁/Sa	−19.85
4608	+10	SB0₃/a	−19.65
4643	+2	SB0₃/SBa	−20.48
4665	+3	SB0₁/₃/SBa:	−19.07
4767	−39	S0/a	−21.29
4856	−14	S0₁(6)/Sa	−20.22
5121	−37	S0₁(4)Sa	−19.80
5273	+35	S0/a	−19.23
5631	+56	S0₃(2)/Sa	−20.67
6875	−46	S0/a (merger)	−21.25
5063*	−57	S0₃(3) pec/Sa	−20.95
7007	−52	(S0₂/a)	−20.87
7020	−64	RS0₂(5)/RSa	−21.40
7049	−48	S0₃(4)/a	−21.57
7377	−22	S0₂/₃/Sa pec	−21.62
7585	−4	S0₁(3)/Sa	−21.85

Sa

NGC IC*	δ	TYPE	$M^{o,i}_{B_T}$
718	+3	SaI	−20.46
788	−7	Sa	−21.64
1079	−29	Sa(s)	−21.02
1302	−26	Sa	−21.23
1316	−37	Sa pec (merger?)	−23.08
1317	−37	Sa	−20.36
1350	−33	Sa(r)	−21.38
1357	−13	Sa(s)	−21.13
1371	−25	Sa(s)	−20.76
1386	−36	Sa	−21.36
1415	−22	Sa/SBa late	−20.62
1617	−54	Sa(s)	−20.68
1638	−01	Sa	−21.46
2179	−21	Sa	−20.77
2639	+50	Sa	−22.18
2655	+78	Sa pec	−22.19
2681	+51	Sa	−20.48
2775	+7	Sa(r)	−20.79
2781	−14	Sa(r)	−20.75
2782	+40	Sa(s) pec	−22.06

NGC IC*	δ	TYPE	$M^{o,i}_{B_T}$
		(Sa *continued***)**	
2811	−16	Sa	−21.75
2844	+40	Sa:(r)	−19.62
2855	−11	Sa(r)	−20.85
2992	−14	Sa (tides)	−21.36
3166	+3	Sa(s)	−21.19
3190	+22	Sa	−21.19
3271	−35	Sa	−22.52
3281	−34	Sa	−22.11
3277	+28	Sa(r)I–II	−19.87
3301	+22	Sa	−19.74
3358	−36	Sa(r)I	−21.69
3449	−32	Sa	−21.55
3571	−18	Sa	−22.46
3593	+13	Sa pec	−19.19
3611	+4	Sa	−20.03
3619	+58	Sa	−20.59
3623	+13	Sa(s)II	−21.48
3626	+18	Sa	−20.81
3718	+53	Sa pec?	−21.24
3885	−27	Sa	−20.10
3898	+56	SaI	−21.04
3900	+27	Sa(r)	−21.27
4158	+20	Sa:	−21.04
4220	+48	Sa(r)	−20.36
4224	+7	Sa	−21.40
4235	+7	Sa	−21.39
4274	+29	Sa(s)	−20.87
4293	+18	Sa pec	−21.34
4324	+5	Sa(r) ring	−19.79
4378	+4	Sa(s)	−21.12
4424	+9	S(a?) pec	−20.20
4425	+13	SB0 pec or Sa pec	−18.91
4454	−1	Sa	−20.25
4461	+13	Sa	−19.61
4503	+11	Sa	−19.48
4586	+4	Sa	−20.17
4698	+8	Sa	−20.55
4772	+2	Sa:	−19.66
4845	+1	Sa	−20.22
4866	+14	Sa	−21.11
4984	−15	Sa(s)	−20.49
5064	−47	Sa	−22.27
5377	+47	SBa or Sa	−21.62
5422	+55	Sa or S0₃(8)	−20.26
5448	+49	Sa(s)	−21.79

NGC IC*	δ	TYPE	$M^{o,i}_{B_T}$
		(Sa *continued*)	
5548	+25	Sa	−22.08
5614	+35	Sa(s) (tides)	−22.45
5689	+48	Sa	−20.85
5739	+42	Sa(s)	−22.5
5854	+2	Sa	−20.00
6340	+72	Sa(r)I	−21.05
6902	−43	Sa(r)	−21.41
6935	−52	Sa(r)	−22.46
7096	−64	Sa(r)I	−21.23
5135*	−35	Sa pec	−22.27
7126	−60	Sa(r):	−21.61
7213	−47	Sa(rs)	−21.96
5267*	−43	Sa(r)	−21.53
7679	+3	Sc(s)/Sa (tides?)	−22.38
7702	−56	RSa(r)	−21.66
7727	−12	Sa pec	−21.98
7742	+10	Sa(r!)	−20.91

SBa

NGC IC*	δ	TYPE	$M^{o,i}_{B_T}$
357	−6	SBa	−21.05
1022	−6	SBa(r) pec	−20.83
1169	+46	SBa(r)I	−21.99
1291	−41	SBa	−21.68
1326	−36	RSBa	−21.06
1358	−5	SBa(s)I	−21.63
1415	−22	Sa/SBa late	−20.68
1452	−18	SBa(r)	−19.85
2217	−27	SBa(s)	−21.23
2798	+42	SBa(s) (tides)	−19.81
2983	−20	SBa	−20.35
3081	−22	SBa(s)	−20.67
3185	+21	SBa(s)	−19.18
3783	−37	SBa(r)I	−20.81
4245	+29	SBa(s)	−18.91
4260	+6	SBa(s)	−20.49
4314	+30	SBa(rs) pec	−19.80
4596	+10	SBa (very early)	−20.25
4795	+8	SBa(s) (tides?)	−21.03
5101	−27	SBa	−21.06

NGC IC*	δ	TYPE	$M^{o,i}_{B_T}$
		(SBa *continued*)	
5377	+47	SBa or Sa	−21.62
5566	+4	SBa(r)II	−21.99
5701	+5	(PR)SBa	−20.47
5750	−0	SBa(s)	−21.14
5864	+3	SBa	−19.86
6684	−65	SBa(s)	−19.91
New 5	−44	SBa	−21.24
6942	−54	SBa(s)	−21.42
7079	−44	SBa	−21.23
5240*	−45	SBa(r)	−21.04
7371	−11	SBa(r)II	−21.18
7410	−39	SBa	−22.40
7743	+9	SBa	−21.00

Sab

NGC IC*	δ	TYPE	$M^{o,i}_{B_T}$
7814	+15	S(ab)	−21.70
434	−58	Sab(s)	−22.67
488	+4	Sab(rs)I	−22.86
681	−10	Sab	−20.79
1288	−32	Sab(r)I-II	−22.42
1532	−33	Sab(s)I (tides?)	−21.33
2196	−21	Sab(s)I	−21.95
2460	+60	Sab(s)	−20.62
2551	+73	Sab(s)I:	−21.17
2654	+60	Sab:	−20.99
2985	+72	Sab(s)	−21.74
2993	−14	Sab (tides)	−20.46
3285	−27	Sab(s)	—
3312	−27	Sab(r)	−21.85
3329	+77	Sab	−20.92
3368	+12	Sab(s)II	−21.41
3705	+9	Sab(r)I-II	−20.32
3865	−8	Sab(rs)	−22.94
4138	+43	Sab(r)	−20.21
4151	+39	Sab	−20.93
4380	+10	Sab(s)	−20.04
4388	+12	Sab	−21.05
4450	+17	Sab pec	−21.39
4469	+09	Sab (on edge)	−20.41
4569	+13	Sab(s)I-II	−22.31

NGC IC*	δ	TYPE	$M^{o,t}_{B_T}$
		(Sab *continued*)	
4579	+12	Sab(s)II	−21.69
4594	−11	Sa⁺/Sb⁻	−22.81
4699	−8	Sab(sr)	−22.24
4736	+41	RSab(s)	−20.81
4818	−8	Sab:	−20.24
4826	+21	Sab(s)II	−20.61
4941	−5	Sab(s)II	−20.07
5037	−16	Sab(s)	−20.73
5641	+29	S(B)abI	−22.60
6887	−52	Sab(s)I–II	−22.42
6890	−44	Sab(s)II–III	−21.06
5020*	−33	Sab(r)	−21.6
7177	+17	Sab(r)II.2	−21.10
7469	+8	Sab pec	−23.10
7690	−51	Sab(s)	−20.24
7716	+0	Sab(r)I	−21.26

SBab

175	−20	SBab(r)I–II	−22.17
1398	−26	SBab(r)I	−22.30
3275	−36	SBab(r)I	−22.28
4419	+15	SBab:	−20.58
4462	−22	SBab(s)I–II	−20.97
New 2	−39	SBab(rs)I	−21.96
5641	+29	S(B)abI	−22.60
6782	−60	SBab(s)	−22.57
7582	−42	SBab(rs)	−21.75

Sb

23	+25	SbI–II	−22.86
210	−14	Sb(rs)I	−21.86
224	+40	SbI–II	−21.61
473	+16	Sb(r)	−20.71
615	−7	Sb(r)I–II	−21.59
670	+27	Sb:	−22.34
772	+18	Sb(rs)I	−23.29
779	−6	Sb(rs)I–II	−21.57
891	+42	Sb on edge	−21.66
955	−1	Sb	−20.74

NGC IC*	δ	TYPE	$M^{o,i}_{B_T}$
		(Sb *continued*)	
972	+29	Sb pec	−21.56
1068	−0	Sb(rs)II	−22.93
1140	−10	Sb pec:	−20.36
1309	−15	Sb(rs)II	−21.61
1325	−21	Sb	−21.15
1417	−4	Sb(s)I.3	−22.57
1425	−30	Sb(r)II	−21.53
1515	−54	Sb(s)II	−20.76
1672	−59	Sb(rs)II	−21.37
1964	−21	SbI–II	−22.01
1961	+69	Sb(rs)II pec	−23.68
2146	+78	SbII pec	−21.36
2347	+64	Sb(r)I–II	−22.32
2613	−22	Sb(s)(II)	−22.71
2683	+33	Sb (nearly on edge)	−20.17
2764	+21	Amorphous or Sb pec	−20.29
2815	−23	Sb(s)I–II	−22.00
2841	+51	Sb	−21.53
2889	−11	Sb(r)II	−22.19
3038	−32	Sb(s)II	−21.44
3031	+69	Sb(r)I–II	−20.75
3067	+32	Sb(s)III	−20.52
3169	+3	Sb(r)I–II (tides)	−21.09
3147	+73	Sb(s)I.8	−22.94
3177	+21	Sb(s)II	−19.49
3200	−17	Sb(r)I	−22.95
3223	−34	Sb(s)I–II	−22.69
3227	+20	Sb(s)III	−20.80
3241	−32	Sb(r)II	−20.80
3256	−43	Sb(s) pec	−22.80
3254	+29	Sb(s)II	−20.75
3259	+65	SbIII	−20.90
3390	−31	S0₃(8) or (Sb)	−20.65
3504	+28	Sb(s)/SBb(s)I–II	−21.11
3506	+11	Sb(s)I–II	−22.55
3521	+0	Sb(s)II–III	−21.65
3583	+48	Sb(s)II	−21.65
3627	+13	Sb(s)II.2	−21.48
3642	+59	Sb(r)I	−21.69
3675	+43	Sb(r)II	−20.88
3717	−30	Sb(s)	−21.57
3887	−16	Sb(r)I–II	−20.32
3981	−19	Sb:I	−21.07
750*	+43	S(b)	−18.77
4032	+20	S(b):	−19.38

NGC IC*	δ	TYPE	$M^{o,i}_{B_T}$
		(Sb *continued*)	
4102	+52	Sb(r)II	−19.80
764*	−29	Sb(r)I–II	−21.60
4192	+15	SbII:	−21.85
4216	+13	Sb(s)	−21.94
4217	+47	Sb:	−21.46
4256	+66	Sb(s)	−22.34
4258	+47	Sb(s)II	−22.05
4307	+9	Sb?	−19.50
4438	+13	Sb (tides)	−21.73
4448	+28	Sb(r)I–II	−19.54
4457	+3	RSb(rs)II	−20.58
4527	+2	Sb(s)II	−22.19
4565	+26	Sb	−22.79
4679	−39	Sb(s)I–II	−22.55
4725	+25	Sb/SBb(r)II	−22.47
4750	+73	Sb(r)II pec	−21.10
4800	+46	Sb(rs)II–III	−19.32
4814	+58	Sb(s)I	−21.41
4868	+37	Sc: or Sb:	−22.15
5005	+37	Sb(s)II	−21.78
5054	−16	Sb(s)I–II	−21.67
5134	−20	Sb(s)(II–III)	−19.96
5150	−29	Sb(r)I–II	−21.86
5172	+17	SbI	−22.64
5170	−17	Sb:	−21.56
5362	+41	S(b or c)	−20.90
5371	+40	Sb(rs)I/SBb(rs)I	−22.78
4351*	−29	Sb	−22.52
5395	+37	SbII	−22.69
5533	+35	Sb(s)I	−22.48
5600	+14	Sb pec	−20.55
5612	−78	Sb(s)II	−21.65
5691	−0	S(B)b pec III	−20.34
5740	+1	Sb(r)I	−20.51
5746	+2	Sb(s)	−22.34
5806	+2	Sb(s)II.8	−20.23
5879	+57	Sb(s)II	−20.24
5878	−14	Sb(s)I.2	−21.63
5908	+55	Sb (on edge)	−22.28
6384	+7	Sb(r)I	−22.28
6753	−57	Sb(r)I	−22.64
6769	−60	Sb(r)II	−22.57
6810	−58	Sb	−21.87
6951	+65	Sb/SBb(rs)I.3	−21.36
7083	−64	Sb(s)I–II	−22.81

NGC IC*	δ	TYPE	$M^{o,i}_{B_T}$
		(Sb *continued*)	
7171	−13	Sb(r)I	−21.46
7184	−21	Sb(r)II	−23.10
7205	−57	Sb(r)II.8	−21.48
5156*	−34	Sb(s)II–III	−20.4
7217	+31	Sb(r)II–III	−21.66
7232	−46	S0₃(7) or Sb	−19.79
7331	+34	Sb(rs)I–II	−22.60
5271*	−34	Sb(rs)II	−20.73
7606	−8	Sb(r)I	−22.69
7782	+7	Sb(s)I–II	−22.88

SBb

NGC IC*	δ	TYPE	$M^{o,i}_{B_T}$
613	−29	SBb(rs)II	−22.24
782	−58	SBb(r)I–II	−22.99
986	−39	SBb(rs)I–II	−21.81
1300	−19	SBb(s)I.2	−21.99
1365	−36	SBb(s)I	−22.95
1433	−47	SBb(s)I–II	−21.15
1512	−43	SBb(rs)I pec	−20.14
1832	−15	SBb(r)I	−21.53
2523	+73	SBb(r)I	−22.45
2642	−3	SBb(rs)I–II	−22.77
2633	+74	SBb(s)I.3	−21.33
2712	+45	SBb(s)I	−21.00
2935	−20	SBb(s)I.2	−21.76
3347	−36	SBb(r)I	−22.31
3351	+11	SBb(r)II	−20.66
3504	+28	Sb(s)/SBb(s)I–II	−21.11
3673	−26	SBbII	−20.96
3681	+17	SBb(r)I–II	−19.84
3992	+53	SBb(rs)I	−21.83
4050	−16	SBb(rs)I–II	−21.03
4290	+58	SBb	−21.81
4394	+18	SBb(sr)I–II	−20.42
4548	+14	SBb(rs)I–II	−21.27
4593	−5	SBb(rs)I–II	−22.35
4639	+13	SBb(r)II	−20.13
4691	−3	SBb pec	−20.22
4725	+25	Sb/SBb(r)II	−22.47
4902	−14	SBb(s)I–II	−22.04
4999	+1	SBb(r)	−21.74
5135	−29	SBb:	−22.55

NGC IC*	δ	TYPE	$M^{o,i}_{B_T}$
		(SBb *continued*)	
5347	+33	SBb(s)I–II	−20.54
5351	+38	SBb(rs)I	−22.07
5371	+40	Sb(rs)I/SBb(rs)I	−22.78
5383	+42	SBb(s)I–II	−21.79
5430	+59	SBb(r)II	−21.80
5691	−0	S(B)b pec III:	−20.34
5728	−17	SBb(s)II	−22.47
5757	−18	SBb(rs)II	−21.55
5792	−0	SBb(s)I.3	−22.35
5850	+1	SBb(sr)I–II	−22.23
5905	+55	SBb(rs)I	−22.48
5985	+59	SBb(r)I	−22.65
6300	−62	SBb(s)II pec	−21.32
6951	+65	Sb/SBb(rs)I.3	−21.36
7723	−13	SBb(rs)I–II	−21.75

Sbc

NGC IC*	δ	TYPE	$M^{o,i}_{B_T}$
134	−33	Sbc(s)II–III:	−22.28
150	−28	Sbc(s)II	−21.31
245	−1	SbcII.2: pec	−21.79
278	+47	Sbc(s)II.2	−20.50
470	+3	Sbc(s)II.3	−21.46
1783*	−33	Sbc(rs)II	−21.44
864	+5	Sbc(r)II–III	−21.50
1788*	−31	Sbc(s)II	−21.61
958	−3	Sbc(s)II	−23.03
976	+20	Sbc(r)I–II	−22.01
1055	+0	Sbc(s)II	−20.92
1353	−20	Sbc(r)II	−20.75
1546	−56	Sbc(s)III	−19.65
1625	−3	Sb/Sc	−21.59
1808	−37	Sbc pec	−20.96
2268	+84	Sbc(s)II	−21.83
2369	−62	Sbc(s)I pec	−22.13
2608	+28	Sbc(s)II	−20.88
2713	+3	Sbc(s)I	−22.47
3021	+33	Sbc(s)II	−19.80
3162	+22	Sbc(s)I.8	−20.12
3310	+53	Sbc(r) pec	−20.82
3338	+14	Sbc(s)I–II	−20.96
3430	+33	Sbc(r)I–II	−20.78
3403	+73	SbcIII:	−20.20

NGC IC*	δ	TYPE	$M^{o,i}_{B_T}$
		(Sbc *continued*)	
3549	+53	Sbc(s)II	−21.79
3628	+13	Sbc	−21.30
3646	+20	Sbc(r)II	−23.13
3720	+1	Sbc(s)I	−21.94
3982	+55	Sbc(r)II–III	−20.30
4013	+44	Sbc:	−20.02
4030	−0	Sbc(r)I	−21.42
4045	+2	Sbc(s)I–II	−20.48
4051	+44	Sbc(s)II	−20.31
4094	−14	Sbc(s)II	−19.99
4157	+50	Sbc	−20.43
4219	−43	Sbc(s)(II–III)	−21.26
4433	−8	SbcIII	−21.27
4460	+45	Sbc	−19.02
4501	+14	Sbc(s)II	−21.93
4522	+9	Sc/Sb:	−19.73
4580	+5	Sbc(r)II	−19.39
4666	−0	SbcII.3	−21.49
4701	+3	Sbc(s)II	−18.99
4928	−7	Sbc(s)III.3	−19.31
4939	−10	Sbc(rs)I	−22.77
4947	−35	Sbc(s)I–II pec	−21.13
4995	−7	Sbc(s)II	−21.10
5033	+36	Sbc(s)I–II	−21.16
5055	+42	Sbc(s)II–III	−21.34
5194	+47	Sbc(s)I–II	−21.60
5248	+9	Sbc(s)I–II	−21.19
5324	−5	Sbc(r)I.3	−21.64
5376	+59	Sbc(s)II	−20.67
5426	−5	Sbc(rs)I.2	−21.18
5427	−5	Sbc(s)I	−21.79
5592	−28	Sbc(s)I–II	−21.88
5605	−12	Sbc(s)II	−21.29
5633	+46	Sbc(s)II	−21.00
5713	−0	Sbc(s) pec	−21.07
6221	−59	Sbc(s)II–III	−21.55
6574	+14	Sbc(s)II.3	−21.31
6699	−57	Sbc(s)I.2	−21.92
6744	−63	Sbc(r)II	−21.98
6754	−50	Sbc(s)II–III	−21.62
6780	−55	Sbc(rs)I–II	−21.51
6814	−10	Sbc(rs)I–II	−21.21
6925	−32	Sbc(r)I	−22.37
6943	−68	Sbc(rs)I	−22.33
7038	−47	Sbc(s)I.8	−23.06

NGC IC*	δ	TYPE	$M_{B_T}^{o,i}$
		(Sbc *continued*)	
7124	−50	SbcI	−22.50
7162	−43	Sbc(rs)II	−20.54
7392	−20	Sbc(s)I-II	−21.73
7531	−43	Sbc(r)I-II	−21.00
7721	−6	Sbc(s)II.2	−21.50
7755	−30	SBbc(r)/Sbc(r)I-II	−22.14
7769	+19	Sbc(s)II (tides?)	−22.38

SBbc

NGC IC*	δ	TYPE	$M_{B_T}^{o,i}$
151	−9	SBbc(rs)II	−22.70
289	−31	SBbc(rs)I-II	−21.41
491	−34	SBbc(r)II	−21.60
1097	−30	RSBbc(rs)I-II	−22.30
1187	−23	SBbc(s)I-II	−21.70
1241	−9	SBbc(s)I.2	−22.34
1953*	−21	SBbc(rs)II	−20.93
1640	−20	SBbc(r)I-II	−20.57
1784	−11	SBbc(rs)I-II	−21.45
2223	−22	SBbc(r)I.3	−22.04
2336	+80	SBbc(r)I	−22.94
2442	−69	SBbc(rs)II	−21.20
3001	−30	SBbc(s)I-II	−21.20
3054	−25	SBbc(s)I	−21.46
3124	−18	SBbc(r)I	−22.23
3145	−12	SBbc(rs)I	−22.44
3261	−44	SBbc(rs)I-II	−22.09
3318	−41	SBbc(rs)II.2	−21.49
3344	+25	SBbc(rs)I	−20.31
3485	+15	SBbc(s)II	−19.98
3686	+17	SBbc(s)I-II	−19.95
3687	+29	SBbc(r)I.2	−20.89
3953	+52	SBbc(r)I-II	−21.30
4123	+3	SBbc(rs)	−20.35
4304	−33	SBbc(s)II	−20.97
4385	+0	SBbc(s)II	−20.38
4412	+4	SBbc(s)II	−19.73
4618	+41	SBbc(rs)II.2 pec	−19.39
4763	−16	SBbc(r)II	−21.71
4891	−13	SBbc(r)I-II	−21.17
4904	+0	SBbc(rs)II-III	−19.47
4961	+28	SBbc(s)III	−20.00
4981	−6	SBbc(sr)II	−20.91
5156	−48	SBbc(rs)I	−21.49
5188	−34	SBbc(s)II-III pec	−21.18

NGC IC*	δ	TYPE	$M_{B_T}^{o,i}$
		(SBbc *continued*)	
5350	+40	SBbc(rs) I-II	−21.48
5483	−43	SBbc(s)II	−20.94
5534	−7	SBbc(s)II (merger?)	−20.51
5915	−12	SBbc(s) pec	−20.75
5921	+5	SBbc(s)I-II	−21.14
5970	+12	SBbc(r)II	−21.37
6217	+78	RSBbc(s)II	−21.11
6907	−24	SBbc(s)II	−22.49
6923	−31	SBbc(s)II	−21.61
6984	−52	SBbc(r)I.8	−21.90
7329	−66	SBbc(r)I-II	−22.08
7421	−37	SBbc(rs)II-III	−20.45
7479	+12	SBbc(s)I-II	−22.34
7552	−42	SBbc(s)I-II	−21.49
7678	+22	SBbc(s)I-II	−22.05
7755	−30	SBbc(r)/Sbc(r)I-II	−22.14

Sc

NGC IC*	δ	TYPE	$M_{B_T}^{o,i}$
24	−25	Sc(s)II-III	−19.12
55	−39	Sc	−20.15
95	+10	Sc(s)I.8	−22.16
157	−8	Sc(s)I-II	−22.19
178	−14	ScIV	−19.90
214	+25	Sc(r)I	−22.41
237	−0	Sc(rs)I-II	−21.41
247	−21	Sc(s)III-IV	−18.62
253	−25	Sc(s)	−20.72
300	−37	ScII.8	−18.59
309	−10	Sc(r)I	−23.25
337	−7	Sc(s)II.2 pec	−21.07
406	−70	Sc(s)II	−20.29
428	+0	Sc(s)III	−20.61
450	−1	Sc(s)II.3	−20.72
514	+12	Sc(s)II	−21.53
578	−22	Sc(s)I-II	−21.59
598	+30	Sc(s)II-III	−19.07
628	+15	Sc(s)I	−21.75
701	−9	Sc(s)III	−20.56
753	+35	Sc(rs)I	−22.67
877	+14	Sc(s)I-II	−22.50
895	−5	Sc(r)I	−21.47
908	−21	Sc(s)I-II	−22.15
922	−25	Sc(s)II.2 pec	−21.69

NGC IC*	δ	TYPE	$M_{B_T}^{o,i}$
		(Sc *continued*)	
949	+36	Sc(s)III	−19.28
991	−7	Sc(rs)II	−20.42
1035	−8	Sc:II	−19.67
1042	−8	Sc(rs)I-II	−21.15
1058	+37	Sc(s)II-III	−19.27
1084	−7	Sc(s)II.2	−21.62
1087	−0	Sc(s)III.3	−21.43
1232	−20	Sc(rs)I	−22.57
1255	−25	Sc(s)II	−21.42
1292	−27	Sc(s)II	−20.16
1337	−8	Sc(s)I-II	−20.52
1954*	−52	Sc(s)II.2	−19.77
1359	−19	Sc(s)II-III	−20.72
1376	−5	Sc(s)II	−22.19
1385	−24	ScIII:	−21.77
1406	−31	Sc(II)	−19.73
1421	−13	ScIII:	−21.96
1437	−36	Sc(s)II	−20.22
1448	−44	Sc(II):	−21.14
1511	−67	Sc pec	−20.48
1507	−2	Sc	−19.39
1518	−21	ScIII	−19.62
2056*	−60	Sc(s)II	−19.56
1566	−55	Sc(s)I	−22.29
1659	−4	Sc(s)II-III	−22.08
1667	−6	Sc(r):II pec	−22.54
1792	−38	Sc(s)II	−21.39
HA85-1	−14	Sc(s)II	−20.88
2082	−64	Sc(s)II-III	−19.12
2090	−34	Sc(s)II	−19.72
2207	−21	Sc(s)I.2	−22.97
2280	−27	Sc(s)I.2	−21.63
2276	+85	Sc(r)II-III	−22.09
2397	−68	Sc(s)III	−19.40
2403	+65	Sc(s)III	−19.47
2427	−47	Sc(s)II-III	−19.47
2441	+73	Sc(r)I-II	−21.86
2500	+50	Sc(s)II.8	−18.66
2537	+46	ScIII pec	−18.13
2541	+49	Sc(s)III	−18.93
2552	+50	Sc or SdIV	−18.14
2701	+53	Sc(s)II-III	−21.12
2715	+78	Sc(s)II	−21.21
2742	+60	Sc(rs)II	−20.54
2763	−15	Sc(r)II	−20.48

NGC IC*	δ	TYPE	$M_{B_T}^{o,i}$
		(Sc *continued*)	
2748	+76	Sc(s)II-III	−20.95
2776	+45	Sc(s)I	−21.80
2793	+34	ScIII pec	−20.08
2848	−16	Sc(s)II	−20.78
2903	+21	Sc(s)I-II	−20.96
2942	+34	Sc(s)I.3	−22.33
2955	+36	Sc(s)I	−22.85
2967	+0	Sc(rs)I-II	−21.17
2964	+32	Sc(s)II.2	−20.53
2989	−18	Sc(s)I	−21.60
2997	−30	Sc(s)I.3	−21.40
2990	+5	ScII:	−21.26
2998	+44	Sc(rs)I	−22.84
3003	+33	Sc:III:	−20.91
3041	+16	Sc(rs)II	−20.31
3052	−18	Sc(r)II	−21.85
3055	+4	Sc(s)II	−20.54
2522*	−32	Sc/SBc(s)I-II	−21.74
3089	−28	Sc(s)II	−20.94
3095	−31	Sc(s)I-II pec	−21.73
3079	+55	Sc pec:	−21.64
2537*	−27	Sc(s)I-II	−21.23
3175	−28	Sc(s)III: pec	−19.52
3184	+41	Sc(r)II.2	−20.28
3198	+45	Sc(rs)I-II	−20.39
3294	+37	Sc(s)I.3	−20.79
3320	+47	Sc(s)II-III	−20.98
3370	+17	Sc(s)I-II	−20.25
3389	+12	Sc(s)II.2	−19.91
3395	+33	Sc(s)II-III	−20.58
3396	+33	Sc	−20.56
3423	+6	Sc(s)II-III	−19.84
3433	+10	Sc(r)I.3	−21.58
3432	+36	Sc(II-III:)	−19.50
3437	+23	Sc(s)(III)	−19.74
3445	+57	Sc(s)III	−20.61
3455	+17	Sc(s)II:	−19.12
3464	−20	Sc(rs)I	−21.96
3478	+46	Sc(s)?	−23.27
3486	+29	Sc(r)I-II	−20.05
3495	+3	Sc(s)III	−19.78
3511	−22	Sc(s)II.8	−20.56
3512	+28	Sc(rs)I-II	−19.45
3547	+10	ScIII	−19.57
2627*	−23	Sc(r)I-II	−20.60

NGC IC*	δ	TYPE	$M_{B_T}^{o,i}$
		(Sc *continued*)	
3556	+55	Sc(s)III	−21.02
3596	+15	Sc(r)II.2	−20.30
3614	+46	Sc(r)I	−21.62
3621	−32	Sc(s)II.8	−20.29
3629	+27	Sc(s)II–III	−19.89
3631	+53	Sc(s)I–II	−21.26
3655	+16	Sc(s)III pec	−20.33
3659	+18	Sc(s)III	−19.42
3666	+11	ScII–III	−19.68
3672	−9	Sc(s)I–II	−21.49
3684	+17	Sc(s)II	−19.74
3683	+57	Sc(III)	−19.97
3689	+25	Sc(r)II	−21.01
3726	+47	Sc(r)I–II	−20.74
3732	−9	Sc(r) pec	−20.03
3735	+70	Sc(II–III)	−22.15
3756	+54	Sc(s)I–II	−20.55
3780	+56	Sc(r)II.3	−21.56
3810	+11	Sc(s)II	−20.22
3813	+36	Sc(s)II.8	−20.55
3877	+47	ScII.2	−20.35
3888	+56	Sc(s)I–II	−20.73
3893	+48	Sc(s)I.2	−20.91
3917	+52	Sc(s)III	−19.94
3936	−26	Sc(s)I–II	−20.85
3938	+44	Sc(s)I	−20.54
3949	+48	Sc(s)III	−20.23
3956	−20	Sc(s)II	−20.44
3976	+7	Sc(s)I–II	−21.77
3995	+32	ScIII	−21.93
4027	−18	Sc(s)III	−21.06
4038	−18	Sc pec	−21.40
4041	+62	Sc(s)II–III	−20.83
4047	+48	Sc(s)I–II	−21.40
4062	+32	Sc(s)II–III	−19.44
4085	+50	ScIII::	−18.87
4088	+50	Sc(s)II–III/SBc	−20.53
2995*	−27	Sc(s)III	−20.55
4096	+47	Sc(s)II–III	−20.15
4100	+49	Sc(s)I–II	−20.82
4129	−8	ScIII:	−19.03
4136	+30	Sc(r)I–II	−18.28
4152	+16	Sc(r)I.4	−20.93
4162	+24	Sc(s)I–II	−21.69
4212	+14	Sc(s)II–III	−20.26

NGC IC*	δ	TYPE	$M_{B_T}^{o,i}$
		(Sc *continued*)	
4237	+15	Sc(r)II.8	−19.59
4254	+14	Sc(s)I.3	−21.59
4298	+14	Sc(s)III	−20.09
4302	+14	Sc (on edge)	−20.01
4303	+4	Sc(s)I.2	−21.84
4321	+16	Sc(s)I	−21.91
3253*	−34	Sc(s)II–III	−21.84
4369	+39	Sc(s)III–IV	−19.66
4414	+31	Sc(sr)II.2	−20.26
4420	+2	Sc(s)III	−20.23
4428	−7	Sc(s)II.3	−21.00
4455	+23	Sc on edge	−19.43
4504	−7	Sc(s)II	−19.50
4517	+0	Sc	−21.08
4536	+2	Sc(s)I	−22.15
4559	+28	Sc(s)II–III	−21.15
4567	+11	Sc(s)II–III	−20.03
4568	+11	Sc(s)II–III	−20.57
4571	+14	Sc(s)II–III	−20.21
4595	+15	Sc(s)II.8	−18.91
4605	+61	Sc(s)III	−18.34
4602	−4	Sc(s)I–II	−21.71
4603	−40	Sc(s)I–II	−21.66
4631	+32	Sc on edge	−21.44
4632	+0	Sc(s)II.3	−20.86
4635	+20	ScII–III	−19.16
4647	+11	Sc(rs)III	−20.04
4651	+16	Sc(r)I–II	−20.75
4653	−0	Sc(rs)I.3	−20.93
4682	−9	Sc(s)II.4	−20.74
4689	+14	Sc(s)II.3	−20.48
4700	−11	Sc or Sm	−19.95
4712	+25	Sc(s)II	−21.66
4771	+1	ScII–III:	−19.69
4775	−6	Sc(s)II.8	−20.76
4781	−10	Sc(s)II.8	−19.55
4793	+29	Sc(s)II.2	−21.65
New 4	+0	Sc(s)III	−19.73
4808	+4	Sc(s)III	−18.51
4835	−45	Sc(s)(I–II)	−21.52
4868	+37	Sc: or Sb:	−22.15
4900	+2	ScIII–IV	−19.32
4899	−13	Sc(s)II.8	−21.34
4951	−6	Sc(s)II:	−19.54
4945	−49	Sc	−20.90

NGC IC*	δ	TYPE	$M_{B_T}^{o,i}$
\multicolumn{4}{c}{(Sc *continued*)}
5012	+23	Sc(rs)I–II	−21.63
5016	+24	Sc(r)II	−20.97
5085	−24	Sc(r)I–II	−21.04
5088	−12	ScIII	−19.51
5112	+38	Sc(rs)II	−20.07
5116	+27	Sc(s)II	−21.26
5147	+2	Sc(s)III–IV	−19.47
5161	−32	Sc(s)I	−21.89
5230	+13	Sc(s)I	−23.22
5247	−17	Sc(s)I–II	−21.09
5297	+44	Sc(s)II	−22.19
5301	+46	Sc(s)	−20.83
5300	+4	Sc(s)II	−20.09
5362	+41	S(b or c)	−20.90
5364	+5	Sc(r)I	−21.15
HA72	−45	Sc(s)II–III	−19.79
5406	+39	Sc(s)I.2	−22.52
5457	+54	Sc(s)I	−21.51
5468	−5	Sc(s)II	−21.71
5480	+50	Sc(s)III	−20.50
5496	−0	Sc(s)	−20.48
5494	−30	Sc(s)I–II	−21.21
5523	+25	Sc(s)II–III	−19.83
5530	−43	Sc(s)II.8	−20.24
5584	−0	Sc(s)I–II	−20.84
5595	−16	Sc(s)II	−21.35
5653	+31	Sc(s)III pec	−21.72
5660	+49	Sc(s)I.8	−21.45
5645	+7	ScIII pec	−19.85
4444*	−43	Sc(s)II	−21.22
5665	+8	Sc(s)IV pec	−20.84
5669	+10	Sc/SBc(r)I–II	−20.46
5678	+58	Sc(s)II–III	−21.90
5668	+4	Sc(s)II–III	−20.52
5676	+49	Sc(s)II	−22.11
5690	+2	ScII:	−20.79
5756	−14	Sc(s)II	−20.43
5768	−2	Sc(s)III	−20.44
5775	+3	Sc (on edge)	−20.91
5861	−11	Sc(s)II	−20.94
F703	−15	Sc(s)II.2	−21.18
5899	+42	Sc(s)II	−21.62
5907	+56	Sc (on edge)	−20.68
5949	+64	Sc	−18.13
5936	+13	Sc(r)I–II	−21.81

NGC IC*	δ	TYPE	$M_{B_T}^{o,i}$
\multicolumn{4}{c}{(Sc *continued*)}
5962	+16	Sc(r)II.3	−21.28
5967	−75	Sc(rs)II.2	−21.66
6015	+62	Sc(s)II–III	−20.48
6070	+0	Sc(s)I	−21.22
6106	+7	Sc(rs)II.3	−20.10
6118	−2	Sc(s)I.3	−21.20
6181	+19	Sc(s)II	−21.56
6207	+36	Sc(s)III	−19.96
6215	−58	Sc(s)II	−21.33
6412	+75	SBc(s)/Sc(s)I–II	−20.60
6503	+70	Sc(s)II.8	−18.76
6643	+74	Sc(s)II	−21.64
4721*	−58	Sc(s)II	−21.21
4837*	−54	Sc(s)II–III	−21.52
6808	−70	Sc(s)II	−21.44
6878	−44	Sc(r)I.3	−21.74
6946	+59	Sc(s)II	−20.30
5039*	−30	Sc(sIII)	−21.27
6970	−48	Sc(s)II	−22.21
New 6	−45	Sc(s)I	−21.80
7059	−60	Sc(s)II	−20.25
7119	−46	Sc(s)II	−23.21
7125	−60	Sc(rs)I	−21.42
7137	+21	Sc(rs)II.8	−20.42
7218	−16	Sc(s)II.8	−20.74
5179*	−37	Sc(s)II–III	−22.39
7300	−14	Sc(s)I–II	−21.83
7309	−10	Sc(rs)I–II	−21.81
7314	−26	Sc(s)III	−21.26
7361	−30	ScII–III:	−19.82
7412	−42	Sc(rs)I–II	−20.98
7418	−37	Sc(rs)I.8	−20.66
7424	−41	Sc(s)II.3	−20.67
7448	+15	Sc(r)II.2	−21.97
7456	−39	Sc(s)II–III	−20.57
7541	+4	Sc(s)II	−21.99
7590	−42	Sc(s)II	−20.78
7599	−42	Sc(s)II	−21.26
5325*	−41	Sc(s)II–III	−20.30
7679	+3	Sc(s)/Sa (tides?)	−22.38
7689	−54	Sc(rs)II	−20.86
5332*	−36	Sc(s)II–III	−19.90
7713	−38	Sc(s)II–III	−19.60

NGC IC*	δ	TYPE	$M_{B_T}^{o,i}$
		SBc	
255	−11	SBc(r)II.3	−20.66
268	−5	SBc(r)I–II	−22.37
New 1	−6	SBc(s)II.2	−19.85
521	+1	SBc(rs)I	−22.88
672	+27	SBc(s)III	−19.87
685	−53	SBc(r)II	−20.39
925	+33	SBc(s)II–III	−21.07
1073	+1	SBc(rs)II	−20.90
1090	−0	SBc(s)I–II	−21.74
1179	−19	SBc(rs)I–II	−20.88
1249	−53	SBc(s)II	−19.98
1313	−66	SBc(s)III–IV	−19.66
1933*	−52	SBc(s)II–III	−18.76
1341	−37	SBc(s)II–III	−19.51
1493	−46	SBc(rs)III	−19.84
1536	−56	SBc(s)pec	−19.14
1559	−62	SBc(s)II.8	−21.26
1637	−2	SBc(s)II.3	−19.72
1688	−59	SBc(s)II–III	−19.55
1796	−61	SBc(s)II	−18.47
2139	−23	SBc(s)II.3	−21.15
2339	+18	SBc(s)II	−21.83
2525	−11	SBc(s)II	−20.92
2545	+21	SBc(r)I–II	−21.54
2835	−22	SBc(rs)I.2	−20.23
3059	−73	SBc(s)III	−20.14
2522*	−32	Sc/SBc(s)I–II	−21.74
3319	+41	SBc(s)II.4	−19.66
3346	+15	Sbc(rs)II.2	−19.93
3359	+63	SBc(s)I.8 pec	−21.30
3367	+14	SBc(s)II	−22.08
3510	+29	SBc(s)	−18.12
3513	−22	SBc(s)II.2	−19.61
3769	+48	SBc(s)II	−19.15
3963	+58	SBc(rs)I–II	−22.02
749*	+43	SBc(rs)II–III	−18.65
4037	+13	SBc(s)II.3	−19.51
4064	+18	SBc(s):	−20.00
4088	+50	Sc(s)II–III/SBc	−20.53
4116	+2	SBc(r)III	−19.88
4145	+40	SBc(r)II	−20.45
4178	+11	SBc(s)II	−20.44
4189	+13	SBc(sr)II.2	−19.50
4234	+3	SBcIII.4	−19.86
4273	+5	SBc(s)II	−21.31

NGC IC*	δ	TYPE	$M_{B_T}^{o,i}$
		(SBc *continued*)	
4294	+11	SBc(s)II–III	−19.68
4487	−7	SBc(s)II.2	−19.83
4496	+4	SBcIII–IV	−20.36
4519	+8	SBc(rs)II.2	−19.76
4535	+8	SBc(s)I.3	−21.58
4561	+19	SBcIV	−19.09
4597	−5	SBc(r)III:	−19.10
4654	+13	SBc(rs)II	−21.02
4658	−9	SBc(s)I–II	−21.05
4668	−0	SBc(s)III	−19.31
4688	+4	SBc(s)II	−18.96
4713	+5	SBc(s)II–III	−19.92
4731	−6	SBc(s)III:	−21.06
4747	+26	SBc:	−19.44
5068	−20	SBc(s)II–III	−19.05
5236	−29	SBc(s)II	−21.12
5398	−32	SBc(s)II–III	−19.16
5556	−29	SBc(sr)II–III	−20.41
5597	−16	SBc(s)II	−21.25
5643	−43	SBc(s)II–III	−21.20
5669	+10	Sc/SBc(r)I–II	−20.46
5885	−9	SBc(s)II	−21.07
6239	+42	SBcIII pec	−19.53
6412	+75	SBc(s)/Sc(s)I–II	−20.60
7070	−43	SBc(s)II.8	−20.89
7090	−54	SBc: (on edge)	−20.71
7307	−41	SBc(s)II	−20.85
5273*	−37	SBc(s)II–III	−20.56
7462	−41	SBc(s)	−19.63
7496	−43	SBc(s)II.8	−20.89
7640	+40	SBc(s)II:	−20.30
7741	+25	SBc(s)II.2	−20.20
		Scd	
45	−23	Scd(s)III	−19.45
941	−1	ScdIII	−20.12
1494	−49	Scd(s)II	−19.68
2188	−34	ScdIII	−18.86
3044	+1	Scd (on edge)	−20.30
4144	+46	ScdIII	−17.78
4183	+43	Scd (on edge)	−19.90
4244	+38	Scd	−18.76
4490	+41	ScdIII pec	−20.70
4540	+15	Scd(s)III–IV	−19.19

NGC IC*	δ	TYPE	$M_{B_T}^{o,i}$
		(Scd *continued***)**	
4592	−0	ScdIII	−19.82
5474	+53	Scd(s)IV pec	−18.39
7064	−52	Scd (on edge)	−18.65

SBcd

NGC IC*	δ	TYPE	$M_{B_T}^{o,i}$
1744	−26	SBcd(s)II-III	−19.40
3287	+21	SBcd(s)III	−19.62
New 3	−9	SBcd(s)III	−19.98
5984	+14	SBcdIII:	−19.60
5201*	−46	SBcdII	−19.82

Sd, Sdm

NGC IC*	δ	TYPE	$M_{B_T}^{o,i}$
2552	+50	Sc or SdIV	−18.14
2976	+68	SdIII-IV	−17.51
3738	+54	SdIII	−17.21
4299	+11	Sd(s)III	−19.14
4395	+33	SdIII-IV	−18.57
R80	+0	SdIV	−19.91
4765	+4	SdIII:	−17.60
4790	−9	SdII	−19.43
5204	+58	SdIV	−18.11
5585	+56	Sd(s)IV	−18.46
5052*	−69	Sd (on edge)	−16.08
5152*	−51	SdmIV-V	−14.6
7793	−32	Sd(s)IV	−18.85

SBd

NGC IC*	δ	TYPE	$M_{B_T}^{o,i}$
4236	+69	SBdIV	−18.41
4242	+45	SBdIII	−19.09
4710*	−67	SBd(s)IV	−18.28

Sm, Im

NGC IC*	δ	TYPE	$M_{B_T}^{o,i}$
SMC	−73	ImIV-V	−16.99
625	−41	Amorphous or ImIII	−17.33
1156	+25	SmIV	−18.32
1569	+64	SmIV	−16.22
3109	−25	SmIV	−17.28
3952	−3	S or Sm	−19.30
4190	+36	SmIV	−15.48
4449	+44	SmIV	−18.84
4532	+6	SmIII-IV	−19.70
4656	+32	Im	−20.03
4700	−11	Sc or Sm	−19.95
4662*	−64	ImIII	−17.18
6822	−14	ImIV-V	−15.25

SBm, SBc/SBm, IBm

NGC IC*	δ	TYPE	$M_{B_T}^{o,i}$
LMC	−69	SBmIII	−18.43
2366	+69	SBmIV-V	−16.73
3664	+3	SBmIII-IV	−19.39
3782	+46	SBmIV	−18.11
4214	+36	SBmIII	−18.79
4861	+35	SBmIV-V:	−18.64
5464	−29	IBmIII	−20.65
7107	−45	SBc(s)/SBmIII-IV	−20.80
7764	−41	SBmIII	−20.14

S

NGC IC*	δ	TYPE	$M_{B_T}^{o,i}$
275	−7	S pec (tidal)	−20.27
1487	−42	S pec (tides)	−19.01
3274	+27	SIV	−17.05
3691	+17	S	−18.23
3690	+58	S pec	−22.30
3952	−3	S or Sm	−19.30
3955	−22	S pec	−19.95
3985	+48	S	−19.04
4348	−3	S on edge	−21.01
4485	+41	S (tidal)	−19.22

NGC IC*	δ	TYPE	$M_{B_T}^{o,i}$
		(S continued)	
4630	+4	S	−19.23
5074	+31	S	−21.27
5128	−42	S0+S pec	−22.6
5313	+40	S:	−20.88
6052	+20	S pec	−21.69
7625	+16	S pec	−20.38

SB

NGC IC*	δ	TYPE	$M_{B_T}^{o,i}$
3729	+53	SB (ring) pec	−20.16
3912	+26	SB (late) pec	−20.15
4389	+45	SB pec	−18.24
4670	+27	SB pec	−19.01
5334	−0	SB:	−20.55

Special Types

NGC IC*	δ	TYPE	$M_{B_T}^{o,i}$
520	+3	Amorphous	−21.3
625	−41	Amorphous or Im III	−17.33
1531	−32	Amorphous	−18.9
1705	−53	Amorphous	−17.0
1800	−32	Amorphous	−17.3
2968	+32	Amorphous or S0₃ pec	−19.73
3034	+69	Amorphous	−18.6
3043	+59	?	−21.5
3077	+68	Amorphous	−17.2
3125	−29	Amorphous	−18.2
3353	+56	?	−18.5
3448	+54	Amorphous?	−20.2
3773	+12	pec jet	−18.2
4694	+11	Amorphous	−19.49
5253	−31	Amorphous	−18.2
5326	+39	?	−20.7
6835	−12	Amorphous?	−19.8
7252	−24	merger	−22.02

PART IV

Some Statistical Properties of the Catalog

THIS REVISED SHAPLEY-AMES (*RSA*) catalog provides a particularly useful sample for statistical studies because the velocity coverage is nearly complete and because the catalog completeness function $f(m)$ is well determined (page 4). The luminosity and density functions of the nearby galaxies can be obtained from the *RSA* data from calculations of the bias (Sandage, Tammann, and Yahil, 1979; Tammann, Yahil, and Sandage, 1979; Yahil, Sandage, and Tammann, 1980) that start from the apparent distributions of velocities, apparent magnitudes, and absolute magnitudes. Because the distributions are of general interest in themselves, we summarize some of them in this section.

Distribution of Morphological Types

Histograms of the types are given in Figure 1, divided into the ordinary and the barred families. The types in the main catalog have a somewhat finer subdivision than shown in this figure, as we have combined the transition cases (such as E/S0, S0/a, Sab, Sbc) with the

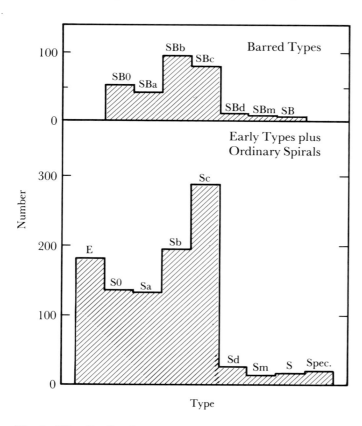

Fig. 1. The distribution of types in the complete *RSA*. Intermediate and transitional types have been combined with the main types in these histograms.

main groups. In those cases where the type is in doubt and where two possibilities are given [such as NGC 3390, listed as type S0₃(8) or (Sb)], the galaxy has been counted twice, once in each bin. Hence the sum of the numbers is greater than the 1246 entries in the catalog.

The distribution of the types is as follows:

Ordinary		*Barred*	
E + E/S0	173	SB0 + SB0/SBa	48
S0 + S0/a	142	SBa + SBab	42
Sa + Sab	123	SBb + SBbc	96
Sb + Sbc	187	SBc	77
Sc	293	SBcd + SBd	8
Scd + Sd	26	SBm + IBm	9
Sm + Im	13	SB	5
S	16		
Special	18		
	991		285

Note the very few galaxies of types Sd, SBd, and later. This is due entirely to the observational bias in the apparent-magnitude-limited *RSA* caused by the fainter mean absolute magnitude of these types compared with Sc, SBc, and earlier galaxies. The density of Sd and later types per unit volume of space, in fact, dominates the true distribution (see Tammann *et al.*, 1979).

Distribution of Velocities

The distribution of velocities v_0, i.e., reduced to the centroid of the Local Group, is shown in Figure 2, binned in 250 km s^{-1} intervals. Only nine galaxies of the 1245 listed have negative velocities, and these are either in the Local Group or are within 4° of the center of the Virgo Cluster. The Virgo cases are clearly in the tail of the virial velocity distribution of that cluster.

This observed distribution diagram contains the information which, together with the distribution of apparent and absolute magnitudes, permits the luminosity, completeness, and density functions to be calculated. The calculation starts by noting that the number of galaxies with velocity v in the velocity interval Δv that are listed in the *RSA* in a particular region of the sky of solid angle Ω is

$$N(v) \Delta v = \Omega\, v^2\, \Delta v\, H_0^{-3} \int_{-\infty}^{+\infty} \varphi(M) f(m) D(v)\, dM,$$

where H_0 is the Hubble constant, $\varphi(M)$ is the differential luminosity function (i.e., the number of galaxies per unit volume at M per unit magnitude interval), $f(m)$ the

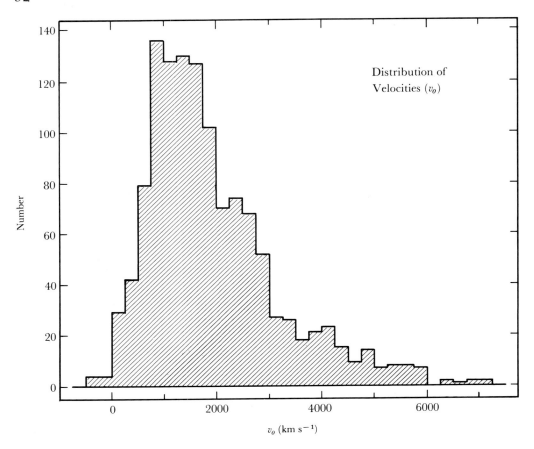

Distribution of
Velocities (v_0)

Fig. 2. The distribution of reduced velocities v_0 in the *RSA* ($n = 1245$), binned in 250 km s^{-1} intervals. (NGC 7119 with $v_0 = 9825$ km s^{-1} is not plotted.)

v_0 (km s^{-1})

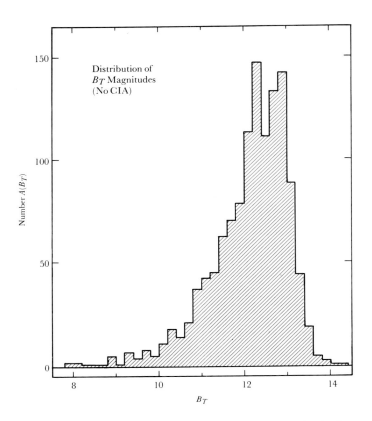

Distribution of
B_T Magnitudes
(No CIA)

B_T

Fig. 3. The number of galaxies in the *RSA* at magnitude B_T (not corrected for galactic or internal absorption) in the interval $\Delta B_T = 0^m2$ mag.

completeness function, and $D(v)$ the density of galaxies [normalized to $D(v) = 1$ for the homogeneous case]. A linear velocity-distance relation is assumed, and the variables are connected by $m = M + 5 \log v + 16.51$, which assumes a Hubble constant of 50 km s^{-1} Mpc.

Use of the $\varphi(M), f(m)$, and $D(v)$ functions determined from these data (Sandage *et al.*, 1979; Tamman *et al.*, 1979; Yahil *et al.*, 1980) reproduces the histogram in Figure 2 by summing the separate calculations from this equation, providing that the sky is divided into coherent regions over which particular values of the density $D(v)$ have relevance.

Note from Figure 2 the few numbers of *RSA* galaxies with $v_0 > 4000$ km s^{-1}. Hence, the grasp of the catalog is hardly further than ~ 80 Mpc with any statistical significance.

Distribution of Apparent Magnitudes and the Completeness Factors

Figure 3 shows the distribution of B_T magnitudes, not corrected for galactic absorption (A^0 of column 13) nor for internal absorption (A^i of column 14). A histogram (not shown) of *corrected* magnitudes $B_T{}^{0,i}$ is similar, but is, of course, shifted toward brighter magnitudes. The

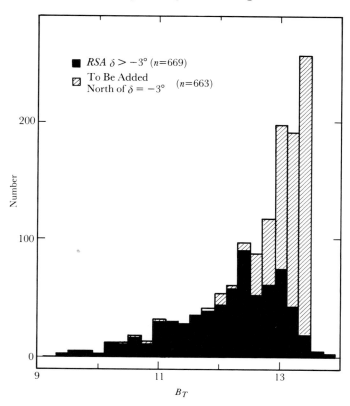

Fig. 4. Illustrates the incompleteness of the *RSA* as listed. The solid histogram is the distribution of apparent B_T magnitudes for all galaxies in the *RSA* north of declination $-3°$. The hatched additions are the galaxies north of $\delta = -3°$ not listed in the *RSA* that are brighter than $B_T = 13^m4$, found by reducing the Zwicky Catalogs to the B_T system.

expected count per magnitude interval $A(B_T)$ can be calculated from the fundamental equation of stellar statistics with the adopted $\varphi(M), f(m)$, and density functions. And because these functions were determined from the reverse analysis of Figures 2 and 3, the agreement of the prediction with the observed distribution of Figure 3 is of course good.

The incompleteness of the *RSA* is shown in Figure 4, where the solid histogram represents counts in the *RSA* for galaxies with declinations north of $-3°$ The hatched histogram is for galaxies from the Table of Additional Bright Galaxies in Appendix A. These should have been included in the original Shapley-Ames but were not. The completeness function $f(m)$ agrees well with the ratio of the hatched to the solid histograms at any given apparent magnitude.

The incompleteness begins at about $B_T \simeq 12^m$ and becomes severe by $B_T = 12^m5$. Surprisingly, however, there are a number of galaxies even brighter than $B_T = 12^m0$ that should also have been included. Ten of these are low-surface-brightness dwarfs ($M_B \lesssim -17^m0$). Two

additional galaxies (IC 342 and the Circinus system) lie at very low galactic latitude. This shows the strong bias of the *SA* against low-surface-brightness galaxies. The brightest full-sized systems whose absence in the *SA* cannot be explained in this way are NGC 676, NGC 3507, and NGC 660.

For convenience we list the 20 known galaxies that are brighter than $B_T = 12^m0$ missing from the *RSA*. The absolute magnitudes are from Kraan-Korteweg and Tammann (1979).

Missing Galaxies Brighter than $B_T = 12.0$

Name	B_T	b	M_B
Sculptor	9.00	-83	-10.6
Fornax	9.04	-65	-12.0
IC 342	9.10	$+10$	-20.7
IC 1613	9.96	-60	-14.8
NGC 676	10.20	-54	$\ldots$
U 7658	10.80	$+74$	-20.4
Leo I	10.81	$+49$	-9.6
NGC 3507	11.03	$+63$	$\ldots$
IC 2574	11.03	$+43$	-17.0
Circinus	11.25	-3	-19.2
Ho II	11.27	$+32$	-16.7
WLM	11.29	-73	-15.3
NGC 660	11.62	-47	$\ldots$
IC 520	11.70	$+34$	$\ldots$
IC 10	11.71	-3	-16.2
NGC 2805	11.78	$+40$	$\ldots$
NGC 2770	11.80	$+42$	$\ldots$
Sextans B	11.89	$+43$	-15.5
IC 239	11.93	-19	$\ldots$
Sextans A	11.93	$+39$	-15.2

Distribution of Absolute Magnitudes

The distribution of absolute magnitudes for all galaxies in the catalog with redshifts is shown in Figure 5. The very few galaxies fainter than $M_{B_T}{}^{o,i} = -18^m$ is a result of the *intrinsic* bias of the magnitude-limited catalog. The absolutely fainter galaxies are denied entry into the listing in appreciable numbers because the apparent magnitude limit is too bright for distances where the volume becomes sufficiently large. This natural bias is so severe that the true differential luminosity function rises monotonically from $M_B \simeq -23^m$ to at least -16^m, whereas the apparent distribution in Figure 5 begins to fall already fainter than $M_B \simeq -22^m$. The method of calculating this apparent distribution from the luminosity and completeness functions is given elsewhere (Sandage, Tammann, and Yahil, 1979).

For convenience we list here the 13 *RSA* galaxies that are brighter than $M_{B_T}^{o,i} = -23^m0$ and the 11 galaxies fainter than $M_{B_T}^{o,i} = -17^m0$.

Brightest Galaxies

Name	$M_{B_T}^{o,i}$	Type
NGC 1961	-23.68	Sb(rs)II pec
2832	-23.32	E3
772	-23.29	Sb(rs)I
1275	-23.27	E pec
3478	-23.27	Sc(s)?
309	-23.25	Sc(r)I
5230	-23.22	Sc(s)I
7119	-23.21	Sc(s)II
3646	-23.13	Sbc(r)II
7184	-23.10	Sab pec
7469	-23.06	Sbc(s)I.8
1316	-23.08	Sa pec(merger?)
958	-23.03	Sbc(s)II

Faintest Galaxies

Name	$M_{B_T}^{o,i}$	Type
NGC 147	-14.36	dE5
185	-14.59	dE3 pec
IC 5152	-14.60	SdmIV–V
NGC 6822	-15.25	ImIV–V
4190	-15.51	SmIV
221	-15.53	E2
205	-15.72	S0/E5pec
4150	-15.73	S0₃(4)/Sa
1569	-16.22	SmIV
2366	-16.73	SBmIV–V
SMC	-16.99	ImIV–V

The comparison of the maximum luminosity of E and spiral galaxies depends, of course, on the adopted correction for intrinsic absorption. Without corrections, the brightest spiral is NGC 1961 with $M_{B_T}^{o,i} = -23^m04$ which is ~ 0.3 fainter than the brightest elliptical.

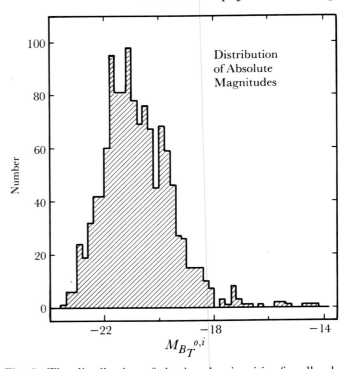

Fig. 5. The distribution of absolute luminosities for all galaxies in the *RSA* that have redshifts, using magnitudes corrected for internal and galactic absorption. The true luminosity function (i.e., the distribution per unit volume) rises monotonically. The fall of the apparent function fainter than -22 is due to the observational bias.

PART V

The Illustrations

The system of luminosity classes introduced by van den Bergh (1960a, b, c) is a major advance in galaxy classification. The principal observational materials available to van den Bergh were the paper prints of the National Geographic–Palomar Sky Survey, and his illustrations of the system were taken from them. Although satisfactory to define the principles of the system, these materials are sometimes inadequate owing to small scale and insufficient photographic latitude in the centers of high-surface-brightness spirals.

With this in mind, we have adopted the precepts of van den Bergh but have set up the standards anew. The system of the *RSA* is defined by these new type examples and is illustrated in the set of 15 panels that follow.

Each of the first 13 panels contains galaxies of the same luminosity class. The galaxies within each panel are arranged in order of their absolute magnitudes, so as to visualize at a glance how the form changes (if at all) with luminosity. The forms within any given luminosity class are similar, despite differences of at least a factor of 10 in absolute luminosity. From this, and from a detailed analysis (Sandage, Tammann, and Yahil, 1979; Tammann, Yahil, and Sandage, 1979), it is clear that although the luminosity-class designation is very useful as a descriptive device, the original hope that it is a good indicator of absolute luminosity has not been realized.

The great dispersion in absolute magnitude is illustrated explicitly in the last two panels, where extreme examples of the dispersion are shown.

Technical details and descriptions of the galaxies are given on the page facing each of the 15 sets of reproductions. The symbols preceding the plate number identify the telescope; the letters that follow identify the observer. The telescopes are coded as follows: P200 for the Palomar Hale 5-meter reflector, P48 for the 1.2-meter Palomar-Schmidt, W100 for the 2.5-meter Mount Wilson Hooker, W60 for the 1.5-meter Mount Wilson 60-inch, C100 for the Las Campanas 2.5-meter du Pont, and W10 for the Mount Wilson 10-inch refractor (used by Henize in South Africa for the SMC plate). Of the 84 galaxies illustrated (of which six are shown twice), 51 were photographed with the P200, 17 with the C100, 11 with the W100, 2 with the W60, 2 with the P48, and 1 with the W10.

The observers are coded as follows: B = Baade, Bm = Baum, Dr = Dressler, He = Henize, H = Hubble, MH = Humason, Ro = Rose, and S = Sandage.

Other information such as absolute magnitude, redshift, and orientation of the photograph are given in the legends. The scale of each photograph is indicated by the horizontal line marked on each reproduction. Most of these marks are 120 arcsec long, but a few are one-tenth of this. Note the differences in enlargement. Those prints having the longest horizontal lines are, of course, of galaxies with the smallest angular diameter, and hence the images contain fewer resolution elements. Note therefore that these generally show the most grain and the largest star images owing to the finite seeing.

The galaxies illustrated in the 15 panels are listed in Table 3.

TABLE 3. GALAXIES ILLUSTRATED AS TYPE EXAMPLES

NGC/Name	Type	$M_{B_T}^{o,i}$	v_o km s^{-1}	Telescope*	NGC/Name	Type	$M_{B_T}^{o,i}$	v_o km s^{-1}	Telescope*
23	SbI–II	−22.86	4836	P200	4321	Sc(s)I	−21.91 V	1464	P200
157	Sc(s)I–II	−22.19	1813	P200	4395	SdIII–IV	−18.57	304	P200
210	Sb(rs)I	−21.86	1875	P200	4540	Scd(s)III–IV	−19.19 V	1184	W100
224	SbI–II	−21.61 L	−10	P48	4569	Sab(s)I–II	−22.31 V	−373	P200
247	Sc(s)III–IV	−18.62 S	227	C100	4592	ScdIII	−19.82	903	W100
598	Sc(s)II–III	−19.07 L	69	P48	4593	SBb(rs)I–II	−22.35	2505	P200
613	SBb(rs)II	−22.24	1534	C100	4725	Sb/SBb(r)II	−22.47	1167	W100
615	Sb(r)I–II	−21.59	1971	P200	4800	Sb(rs)II–III	−19.32	808	W60
628	Sc(s)I	−21.75	861	P200	5005	Sb(s)II	−21.78	982	W100
864	Sbc(r)II–III	−21.50	1707	P200	5055	Sbc(s)II–III	−21.34	550	W100
1058	Sc(s)II–III	−19.27	746	P200	5204	SdIV	−18.11 M	329	P200
1087	Sc(s)III.3	−21.43	1628	W100	5248	Sbc(s)I–II	−21.19	1049	P200
1156	SmIV	−18.32	558	P200	5364	Sc(r)I	−21.16	1144	P200
1232	Sc(rs)I	−22.57	1775	P200	5395	SbII	−22.69	3584	W100
1313	SBc(s)III–IV	−19.66	261	C100	5457	Sc(s)I	−21.51 M	372	P200
1437	Sc(s)II	−20.22 F	1067	C100	5585	Sd(s)IV	−18.46 M	441	P200
1493	SBc(rs)III	−19.84	910	C100	5676	Sc(s)II	−22.11	2239	W60
1569	SmIV	−16.22	144	P200	5806	Sb(s)II.8	−20.23	1260	W100
1637	SBc(s)II.3	−19.72	715	P200	5985	SBb(r)I	−22.65	2694	P200
2146	SbII pec	−21.36	1106	P200	6643	Sc(s)II	−21.64	1743	P200
2223	SBbc(r)I.3	−22.04	2529	C100	6699	Sbc(s)I.2	−21.91	3360	C100
2276	Sc(r)II–III	−22.09	2648	P200	6753	Sb(r)I	−22.64	3001	C100
2366	SBmIV–V	−16.73 N	281	P200	6822	ImIV–V	−15.25 L	15	P200
2403	Sc(s)III	−19.47 N	299	P200	7205	Sb(r)II.8	−21.48	1379	C100
2427	Sc(s)II–III	−19.47	707	C100	7217	Sb(r)II–III	−21.66	1234	P200
2500	Sc(s)II.8	−18.66	615	P200	7331	Sb(rs)I–II	−22.60	1114	P200
2523	SBb(r)I	−22.45	3638	P200	7769	Sbc(s)II–III	−22.38	4606	P200
2525	SBc(s)II	−20.92	1395	C100	7793	Sd(s)IV	−18.85 S	241	C100
2541	Sc(s)III	−18.93	646	P200	IC 749	SBc(rs)II–III	−18.65	827	P200
2763	Sc(r)II	−20.48	1658	C100	IC 1613	ImV	−14.59 L	−66	P200
2903	Sc(s)I–II	−20.96	472	P200	Ho I	ImV	−14.40 N	310	P200
2976	SdIII–IV	−17.51 N	168	P200	Ho II	ImIV–V	−16.78 N	337	P200
3031	Sb(r)I–II	−20.75 N	124	P200	Ho IX	ImV	−13.54 N	175:	P200
3059	SBc(s)III	−20.14	984	C100	Leo A	ImV	(−13.1) L	−10	P200
3109	SmIV	−17.28	129	C100	Peg Dwarf	Im V	(−11.5) L	61	P200
3294	Sc(s)I.3	−20.79	1566	W100	Sextans A	ImV	(−15.2) L	117	P200
3347	SBb(r)I	−22.31	2626	C100	Sextans B	ImIV–V	(−15.5) L	132	P200
3351	SBb(r)II	−20.66	641	P200	SMC	ImIV–V	−16.99 L	−19	W10
3504	Sb(s)/SBb(s)I–II	−21.11	1480	P200	WLM	ImIV–V	(−15.5) L	−5	P200
3627	Sb(s)II.2	−21.48	593	W100					
3646	Sbc(r)II	−23.13	4100	W100					
3756	Sc(s)I–II	−20.55	1372	P200					
3992	SBb(rs)I	−21.83	1134	P200					
4254	Sc(s)I.3	−21.59 V	2301	P200					
4304	SBbc(s)II	−20.97	2327	C100					

* Telescope used for the plates in this volume.

97

ScI

Galaxies of this luminosity class have a well-defined global spiral pattern, which appears at first glance to be highly regular. In the cases of NGC 4321 (M100), NGC 628, and NGC 3294, there exist two principal arms emerging from the central regions. These are thin and well formed for nearly three-fourths of a revolution. The arms do, however, branch in the outer regions, where they appear to be composed of separate fragments rather than to be coherent structures of a double-arm system.

The fragmentation and branching is especially well seen in NGC 1232, the brightest galaxy shown here. The fragmentation is also pronounced over the outer two-thirds of M101.

The two very regular arms in NGC 5364 are relatively easy to trace in the outer regions, although the SW major arm *is* fragmented there. However, the connections of these arms onto the inner ring suggest that they cross one another near the ring at the NE major axis. Some color is given to this suggestion by the absorption pattern of one arm as it is silhouetted against the other near this crossing.

The first five galaxies in the panel are within ~ 1 mag of the same absolute luminosity. The faintest galaxy (NGC 3294) is 1.8 mag fainter than NGC 1232.

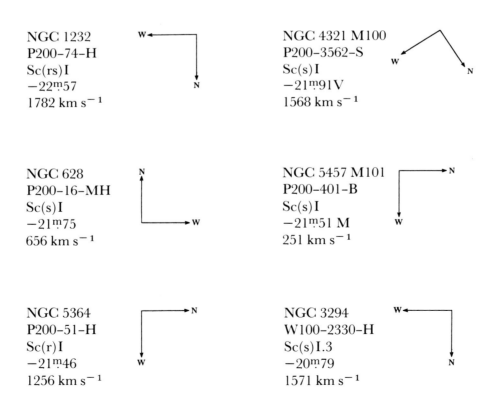

NGC 1232
P200–74–H
Sc(rs)I
$-22\overset{m}{.}57$
1782 km s^{-1}

NGC 4321 M100
P200–3562–S
Sc(s)I
$-21\overset{m}{.}91$V
1568 km s^{-1}

NGC 628
P200–16–MH
Sc(s)I
$-21\overset{m}{.}75$
656 km s^{-1}

NGC 5457 M101
P200–401–B
Sc(s)I
$-21\overset{m}{.}51$ M
251 km s^{-1}

NGC 5364
P200–51–H
Sc(r)I
$-21\overset{m}{.}46$
1256 km s^{-1}

NGC 3294
W100–2330–H
Sc(s)I.3
$-20\overset{m}{.}79$
1571 km s^{-1}

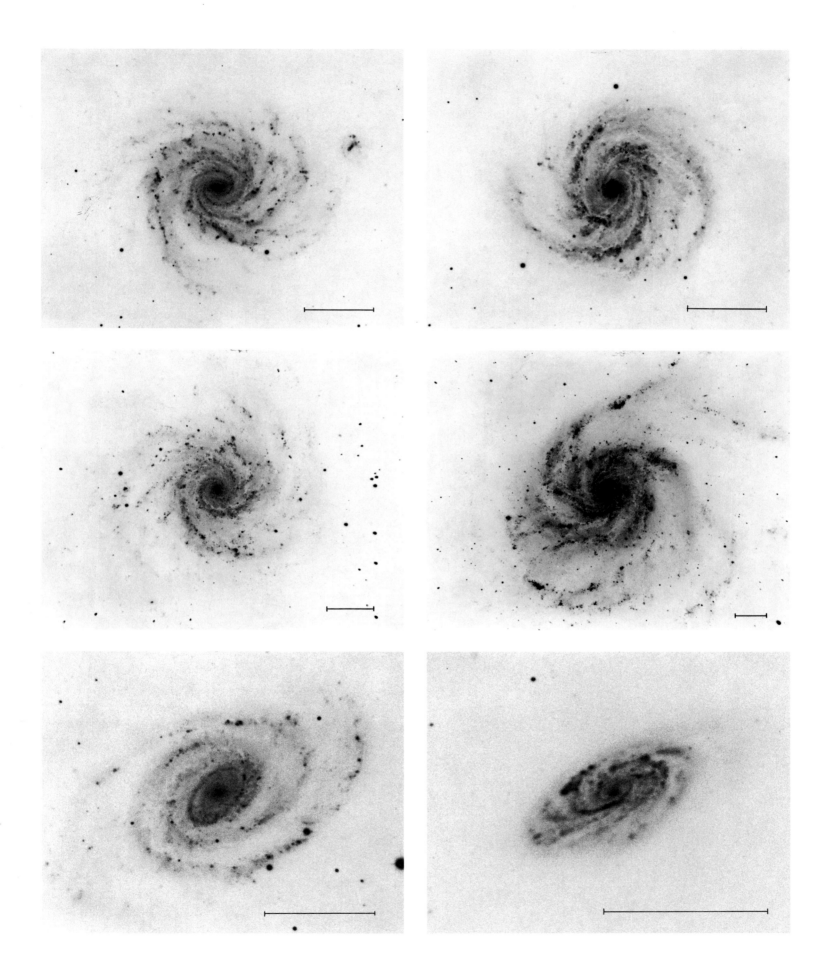

ScI-II

The arms in galaxies of this luminosity class are not as narrow or well defined as those of ScI. Two examples of thick-arm spirals are NGC 157 and NGC 4254 in the Virgo Cluster. Of the remaining four, NGC 2223, NGC 2903, and NGC 3756 have thin arms, while the arms in NGC 5248 (of Sbc type) are thick over the inner bright disk but become very thin and are of low surface brightness beyond the lens.

The arm pattern for all galaxies of this class is still nearly as well defined as in ScI systems but, as in NGC 4254, has a raggedness not present in ScI systems.

The spread in absolute luminosities for galaxies of types ScI and ScI-II is large, ranging from -18^m3 to -23^m4 (Tammann, Yahil, and Sandage, 1979), with the bulk of the distribution from $-20^m > M_{B_T}^{o,i} > -23^m$. This is a factor of 15 in luminosity (and presumably a comparable range in mass). The similarity of all galaxies here and in the ScI panel shows that the form does not appreciably change over this large range in absolute magnitude, and hence that luminosity is not the chief factor that governs the luminosity class of a galaxy.

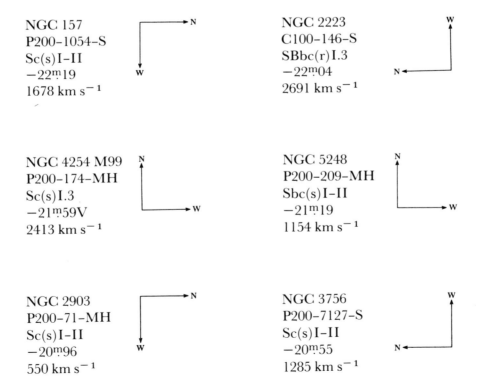

NGC 157
P200-1054-S
Sc(s)I-II
-22^m19
1678 km s^{-1}

NGC 2223
C100-146-S
SBbc(r)I.3
-22^m04
2691 km s^{-1}

NGC 4254 M99
P200-174-MH
Sc(s)I.3
-21^m59V
2413 km s^{-1}

NGC 5248
P200-209-MH
Sbc(s)I-II
-21^m19
1154 km s^{-1}

NGC 2903
P200-71-MH
Sc(s)I-II
-20^m96
550 km s^{-1}

NGC 3756
P200-7127-S
Sc(s)I-II
-20^m55
1285 km s^{-1}

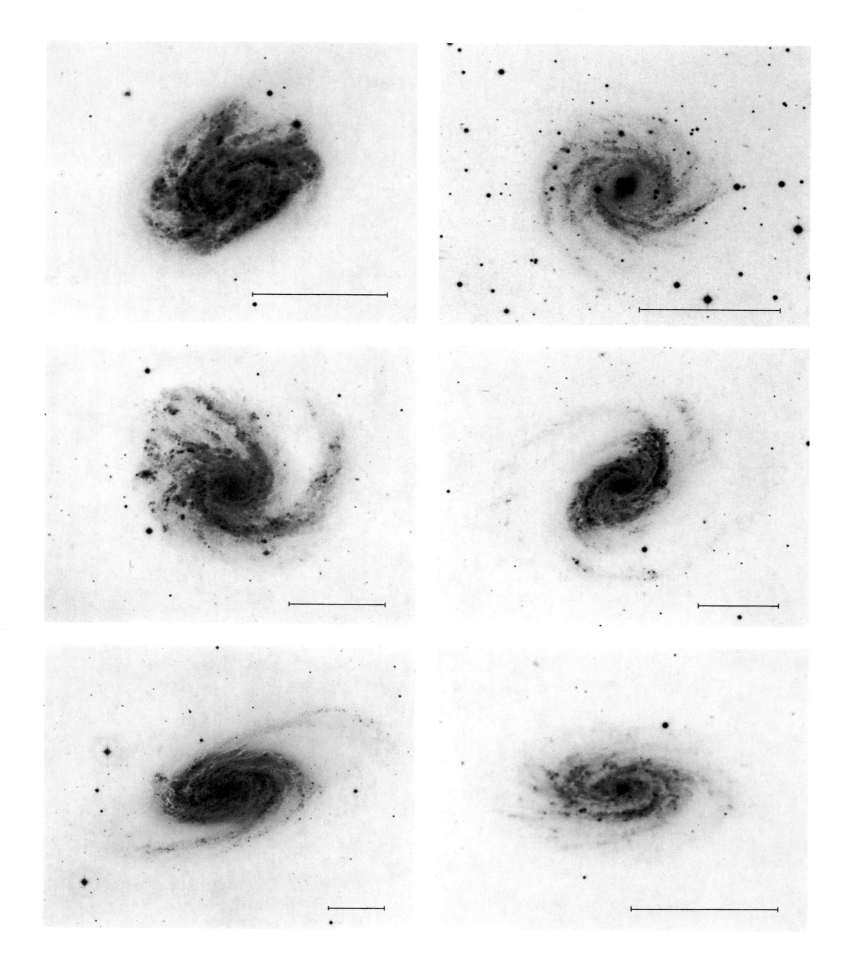

101

ScII

The pattern of the arms has now become more ragged than in ScI–II systems, but the arms are still moderately easy to trace. They are thicker than in ScI systems and cover a larger fraction of the underlying disk.

Although the range of absolute luminosities here is ~ 2 mag, again there is no appreciable difference in the appearance of NGC 5676 (the brightest) and NGC 1437 (the faintest). Note also that the surface brightness of the arm system (i.e., of the population I) is closely the same within this group and in fact is not fainter than for the galaxies illustrated in the ScI and ScI–II panels.

The two main inner arms in the barred spirals (NGC 4304 and NGC 2525) spring from the ends of the bar, as in NGC 1300 (Sandage, 1961, p. 45), and the arms are well defined for about half a revolution beyond their junction with the bar. However, in NGC 4304 especially, the arms beyond this point begin to fragment and decrease in surface brightness. The presence of these faint fossil outer arms becomes a common feature in galaxies of later luminosity class.

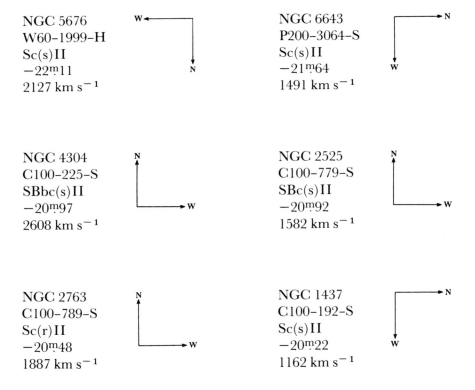

NGC 5676
W60–1999–H
Sc(s)II
$-22^{m}11$
2127 km s^{-1}

NGC 6643
P200–3064–S
Sc(s)II
$-21^{m}64$
1491 km s^{-1}

NGC 4304
C100–225–S
SBbc(s)II
$-20^{m}97$
2608 km s^{-1}

NGC 2525
C100–779–S
SBc(s)II
$-20^{m}92$
1582 km s^{-1}

NGC 2763
C100–789–S
Sc(r)II
$-20^{m}48$
1887 km s^{-1}

NGC 1437
C100–192–S
Sc(s)II
$-20^{m}22$
1162 km s^{-1}

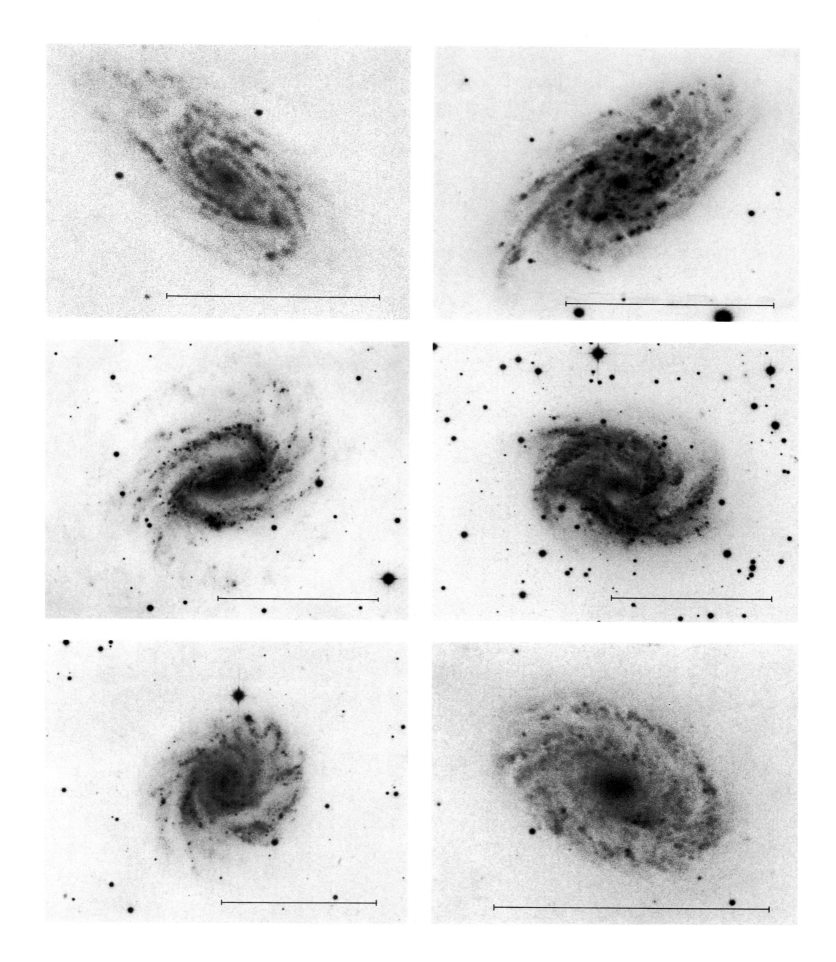

103

ScII–III

The chief characteristic of this class is a definite but chaotic arm structure, with most of the underlying disk covered by the Population I material whether in the regions of the wide diffuse arms or in the "interarm" region. The arms are not nearly as well separated as in ScI systems.

For the classifier, one puts galaxies into the ScII–III bin by asking "is the galaxy as regular as ScII systems or as chaotic as ScIII"? The systems M33 (ScII–III) and NGC 2403 (ScIII) served as the archetypes. Our use of M33, the faintest of the six shown here, follows van den Bergh (1960a,c).

Five of the six galaxies here are similar. NGC 2276 is the brightest at $M_{B_T}^{o,i} = -22^m09$. It has a more easily traced global pattern and better-defined filamentary segments to the arms than NGC 2427 or NGC 1058, for example; yet the entire face of the lens is covered with these fragments. They are not as organized as in ScI or even ScII systems—hence the classification ScII–III is based entirely on the degree of disorder of the arm system.

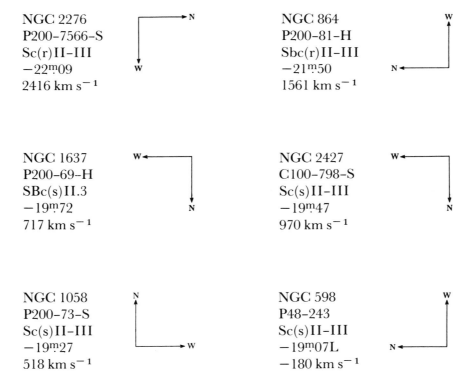

NGC 2276
P200-7566-S
Sc(r)II-III
-22^m09
2416 km s^{-1}

NGC 864
P200-81-H
Sbc(r)II-III
-21^m50
1561 km s^{-1}

NGC 1637
P200-69-H
SBc(s)II.3
-19^m72
717 km s^{-1}

NGC 2427
C100-798-S
Sc(s)II-III
-19^m47
970 km s^{-1}

NGC 1058
P200-73-S
Sc(s)II-III
-19^m27
518 km s^{-1}

NGC 598
P48-243
Sc(s)II-III
-19^m07L
-180 km s^{-1}

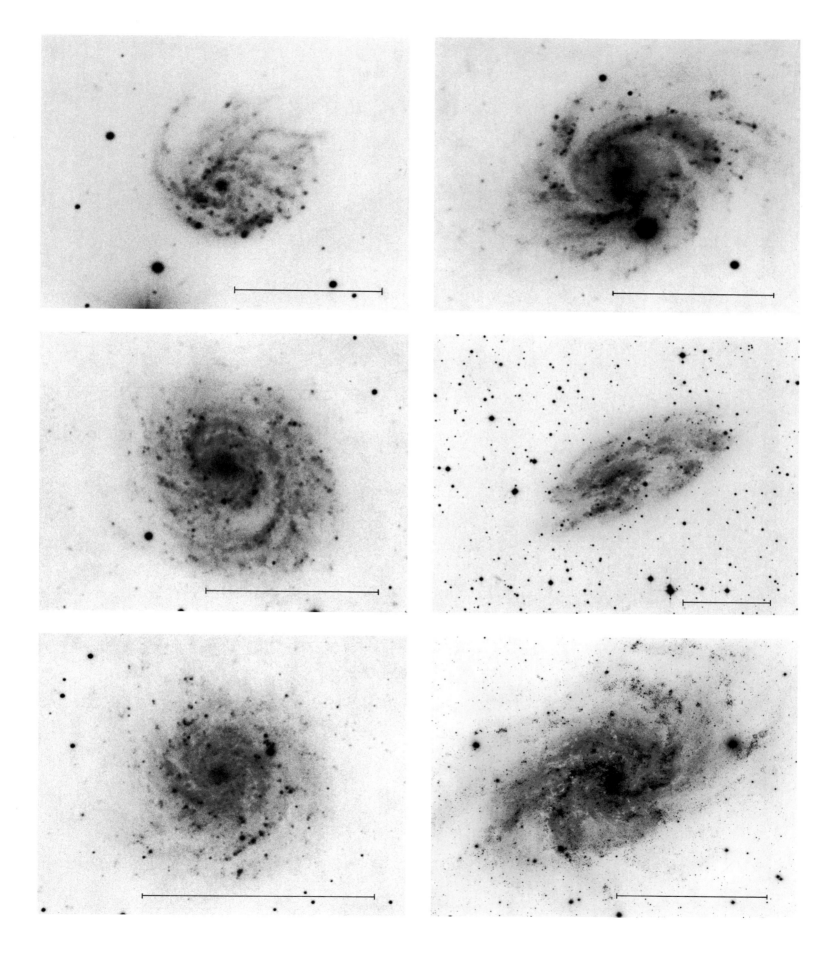

105

ScIII

By now the arms are difficult to trace, and nearly the whole of the face of the galaxy is covered with young star-producing regions. The brightest of the galaxies is NGC 1087 ($M_{B_T}{}^{o,i} = -21^m4$), which clearly is of later luminosity class than any of the galaxies shown in the ScI, ScI–II, ScII, and ScII–III panels. Hence, the range in absolute magnitude among ScIII galaxies is large, with a spread of 2.8 mag among the six illustrated galaxies. The faintest is NGC 2500 at $M_{B_T}{}^{o,i} = -18^m66$; yet its form is more regular than that of NGC 3059, which is 1.4 mag brighter and is certainly more regular than NGC 1087. The total range in M for galaxies classified as ScIII in the *RSA* is ~ 3.5 mag. And although better plates are needed for some of these, there is no question that the range is large, since the absolute magnitude of NGC 7314 ($M_{B_T}{}^{o,i} = -21^m26$) and of NGC 4808 ($M_{B_T}{}^{o,i} = -18^m51$), for example, is secure.

The phenomenon of outer, faint-surface-brightness "fossil arms" is clearly shown in several of the galaxies in this panel. Note particularly the very faint outer fragments of arms in NGC 3059, NGC 1493, and NGC 2403. We took NGC 2403 to be the type example of ScIII.

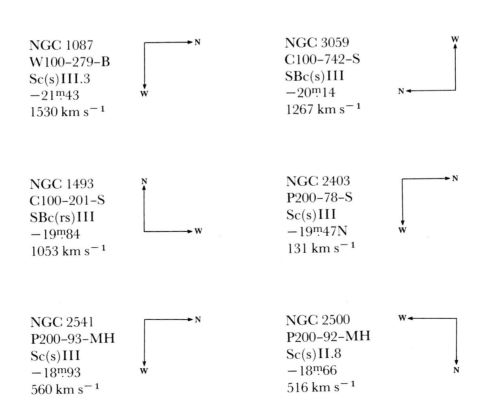

NGC 1087
W100–279–B
Sc(s)III.3
−21^m43
1530 km s⁻¹

NGC 3059
C100–742–S
SBc(s)III
−20^m14
1267 km s⁻¹

NGC 1493
C100–201–S
SBc(rs)III
−19^m84
1053 km s⁻¹

NGC 2403
P200–78–S
Sc(s)III
−19^m47N
131 km s⁻¹

NGC 2541
P200–93–MH
Sc(s)III
−18^m93
560 km s⁻¹

NGC 2500
P200–92–MH
Sc(s)II.8
−18^m66
516 km s⁻¹

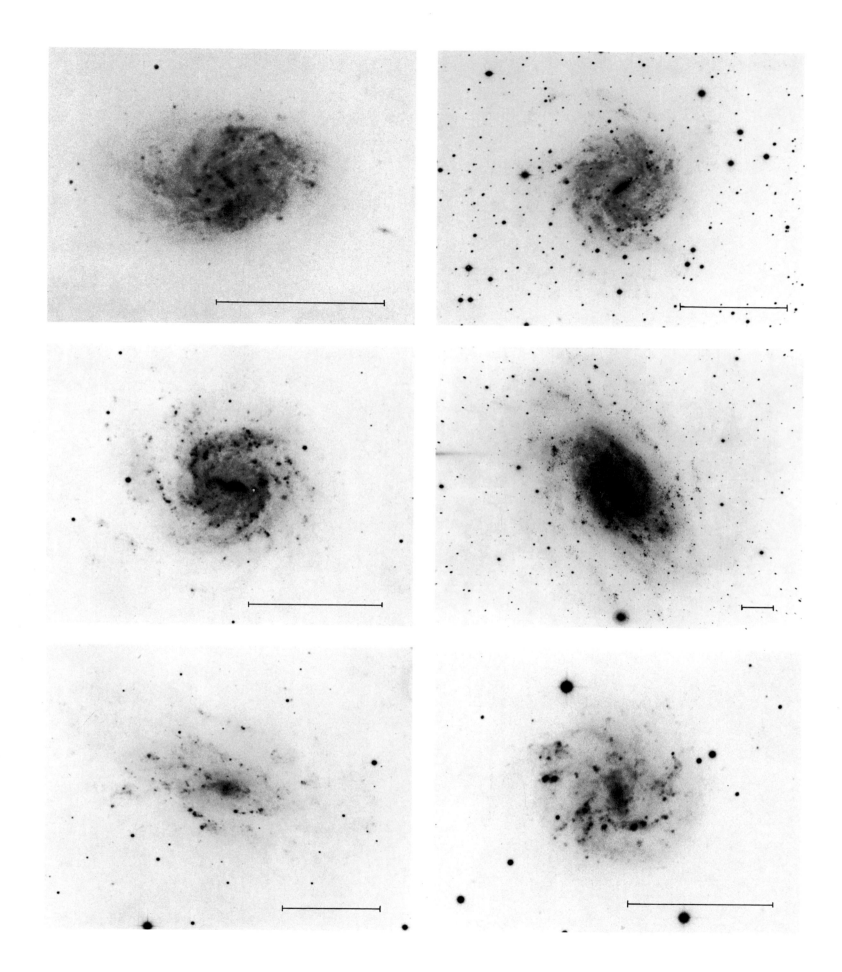

ScIII–IV

A spiral pattern is still traceable in galaxies of this luminosity class, but with some difficulty in certain cases such as NGC 4540. The *pattern* is evident, but coherent arms hardly exist. At most, one traces only fragments, such as those on the north side of NGC 2976 and the generally chaotic pieces in NGC 1313 and NGC 4395.

Notice also the great difference in average surface brightness among galaxies of this class. The SdIII–IV system of NGC 4395/4401 is of much lower surface brightness than NGC 4540; yet the highest-surface-brightness galaxy among those shown here is NGC 2976, which has the faintest absolute magnitude at $M_{B_T}^{o,i} = -17^m51$. Clearly, surface brightness is not an indicator of absolute luminosity for these Population I systems (although there *is* a pronounced absolute magnitude–surface brightness relation for E and S0 galaxies over the range $-23^m < M < -12^m$).

The range in absolute magnitude of the galaxies shown here is ~ 2.2 mag. The range is ~ 2.8 mag among all the galaxies in the *RSA* of this type.

Note that the six illustrated galaxies contain some type Sd systems (NGC 4395/4401, and NGC 2976) and two intermediate Scd systems (NGC 4592 and NGC 4540). The difference between the Sc and Sd subtypes rests in the clarity of the arm pattern.

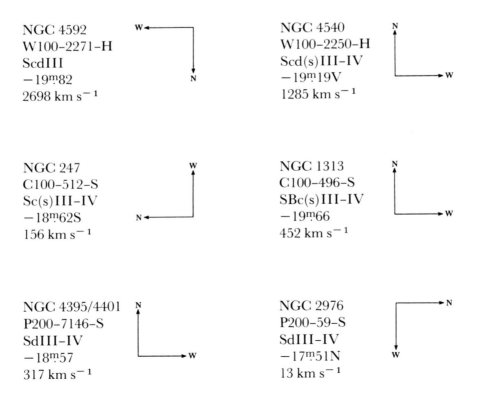

NGC 4592
W100–2271–H
ScdIII
-19^m82
2698 km s^{-1}

NGC 4540
W100–2250–H
Scd(s)III–IV
-19^m19V
1285 km s^{-1}

NGC 247
C100–512–S
Sc(s)III–IV
-18^m62S
156 km s^{-1}

NGC 1313
C100–496–S
SBc(s)III–IV
-19^m66
452 km s^{-1}

NGC 4395/4401
P200–7146–S
SdIII–IV
-18^m57
317 km s^{-1}

NGC 2976
P200–59–S
SdIII–IV
-17^m51N
13 km s^{-1}

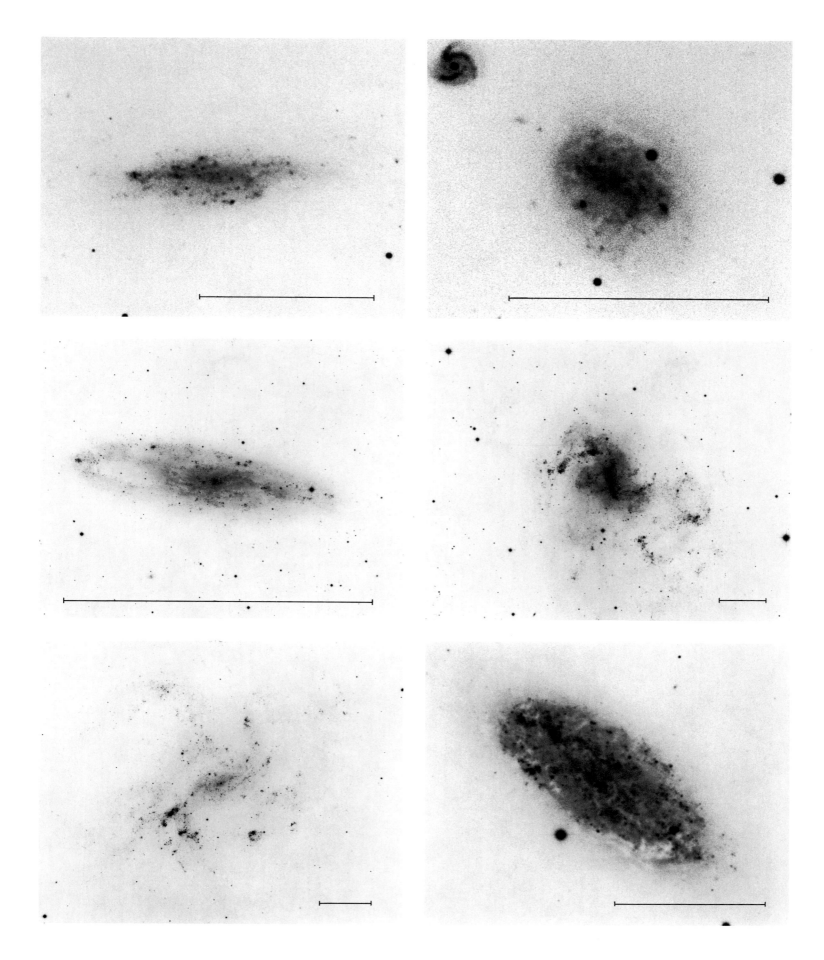

109

SdIV–SmIV

Luminosity class IV is the last in which any appreciable spiral pattern is seen, albeit often only with some imagination. Galaxies of this class are usually no longer typed as Sc, but rather Sd or Sm.

The spiral pattern is most easily traced in NGC 7793, which is the brightest of the six at $M_{B_T}^{o,i} = -18\overset{m}{.}5$. (This galaxy could perhaps be classed as SdIII–IV by comparison with the last panel, though we have not done so.) A single spiral plume, highly resolved into stars, is seen on the NW side of NGC 5585 (a companion to M101). A few "non-random" features in NGC 1156 suggest a spiral pattern similar to the imaginative case of the LMC. The pattern is not quite so subtle in NGC 5204 (another companion to M101; see Sandage and Tammann 1974c, table 3), and hence the galaxy is classed Sd.

Any spiral pattern in NGC 3109 and NGC 1569 (which are nearly edge-on) remains suggestive rather than visible. These systems are classed as SIV rather than SIV–V because of their high surface brightness.

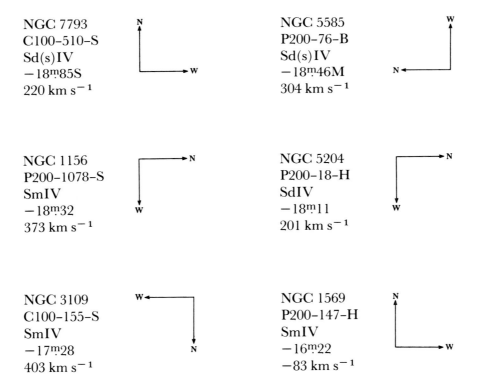

NGC 7793
C100–510–S
Sd(s)IV
$-18\overset{m}{.}85$S
220 km s^{-1}

NGC 5585
P200–76–B
Sd(s)IV
$-18\overset{m}{.}46$M
304 km s^{-1}

NGC 1156
P200–1078–S
SmIV
$-18\overset{m}{.}32$
373 km s^{-1}

NGC 5204
P200–18–H
SdIV
$-18\overset{m}{.}11$
201 km s^{-1}

NGC 3109
C100–155–S
SmIV
$-17\overset{m}{.}28$
403 km s^{-1}

NGC 1569
P200–147–H
SmIV
$-16\overset{m}{.}22$
-83 km s^{-1}

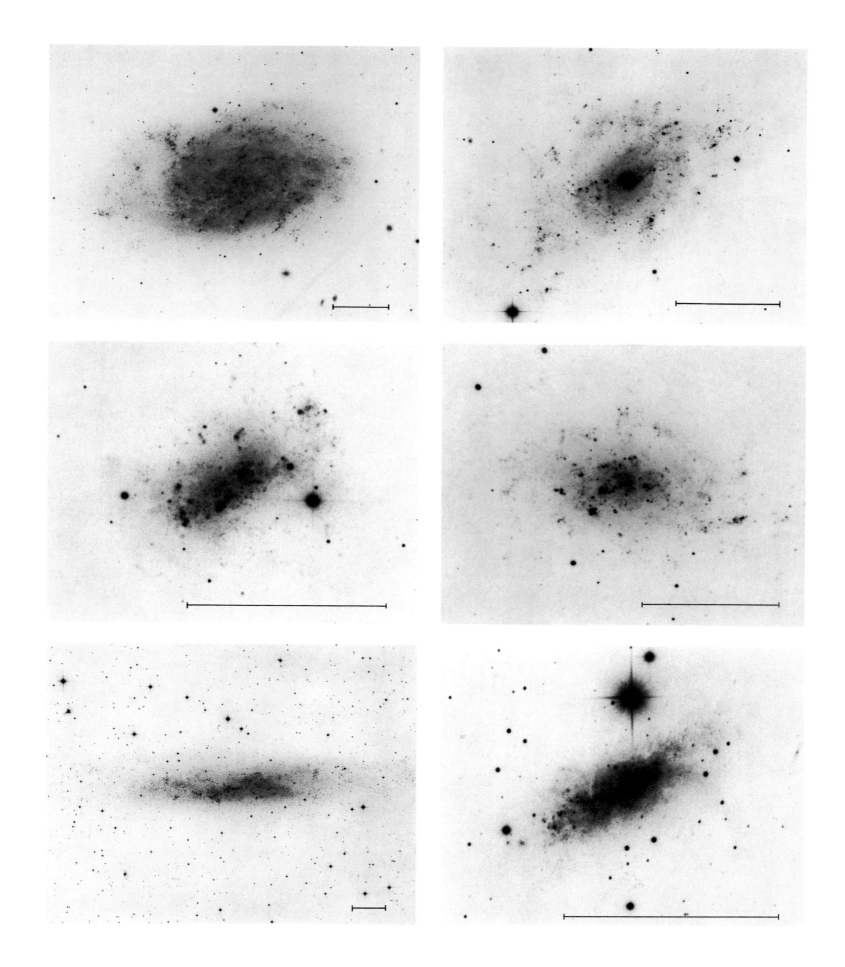

Im/SBmIV–V

No trace of spiral structure is present in galaxies of this luminosity class. All galaxies of this and of class V in the next panel have very faint absolute luminosities. Furthermore, they have such low surface brightness that they are generally absent from the *SA* (and hence the *RSA*). Of the six illustrated galaxies, only SMC, NGC 2366, and NGC 6822 are listed in the main catalog, and the exclusion becomes complete in the next panel.

The galaxies shown here are nearby. Members of the Local Group are SMC, WLM, and NGC 6822. Just beyond the Local Group, and exhibiting a slight velocity of recession, is Sextans B. The two most distant are Holmberg II and NGC 2366, which we consider to be in the M81/NGC 2403 group. Cepheid variables have been found, of course, in the two classical members of the Local Group (SMC and NGC 6822), and now also in Sextans B and WLM (Sandage, unpublished). There is no doubt that they could be found in NGC 2366 and Ho II as easily as in NGC 2403 itself (Tammann and Sandage,1968).

The resolved stars in each of these galaxies are blue and red supergiants brighter than $M_B \simeq -7^m$. These form a Population I overlay to a resolved disk of Population II stars that has been found in SMC, Sextans B, WLM, and NGC 6822. This sheet of background red stars resolves suddenly at $M_V = -3^m$, just as Baade showed for the background disk of M31. Hence, these galaxies, dominated by young Population I stars, are in fact old.

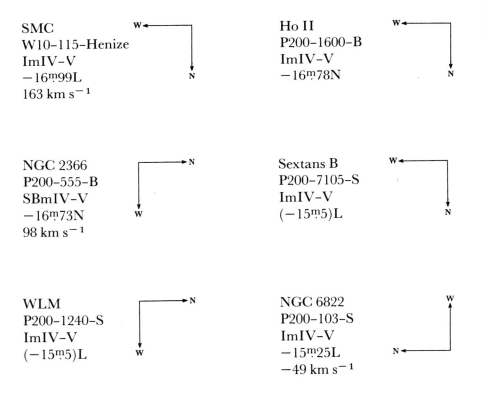

SMC
W10–115–Henize
ImIV–V
-16^m99L
163 km s^{-1}

Ho II
P200–1600–B
ImIV–V
-16^m78N

NGC 2366
P200–555–B
SBmIV–V
-16^m73N
98 km s^{-1}

Sextans B
P200–7105–S
ImIV–V
(-15^m5)L

WLM
P200–1240–S
ImIV–V
(-15^m5)L

NGC 6822
P200–103–S
ImIV–V
-15^m25L
-49 km s^{-1}

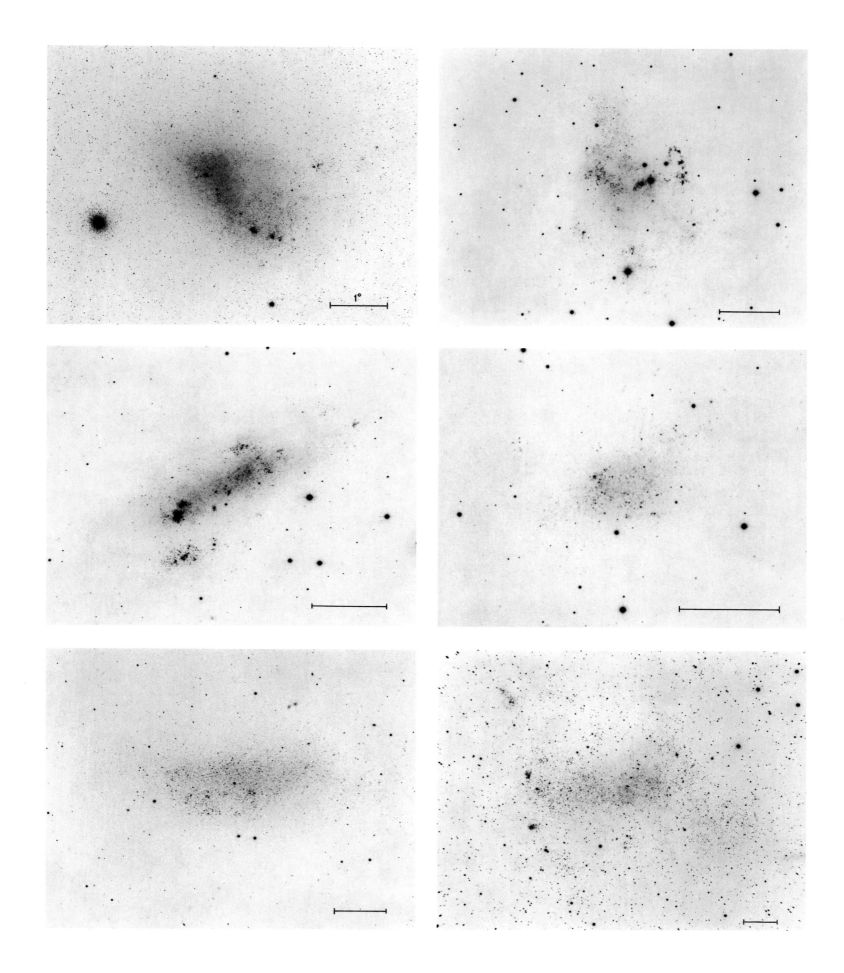

113

ImV

Galaxies of this type are highly resolved into Population I supergiants. The surface brightness is even lower than for galaxies of class IV–V.

None of the galaxies shown here are in the *RSA*. Their surface brightness is too low despite the fact that in some cases their integrated apparent magnitude is brighter than the *SA* limit.

Cepheids have been found, of course, in IC 1613 by Baade and now in Sextans A and Leo A. The background sheet of old red stars that starts at $M_V = -3^m$ has been found in IC 1613 and Sextans A, and perhaps in Leo A and the Pegasus Dwarf.

We consider these systems, except Ho I and Ho IX, to be in or very near the Local Group. These two galaxies are in the M81/NGC 2403 group. Ho IX is the dwarf companion to M81, near to the main body on the north side. It resolves into fainter blue supergiants than M81 itself (as is expected from the correlation of the brightness of the blue supergiants with that of the parent galaxy), but the red supergiants resolve at $V \simeq 20$, which is consistent with $M_V = -8^m0 \pm 0^m1$ for these stars independent of the parent's luminosity (Sandage and Tammann, 1974c). Galaxies of this type and luminosity class are expected to provide improved calibration of the absolute magnitude of the brightest resolved stars as distance indicators.

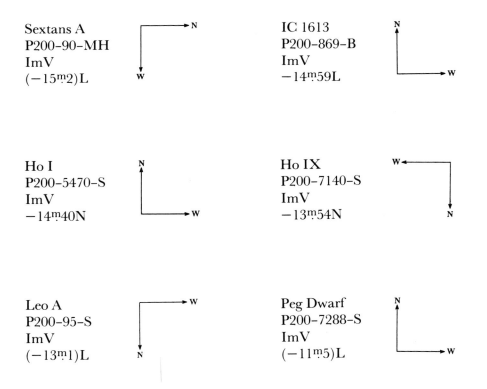

Sextans A
P200–90–MH
ImV
(-15^m2)L

IC 1613
P200–869–B
ImV
-14^m59L

Ho I
P200–5470–S
ImV
-14^m40N

Ho IX
P200–7140–S
ImV
-13^m54N

Leo A
P200–95–S
ImV
(-13^m1)L

Peg Dwarf
P200–7288–S
ImV
(-11^m5)L

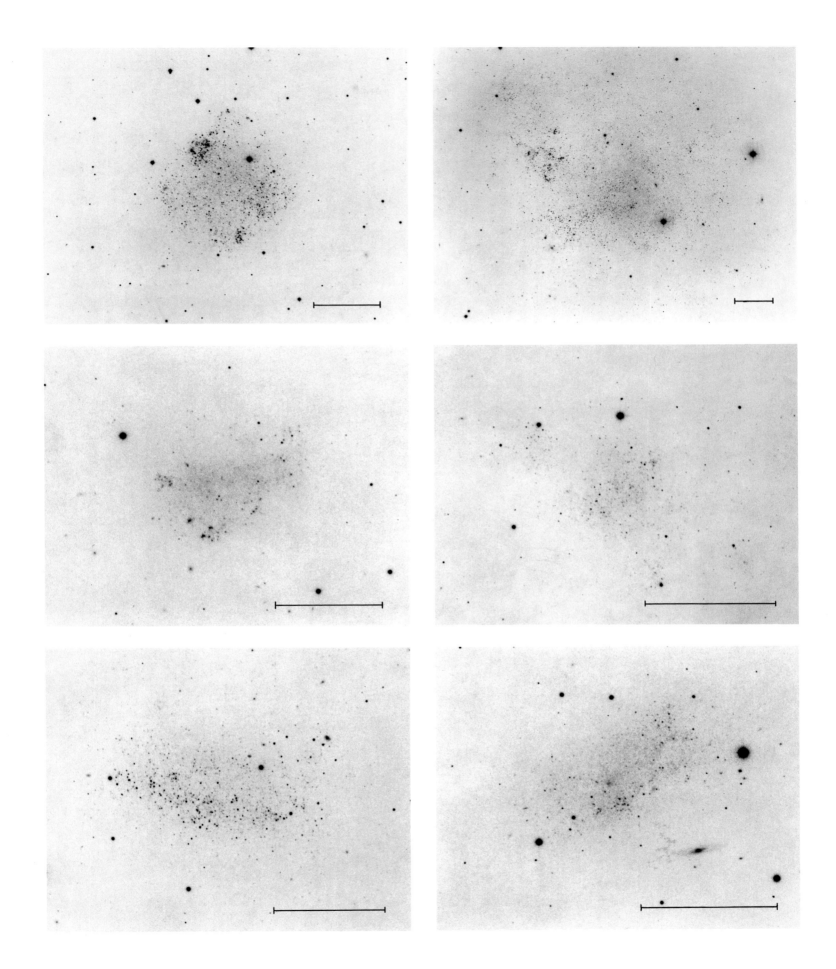

115

SbI

Luminosity classes in Sb galaxies are also assigned on the basis of the degree of order in the arm pattern. But unlike Sc galaxies, there are no entirely chaotic Sb forms. Hence the luminosity classes do not extend beyond SbIII in the *RSA* and in van den Bergh's (1960c) original list. There are no dwarf Sb galaxies. The physical reason for this may be the presence of the large central spheroid in Sb's and its absence in Sc, Sd, and Sm galaxies. This stronger central mass concentration changes the nature of the variation of rotational velocity with radius and hence, presumably, the character of the spiral pattern. Clearly the central spheroid causes a more ordered spiral pattern. In this regard note that the arms in Sa galaxies are generally even more regular than in Sb systems.

The SbI galaxies shown here cover the small range of absolute magnitude $-22\overset{m}{.}6 < M_{B_T}{}^{o,i} < -21\overset{m}{.}8$. The arms are thin, regular, and well separated. The interarm region is well defined in the multiple arm cases such as NGC 5985 and NGC 3992. There is, however, considerable branching of the arms, and in several cases two systems of arms (an inner and an outer set) exist. This is particularly true in NGC 6753 and NGC 210, where the inner set is tightly wound close to the central spheroid and the outer set is more open and slightly fragmented.

A particularly interesting galaxy is NGC 3347, with its two principal arms. Note the discontinuous break in the north arm at a bright knot. Notice also that the dust in this arm is not along the inner edge but threads the middle.

The inner arms of NGC 5985 are thin and well formed. On the west side, the outer structures are branched into a series of more radial twigs that clearly have a different pitch angle than the brighter main arm from which they radiate.

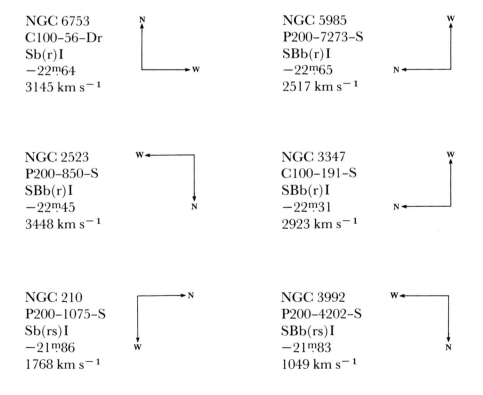

NGC 6753
C100–56–Dr
Sb(r)I
$-22\overset{m}{.}64$
3145 km s^{-1}

NGC 5985
P200–7273–S
SBb(r)I
$-22\overset{m}{.}65$
2517 km s^{-1}

NGC 2523
P200–850–S
SBb(r)I
$-22\overset{m}{.}45$
3448 km s^{-1}

NGC 3347
C100–191–S
SBb(r)I
$-22\overset{m}{.}31$
2923 km s^{-1}

NGC 210
P200–1075–S
Sb(rs)I
$-21\overset{m}{.}86$
1768 km s^{-1}

NGC 3992
P200–4202–S
SBb(rs)I
$-21\overset{m}{.}83$
1049 km s^{-1}

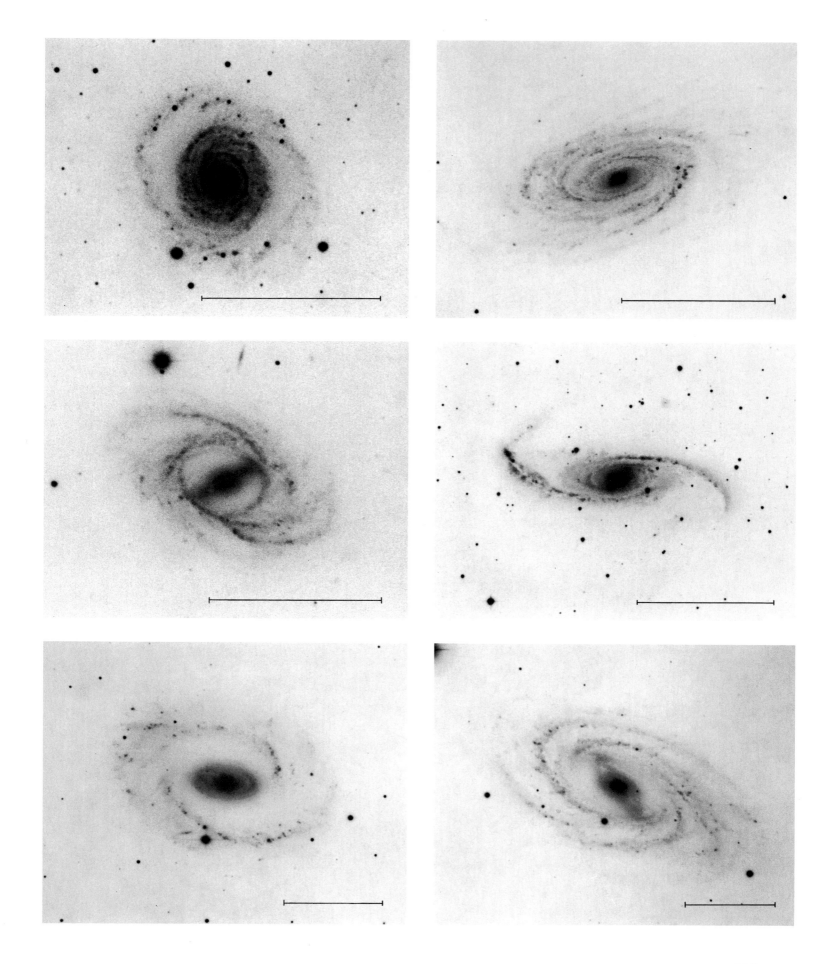

117

SbI–II

The arms here are generally thicker and slightly less regular than in SbI galaxies. The range in absolute luminosity of the illustrated galaxies is only 1.5 mag from $-22^{m}60$ to $-21^{m}11$.

A particularly interesting case is NGC 4569 (M90), with its massive, smooth, but regular system of inner and outer arms. The whole of the disk is covered by the spiral pattern, with prominent dust lanes defining the inner arms.

Notice the very regular but faint outer arms in NGC 3504, which is a transition galaxy to an SBb system. The one nearly linear dust lane on the SE side is characteristic of classical SBb systems such as NGC 1300 (Sandage, 1961, p. 45) and serves, in this case, as a diagnostic. There is a similar but less pronounced linear dust feature along the NE bar in the SB galaxy NGC 4593 shown in the upper right. Note also the low surface brightness of the outer arms of this galaxy.

The arms in NGC 7331, the brightest galaxy shown, are relatively thick, as in M31 which is represented here from a 1.2-meter Palomar Schmidt plate. The thickness and multiplicity of the arms in NGC 615 is also similar.

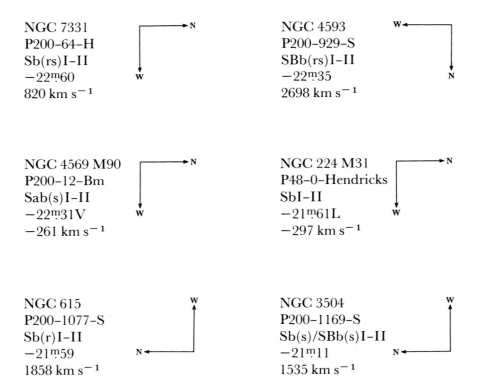

NGC 7331
P200-64-H
Sb(rs)I–II
$-22^{m}60$
820 km s^{-1}

NGC 4593
P200-929-S
SBb(rs)I–II
$-22^{m}35$
2698 km s^{-1}

NGC 4569 M90
P200-12-Bm
Sab(s)I–II
$-22^{m}31$V
-261 km s^{-1}

NGC 224 M31
P48-0-Hendricks
SbI–II
$-21^{m}61$L
-297 km s^{-1}

NGC 615
P200-1077-S
Sb(r)I–II
$-21^{m}59$
1858 km s^{-1}

NGC 3504
P200-1169-S
Sb(s)/SBb(s)I–II
$-21^{m}11$
1535 km s^{-1}

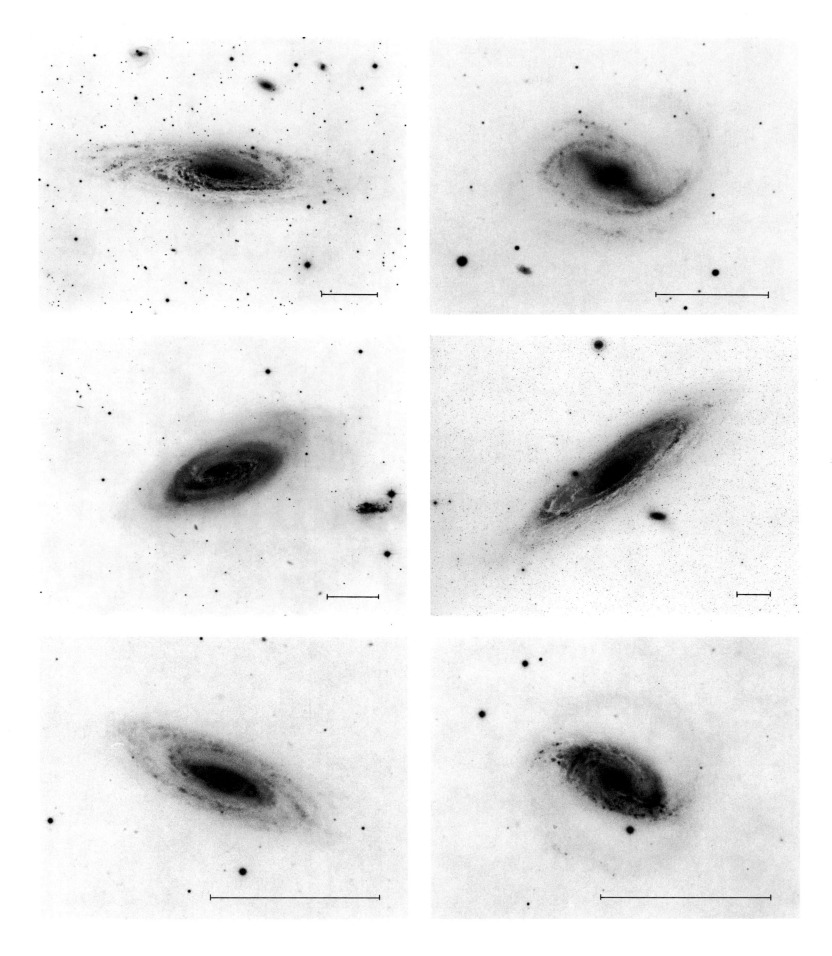

119

SbII

The progression of the arms in their degree of disorder from the SbI–II cases is evident here. The arms are generally more fragmentary and cover more of the face of the outer disk. Note the multiple nature of the arm fragments in NGC 5005 and NGC 3627, and the large amount of dust associated with these galaxies.

The twisted arm pattern in NGC 2146 suggests a warped outer disk beyond the plane defined by the flattened central spheroid and its pattern of associated dust.

Notice the very faint smooth outer arm in NGC 4725. This is particularly well seen on the paper prints of the National Geographic–Palomar Sky Survey. The inner tightly wound arms are only moderately well defined. They are difficult to trace as a coherent pattern, but exist in the form of fragments that begin at the rim of the lens at what may be the inner Lindblad resonance. These fragments can be traced for at most $\sim 100°$, and many are shorter.

A similar non-coherence of the arms is present in NGC 3351. Here the arms are thick and are of low surface brightness. The arm fragments cover much of the disk outside the inner ring.

Note the characteristic linear dust lanes in the SBb galaxy NGC 613. The lanes are also present in NGC 4725, but are not as pronounced. The four principal arms in NGC 613 have different projected forms. Either the pitch angles themselves are different, or the optical plane is warped.

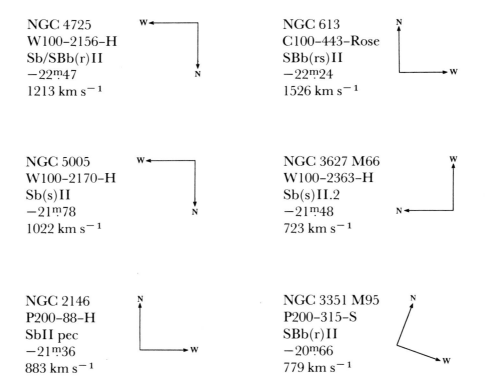

NGC 4725
W100–2156–H
Sb/SBb(r)II
$-22^{m}47$
1213 km s^{-1}

NGC 613
C100–443–Rose
SBb(rs)II
$-22^{m}24$
1526 km s^{-1}

NGC 5005
W100–2170–H
Sb(s)II
$-21^{m}78$
1022 km s^{-1}

NGC 3627 M66
W100–2363–H
Sb(s)II.2
$-21^{m}48$
723 km s^{-1}

NGC 2146
P200–88–H
SbII pec
$-21^{m}36$
883 km s^{-1}

NGC 3351 M95
P200–315–S
SBb(r)II
$-20^{m}66$
779 km s^{-1}

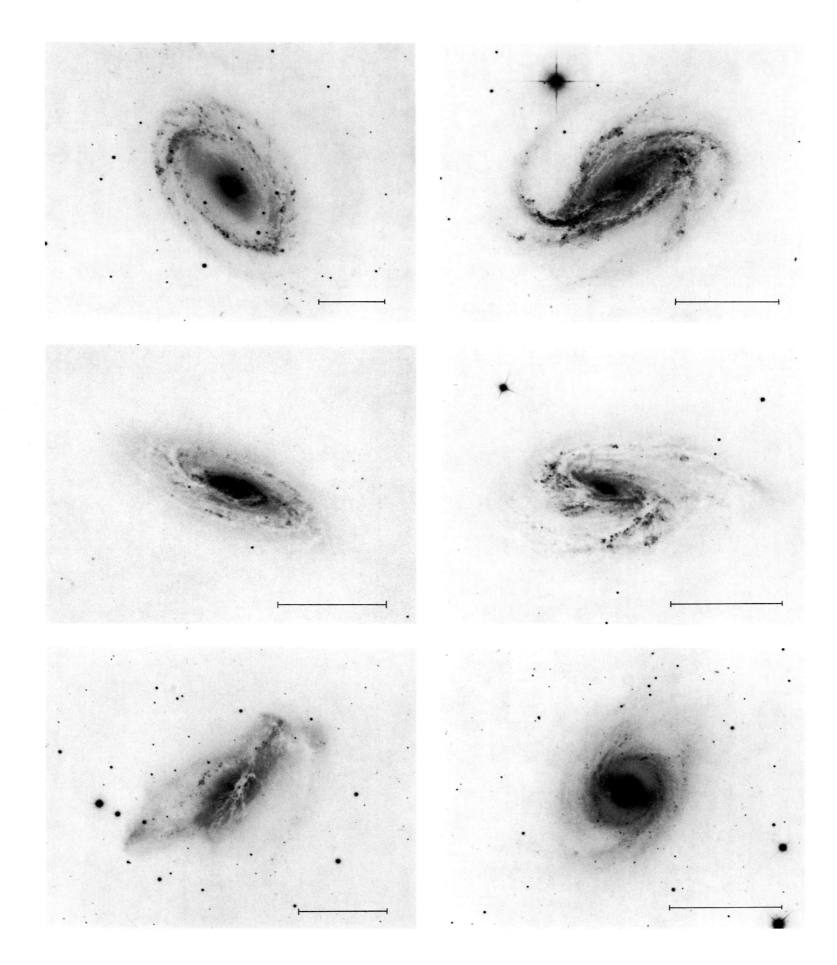

121

SbII-III

The arm pattern in Sb systems reach their maximum degree of disorder in galaxies of this luminosity class. Perhaps the most chaotic galaxy shown here is NGC 5055, classed Sbc rather than pure Sb. The fragmented filamentary arms cannot be traced, yet the general spiral pattern is clear albeit not coherent. The same comments apply to NGC 7217, which at first glance appears to have a highly regular arm pattern but which in fact again has only fragmented arms. Both NGC 7217 and NGC 5055 are late examples of NGC 2841 (*Hubble Atlas*, Sandage, 1961, p. 14) which is the type-example for the filamentary galaxy type. Many other examples of Sb galaxies with this form are given in the *Hubble Atlas* (pp. 14–18). The group also includes NGC 4800, shown here in the lower right from a W60 plate.

The absolute luminosities of the illustrated SbII–III galaxies show a wider range than in the previous three Sb panels, going from -22^m38 for NGC 7769 to -19^m32 for NGC 4800. Despite this 3-mag difference, the appearance of these galaxies does not progressively change from the upper left to the lower right. Once again we take this to mean that luminosity is not the primary factor that determines the luminosity class of a given galaxy.

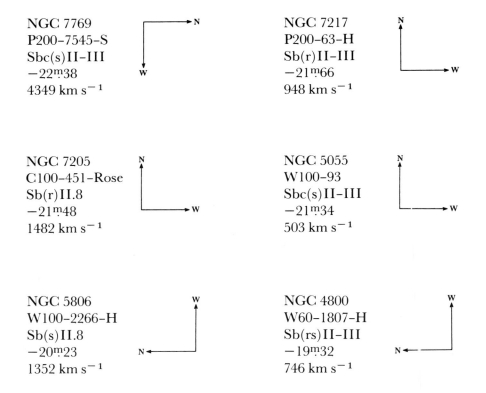

NGC 7769
P200-7545-S
Sbc(s)II–III
-22^m38
4349 km s^{-1}

NGC 7217
P200-63-H
Sb(r)II–III
-21^m66
948 km s^{-1}

NGC 7205
C100-451-Rose
Sb(r)II.8
-21^m48
1482 km s^{-1}

NGC 5055
W100-93
Sbc(s)II–III
-21^m34
503 km s^{-1}

NGC 5806
W100-2266-H
Sb(s)II.8
-20^m23
1352 km s^{-1}

NGC 4800
W60-1807-H
Sb(rs)II–III
-19^m32
746 km s^{-1}

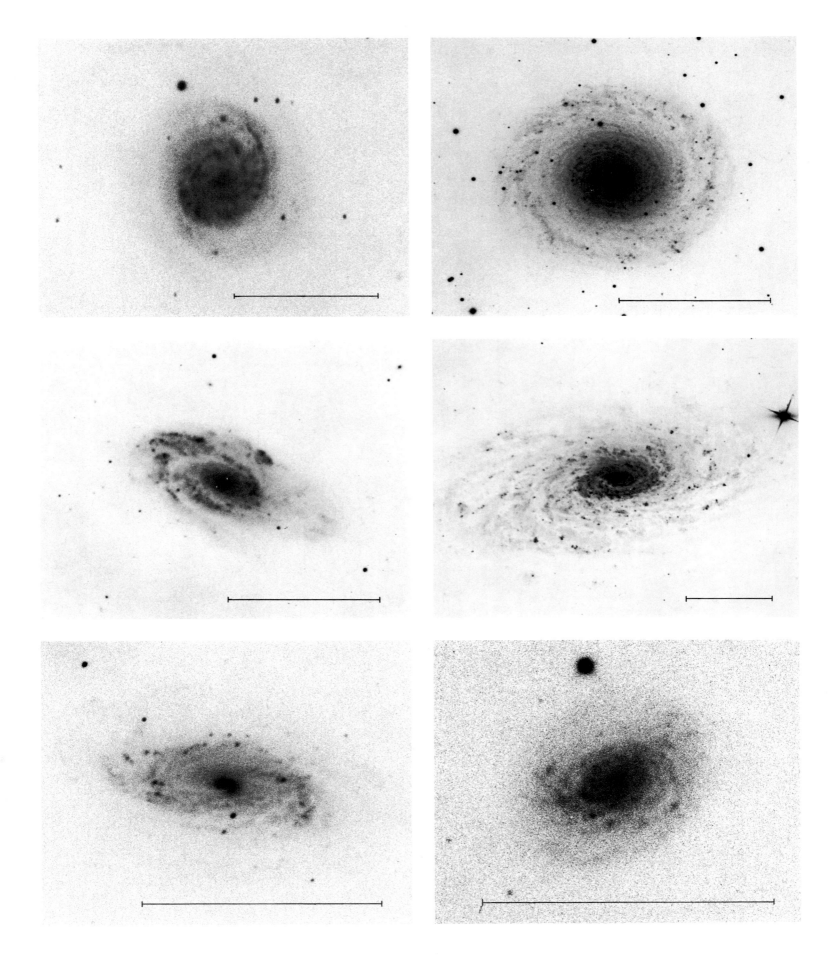

123

Intrinsic Disprion Sb

In this panel we compare Sb galaxies to show again that appearance does not correlate well with absolute luminosity.

The upper comparison is NGC 23 ($M_{B_T}^{o,i} = -22^m86$; SbI–II) with NGC 3031 (M81; $M_{B_T}^{o,i} = -20^m75$; SbI–II); NGC 23 is 2.2 mag brighter than M81, yet appears less developed even taking into account the degraded resolution due to its large redshift of 4658 km s^{-1}.

The second comparison is the pair of NGC 5394/95 with NGC 224 (M31; $M_{B_T}^{o,i} = -21^m66$; SbI–II). The larger galaxy of the double is NGC 5395, which has a redshift of 3628 km s^{-1}, while its companion, NGC 5394, has $v = 3441$ km s^{-1}; hence they are a physical pair. NGC 5395 is of type SbII, has only a single pair of arms and a small nucleus, yet is $\Delta M_{B_T}^{o,i} = 1$ mag brighter than the impressive Andromeda Nebula, which is more regular.

The final comparison is NGC 4725 [$M_{B_T}^{o,i} = -22^m47$; Sb/SBb(r)II] with NGC 3351 ($M_{B_T}^{o,i} = -20^m66$; SBbII). These galaxies are of the same luminosity class, and except for the lower surface brightness arms in NGC 3551, look similar; yet NGC 4725 is 1.8 mag brighter than NGC 3351.

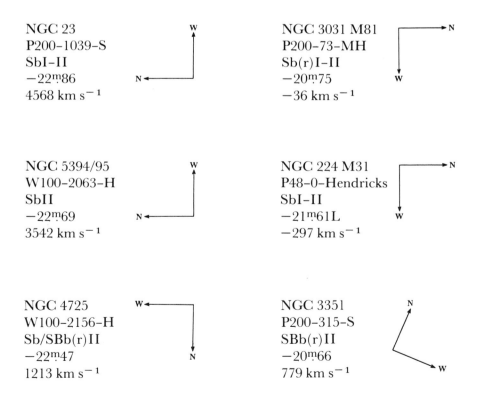

NGC 23
P200-1039-S
SbI–II
−22^{m}86
4568 km s^{-1}

NGC 3031 M81
P200-73-MH
Sb(r)I–II
−20^{m}75
−36 km s^{-1}

NGC 5394/95
W100-2063-H
SbII
−22^{m}69
3542 km s^{-1}

NGC 224 M31
P48-0-Hendricks
SbI–II
−21^{m}61L
−297 km s^{-1}

NGC 4725
W100-2156-H
Sb/SBb(r)II
−22^{m}47
1213 km s^{-1}

NGC 3351
P200-315-S
SBb(r)II
−20^{m}66
779 km s^{-1}

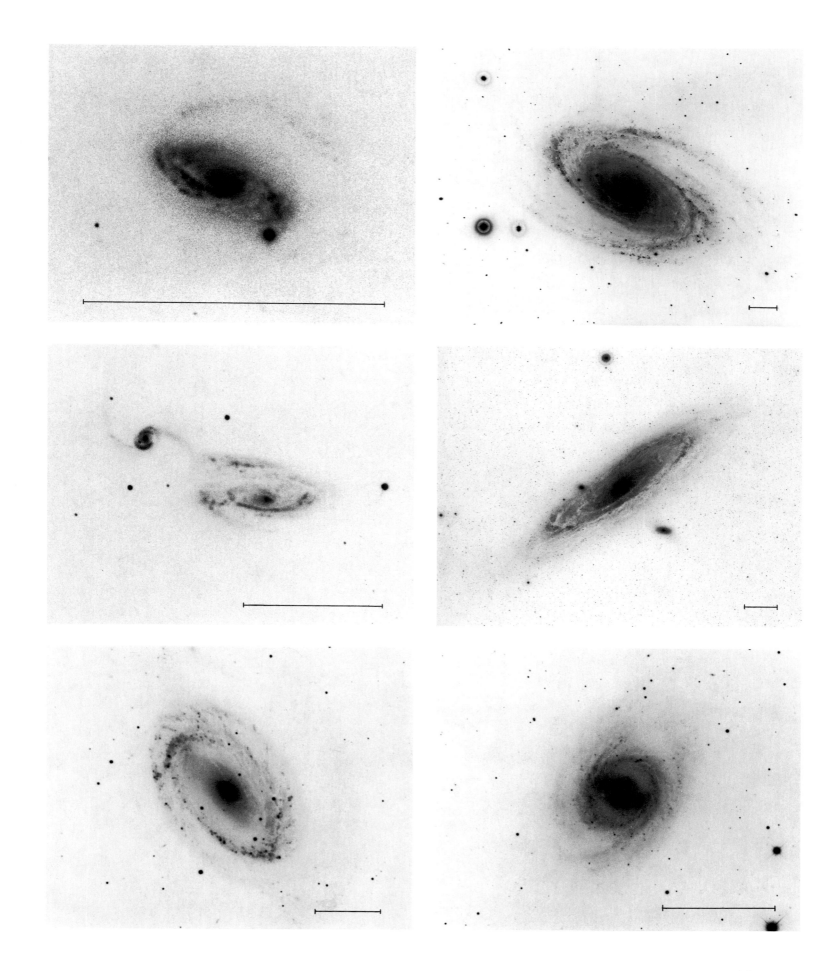

125

Intrinsic Dispersion Sc

In this final panel we give examples of pairs of Sc galaxies that have either similar appearances but greatly different absolute magnitudes or dissimilar appearances where the more chaotic of the pair has the brighter absolute magnitude. Both types of comparisons show again that luminosity class is not primarily a measure of absolute magnitude.

The first comparison is NGC 2276 ($M_{B_T}{}^{o,i} = -22^m09$; ScII–III) at the upper left with NGC 3294 ($M_{B_T}{}^{o,i} = -19^m79$; ScI.3) at the upper right. The arm pattern of NGC 3294 is more regular than that in NGC 2276, yet the two galaxies differ by $\Delta M_{B_T}{}^{o,i} = 2.3$ mag, with NGC 2276 being the brighter.

The middle comparison is NGC 3646 ($M_{B_T}{}^{o,i} = -23^m13$; SbcII) with NGC 6699 ($M_{B_T}{}^{o,i} = -21^m92$; SbcI.2). NGC 6699 is by far the more regular. The arms are well formed and are hardly fragmented, yet this galaxy is 1.2 mag fainter than the more chaotic NGC 3646 on the left. Although the broken arm pattern of NGC 3646 could possibly be due to tidal interaction with the small faint SBa galaxy NGC 3649 8 arc min away, this seems unlikely, as the projected distance is already 200 kpc and the companion is at least 3 mag fainter. (The redshift of NGC 3649 is unknown.)

The bottom comparison is NGC 1087 ($M_{B_T}{}^{o,i} = -21^m43$; ScIII.3) with IC 749 ($M_{B_T}{}^{o,i} = -18^m65$; SBcII–III). The latter is more regular by far than NGC 1087, yet it is 2.8 mag fainter. Furthermore, the very obvious later luminosity class of NGC 1087 makes its very bright luminosity of -21^m43 even more surprising.

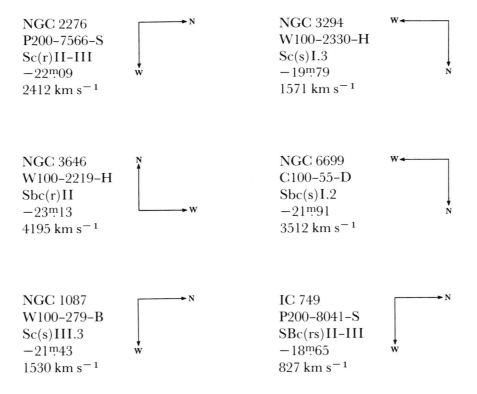

NGC 2276		NGC 3294
P200–7566–S		W100–2330–H
Sc(r)II–III		Sc(s)I.3
-22^m09		-19^m79
2412 km s^{-1}		1571 km s^{-1}

NGC 3646		NGC 6699
W100–2219–H		C100–55–D
Sbc(r)II		Sbc(s)I.2
-23^m13		-21^m91
4195 km s^{-1}		3512 km s^{-1}

NGC 1087		IC 749
W100–279–B		P200–8041–S
Sc(s)III.3		SBc(rs)II–III
-21^m43		-18^m65
1530 km s^{-1}		827 km s^{-1}

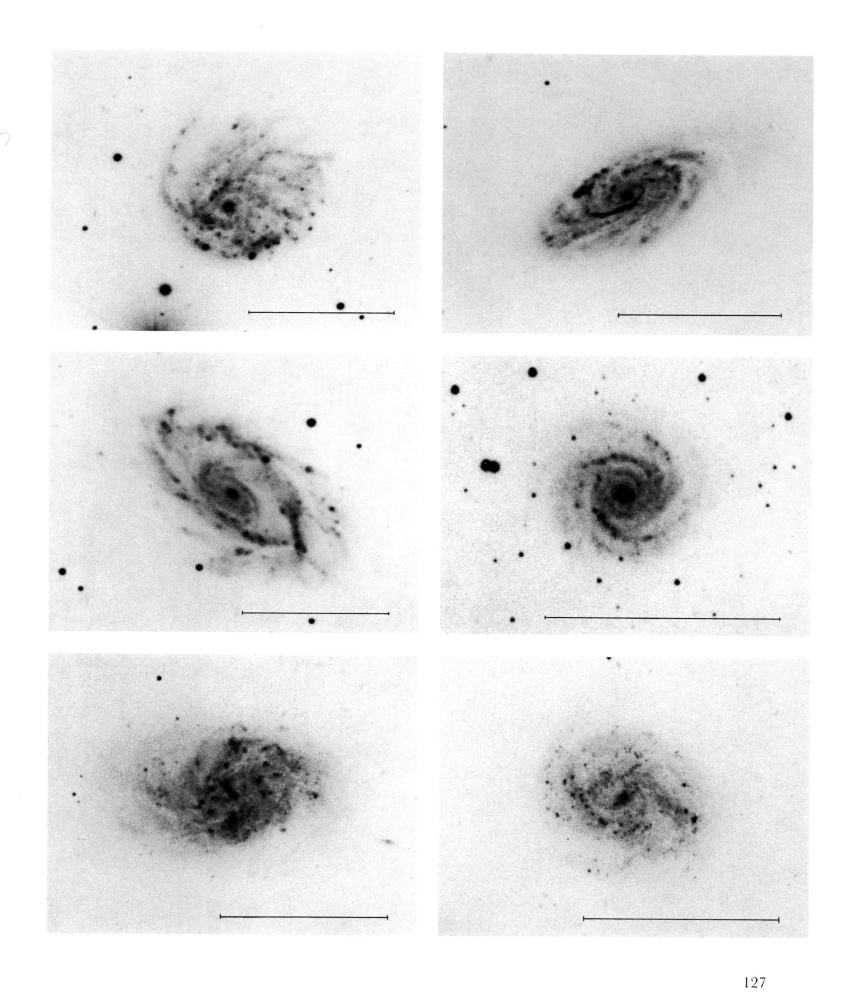

127

PART VI

Appendices

Appendix A. Table of Additional Bright Galaxies

The following tabulation contains 822 galaxies not in the *SA* but known to be brighter than $B \sim 13^m4$. Although the available information on the magnitudes of some entries is still of low quality, the tabulation provides a search list for use in any future attempt to compile a more complete catalog.

The list itself has no claim to completeness. The inclusion of a galaxy depends entirely on the availability of a magnitude value from some source. Most are drawn from the Zwicky catalog, which is limited to $\delta > -3°$. For this reason, the data for the northern hemisphere are much more complete than for the southern.

The available magnitudes are not on a uniform system. The dwarf galaxies whose magnitudes by Fisher and Tully (1975) cannot be transformed into the B_T system are listed separately at Appendix B. All other magnitudes either are published in the B_T system or have been reduced to it, as explained in the key to the sources in the footnote ending Appendix A. The important exceptions are the Zwicky magnitudes. These were transformed into the B_T system in the following way:

The B_T magnitudes between 12^m5 and 14^m5 in the *RC2* (de Vaucouleurs *et al.*, 1977) that are *not* contained in the *SA* were compared with the Zwicky magnitudes. The exclusion of the *SA* galaxies is necessary because Zwicky used the *SA* magnitudes as one set of data for his adopted system. With this exclusion, however, the overlap between the two catalogs is small, and we could detect no significant magnitude equation as a function of galaxy type or apparent magnitude diameter. But there is a well-determined zero point correction, which varies for the different volumes of the Zwicky catalog as follows:

Zwicky Volume	$B_T - m$ (Zwicky)	number	$\sigma(m)$	adopted
I	-0.40 ± 0.03	49	0.23	-0.4
II	-0.39 ± 0.05	47	0.31	-0.4
III	-0.30 ± 0.06	26	0.32	-0.3
IV	-0.18 ± 0.03	28	0.68	-0.2
V	-0.31 ± 0.08	37	0.48	-0.3
VI	-0.33 ± 0.07	37	0.42	-0.3

These corrections have been applied in the main table of this appendix.

De Vaucouleurs and Pence (1979) have reduced a set of Zwicky magnitudes for galaxies in the Virgo region into the B_T system. They employed an elaborate transformation equation determined from a considerable number of local standard galaxies. Because of the obvious variations of the magnitude systems of the different volumes of the Zwicky catalog, it would not be justified to use their transformation for all Zwicky magnitudes. Hence, we have applied only the zero point corrections as given above. A comparison of the 33 galaxies which de Vaucouleurs and Pence reduced to the B_T system with our values shows that B (de Vaucouleurs and Pence) $- B$ (here) $= +0^m12 \pm 0^m05$, with a scatter of $\sigma(B) = 0^m28$. The external errors may of course be larger, but because photoelectric checks of Zwicky magnitudes also show reasonably small error similar to our values, the converted Zwicky magnitudes in the following list should be useful for future work.

Name	Dec	Type	(B_T)	Source*
NGC 1	+27	S	13.1	Z
IC 1530	+32	S	13.1	Z
NGC 14	+15	I	13.0	Z
NGC 29	+33	S	13.2	Z
NGC 57	+17	EL	13.4	Z
NGC 63	+11	S	12.3	Z
IC 10	+10	I	11.71	4
NGC 80	+22	EL	13.10	1
NGC 97	+29	EL	13.2	Z
NGC 108	+28	EL	13.0	Z
NGC 125	+02	S	13.20	1
NGC 145	−05	S	13.20	1
NGC 160	+23	EL	13.4	1
NGC 194	+02	EL	13.00	1
NGC 234	+14	S	13.2	Z
U480	+36	S	13.3	Z
NGC 252	+27	EL	13.1	Z
NGC 257	+08	S	13.4	Z
NGC 266	+32	S	12.3	Z
NGC 271	−02	S	12.9	Z
NGC 295	+31	S	13.2	Z
NGC 315	+30	EL	12.2	Z
Sculptor S.	−33	EL	9.0	1
IC 1613	+01	I	9.96	2
NGC 383	+32	EL	13.3	Z
NGC 393	+39	EL	13.0	Z
NGC 403	+32	S	13.0	Z
NGC 410	+32	EL	12.3	Z
NGC 420	+31	EL	13.1	Z
NGC 425	+38	S	13.2	Z
NGC 430	−00	EL	13.3	Z
NGC 448	−01	EL	12.9	Z
NGC 467	+03	EL	12.93	1
NGC 489	+05	S	13.1	2
NGC 493	+00	S	12.95	1
NGC 499	+33	EL	13.11	1, 6
NGC 507	+32	EL	12.5	1, 6
NGC 513	+33	—	13.1	Z
NGC 517	+33	EL	13.3	Z
NGC 523	+33	—	13.2	Z
NGC 528	+33	EL	13.4	Z
NGC 529	+34	EL	12.8	Z
NGC 532	+09	S	13.2	Z
NGC 536	+34	S	12.9	Z
NGC 541	−01	EL	13.00	1

Name	Dec	Type	(B_T)	Source*
NGC 545	−01	EL	13.4	Z
NGC 547	−01	S	13.3	Z
NGC 550	+01	S	13.3	Z
NGC 551	+36	S	13.2	Z
U 1068	+45	S	13.4	Z
NGC 573	+41	—	13.2	Z
NGC 579	+33	S	13.3	Z
NGC 582	+33	S	13.4	Z
NGC 587	+35	S	13.4	Z
NGC 600	−07	S	13.0	1
NGC 632	+05	El	13.2	Z
NGC 656	+25	EL	13.2	Z
NGC 658	+12	S	13.3	Z
NGC 660	+13	S	11.62	4
NGC 661	+28	EL	12.7	Z
NGC 665	+10	EL	13.2	Z
NGC 666	+34	—	13.3	Z
NGC 668	+36	S	13.2	Z
NGC 669	+35	S	12.6	Z
NGC 673	+11	S	13.3	Z
U 1219	+17	S	13.3	Z
IC 1727	+27	S	12.13	4
NGC 676	+05	EL	10.2	Z
NGC 678	+21	S	13.0	Z
U 1281	+32	S	12.7	Z
NGC 679	+35	EL	13.25	1
NGC 680	+21	EL	12.7	Z
NGC 684	+27	S	12.9	Z
NGC 687	+36	EL	13.0	Z
NGC 688	+35	S	13.0	Z
NGC 691	+21	S	13.2	Z
NGC 693	+05	S	13.2	Z
NGC 695	+22	EL	13.4	Z
NGC 697	+22	S	12.4	Z
NGC 706	+07	S	12.9	Z
NGC 736	+32	EL	13.20	1
NGC 759	+36	EL	13.4	Z
NGC 769	+13	S	13.1	Z
NGC 776	+23	S	13.1	Z
IC 179	+37	EL	13.1	Z
NGC 783	+31	S	12.5	Z
NGC 784	+28	S	12.26	1
NGC 797	+37	S	12.8d	Z
NGC 801	+38	S	13.2	Z
NGC 803	+15	S	13.01	1

Name	Dec	Type	(B_T)	Source*
NGC 813	+44	S	12.5	Z
NGC 818	+38	S	12.4	Z
NGC 820	+14	S	13.4	Z
NGC 828	+38	S	12.7	Z
NGC 834	+37	S	12.9	Z
NGC 835	−10	S	13.0	1
NGC 841	+37	S	12.5	Z
NGC 846	+44	S	12.9	Z
NGC 855	+27	EL	12.7	Z
U 1757	+38	S	13.3	Z
U1772	+37	—	13.4	Z
U1810	+39	S	13.4	Z
U1886	+39	S	12.8	Z
NGC 930	+20	S	13.4	Z
NGC 940	+31	EL	13.1	Z
NGC 959	+35	S	12.2	Z
NGC 969	+32	EL	13.2	Z
NGC 973	+32	S	13.4	Z
NGC 978	+32	EL	13.0d	Z
NGC 980	+40	S	12.9	Z
U 2069	+37	S	12.9	Z
IC 239	+38	S	11.93	1
NGC 987	+33	S	13.1	Z
NGC 992	+20	S	13.2	2
NGC 1003	+40	S	12.02	4
NGC 1012	+29	S	12.8	Z
NGC 1015	−01	S	13.2	Z
NGC 1016	+01	EL	13.0	Z
NGC 1032	+00	S	12.9	Z
IC 1830	−27	S	13.2	1
NGC 1036	+19	—	13.2	Z
Fornax S.	+01	I	9.04	2
NGC 1050	+34	S	13.2	Z
NGC 1056	+38	S	13.2	Z
NGC 1060	+32	EL	13.1	Z
NGC 1070	+04	S	12.7	Z
NGC 1085	+03	S	13.3	Z
NGC 1086	+41	S	13.3	Z
NGC 1094	−00	S	13.2	Z
U 2296	+18	—	12.8	Z
NGC 1106	+41	EL	13.4	Z
NGC 1121	−01	S	13.4	Z
NGC 1122	+42	S	12.7	Z
NGC 1134	+12	S	12.9	Z
NGC 1137	+02	S	13.2	Z

Name	Dec	Type	(B_T)	Source*
NGC 1153	+03	—	13.2	Z
NGC 1160	+44	S	12.7	Z
NGC 1161	+44	EL	12.3	Z
NGC 1171	+43	S	13.3	Z
U 2526	+36	S	13.2	Z
NGC 1184	+80	S	13.2	Z
NGC 1186	+42	S	12.2	Z
NGC 1207	+38	S	13.4	Z
NGC 1211	−00	S	13.2	Z
NGC 1219	+01	S	13.2	Z
IC 334	+76	I	13.0	Z
IC 342	+67	S	9.10	2
NGC 1485	+70	S	13.4	Z
IC 356	+69	S	11.43	2
NGC 1530	+75	S	13.2	Z
NGC 1560	+71	S	12.24	1
NGC 1587	+00	EL	12.83	6
NGC 1620	−00	S	13.3	Z
NGC 1622	−03	S	13.15	1
NGC 1635	−00	S	13.2	Z
NGC 1642	+00	S	13.3	Z
NGC 1653	−02	EL	12.6	Z
IC 391	+78	S	13.0	1
NGC 1691	+03	S	12.9	Z
IC 396	+68	S	13.0	Z
NGC 1762	+01	S	13.2	Z
U 3253	+84	S	12.9	Z
NGC 1819	+05	EL	13.4	Z
DDO 231	−33	I	13.20	1
NGC 1888	−11	S	12.90	1
U 3327	+31	EL	13.01	7
U 3431	+76	EL	13.4	Z
IC 2166	+59	S	13.3	Z
U 3478	+63	S	13.1	Z
U 3504	+60	S	13.1	Z
U 3511	+65	S	12.8	Z
NGC 2258	+74	EL	13.0	Z
NGC 2272	−27	EL	12.85	1
NGC 2273	+60	S	12.3	Z
NGC 2274	+33	EL	13.3	Z
U 3580	+69	S	12.7	Z
U 3596	+39	EL	13.2	Z
U 3608	+46	S	13.4	Z
U 3642	+64	EL	13.3	Z
U 3660	+63	S	13.4	Z

Name	Dec	Type	(B_T)	Source*
U 3685	+61	S	12.9	Z
U 3691	+15	S	13.0	Z
U 3697	+71	S	12.9	Z
U 3714	+71	S	12.5	Z
IC 2179	+65	—	13.2	Z
NGC 2329	+48	EL	13.4	Z
NGC 2337	+44	I	12.8	Z
NGC 2341	+20	—	13.3	Z
NGC 2342	+20	S	12.2	Z
NGC 2344	+47	S	12.85	I
U 3789	+59	S	13.1	Z
U 3804	+71	S	12.8	Z
U 3816	+58	EL	13.2	Z
U 3828	+58	Sb	12.5	Z
U 3829	+33	—	13.4	Z
U 3831	+49	S	13.3	Z
IC 467	+79	S	12.5	Z
U 3845	+47	S	13.3	Z
U 3859	+73	S	13.1	Z
NGC 2389	+33	S	13.2	Z
IC 2199	+31	S	13.2	Z
NGC 2415	+35	I	12.64	1, 7
NGC 2418	+18	EL	13.3	Z
IC 469	+85	S	13.4	Z
U 4028	+74	S	12.5	Z
U 4041	+73	S	13.4	Z
U 4079	+55	S	13.3	Z
U 2469	+56	S	13.0	Z
U 4151	+77	S	12.9	Z
U 4169	+61	S	13.3	Z
IC 2233	+54	S	13.3	Z
NGC 2435	+31	S	13.1	Z
NGC 2476	+40	EL	13.1	Z
NGC 2481	+23	S	13.0	Z
NGC 2485	+07	S	12.9	Z
NGC 2493	+39	EL	12.8	Z
NGC 2513	+09	EL	13.3	Z
U 4227	+39	S	13.2	Z
NGC 2524	+39	S	13.4	Z
U 4238	+76	S	13.3	Z
NGC 2532	+34	S	13.0	1
NGC 2535	+25	S	13.1	1
NGC 2538	+03	S	13.4	Z
NGC 2543	+36	S	12.4	Z
Ho II	+70	I	11.27	1

Name	Dec	Type	(B_T)	Source*
NGC 2544	+74	S	13.2	Z
NGC 2550	+74	S	12.9	Z
NGC 2554	+23	S	13.1	Z
NGC 2555	+00	S	13.1	Z
NGC 2563	+21	EL	13.3	Z
NGC 2565	+22	S	13.4	Z
NGC 2577	+22	EL	13.4	Z
IC 499	+85	S	13.3	Z
NGC 2591	+78	S	12.6	Z
NGC 2592	+26	EL	13.2	Z
U 4393	+46	S	13.3	Z
U 4397	+73	S	13.3	Z
NGC 2599	+22	S	13.0	Z
NGC 2604	+29	S	13.1	Z
NGC 2615	−02	S	13.1	Z
NGC 2619	+28	S	13.2	Z
U 4551	+49	EL	12.8	Z
NGC 2629	+73	EL	12.6	Z
IC 2389	+73	S	13.0	Z
NGC 2634	+74	EL	12.4	Z
NGC 2638	+37	S	13.4	Z
NGC 2644	+05	—	13.0	Z
NGC 2646	+73	EL	12.95	1
NGC 2648	+14	S	12.6	Z
NGC 2649	+34	S	12.8	Z
U 4621	+35	—	13.3	Z
U 4623	+76	S	13.3	Z
IC 512	+85	S	13.0	Z
IC 520	+73	S	11.7	Z
NGC 2684	+49	S	13.1	Z
NGC 2695	−02	—	12.9	Z
NGC 2697	−02	—	13.2	Z
NGC 2698	−03	S	12.8	Z
U 4671	+52	S	13.3	Z
NGC 2699	−02	—	13.2	Z
NGC 2706	−02	S	13.4	Z
NGC 2708	−03	S	13.2	Z
NGC 2716	+03	EL	13.3	1
NGC 2718	+06	S	12.9	Z
U 4713	+52	S	13.4	Z
NGC 2719	+35	I	13.4	Z
NGC 2726	+60	S	12.9	Z
NGC 2730	+17	S	13.3	Z
NGC 2738	+22	S	13.4	Z
U 4749	+51	S	13.3	Z

Name	Dec	Type	(B_T)	Source*
NGC 2750	+25	S	12.3	Z
NGC 2756	+54	S	12.9	Z
NGC 2765	+03	EL	12.9	Z
NGC 2770	+33	S	11.8	Z
NGC 2778	+35	EL	12.8	Z
Ho III	+74	S	13.07	1
U 4861	+12	S	13.4	Z
NGC 2789	+29	S	13.4	Z
U 4883	+74	S	12.6	Z
IC 529	+73	S	12.66	1
U 4906	+53	S	13.1	Z
NGC 2805	+64	S	11.78	1
NGC 2810	+72	EL	13.2	2
NGC 2820	+64	S	12.9	Z
NGC 2822	−69	EL	12.07	7
IC 529	+73	S	12.66	1
NGC 2858	+03	S	13.4	2
NGC 2862	+26	S	13.4	Z
NGC 2872	+11	EL	12.6	Z
NGC 2874	+11	S	13.1	Z
NGC 2882	+08	S	13.1	Z
NGC 2893	+29	EL	13.2	Z
NGC 2894	+07	S	13.0	Z
NGC 2906	+08	S	12.7	Z
NGC 2915	−76	I	13.20	1
NGC 2916	+21	S	12.65	1
U 5151	+48	—	13.2	Z
NGC 2918	+31	EL	13.2	Z
NGC 2919	+10	S	13.2	Z
NGC 2939	+09	S	13.1	Z
U 5189	+09	—	13.3d	Z
U 5215	+09	S	13.4	Z
NGC 2948	+07	S	13.4	Z
NGC 2954	+15	EL	13.1	Z
NGC 2960	+03	S	13.2	Z
NGC 2977	+75	S	12.5	Z
NGC 3016	+12	S	13.3	Z
A0947+28	+28	EL	12.3	1
NGC 3020	+43	S	12.9	Z
NGC 3023	+00	S	13.1	Z
NGC 3024	+13	S	13.3	Z
NGC 3026	+28	I	13.4	Z
NGC 3027	+72	S	12.45	1
NGC 3042	+58	EL	13.4	Z
NGC 3049	+09	S	13.1	Z

Name	Dec	Type	(B_T)	Source*
NGC 3053	+16	S	13.3	Z
NGC 3060	+17	S	13.4	Z
NGC 3070	+32	S	12.8	Z
Leo A	+30	I	13.09	1
Sex B	+05	I	11.89	4
NGC 3094	+16	S	13.1	Z
NGC 3100	−31	EL	12.45	Z
U 5425	+13	S	13.2	Z
U 5435	+59	—	13.4	Z
U 5456	+10	—	13.1	Z
NGC 3126	+32	S	13.1	Z
Leo I	+12	EL	10.81	4
IC 2554	−06	S	12.52	7
Sex A	−04	I	11.93	2
NGC 3153	+12	S	13.2	Z
IC 600	−03	—	12.9	Z
IC 602	+07	S	13.0	Z
NGC 3182	+58	S	12.8	Z
NGC 3183	+74	S	12.70	1
NGC 3187	+22	S	13.4	Z
NGC 3206	+57	S	12.5	Z
NGC 3225	+58	S	13.1	Z
Anon[1]	−02	—	13.0	Z
NGC 3239	+17	I	13.1	Z
NGC 3246	+04	S	13.4	Z
IC 2574	+68	S	11.03	1
NGC 3266	+65	EL	13.3	Z
NGC 3267	−35	EL	12.92	7
IC 2584	−34	EL	12.7	7
NGC 3269	−34	EL	12.6	7
NGC 3273	−35	EL	13.02	7
U 5720	+54	I	12.9	Z
U 5747	−01	—	13.4	Z
NGC 3306	+37	S	13.3	Z
NGC 3311	−27	EL	13.03	1,7
NGC 3332	+12	S	13.4	Z
NGC 3339	−00	S	13.2	Z
U 5832	+13	S	13.4	Z
NGC 3356	+07	S	12.9	Z
NGC 3362	+06	S	13.2	Z
NGC 3380	+28	S	13.2	Z
NGC 3381	+34	S	12.5	Z
NGC 3385	+05	EL	13.3	Z
NGC 3391	+14	—	13.1	Z
NGC 3394	+65	S	12.9	Z

[1] $10^h 21^m4, -02°56'$

Name	Dec	Type	(B_T)	Source*
IC 651	−01	—	12.5	Z
NGC 3406	+51	—	13.4	Z
NGC 3413	+33	EL	12.8	Z
U 5953	+44	—	12.9	Z
NGC 3419	+14	EL	13.0	Z
NGC 3424	+33	S	12.9	Z
NGC 3434	+04	S	13.0	Z
NGC 3442	+34	S	12.9	Z
U 6062	+09	EL	13.3	Z
U 6070	+33	—	13.0	Z
U 6132	+38	—	12.8	Z
NGC 3451	+27	S	13.1	Z
NGC 3457	+17	—	12.6	Z
NGC 3462	+07	EL	13.0	Z
NGC 3471	+61	S	12.8	Z
U 6103	+45	—	13.1	Z
NGC 3501	+18	S	13.4	Z
NGC 3507	+18	S	11.0	Z
U 6135	+45	S	12.7	Z
NGC 3524	+11	S	13.0	Z
NGC 3526	+07	S	13.3	Z
NGC 3557B	−37	EL	13.2	1
U 6255	+47	S	13.3	Z
NGC 3559	+12	S	13.4	Z
NGC 3562	+73	EL	13.0	Z
IC 676	+09	EL	13.0	Z
Leo II	+22	EL	12.38	1
IC 677	+12	S	13.2	Z
NGC 3568	−37	S	12.07	7
NGC 3595	+47	—	12.7	Z
NGC 3598	+17	EL	13.1	Z
U 6320	+19	—	13.2	Z
NGC 3599	+18	EL	12.75	1
NGC 3600	+41	S	12.3	Z
U 6309	+51	S	13.4	Z
NGC 3648	+40	EL	13.2	Z
NGC 3652	+38	S	12.3	Z
NGC 3654	+69	S	13.2	Z
NGC 3656	+54	I	13.1	Z
NGC 3657	+53	S	12.8	Z
NGC 3658	+38	EL	13.0	Z
NGC 3662	−00	S	13.4	Z
NGC 3668	+63	S	12.9	Z
NGC 3669	+57	S	12.7	Z
NGC 3674	+57	EL	12.9	Z

Name	Dec	Type	(B_T)	Source*
NGC 3677	+47	EL	13.2	Z
NGC 3682	+66	EL	13.2	Z
NGC 3692	+09	S	12.5	Z
NGC 3694	+35	—	13.2	Z
U 6484	+57	S	12.4	Z
NGC 3719	+01	S	13.4	Z
U 6534	+63	S	13.1	Z
NGC 3757	+58	EL	13.3	Z
NGC 3733	+55	S	12.9	Z
NGC 3762	+62	S	13.1	Z
NGC 3768	+18	EL	13.3	Z
NGC 3770	+59	S	13.3	Z
NGC 3786	+32	S	13.1	Z
NGC 3788	+32	S	12.8	Z
IC 719	+09	EL	13.2	Z
NGC 3796	+60	S	13.2	Z
NGC 3800	+15	S	12.7	Z
NGC 3801	+18	EL	13.0	Z
NGC 3805	+20	EL	13.4	Z
NGC 3809	+60	EL	13.4	Z
NGC 3811	+47	S	12.7	Z
NGC 3816	+20	EL	13.2	Z
NGC 3821	+20	S	13.4	Z
NGC 3822	+10	EL	13.3	Z
U 6665	+00	—	13.3	Z
NGC 3825	+10	S	13.4	Z
NGC 3827	+19	—	13.2	Z
IC 724	+09	S	13.4	Z
NGC 3835	+60	S	12.8	Z
NGC 3838	+58	S	12.5	Z
NGC 3839	+11	S	13.2	Z
NGC 3842	+20	EL	12.9	Z
NGC 3853	+16	EL	13.1	Z
U 6730	+09	S	13.0	Z
U 6732	+59	—	13.3	Z
NGC 3869	+11	S	13.1	Z
NGC 3870	+50	EL	12.9	Z
NGC 3879	+69	S	13.3	Z
NGC 3891	+30	S	13.3	Z
NGC 3894	+59	EL	12.7	Z
NGC 3914	+06	S	13.4	Z
NGC 3921	+55	S	13.1	Z
NGC 3928	+48	EL	12.8	Z
NGC 3930	+38	S	13.2	Z
IC 745	+00	—	13.3	Z

Name	Dec	Type	(B_T)	Source*
NGC 3958	+58	S	12.9	Z
NGC 3968	+12	S	12.9	Z
NGC 3972	+55	S	12.6	Z
NGC 3978	+60	S	13.0	Z
NGC 4010	+47	S	12.8	Z
NGC 4014	+16	S	13.1	Z
NGC 4016		—	13.1	Z
NGC 4020	+30	S	12.8	Z
NGC 4067	+11	S	12.8	Z
NGC 4068	+52	I	13.0	Z
NGC 4081	+64	S	13.4	Z
NGC 4106	+28	EL	13.3	Z
NGC 4108	+67	S	12.8	Z
NGC 4127	+77	S	13.3	Z
NGC 4133	+75	S	12.9	Z
NGC 4134	+29	S	13.4	Z
NGC 4146	+26	S	13.4	Z
NGC 4163	+36	I	13.4	Z
NGC 4169	+29	EL	12.5	Z
NGC 4173	+29	S	13.3	Z
NGC 4180	+07	S	12.8	Z
NGC 4185	+28	S	13.1	Z
NGC 4193	+13	S	13.20	5
NGC 4194	+54	I	12.95	1
NGC 4196	+28	EL	13.3	Z
NGC 4197	+06	S	13.4	Z
NGC 4206	+13	S	12.77	5
NGC 4207	+09	—	13.3	Z
NGC 4210	+66	S	13.2	Z
NGC 4218	+48	S	12.9	Z
NGC 4221	+66	EL	13.4	Z
NGC 4239	+16	EL	13.1	Z
NGC 4241	+06	S	12.99	5
NGC 4248	+47	I	13.19	1
NGC 4250	+71	EL	12.8	Z
NGC 4253	+30	S	13.3	Z
NGC 4255	+05	EL	13.1	Z
U 7367	+50	S	13.4	Z
NGC 4275	+27	S	13.0	Z
NGC 4305	+13	S	13.25	1
NGC 4310	+29	EL	13.1	Z
NGC 4312	+15	S	12.56	5
NGC 4313	+12	S	12.8	Z
NGC 4319	+75	S	12.8	Z
NGC 4332	+66	S	13.0	Z

Name	Dec	Type	(B_T)	Source*
NGC 4336	+19	S	13.2	Z
NGC 4343	+07	S	13.29	1
NGC 4344	+17	EL	13.3	Z
NGC 4351	+12	S	12.8	1
NGC 4357	+49	S	13.2	Z
NGC 4384	+54	S	13.2	Z
NGC 4387	+13	EL	12.97	5, 6
NGC 4390	+10	S	13.3	Z
NGC 4393	+27	S	13.4	Z
NGC 4396	+15	S	13.3	Z
NGC 4402	+13	S	12.56	5
NGC 4405	+16	S	12.5	Z
NGC 4410	+09	—	13.2d	Z
NGC 4411B	+09	S	12.92	5
NGC 4413	+12	S	13.06	6
NGC 4416	+08	S	13.1	Z
NGC 4421	+15	S	12.45	5
NGC 4430	+06	S	13.0	Z
NGC 4434	+08	EL	12.8	Z
NGC 4440	+12	S	12.73	5
NGC 4441	+65	EL	13.3	Z
IC 3392	+15	S	12.9	Z
NGC 4458	+13	EL	12.83	5, 6
NGC 4470	+08	S	12.5	Z
NGC 4480	+04	S	13.09	5
NGC 4488	+08	S	13.4	Z
NGC 4489	+17	EL	12.8	Z
U 7658	+12	EL	10.8	Z
NGC 4492	+08	S	13.2	Z
NGC 4498	+17	S	12.4	Z
NGC 4500	+58	S	13.0	Z
Anon[2]	+42	—	13.4	Z
IC 3476	+14	I	13.1	Z
U 7699	+37	S	13.1	Z
NGC 4515	+16	EL	12.9	Z
NGC 4521	+64	S	12.8	Z
NGC 4525	+30	S	12.6	Z
NGC 4528	+11	EL	12.70	5
NGC 4531	+13	S	12.9	Z
NGC 4534	+35	—	12.9	Z
NGC 4539	+18	S	12.81	5
NGC 4545	+63	S	12.9	Z
NGC 4551	+12	EL	12.72	5, 6
NGC 4555	+26	EL	13.1	Z
U 7767	+73	EL	13.3	Z

[2] $12^h 30^m$, $+42°59'$

Name	Dec	Type	(B_T)	Source*
NGC 4575	−40	S	13.17	7
NGC 4581	+01	EL	13.0	Z
NGC 4599	+01	S	13.3	Z
NGC 4606	+12	S	12.69	5
NGC 4615	+26	S	13.4	Z
NGC 4619	+35	S	13.2	Z
NGC 4625	+41	S	12.90	4
NGC 4627	+32	EL	12.88	4
NGC 4634	+14	S	13.19	5
NGC 4642	−00	S	13.4	Z
NGC 4648	+74	EL	12.4	Z
NGC 4659	+13	EL	12.9	Z
NGC 4664		—	12.1	6
NGC 4673	+27	EL	13.3	Z
NGC 4685	+19	EL	13.4	Z
NGC 4686	+54	S	13.4	Z
NGC 4709	−41	EL	12.53	7
NGC 4733	+11	EL	12.8	Z
NGC 4746	+12	S	12.9	Z
NGC 4779	+10	S	13.1	Z
NGC 4789	+27	EL	13.1	1
NGC 4841	+28	EL	12.5d	1
NGC 4874	+28	EL	12.9	1
NGC 4921	+28	S	13.0	1
NGC 4944	+28	S	12.9	Z
NGC 4952	+29	EL	13.2	Z
NGC 4956	+35	EL	13.2	Z
NGC 5014	+36	S	13.2	Z
NGC 5020	+12	S	13.0	Z
NGC 5023	+44	S	12.9	Z
NGC 5026	−42	S	12.71	7
NGC 5032	+28	S	13.2	Z
NGC 5056	+31	S	13.2	Z
NGC 5103	+43	—	13.3	Z
NGC 5107	+38	S	13.4	Z
NGC 5109	+57	S	13.4	Z
NGC 5123	+43	S	13.2	Z
NGC 5125	+09	S	13.1	Z
NGC 5129	+14	EL	12.9	Z
NGC 5140	−33	EL	12.80	1
NGC 5144	+70	S	13.0	Z
NGC 5145	+43	S	13.3	Z
NGC 5158	+18	S	13.4	Z
NGC 5173	+46	EL	13.2	Z
NGC 5174	+11	S	13.3	Z

Name	Dec	Type	(B_T)	Source*
NGC 5183	−01	S	13.2	Z
NGC 5184	−01	S	13.3	Z
NGC 5190	+18	S	13.3	Z
NGC 5205	+62	S	13.3	Z
U 8517	+20	S	13.4	Z
NGC 5218	+63	S	12.9	Z
NGC 5257	+01	S	13.3	Z
NGC 5258	+01	S	13.4	Z
NGC 5266A	−48	—	12.93	7
NGC 5278	+55	S	13.3	Z
NGC 5289	+41	S	13.2	Z
NGC 5290	+41	S	13.0	Z
NGC 5302	−30	EL	13.20	1
NGC 5303	+38	—	12.9	Z
1346-35	−35	I	12.6	8
NGC 5311	+40	S	13.4	Z
NGC 5318	+33	EL	13.2	Z
NGC 5320	+41	S	12.8	Z
NGC 5336	+43	S	13.3	Z
NGC 5337	+39	S	13.1	Z
NGC 5345	−01	—	13.4	Z
NGC 5354	+40	EL	12.45	1
Ho IV	+54	S	13.10	1
NGC 5374	+06	S	13.3	Z
NGC 5375	+29	S	12.8	Z
NGC 5386	+06	S	13.3	Z
NGC 5389	+59	S	13.0	Z
NGC 5394	+37	S	13.4	Z
NGC 5414	+10	—	13.4d	Z
NGC 5416	+09	S	13.2	Z
NGC 5417	+08	S	13.4	Z
NGC 5443	+56	S	12.9	Z
NGC 5475	+55	S	13.1	Z
NGC 5481	+50	EL	13.08	6
NGC 5490	+17	EL	13.0	Z
NGC 5492	+19	S	13.3	Z
Circinus	−65	S	11.25	1
NGC 5506	−02	S	13.2	Z
NGC 5507	−02	EL	13.4	Z
NGC 5515	+39	S	13.4	Z

Name	Dec	Type	(B_T)	Source*
NGC 5520	+50	S	13.0	Z
NGC 5529	+36	S	12.6	Z
NGC 5532	+11	EL	13.00	1
NGC 5541	+39	S	13.1	Z
NGC 5544	+36	S		
			12.9	Z
NGC 5545	+36	S		
NGC 5560	+04	S	13.2	1
NGC 5577	+03	S	13.2	Z
NGC 5582	+39	EL	12.7	Z
NGC 5590	+35	EL	13.3	Z
NGC 5602	+50	S	13.2	Z
U 9215	+01	S	13.2	Z
NGC 5604	−03	S	13.4	Z
NGC 5611	+33	EL	13.2	Z
NGC 5612	−78	EL	13.16	6
NGC 5623	+33	EL	13.4	Z
NGC 5630	+41	S	13.3	Z
NGC 5652	+06	S	13.4	Z
NGC 5656	+35	S	12.4	Z
NGC 5666	+10	—	13.1	Z
NGC 5667	+59	—	12.9	Z
IC 1029	+50	S	13.4	Z
NGC 5674	+05	S	13.3	Z
NGC 5692	+03	—	12.9	Z
NGC 5707	+51	S	13.0	Z
NGC 5719	−00	S	13.4	Z
NGC 5735	+28	S	13.4	Z
IC 1067	+03	S	13.2	Z
NGC 5774	+03	S	12.82	1
NGC 5784	+42	EL	13.4	Z
NGC 5797	+49	S	13.3	Z
NGC 5798	+30	I	13.1	Z
NGC 5827	+26	S	13.3	Z
NGC 5832	+71	S	13.1	Z
NGC 5845	+01	EL	13.1	1
NGC 5859	+19	S	13.25	1
NGC 5865	+00	EL	13.1	Z
NGC 5875	+52	S	13.1	Z
NGC 5894	+60	S	13.0	Z
NGC 5928	+18	EL	13.4	Z
NGC 5929	+41	S		
NGC 5930	+41	S	12.7	Z
NGC 5937	−02	S	12.7	Z
NGC 5951	+15	S	13.4	Z
NGC 5953	+15	S	13.06	7

Name	Dec	Type	(B_T)	Source*
NGC 5954	+15	S	12.90	7
NGC 5956	+11	S	12.9	Z
NGC 5957	+12	S	12.9	Z
NGC 5958	+28	S	12.8	Z
NGC 5963	+56	S	12.8	Z
NGC 5964	+06	S	13.2	Z
IC 4567	+43	S	13.21	Z
NGC 5980	+15	S	12.9	Z
NGC 5987	+58	S	13.1	Z
NGC 5989	+59			
NGC 5990	+02	S	12.7	Z
NGC 5996	+18	S	12.8d	Z
NGC 6004	+19	S	13.0	Z
U 10070	+47	S	13.3	Z
NGC 6010	+00	S	12.9	Z
NGC 6012	+14	S	12.7	Z
NGC 6014	+06	EL	13.4	Z
NGC 6017	+06	—	13.4	Z
IC 1151	+17	S	13.0	Z
IC 1153	+48	EL	13.3	Z
NGC 6048	+70	EL	13.4	Z
NGC 6068	+79	S	13.1	Z
U 10200	+41	—	13.3	Z
NGC 6127	+58	EL	12.8	Z
NGC 6140	+65	S	12.4	Z
NGC 6155	+48	S	12.7	Z
NGC 6166	+39	EL	13.05	1
NGC 6189	+59	S	13.1	Z
NGC 6190	+58	S	13.0	Z
U 10502	+72	S	12.9	Z
NGC 6223	+61	—	12.9	Z
U 10528	+22	EL	13.1	Z
NGC 6232	+70	S	13.3	Z
NGC 6236	+70	S	12.5	Z
NGC 6247	+63	—	13.3	Z
U 10599	+39	—	13.4	Z
NGC 6283	+50	S	13.4	Z
NGC 6324	+75	S	13.3	Z
NGC 6339	+40	S	13.4	Z
U 10731	+63	S	12.9	Z
U 10803	+73	—	12.7	Z
NGC 6368	+11	S	13.3	Z
NGC 6381	+60	S	13.4	Z
NGC 6389	+16	S	13.2	Z
NGC 6395	+71	S	12.6	Z

Name	Dec	Type	(B_T)	Source*
NGC 6411	+60	EL	13.0	Z
NGC 6434	+72	S	13.0	Z
U 11057	+12	S	13.4	Z
NGC 6438	−85	—	12.53	3
NGC 6484	+24	S	13.1	Z
NGC 6495	+18	EL	13.4	Z
NGC 6500	+18	S	12.92	7
NGC 6501	+18	EL	13.20	1, 7
NGC 6504	+33	S	13.1	Z
NGC 6509	+06	S	13.0	Z
NGC 6548	+18	EL	12.7	Z
NGC 6555	+17	S	13.0	Z
NGC 6570	+14	S	12.8	Z
NGC 6585	+39	S	13.3	Z
NGC 6587	+18	EL	13.15	Z
NGC 6599	+24	EL	13.3	Z
NGC 6621	+68	S	13.4d	Z
NGC 6632	+27	S	12.8	Z
NGC 6646	+39	S	13.4	Z
NGC 6654	±73	S	12.45	1
NGC 6661	+22	S	13.00	1, 6
NGC 6671	+26	S	13.4	Z
NGC 6674	+25	S	12.85	1
NGC 6675	+40	S	13.0	Z
NGC 6677	+67	—	13.4d	Z
NGC 6689	+70	S	12.4	Z
U 11332	+73	S	13.4	Z
NGC 6701	+60	S	12.7	Z
NGC 6703	+45	EL	12.37	1, 6
NGC 6745	+40	—	13.0d	Z
NGC 6764	+50	S	12.9	Z
U 11466	+45	—	13.2	Z
NGC 6770	−60	S	12.95	3
NGC 6792	+43	S	13.1	Z
NGC 6796	+61	S	13.3	Z
NGC 6824	+55	S	12.7	Z
NGC 6869	+66	EL	12.6	Z
NGC 6870	−48	S	13.15	1
NGC 6872	−70	S	12.34	1, 7
NGC 6926	−02	S	13.1	1
NGC 6956	+12	S	13.2	Z
NGC 6962	+00	S	12.85	1
NGC 7013	+29	EL	12.6	Z
NGC 7015	+11	S	12.9	Z
NGC 7042	+13	S	12.7	Z

Name	Dec	Type	(B_T)	Source*
NGC 7081	+02	S	13.4	Z
IC 1392	+35	EL	12.7	Z
U 11781	+35	EL	13.4	Z
NGC 7156	+02	S	13.2	Z
NGC 7162A	−43	S	13.08	3
NGC 7172	−32	S	12.98	1, 7
NGC 7173	−32	EL	13.17	1, 7
NGC 7176	−32	EL	12.9	1
NGC 7214	−28	S	13.0	1
NGC 7219	−64	—	12.97	7
NGC 7223	+40	S	13.2	Z
NGC 7242	+37	EL	13.15	Z
U 11909	+47	S	13.0	Z
U 11920	+48	S	12.7	Z
U 11973	+41	S	13.2	Z
NGC 7248	+40	EL	13.3	Z
NGC 7250	+40	S	12.8	Z
NGC 7265	+35	EL	13.4	Z
NGC 7280	+15	EL	13.3	Z
NGC 7286	+28	S	13.1	Z
NGC 7292	+30	I	12.8	Z
NGC 7303	+30	S	13.4	Z
NGC 7311	+05	S	13.1	Z
NGC 7316	+20	S	13.4	Z
NGC 7330	+38	EL	13.3	Z
NGC 7339	+23	S	13.0	1
U 12173	+38	S	13.4	Z
U 12177	+33	S	13.2	Z
NGC 7391	−01	EL	13.4	Z
U 12234	+33	S	13.0	Z
NGC 7416	−05	S	13.10	1
NGC 7426	+36	EL	13.3	Z
NGC 7454	+16	EL	13.3	Z
NGC 7463	+15	S	13.2	Z
NGC 7465	+15	EL	13.0	Z
NGC 7490	+32	S	13.2	Z
NGC 7497	+17	S	13.0	Z
NGC 7513	−28	S	12.6	1
NGC 7514	+34	S	13.2	Z
NGC 7539	+23	EL	13.4	Z
NGC 7562	+06	EL	12.70	1, 6
NGC 7620	+23	S	13.2	Z
NGC 7634	+08	EL	13.4	Z
NGC 7648	+09	EL	13.2	Z
NGC 7664	+24	S	13.0	Z

Name	Dec	Type	(B_T)	Source*
NGC 7673	+23	S	13.0	1
NGC 7674	+08	S	13.3d	Z
Pegasus S.	+14	I	12.63	1
NGC 7680	+32	EL	13.2	Z
U 12667	+29	S	13.2	Z
NGC 7712	+23	—	13.4	Z
NGC 7714	+01	S	12.8	Z
NGC 7722	+15	S	13.4	Z
NGC 7753	+29	S	12.9	Z
NGC 7771	+19	S	13.1	1

Name	Dec	Type	(B_T)	Source*
NGC 7779	+07	S	13.3	Z
IC 1525	+46	S	13.0	Z
NGC 7798	+20	S	12.4	Z
NGC 7800	+14	I	13.1	Z
U 12914	+23	S	12.9	Z
WLM	−15	I	11.29	4
NGC 7817	+07	S	12.4	Z

* Key to sources of magnitudes:

1. de Vaucouleurs, G., de Vaucouleurs, A., and Corwin, H. G. 1977, *Reference Catalogue of Bright Galaxies*, 2nd ed. (Austin: University of Texas Press) (*RC2*).
2. de Vaucouleurs, G. 1977, *Astrophys. J. Suppl. 33*, 211.
3. de Vaucouleurs, G., and Bollinger, G. 1977, *Astrophys. J. Suppl. 33*, 247.
4. de Vaucouleurs, G., and Bollinger, G. 1977, *Astrophys. J. Suppl. 34*, 469.
5. de Vaucouleurs, G., and Head, C. 1978, *Astrophys. J. Suppl. 36*, 439.
6. B_T calculated from Visvanathan, N., and Sandage, A. 1978, *Astrophys. J. 223*, 707 (cf. Introduction, p. 7).
7. B_T calculated from unpublished data by G. Wegner, 1979 (cf. Introduction, p. 7).
8. Peterson, C.-J. 1978, private communication.
Z. Zwicky, F. *et al.* 1961–1968, *Catalogue of Galaxies and Clusters of Galaxies*, Vols. 1–6.

Appendix B. DDO Dwarf Galaxies with $m_{pg} \leq 13^m4$ According to Fisher and Tully.*

Name†	Alias	Dec	Type	m_{pg}	Name	Alias	Dec	Type	m_{pg}
DDO 225	IC 1558	−25	3	12.9	DDO 126		+37	I	12.8
DDO 13		+15	I	13.0	DDO 125		+43	I	12.7
DDO 14		−12	S	13.21	DDO 129		+43	I	13.0
DDO 25		+33	I	13.1	DDO 132	IC 3475	+13	E	13.4§
DDO 24		+40	I	12.9	DDO 133		+31	I	12.4
DDO 28		+03	S	12.4	DDO 135	NGC 4523	+15	S	13.4
DDO 29		+01	S	12.2	DDO 138	IC 3576	+06	S	12.9
DDO 30		−01	S	12.8	DDO 141	IC 3687	+38	S	13.1
DDO 228		−29	S	13.1	DDO 142		−05	S	13.3
DDO 229		−25	S	12.7	DDO 144		+00	S	13.3
DDO 230		−31	S	13.3	DDO 146		−05	I	13.2
DDO 39		+75	I	13.2	DDO 150	NGC 4707	+51	S	13.4
DDO 47		+16	I	12.8	DDO 151		−10	I	13.1
DDO 63	Ho I	+71	I	13.3‡	DDO 165		+67	I	13.4
DDO 235		−31	S	13.2	DDO 168		+46	I	13.0
DDO 67	NGC 3057	+80	S	12.9	DDO 172		+42	S	13.4
DDO 77		+71	E	12.6	DDO 175		+58	I	13.4
DDO 80		+70	S	13.1	DDO 179		+07	I	13.1
DDO 82		+70	S	12.7	DDO 180		−09	S	13.4
DDO 238		−24	S	12.8	DDO 184		+18	I	13.3
DDO 84		+34	I	12.3	DDO 190		+44	I	13.4
DDO 94		+02	I	13.3	DDO 196		+08	S	13.4
DDO 239		−28	I	13.4	DDO 197		−09	Pec	12.7
DDO 100		+52	S	12.8	DDO 199	UMi S.	+67	E	11?
DDO 105		+38	I	12.7	DDO 204		+47	I	13.1
DDO 107	NGC 4025	+38	S	13.21	DDO 208	Draco S.	+57	E	11?
DDO 119	NGC 4288	+46	S	12.7	DDO 213		+321	S	13.0
DDO 120		+46	I	13.4	DDO 217		+40	S	12.7
DDO 122		+70	S	12.6					
DDO 123		+58	I	13.2					

* Fisher, J. R., and Tully, R. B. 1975, *Astron. Astrophys.* *44*, 151.
† In order of Right Ascension. Only galaxies not in Appendix A tabulation are listed here.
‡ $B_T = 13^m41$, from de Vaucouleurs, *et al.*, 1977 (*RC2*).
§ $B_T = 13^m95$, from de Vaucouleurs, *et al.*, 1977 (*RC2*).

APPENDIX C. Finding List for Galaxies with Non-NGC Numbers

Galaxy	Other name	RA (1950)	Galaxy	Other name	RA (1950)
F 703	A 1511-15	15^{h}11^m	IC 4797	...	18^{h}52^m
HA 72	A 1357-45	13 57	IC 4837	...	19 11
HA 85-1	A 0509-14	05 09	IC 4889	...	19 41
HA 85-2	A 1852-54	18 52	IC 5020	...	20 27
IC 749	...	11 56	IC 5052	...	20 47
IC 750	...	11 56	IC 5063	...	20 48
IC 764	...	12 07	IC 5105	...	21 21
IC 1459	...	22 54	IC 5135	...	21 45
IC 1783	...	02 07	IC 5152	...	21 59
IC 1788	...	02 13	IC 5156	...	22 00
IC 1933	...	03 24	IC 5179	...	22 13
IC 1953	...	03 31	IC 5181	...	22 10
IC 1954	...	03 30	IC 5201	...	22 17
IC 2006	...	03 52	IC 5240	...	22 38
IC 2035	...	04 07	IC 5267	...	22 54
IC 2056	...	04 15	IC 5269	...	22 54
IC 2522	...	09 52	IC 5271	...	22 55
IC 2537	...	10 01	IC 5273	...	22 56
IC 2627	...	11 07	IC 5325	...	23 26
IC 2995	...	12 03	IC 5328	...	23 30
IC 3253	...	12 21	IC 5332	...	23 31
IC 3370	...	12 24	LMC	A 0524-69	05 24
IC 3896	...	12 53	New 1	A 0102-06	01 02
IC 4296	...	13 33	New 2	NGC 4507	12 32
IC 4329	...	13 46	New 3	A 1246-09	12 46
IC 4351	...	13 55	New 4	A 1252+00	12 52
IC 4444	...	14 28	New 5	A 2020-44	20 20
IC 4662	...	17 42	New 6	A 2120-46	21 20
IC 4710	...	18 23	R80	NGC 4517A	12 29
IC 4721	...	18 30	SMC	A 0051-73	00 51

APPENDIX D. Cross-Reference Finding List When Two Names Are Used

Other Name	Main Name		Other Name	Main Name
IC 39	NGC 178		M65	NGC 3623
IC 520	Introduction		M66	NGC 3627
IC 629	NGC 3312		M74	NGC 628
IC 1712	NGC 584		M77	NGC 1068
IC 2133	NGC 1961		M81	NGC 3031
IC 2154	NGC 2139		M82	NGC 3034
IC 2571	NGC 3223		M83	NGC 5236
IC 2585	NGC 3271		M84	NGC 4374
IC 2613	NGC 3430		M85	NGC 4382
IC 3011	NGC 4124		M86	NGC 4406
IC 3042	NGC 4178		M87	NGC 4486
IC 3050	NGC 4189		M88	NGC 4501
IC 3098	NGC 4235		M89	NGC 4552
IC 3256	NGC 4342		M90	NGC 4569
IC 3569	NGC 4561		M94	NGC 4736
IC 3588	NGC 4571		M95	NGC 3351
IC 3708	NGC 4654		M96	NGC 3368
IC 4338	NGC 5334		M98	NGC 4192
IC 4895	NGC 6822		M99	NGC 4254
IC 4949	NGC 6861		M100	NGC 4321
IC 5184	IC 5179		M101	NGC 5457
NGC 5186	Introduction		M102	NGC 5866
IC 5228	NGC 7302		M104	NGC 4594
IC 5294	NGC 7552		M105	NGC 3379
M 31	NGC 224		M106	NGC 4258
M32	NGC 221		NGC 643	Introduction
M33	NGC 598		NGC 1048	Introduction
M49	NGC 4472		NGC 2149	Introduction
M51	NGC 5194		NGC 3189	NGC 3190
M58	NGC 4579		NGC 3397	NGC 3329
M59	NGC 4621		NGC 4160	Introduction
M60	NGC 4649		NGC 4507	New 2
M61	NGC 4303		NGC 4517A	R80
M63	NGC 5055		NGC 4657	NGC 4656
M64	NGC 4826		NGC 4872	Introduction
			NGC 6026	Introduction

PART VII

References

References A. The Sources of the Redshifts

As explained in the introductory sections, we have used the original literature to determine the weighted mean redshifts listed in the main table in Part II of this volume. The sources, coded by number in column 21 of the table, are identified here.

The references are given alphabetically from sources 1 through 361 as they were compiled to the middle of 1977. Later references were added as they became available, and these are listed in numerical order from sources 370 to 442.

For those galaxies where the number of references exceeds five, a single source-code, designated by $n \geq 500$, is shown in column 21 of the main table. Each separate reference for that galaxy is then listed after the $n \geq 500$ number by its own code number in the main part of the source list that follows.

1. Agüero, E., and Carranza, G. 1975, *Observatory 95*, 179.
2. Albada, G. D. van, and Shane, W. W. 1975, *Astron. Astrophys. 42*, 433.
3. Allen, R., Dardry, B., and Lauqué, R. 1971, *Astron. Astrophys. 10*, 198.
4. Allen, R. J., Goss, W. M., Sancisi, R., Sullivan, W. T. III, and Woerden, H. van 1974, *I. A. U. Symp. 58*, 425.
5. Allen, R. J., Hulst, J. M. van der, Goss, W. M., and Huchtmeier, W. 1976, *Astron. Astrophys.*, preprint.
6. Anderson, K. S. 1973, *Ap. J. 182*, 369.
7. Anderson, K. S. 1974, *Ap. J. 189*, 195.
8. Anderson, K. S., and Kraft, R. P. 1969, *Ap. J. 158*, 859.
9. Andrillat, Y. 1968, *Ap. J. 73*, 862.
10. Andrillat, Y., and Souffrin, S. 1967, *C. R. Acad. Sc. Paris 264*, B89.
11. Andrillat, Y., and Souffrin, S. 1970, *C. R. Acad. Sc. Paris 270*, B238.
12. Arakelyan, M. A., Dibai, E. A., and Esipov, V. F. 1972, *Astrofizika 8*, 33.
13. Arakelyan, M. A., Dibai, E. A., and Esipov, V. F. 1973, *Astrofizika 9*, 325.
14. Arakelyan, M. A., Dibai, E. A., and Esipov, V. F. 1975, *Astrofizika 11*, 15.
15. Arakelyan, M. A., Dibai, E. A., and Esipov, V. F. 1975, *Astrofizika 11*, 377.
16. Arakelyan, M. A., Dibai, E. A., Esipov, V. F., and Markaryan, B. E. 1970, *Astrofizika 6*, 189.
17. Arakelyan, M. A., Dibai, E. A., Esipov, V. F., and Markaryan, B. E. 1971, *Astrofizika 7*, 177.
18. Argyle, E. 1965, *Ap. J. 141*, 750.
19. Arp, H. 1977, *I. A. U. Coll. 37*, 377 (citing H. Ford *et al.*).
20. Arp, H. 1969, *Astron. Astrophys. 3*, 418.
21. Arp, H. 1970, *Astrophys. Letters 5*, 257.
22. Arp, H. 1976, *Ap. J. Letters 210*, L59.
23. Arp, H., and Bertola, F. 1970, *Astrophys. Letters 6*, 65.
24. Baade, W., and Minkowski, R. 1954, *Ap. J. 119*, 215.
25. Babcock, H. W. 1939, *Lick Obs. Bull. No. 498*.
26. Balick, B., Faber, S. M., and Gallagher, J. S. 1976, *Lick Obs. Bull. No. 726*.
27. Balkowski, C., Bottinelli, L., Gouguenheim, L., and Heidmann, J. 1972, *Astron. Astrophys. 21*, 303.
28. Balkowski, C., Bottinelli, L., Gouguenheim, L., and Heidmann, J. 1973, *Astron. Astrophys. 23*, 139.
29. Barbieri, C., Bertola, F., and di Tullio, G. 1974, *Astron. Astrophys. 35*, 463.
30. Barbon, R., and Capaccioli, M. 1974, *Astron. Astrophys. 35*, 151.
31. Barbon, R., and Capaccioli, M. 1975, *Astron. Astrophys. 42*, 221.
32. Beale, J. S., and Davies, R. D. 1969, *Nature 221*, 531.
33. Benvenuti, P., Capaccioli, M., and D'Odorico, S. 1975, *Astron. Astrophys. 41*, 91.
34. Bergh, S. van den 1969, *Ap. J. Suppl. 19*, 145.
35. Bertola, F. 1965, *Contr. Oss. Astrofis. Asiago, No. 172*, 95.
36. Bertola, F. 1966, *Mem. Soc. Astron. Ital. 37*, 433.
37. Bertola, F. 1972, *I. A. U. Symp. 44*, 34.
38. Bertola, F., and Capaccioli, M. 1975, *Ap. J. 200*, 439.
39. Bertola, F., D'Odorico, S., Ford Jr., W. K., and Rubin, V. C. 1969, *Ap. J. Letters 157*, L27.

40. Bohuski, T. J., Burbidge, E. M., Burbidge, G. R., and Smith, M. G. 1972, *Ap. J. 175*, 329.

41. Bosma, A., Hulst, J. M. v. d., and Sullivan, W. T. 1976, *Astron. Astrophys.*, preprint.

42. Bottinelli, L., Chamaraux, P., Gouguenheim, L., and Heidmann, J. 1973, *Astron. Astrophys. 29*, 217.

43. Bottinelli, L., Chamaraux, P., Gouguenheim, L., and Laugué, R. 1970, *Astron. Astrophys. 6*, 453.

44. Bottinelli, L., and Gouguenheim, L. 1973, *Astron. Astrophys. 26*, 85.

45. Bottinelli, L., and Gouguenheim, L. 1973, *Astron. Astrophys. 29*, 425.

46. Bottinelli, L., and Gouguenheim, L. 1976, *Astron. Astrophys. 47*, 381.

47. Bottinelli, L., Gouguenheim, L., and Heidmann, J. 1972, *Astron. Astrophys. 17*, 445.

48. Bottinelli, L., Gouguenheim, L., Heidmann, J., and Heidmann, N. 1968, *Ann. Astrophys. 31*, 205.

49. Bottinelli, L., Gouguenheim, L., Heidmann, J., Heidmann, N., and Weliachew, L. 1966, *C. R. Acad. Sc. Paris 263*, B223.

50. Boulesteix, J., Dubout-Crillon, R., and Monnet, G. 1970, *Astron. Astrophys. 8*, 204.

51. Brandt, J. C. 1965, *M. N. 129*, 309.

52. Brundage, W. D., and Kraus, J. D. 1966, *Science 153*, 411.

53. Burbidge, E. M., and Burbidge, G. R. 1959, *Ap. J. 129*, 271.

54. Burbidge, E. M., and Burbidge, G. R. 1960, *Ap. J. 132*, 30.

55. Burbidge, E. M., and Burbidge, G. R. 1962, *Ap. J. 135*, 366.

56. Burbidge, E. M., and Burbidge, G. R. 1962, *Nature 194*, 367.

57. Burbidge, E. M., and Burbidge, G. R. 1964, *Ap. J. 140*, 1445.

58. Burbidge, E. M., and Burbidge, G. R. 1965, *Ap. J. 142*, 634.

59. Burbidge, E. M., and Burbidge, G. R. 1965, *Ap. J. 142*, 1351.

60. Burbidge, E. M., and Burbidge, G. R. 1966, *Ap. J. 145*, 661.

61. Burbidge, E. M., and Burbidge, G. R. 1968, *Ap. J. 151*, 99.

62. Burbidge, E. M., and Burbidge, G. R. 1968, *Ap. J. 154*, 857.

63. Burbidge, E. M., and Burbidge, G. R. 1972, *Ap. J. 172*, 37–41.

64. Burbidge, E. M., Burbidge, G. R., Crampin, D. J., Rubin, V. C., and Prendergast, K. H. 1964, *Ap. J. 139*, 539.

65. Burbidge, E. M., Burbidge, G. R., Crampin, D. J., Rubin, V. C., and Prendergast, K. H. 1964, *Ap. J. 139*, 1058.

66. Burbidge, E. M., Burbidge, G. R., and Hoyle, F. 1963, *Ap. J. 138*, 873.

67. Burbidge, E. M., Burbidge, G. R., and Prendergast, K. H. 1959, *Ap. J. 130*, 26.

68. Burbidge, E. M., Burbidge, G. R., and Prendergast, K. H. 1959, *Ap. J. 130*, 739.

69. Burbidge, E. M., Burbidge, G. R., and Prendergast, K. H. 1960, *Ap. J. 131*, 282.

70. Burbidge, E. M., Burbidge, G. R., and Prendergast, K. H. 1960, *Ap. J. 131*, 549.

71. Burbidge, E. M., Burbidge, G. R., and Prendergast, K. H. 1960, *Ap. J. 132*, 640.

72. Burbidge, E. M., Burbidge, G. R., and Prendergast, K. H. 1960, *Ap. J. 132*, 654.

73. Burbidge, E. M., Burbidge, G. R., and Prendergast, K. H. 1960, *Ap. J. 132*, 661.

74. Burbidge, E. M., Burbidge, G. R., and Prendergast, K. H. 1961, *Ap. J. 133*, 814.

75. Burbidge, E. M., Burbidge, G. R., and Prendergast, K. H. 1961, *Ap. J. 134*, 232.

76. Burbidge, E. M., Burbidge, G. R., and Prendergast, K. H. 1961, *Ap. J. 134*, 237.

77. Burbidge, E. M., Burbidge, G. R., and Prendergast, K. H. 1961, *Ap. J. 134*, 874.

78. Burbidge, E. M., Burbidge, G. R., and Prendergast, K. H. 1962, *Ap. J. 136*, 128.

79. Burbidge, E. M., Burbidge, G. R., and Prendergast, K. H. 1962, *Ap. J. 136*, 339.

80. Burbidge, E. M., Burbidge, G. R., and Prendergast, K. H. 1962, *Ap. J. 136*, 704.

81. Burbidge, E. M., Burbidge, G. R., and Prendergast, K. H. 1963, *Ap. J. 137*, 376.

82. Burbidge, E. M., Burbidge, G. R., and Prendergast, K. H. 1963, *Ap. J. 137*, 1022.

83. Burbidge, E. M., Burbidge, G. R., and Prendergast, K. H. 1963, *Ap. J. 138*, 375.

84. Burbidge, E. M., Burbidge, G. R., and Prendergast, K. H. 1965, *Ap. J. 142*, 154.

85. Burbidge, E. M., Burbidge, G. R., and Prendergast, K. H. 1965, *Ap. J. 142*, 641.

86. Burbidge, E. M., Burbidge, G. R., and Prendergast, K. H. 1965, *Ap. J. 142*, 649.

87. Burbidge, E. M., Burbidge, G. R., and Rubin, V. C., 1964, *Ap. J. 140*, 942.

88. Burbidge, E. M., Burbidge, G. R., Rubin, V. C., and Prendergast, K. H. 1964, *Ap. J. 140*, 85.

89. Burbidge, E. M., Burbidge, G. R., Solomon, P. M., and Strittmatter, P. A. 1971, *Ap. J. 170*, 233.

90. Burbidge, E. M., and Demoulin, M.-H. 1969, *Astrophys. Letters 4*, 89.

91. Burbidge, E. M., and Hodge, P. M. 1971, *Ap. J. 166*, 1.

92. Burbidge, E. M., Strittmatter, P. A., Smith, H. E., and Spinrad, H. 1972, *Ap. J. Letters 178*, L43.

93. Burke, B. F., Turner, K. C., and Tuve, M. A. 1963, *Ann. Rep. Director Dept. Terrestrial Magnetism, Carnegie Institution of Washington, 1962–1963*, p. 293.

94. Burley, J. M. 1963, *A. J. 68*, 274.

95. Burns, W. R., and Roberts, M. S. 1971, *Ap. J. 166*, 265.

96. Carozzi, N. 1976, *Astron. Astrophys. 49*, 425.

97. Carozzi, N. 1976, *Astron. Astrophys. 49*, 431.

98. Carozzi, N., Chamaraux, P., and Duflot-Augarde, R. 1974, *Astron. Astrophys. 30*, 21.

99. Carranza, G. J. 1967, *Observatory 87*, 38.

100. Carranza, G. J. 1968, *Asoc. Argent. Astr. Bol., No. 14*.

101. Carranza, G. J., and Agüero, E. L. 1974, *Observatory 94*, 7.

102. Carranza, G., Courtèz, G., Georgelin, Y., Monnet, G., Pourcelot, A., and Astier, N. 1968, *Ann. d'Astrophys. 31*, 63.

103. Carranza, G., Crillon, R., and Monnet, G. 1969, *Astron. Astrophys. 1*, 479.

104. Catchpole, R. M., Evans, D. S., and Jones, D. H. P. 1969, *Observatory 89*, 21.

105. Cheriguène, M. F. 1975, *La dynamique des galaxies spirales*, L. Weliachew, ed., p. 420.

106. Chincarini, G., and Rood, H. J. 1972, *A. J. 77*, 4.

107. Chincarini, G., and Rood, H. J. 1972, *A. J. 77*, 448.

108. Chincarini, G., and Rood, H. J. 1976, *Ap. J. 206* 30.

109. Chincarini, G., and Walker, M. F. 1967, *Ap. J. 147*, 407.

110. Chincarini, G., and Walker, M. F. 1967, *Ap. J. 149*, 487.

111. Chromey, F. R. 1973, *Astron. Astrophys. 29*, 77.

112. Chromey, F. R. 1974, *Astron. Astrophys. 31*, 165.

113. Chromey, F. R. 1974, *Astron. Astrophys. 37*, 7.

114. Cottrell, G. A. 1976, *M. N. 174*, 455.

115. Crillon, R., and Monnet, G. 1969, *Astron. Astrophys. 1*, 449.

116. Crillon, R., and Monnet, G. 1969, *Astron. Astrophys. 2*, 1.

117. Damme, K. J. van 1966, *Australian J. Phys. 19*, 687.

118. Danziger, I. J., and Chromey, F. R. 1972, *Astrophys. Letters 10*, 99.

119. Davies, R. D. 1973, *M. N. 161*, 25P.

120. Davies, R. D., and Lewis, B. M. 1973, *M. N. 165*, 231.

121. Dean, J. F., and Davies, R. D. 1975, *M. N. 170*, 503.

122. Deharveng, J. M., and Pellet, A. 1969, *Astron. Astrophys. 1*, 208.

123. Deharveng, J. M., and Pellet, A. 1970, *Astron. Astrophys. 7*, 210.

124. Delannoy, J., Guélin, M., and Weliachew, L. 1967, private communication.

125. Demoulin, M.-H. 1965, *Publ. l'Observ. Haute-Provence 7*, 44.

126. Demoulin, M.-H. 1965, *Publ. l'Observ. Haute-Provence 8*, 1.

127. Demoulin, M.-H. 1969, *Ap. J. 157*, 69.

128. Demoulin, M.-H. 1969, *Ap. J. 157*, 75.

129. Demoulin, M.-H. 1969, *Ap. J. 157*, 81.

130. Demoulin, M.-H. 1970, *Ap. J. Letters 160*, L79.

131. Demoulin, M.-H., and Burbidge, E. M. 1970, *Ap. J. 159*, 799.

132. Demoulin, M.-H., and Chan, Y. W. Tung 1969, *Ap. J. 156*, 501.

133. Denisyuk, E. K. 1971, *Astron. Tsirk. 621*, 7.

134. Denisyuk, E. K., and Lipovetskii, V. A. 1974, *Astrofizika 10*, 315.

135. Denisyuk, E. K., and Pavlova, N. N. 1973, *Astron. Tsirk. 797*, 1.

136. Dickel, J. R., and Rood, H. J. 1975, *Ap. J. 80*, 584.

137. Dieter, N. H. 1962, *A. J. 67*, 217.

138. Dieter, N. H. 1962, *A. J. 67*, 317.

139. Disney, M. J., and Cromwell, R. H. 1971, *Ap. J. Letters 164*, L35.

140. D'Odorico, S. 1970, *Ap. J. 160*, 3.

141. Duflot, R. 1965, *J. des Observateurs 48*, 247.

142. Duflot, R., Lombard, J., and Perrin, Y. 1976, *Astron. Astrophys. 48*, 437.

143. Du Puy, D. L. 1970, *A. J. 75*, 1143.

144. Du Puy, D. L., and De Veny, J. B. 1969, *P.A.S.P. 81*, 637.

145. Elvins, A. 1964, *Nature 201*, 171.

146. Emerson, D. T., and Baldwin, J. E. 1973, *M. N. 165*, 9P.

147. Epstein, E. E. 1964, *A. J. 69*, 490.

148. Evans, D. S. 1952, *Observatory 72*, 164.

149. Evans, D. S. 1956, *M.N. 116*, 659.

150. Evans, D. S. 1963, *M.N.A.S.S.A. 22*, 140.

151. Evans, D. S. 1967, *Observatory 87*, 224.

152. Evans, D. S., and Harding, G. A. 1961, *M.N.A.S.S.A. 20*, 64.

153. Evans, D. S., and Malin, S. R. 1965, *M.N.A.S.S.A. 24*, 32.

154. Evans, D. S., and Wayman, P. A. 1958, *M.N.A.S.S.A. 17*, 137.

155. Foast, M. W., Thackeray, A. E., and Wesselink, A. J. 1961, *M. N. 122*, 433.

156. Fisher, J. R., and Tully, R. B. 1975, *Astron. Astrophys. 44*, 151.

157. Fisher, J. R., and Tully, R. B. 1976, *Astron. Astrophys. 53*, 397.

158. Fisher, J. R., and Tully, R. B. 1976, private communication.

159. Fisher, J. R., and Tully, R. B. 1976, *Astron. Astrophys. 54*, 661.

160. Fisher, J. R., and Tully, R. B. 1978, private communication.

161. Ford, W. K., Purgathofer, A. T., and Rubin, V. C. 1968, *Ap. J. Letters 153*, L39.

162. Ford, W. K., and Rubin, V. C. 1968, *P.A.S.P. 80*, 466.

163. Ford, W. K., and Rubin, V. C. 1968, *Ann. Rep. Director Dept. Terrestrial Magnetism, Carnegie Institution of Washington, 1967–1968*, p. 286.

164. Ford, W. K., Rubin, V. C., and Roberts, M. S. 1971, *A. J. 76*, 22.

165. Gates, H. S., Zwicky, F., Bertola, F., Ciatti, F., and Rudnicki, K. 1967, *A. J. 72*, 912.

166. Goad, J. W. 1974, *Ap. J. 192*, 311.

167. Gordon, K. J. 1971, *Ap. J. 169*, 235.

168. Gordon, K. J., Remage, N. H., and Roberts, M. S. 1968, *Ap. J. 154*, 845.

169. Gottesmann, S. T., and Davies, R. D. 1970, *M. N. 149*, 263.

170. Gottesmann, S. T., Davies, R. D., and Reddish, V. C. 1966, *M. N. 133*, 359.

171. Gottesmann, S. T., and Weliachew, L. 1975, *Ap. J. 195*, 23.

172. Gottesmann, S. T., and Wright, M. C. H. 1973, *Ap. J. 184*, 71.

173. Gouguenheim, L. 1969, *Astron. Astrophys. 3*, 281.

174. Greenstein, J. L. 1961, *Ap. J. 133*, 335.

175. Guélin, M., and Weliachew, L. 1969, *Astron. Astrophys. 1*, 10.

176. Guélin, M., and Weliachew, L. 1970, *Astron. Astrophys. 7*, 141.

177. Guélin, M., and Weliachew, L. 1970, *Astron. Astrophys. 9*, 155.

178. Heckathorn, H. 1972, *Ap. J. 173*, 501.

179. Heidmann, J. 1961, *B.A.N. 15*, 314.

180. Hoglund, B., and Roberts, M. S. 1965, *Ap. J. 142*, 1366.

181. Hubble, E., and Humason, M. L., in: Mayall, N. U. 1960, *Lick Observ. Bull. No. 566*.

182. Huchra, J., and Sargent, W. L. W. 1973, *Ap. J. 186*, 433.

183. Huchtmeier, W. 1972, *Astron. Astrophys. 17*, 207.

184. Huchtmeier, W. 1973, *Astron. Astrophys. 22*, 27.

185. Huchtmeier, W. 1973, *Astron. Astrophys. 22*, 91.

186. Huchtmeier, W. 1973, *Astron. Astrophys. 23*, 93.

187. Huchtmeier, W. K., and Bohnenstengel, H.-D. 1975, *Astron. Astrophys. 44*, 479.

188. Huchtmeier, W. K., Tammann, G. A., and Wendker, H. J. 1976, *Astron. Astrophys. 46*, 381.

189. Hulst, H. C. van de, Raimond, E., and Woerden, H. van 1957, *B.A.N. 14*, 1.

190. Humason, M. L., Mayall, N. U., and Sandage, A. R. 1956, *A. J. 61*, 97. (Mount Wilson-Palomar list of redshifts.)

191. Humason, M. L., Mayall, N. U., and Sandage, A. R. 1956, *A. J. 61*, 97. (Lick list of redshifts.)

192. Jager, G. de, and Davies, R. D. 1971, *M. N. 153*, 9.

193. Jenner, D. C. 1974, *Ap. J. 191*, 55.

194. Karachentsev, I. D., Pronik, V. I., and Chuvaev, K. K. 1976, *Astron. Astrophys. 51*, 185.

195. Kerr, F. J., and Vaucouleurs, G. de 1955, *Australian J. Phys. 7*, 297.

196. Khachikian, E. Ye. 1973, *Astrofizika 9*, 157.

197. Khachikian, E. Ye., and Panossian, H. A. 1972, *Astron. Tsirk. 698*, 1.

198. Khachikian, E. Ye., and Weedman, D. W. 1971, *Astrofizika 7*, 389.

199. Khachikian, E. Ye., and Weedman, D. W. 1974, *Ap. J. 192*, 581.

200. Kintner, E. C. 1971, *A. J. 76*, 409.

201. Kirshner, R. 1977, *Ap. J. 212*, 319.

202. Knapp, G. R., and Kerr, F. J. 1974, *A. J. 79*, 667.

203. Kormendy, J. 1976, Thesis, Calif. Inst. Techn.

204. Kowal, C. T., Zwicky, F., Sargent, W. L. W., and Searle, L. 1974, *P.A.S.P. 86*, 516.

205. Kruit, P. C. van der 1973, *Ap. J. 186*, 807.

206. Kruit, P. C. van der 1974, *Ap. J. 188*, 3.

207. Kruit, P. C. van der 1974, *Ap. J. 192*, 1.

208. Kruit, P. C. van der 1974, *I. A. U. Symp. 58*, 431.

209. Kruit, P. C. van der 1975, *Ap. J. 195*, 611.

210. Kruit, P. C. van der 1976, *Astron. Astrophys. 49*, 161.

211. Kruit, P. C. van der 1976, *Astron. Astrophys.*, preprint.

212. Krumm, N., and Salpeter, E. E. 1976, *Ap. J. Letters 208*, L7.

213. Kunkel, W. E., and Bradt, H. V. 1971, *Ap. J. Letters 170*, L7.

214. Lewis, B. M. 1967, unpublished Parkes observations in: Lewis, B. M. 1975, *Mem. R. A. S. 78*, 75.

215. Lewis, B. M. 1968, *Proc. Astron. Soc. Australia 1*, 104.

216. Lewis, B. M. 1970, *Observatory 90*, 264.

217. Lewis, B. M. 1972, *Australian Phys. 25*, 315.

218. Lewis, B. M. 1972, *I. A. U. Symp. 44*, 267.

219. Lewis, B. M. 1975, *Mem. R. A. S. 78*, 75.

220. Lewis, B. M., and Davies, R. D. 1973, *M. N. 165*, 213.

221. Lewis, B. M., and Robinson, B. J. 1973, *Astron. Astrophys. 23*, 295.

222. Lynds, C. R., and Sandage, A. R. 1963, *Ap. J. 137*, 1005.

223. McCutcheon, W. H., and Davies, R. D. 1970, *M. N. 150*, 337.

224. Martin, W. L. 1976, *M. N. 175*, 633.

225. Mathewson, D. S., Ford, V. L., and Murray, J. D. 1975, *Observatory 95*, 176.

226. Mayall, N. U. 1960, *Licks Obs. Bull. No. 566*.

227. Mayall, N. U., and Aller, L. H. 1942, *Ap. J. 95*, 5.

228. Mayall, N. U., Scott, E. L., and Shane, C. D. 1960, *Bull. Inst. Internat. Statist. 37*, 35.

229. Mayall, N. U., and Vaucouleurs, A. de 1962, *A. J. 67*, 363.

230. Meng, S. Y., and Kraus, J. D. 1966, *A. J. 71*, 170.

231. Minkowski, R. 1960, *Ann d'Astrophys. 23*, 385.

232. Minkowski, R. 1968, *A. J. 73*, 842.

233. Monnet, G. 1970, *I. A. U. Symp. 38*, 73.

234. Moore, J. H. 1915, *P. A. S. P. 27*, 192.

235. Morton, D. C., and Chevalier, R. A. 1972, *Ap. J. 174*, 489.

236. Morton, D. C., and Chevalier, R. A. 1973, *Ap. J. 179*, 55.

237. Munch, G. 1959, *P. A. S. P. 71*, 101.

238. Osmer, P. S., Smith, M. G., and Weedman, D. W. 1974, *Ap. J. 189*, 187.

239. Osmer, P. S., Smith, M. G., and Weedman, D. W. 1974, *Ap. J. 192*, 279.

240. Page, Th. 1967, *A. J. 72*, 821.

241. Page, Th. 1970, *Ap. J. 159*, 791.

242. Pastoriza, M. 1970, *Bol. Assoc. Argentina Astron. 15*, 1.

243. Pease, F. G. 1915, *P. A. S. P. 27*, 133.

244. Pease, F. G. 1920, *Ap. J. 51*, 276.

245. Peterson, B. A. 1970, *A. J. 75*, 695.

246. Peterson, C. J., Rubin, V. C., and Ford, W. K. 1976, *Bull. Amer. Astron. Soc. 8*, 297.

247. Peterson, S. D., and Shostak, G. S. 1974, *A. J. 79*, 767.

248. Raimond, E., and Volders, L. M. J. S. 1957, *B. A. N. 14*, 19.

249. Rickard, J. J. 1975, *Astron. Astrophys. 40*, 339.

250. Roberts, M. S. 1962, *A. J. 67*, 437.

251. Roberts, M. S. 1965, *Ap. J. 142*, 148.

252. Roberts, M. S. 1966, *Ap. J. 144*, 639.

253. Roberts, M. S. 1968, *Ap. J. 73*, 945.

254. Roberts, M. S. 1968, *Ap. J. 151*, 117.

255. Roberts, M. S. 1972, *I. A. U. Symp. 44*, 12.

256. Roberts, M. S. 1973, private communication.

257. Roberts, M. S., and Warren, J. L. 1970, *Astron. Astrophys. 6*, 165.

258. Robinson, B. J., and Damme, K. J. van 1966, *Australian J. Phys. 19*, 111.

259. Rodgers, A. W., and Freeman, K. C. 1970, *Ap. J. Letters 161*, L109.

260. Rogstad, D. H. 1971, *Astron. Astrophys. 13*, 108.

261. Rogstad, D. H., Rougoor, G. W., and Whiteoak, J. B. 1967, *Ap. J. 150*, 9.

262. Rogstad, D. H., and Shostak, G. S. 1972, *Ap. J. 176*, 315.

263. Rood, H. J., and Dickel, J. R. 1976, *Ap. J. 205*, 346.

264. Rood, H. J., Page, T. L., Kintner, E. C., and King, I. R. 1972, *Ap. J. 175*, 627.

265. Rots, A. H., and Shane, W. W. 1974, *Astron. Astrophys. 31*, 245.

266. Rubin, V. C., Burbidge, E. M., and Burbidge, G. R. 1964, *Ap. J. 140*, 94.

267. Rubin, V. C., Burbidge, E. M., and Burbidge, G. R. 1964, *Ap. J. 140*, 1304.

268. Rubin, V. C., Burbidge, E. M., Burbidge, G. R., Crampin, D. J., and Prendergast, K. H. 1965, *Ap. J. 141*, 759.

269. Rubin, V. C., Burbidge, E. M., Burbidge, G. R., and Prendergast, K. H. 1964, *Ap. J. 140*, 80.

270. Rubin, V. C., Burbidge, E. M., Burbidge, G. R., and Prendergast, K. H. 1965, *Ap. J. 141*, 885.

271. Rubin, V. C. and D'Odorico, S. 1969, *Astron. Astrophys. 2*, 484.

272. Rubin, V. C., and Ford, W. K. 1967, *P. A. S. P. 79*, 322.

273. Rubin, V. C., and Ford, W. K. 1968, *Ap. J. 154*, 431.

274. Rubin, V. C., and Ford, W. K. 1970, *Ap. J. 159*, 379.

275. Rubin, V. C., Ford, W. K., Thonnard, N., Roberts, M. S., and Graham, J. A. 1976, *A. J. 81*, 687.

276. Rubin, V. C., Ford, W. K., and D'Odorico, S. 1970, *Ap. J. 160*, 801.

277. Rubin, V. C., Ford, W. K., and Peterson, C. J. 1975, *Ap. J. 199*, 39.

278. Rubin, V. C., Peterson, C. J., and Ford, W. K. 1976, *Bull. Amer. Astron. Soc. 8*, 297.

279. Rubin, V. C., and Thonnard, N. 1974, unpublished.

280. Sakka, K., Oka, S., and Wakamatsu, K. 1973, *Publ. Astron. Soc. Japan 25*, 153.

281. Sakka, K., Oka, S., and Wakamatsu, K. 1973, *Publ. Astron. Soc. Japan 25*, 317.

282. Sancisi, P., Allen, R. J., and Albada, T. S. van 1975, *La dynamique des galaxies spirales*, L. Weliachew, ed., p. 295.

284. Sandage, A. 1978, *A. J. 83*, 904.

287. Sargent, W. L. W. 1970, *Ap. J. 160*, 405.

288. Sargent, W. L. W. 1972, *Ap. J. 173*, 7.

289. Sargent, W. L. W., Schechter, P. L., Boksenberg, A., and Shortridge, K. 1977, *Ap. J. 212*, 326.

290. Sargent, W. L. W., Searle, L., and Kowal, C. T. 1973, *Supernovae and Supernova Remnants*, C. B. Cosmovici, ed., p. 33.

292. Seielstad, G. A., and Whiteoak, J. B. 1965, *Ap. J. 142*, 616.

293. Seielstad, G. A., and Wright, M. C. H. 1973, *Ap. J. 184*, 343.

294. Sérsic, J. L. 1969, *Nature 224*, 253.

295. Sérsic, J. L., and Carranza, G. 1969, *Inf. Bull. Southern Hemisphere 14*, 32.

296. Sérsic, J. L., Carranza, G., and Pastoriza, M. 1972, *Astrophys. Space Sci. 19*, 469.

297. Shobbrook, R. R. 1966, *M. N. 131*, 293.

298. Shobbrook, R. R., and Robinson, B. J. 1967, *Australian J. Phys. 20*, 131.

299. Shostak, G. S. 1973, *Astron. Astrophys. 24*, 411.

300. Shostak, G. S. 1973, unpublished.

301. Shostak, G. S. 1975, *Ap. J. 198*, 527.

302. Siefert, P. T., Gottesman, S. T., and Wright, M. C. H. 1975, *La dynamique des galaxies spirales*, L. Weliachew, ed., p. 425.

303. Simkin, S. M. 1972, *Nature 239*, 43.

304. Simkin, S. M. 1975, *Ap. J. 195*, 293.

305. Slipher, V. M. 1917, *Proc. Am. Phil. Soc. 56*, 403.

306. Strömberg, G. 1925, *Ap. J. 61*, 352.

307. Struve, O., and Linke, W. 1940, *P. A. S. P. 52*, 139.

308. Tifft, W. G. 1973, *Ap. J. 179*, 29.

309. Tifft, W. G., and Gregory, S. A. 1976, *Ap. J. 205*, 696.

310. Tifft, W. G., and Tarenghi, M. 1975, *Ap. J. 199*, 10.

311. Tritton, K. P. 1972, *M. N. 158*, 277.

312. Tully, B. 1974, *Ap. J. Suppl. 27*, 415.

313. Turner, E. L. 1976, *Ap. J. 208*, 20.

314. Turner, K. C., Tuve, M. A., and Burke, B. F. 1963, *A. J. 68*, 295.

315. Ulrich, M.-H. 1971, *Ap. J. 163*, 441.

316. Ulrich, M.-H. 1972, *Ap. J. Letters 171*, L37.

317. Ulrich, M.-H. 1973, *Ap. J. 181*, 51.

319. Vaucouleurs, A. de, Shobbrook, R. R., and Strobel, A. 1976, *A. J. 81*, 219.

320. Vaucouleurs, A. de, and Vaucouleurs, G. de 1961, *Mem. R. A. S. 68*, 69.

321. Vaucouleurs, A. de, and Vaucouleurs, G. de 1967, *A. J. 72*, 730.

322. Vaucouleurs, G. de 1961, *Ap. J. 133*, 405.

323. Vaucouleurs, G. de 1962, *Ap. J. 137*, 720.

324. Vaucouleurs, G. de 1967, *I. A. U. Symp. 30*, 9.

325. Vaucouleurs, G. de 1972, *I. A. U. Symp. 44*, 353.

326. Vaucouleurs, G. de 1975, *Ap. J. Suppl. 29*, 193.

327. Vaucouleurs, G. de, and Vaucouleurs, A. de 1961, *Mem. R. A. S. 68*, 69.

328. Vaucouleurs, G. de, and Vaucouleurs, A. de 1963, *Ap. J. 137*, 363.

329. Vaucouleurs, G. de, and Vaucouleurs, A. de 1973, *Ap. J. 78*, 377.

330. Vaucouleurs, G. de, and Vaucouleurs, A. de 1973, *Astron. Astrophys. 28*, 109.

331. Vaucouleurs, G. de, and Vaucouleurs, A. de 1975, *Observatory 95*, 178.

332. Vaucouleurs, G. de, and Vaucouleurs, A. de 1976, *A. J. 81*, 595.

333. Vaucouleurs, G. de, Vaucouleurs, A. de, and Freeman, C. 1968, *M. N. 139*, 425.

334. Vidal, N. V., and Peterson, B. A. 1975, *Ap. J. Letters 196*, L95.

335. Volders, L. 1959, *B. A. N. 14*, 323.

336. Volders, L., and Högbom, J. A. 1961, *B. A. N. 15*, 307.

337. Volders, L., and Hulst, H. C. van de 1959, *Paris Symp. on Radio Astronomy*, p. 423.

338. Walker, M. F. 1968, *Ap. J. 151*, 71.

339. Walker, M. F., and Chincarini, G. 1967, *Ap. J. 147*, 416.

340. Walker, M. F., and Hayes, S. 1967, *Ap. J. 149*, 481.

341. Warner, P. J., Wright, M. C. H., and Baldwin, J. E. 1973, *M. N. 163*, 163.

342. Weedman, D. W. 1969, *Ap. J. Letters 155*, L129.

343. Weedman, D. W. 1970, *Ap. J. 159*, 405.

344. Weedman, D. W., and Khachikian, E. Ye. 1969, *Astrofizika 5*, 113.

345. Welch, G. A., Chincarini, G., and Rood, H. J. 1975, *A. J. 80*, 77.

346. Welch, G. A., and Wallerstein, G. 1969, *P. A. S. P. 81*, 23.

347. Weliachew, L. 1969, *Astron. Astrophys. 3*, 402.

348. Weliachew, L. 1971, *P. A. S. P. 83*, 609.

349. Weliachew, L. 1974, *Ap. J. 191*, 639.

350. Weliachew, L., and Gottesman, S. T. 1973, *Astron. Astrophys. 24*, 59.

351. West, R. M. 1976, *Astron. Astrophys. 53*, 436.

352. West, R. M. 1977, *Astron. Astrophys. Suppl. 27*, 73.

353. Westphal, J. A., Kristian, J., and Sandage, A. 1975, *Ap. J. Letters 197*, L95.

354. Whitehurst, R. N., and Roberts, M. S. 1972, *Ap. J. 175*, 347.

355. Whiteoak, J. B., and Gardner, F. F. 1971, *Astrophys. Letters 8*, 57.

356. Williams, T. B. 1975, *Ap. J. 199*, 586.

357. Wills, D. 1967, *Ap. J. Letters 148*, L57.

358. Winter, A. J. B. 1975, *M. N. 172*, 1.

359. Yahil, A., Tammann, G. A., and Sandage, A. 1977, *Ap. J. 217*, 903.

360. Zwicky, F. 1964, *Ap. J. 139*, 514.

361. Zwicky, F. 1971, *Catalogue of Selected Compact Galaxies and of Post-Eruptive Galaxies*.

370. Krumm, N. 1977, private communication.

371. Gardner, F. F., and Whiteoak, J. B. 1976, *Proc. A. S. A. 3*, 63.

372. Huchtmeier, W. K., Tammann, G. A., and Wendker, H. J. 1975, *Astron. Astrophys. 42*, 205.

372a. Huchtmeier, W. K., Tammann, G. A., and Wendker, H. J. 1977, *Astron. Astrophys. 57*, 313.

373. Whiteoak, J. B., and Gardner, F. F. 1973, *Astrophys. Letters 15*, 211.

374. Knapp, G. R., Gallagher, J. S., Faber, S. M., and Balick, B. 1977, *A. J. 82*, 106.

375. Barbieri, C., Serego Alighieri, S. di, and Zambon, M. 1977, *Astron. Astrophys. 57*, 353.

376. Bieging, J. H., and Biermann, P. 1977, *Astron. Astrophys. 60*, 361.

377. Bosma, A., Hulst, J. M. van der, and Sullivan, W. T. 1977, *Astron. Astrophys. 57*, 373.

378. Carranza, G. J., and Agüero, G. L. 1977, *Astrophys. Space Sci. 47*, 397.

379. Dawe, J. A., Dickens, R. J., and Peterson, B. A. 1977, *M. N. 178*, 675.

380. Eastmond, T. S., and Abell, G. O. 1978, *P. A. S. P. 90*, 367.

381. Faber, S. M., Balick, B., Gallagher, J. S., and Knapp, G. R. 1977, *Ap. J. 214*, 383.

382. Gregory, S. A., and Thompson, L. A. 1977, *Ap. J. 213*, 345.

383. Woerden, H. van, Mebold, U., Goss, W. M., and Siegman, B. 1977, private communication.

384. Roberts, M. S. 1976, private communication.

385. Peterson, S. D. 1979, *Ap. J. Suppl. 40*, 527.

386. Penston, M. V., Fosbury, R. A. E., Ward, M. J., and Wilson, A. S. 1977, *M. N. 180*, 19.

387. Whiteoak, J. B., and Gardner, F. F. 1977, *Aust. J. Phys. 30*, 187.

388. Wyckoff, S., and Wehinger, P. A. 1977, *Astrophys. Space Sci. 48*, 421.

389. Bieging, J. H. 1977, *Astron. Astrophys. 64*, 23.

390. Combes, F., Gottesman, S. T., and Weliachew, L. 1977, *Astron. Astrophys. 59*, 181.

391. Dickel, J. R., and Rood, H. J. 1978, *Ap. J. 223*, 391.

392. Shostak, G. S. 1978, *Astron. Astrophys. 68*, 321.

393. Agüero, E., and Carrazana, G. J. 1977, *Observatory 97*, 241.

394. Kruit, P. C. van der 1977, *Astron. Astrophys. 61*, 171.

395. Peterson, C. J., Rubin, V. C., Ford, W. K., and Thonnard, N. 1978, *Ap. J. 219*, 31.

396. Bergvall, N. A. S., Borchkhadze, T. M., Breysacher, J., Ekman, A. B. G., Laubert, A., Laustsen, S., Muller, A. B., Schuster, H.-E., Surdej, J., West, R. M., and Westerlund, B. E. 1978, *ESO Preprint No. 17*.

397. Bosma, A. 1978, Ph.D. Thesis, Groningen.

398. Peterson, C. J. 1978, *P. A. S. P. 90*, 10.

399. Peterson, C. J. 1978, private communication.

400. Thonnard, N., Rubin, V. C., Ford, W. K., and Roberts, M. S. 1978, *A. J. 83*, 1564.

401. Rubin, V. C., and Ford, W. K. 1978, in press.

402. Huchtmeier, W. K. 1979, private communication.

403. Carozzi-Meyssonnier, N. 1978, *Astron. Astrophys. 63*, 415.

404. Weliachew, L., Sancisi, R., and Guélin, M. 1978, *Astron. Astrophys. 65*, 37.

405. Heckman, T. M., Balick, B., and Sullivan, W. T. 1978, *Ap. J. 224*, 745.

406. Rubin, V. C., Ford, W. K., Strom, K. M., Strom, S. E., and Romanishin, W. 1978, *Ap. J. 224*, 782.

407. Barbon, R., Capaccioli, M., and Tifft, W. G. 1978, preprint.

408. Allen, R. M., and Shostak, G. S. 1979, *Astron. Astrophys. Suppl. 35*, 163.

409. Krumm, N., and Salpeter, E. E. 1978, preprint.

410. Kruit, P. C. van der, and Bosma, A. 1978, *Astron. Astrophys. Suppl. 34*, 259.

411. Huchra, J. P. 1979, private communication.

412. Silvergate, P. R., and Krumm, N. 1978, *Ap. J. Letters 224*, L99.

413. Knapp, G. R., Faber, S. M., and Gallagher, J. S. 1978, *A. J. 83*, 11.

414. Knapp, G. R., Gallagher, J. S., and Faber, S. M. 1978, *A. J. 83*, 139.

415. Knapp, G. R., Kerr, F. J., and Williams, B. A. 1978 *Ap. J. 222*, 800.

416. Bottinelli, L., and Gouguenheim, L. 1979, *Astron. Astrophys. 76*, 176.

417. Sandage, A. 1975, *Ap. J. 202*, 563.

418. Biermann, P., Clark, J. N., and Fricke, K. J. 1979, *Astron. Astrophys. 75*, 7.

419. Hawarden, T. G., Woerden, H. van, Mebold, U., Goss, W. H., and Peterson, B. A. 1979, *Astron. Astrophys. 76*, 230.

420. Sancisi, R., and Allen, R. J. 1979, *Astron. Astrophys. 74*, 73.

421. Mebold, H., Goss, W. M., Woerden, H. van, Hawarden, T. G., and Siegman, B. 1979, *Astron. Astrophys. 74*, 100.

422. Schechter, P. L., and Gunn, J. E. 1979, *Ap. J. 229*, 472.

423. Rubin, V. C., Ford, W. K., and Roberts, M. S. 1979, *Ap. J. 230*, 35.

424. Rubin, V. C. 1979, private communication.

425. Corwin, H. G. 1979, private communication.

426. Peterson, C. J., Rubin, V. C., Ford, W. K., and Thonnard, N. 1978, *Ap. J. 219*, 31.

427. Peterson, C. J., Rubin, V. C., Ford, W. K., and Roberts, M. S. 1978, *Ap. J. 226*, 770.

428. Rubin, V. C., Ford, K. W., Peterson, C. J., and Lynds, C. R. 1978, *Ap. J. Suppl. 37*, 235.

429. Rubin, V. C., Ford, K. W., and Thonnard, N. 1978, *Ap. J. Letters 225*, L107.

430. Krumm, N., and Salpeter, E. E. 1979, *A. J. 84*, 1138.

431. Vaucouleurs, G. de, Vaucouleurs, A. de, and Nieto, J.-L. 1979, *A. J. 84*, 1811.

432. Allsopp, N. J. 1979, *M. N. 188*, 765.

433. Knapp, G. R., Kerr, F. J., and Henderson, A. P. 1979, *Ap. J. 234*, 448.

434. Gallagher, J. S. 1979, *A. J. 84*, 1281.

435. Balkowski, C. 1979, *Astron. Astrophys. 78*, 190.

436. Sancisi, R., Allen, R. J., and Sullivan, W. T. 1979, *Astron. Astrophys. 78*, 217.

437. Sérsic, J. L., and Cerruti, M. A. 1979, *Observatory 99*, 150.

438. Sérsic, J. L., Arias, J. C., and Araujo, A. 1979, *Observatory 99*, 130.

439. Mebold, U. 1979, private communication.

440. French, H. 1980, private communication.

441. West, R. M. 1980, private communication.

442. Schechter, P. L. 1980, *A. J. 85*, 801.

501: 99, 147, 190, 258, 292, 327, (332), 387.

502: 18, 25, 34, 52, 93, 121, 122, 146, 169, 170, 189, 190, 191, 252, 271, 274, 289, 306, 332, 337, 354.

503: 190, 191, 289, 306, 319, (332), 337.

504: 79, 131, (149), 183, (190), 220, (337), 373, 387, 390.

505: 191, (196), 220, 229, 247, 263, 392.

506: 51, 93, 102, 121, 137, 167, 185, 190, 192, 227, 230, 248, 262, 306, 314, (332), 335, 337, 341.

507: 48, 121, 173, 190, 250, 261, 392.

508: 48, 121, 173, 180, 190, 191, 261, 263, 266, 284, 392, 430.

509: 173, 190, 229, 247, (306), 325, 389, 435.

510: 3, 67, 141, 190, 191, 199, 218, 220, 224, 232, (306), 338, 387, 391, 405.

511: 48, 54, 173, 190, 191, 249.

512: 26, 150, 216, 326, 327, (332), 387, 400, 421.

513: 26, 43, 46, 158, 284, 345, 421, 431, 439.

514: 48, 54, 154, 173, 229, 327.

515: 43, 46, 164, 190, 191, 253, 392.

516: 27, 33, 68, 105, 157, 190, 191.

517: (15), 48, 121, 160, 173, 191, 321, 391, 392.

518: 95, 123, 175, 190, 250, 292, 299.

519: 12, (15), 133, 160, 190, 191, 229, 263, 392.

520: 31, 160, (164), 190, 191, (229), (253), (306), (324).

521: 27, 58, 125, 190, 229, 247, 374, 389, 435.

522: 43, 46, 190, 191, 253, 263, (306), 325, 397.

523: 48, 71, 160, 173, 190, 191, 253, 304, 343.

524: 43, 46, 99, 158, 284, 325, (332), 387, 399, 400.

525: 164, 166, 171, 190, 191, 237, 255, 265, 306, 324, 325, 332, 337, 391.

526: 39, (48), 87, 145, (173), 177, 178, 190, 191, 222, 226, 306, 324, (336), 348, 349.

527: 29, 37, 114, 129, 190, 220, 255.

528: 49, 117, 121, 147, 160, 184, 191, 292, 387.

529: 106, 173, 190, 220, 229, 231, 236, 278, (306), (324), (332), (356).

530: 190, 191, 220, 263, 301, 325.

531: 48, 105, 173, 191, 253, 263, 397.

532: 3, 141, 163, 187, 190, 199, 218, 220, 232, 263, 313, 385, 405.

533: 35, 43, 46, 141, 190, 191, 210, 247, 339.

534: 105, 173, 191, 253, 263, 301.

535: 164, 190, 229, 263, 277, 279, 400.

536: 27, 190, 220, 229, 263, (306), 325.

537: 140, 164, 191, 241, 263, 301.

538: 9, 27, 190, 191, 199, 200, 232, (332), 431.

539: 48, 70, 105, 159, 173, 190, 191, 253, 261, 301, 408, 431.

540: 48, 173, 190, 229, 263, 284, (306), 325, 430.

541: 43, 46, 187, 190, 220, 247, 253, 391.

542: 60, 190, 229, 241, 247, 276, (307).

543: 3, 11, 141, 159, 190, 199, 218, 220, 232, 321, 391, 405.

544: 107, 136, 158, 263, 284, (370).

545: 106, 136, 158, 263, 284, (332).

546: 3, 7, 8, 10, 43, 46, 119, 141, 161, 190, 191, 199, (218), 220, 232, (306), 313, 317, 343, 391, 405.

547: 28, 30, 43, 159, 204, 284, 290, 384.

548: 105, 147, 160, 190, 191, 261, 292, (306), 432.

549: 2, 83, 109, 141, 160, 190, 207, 261, 306, 321.

550: 120, 188, 190, 223, 256, 343, 391, 392.

551: 28, 43, 120, 188, 190, 206, 256, 392.

552: 13, 106, 134, 136, 263, 284.

553: 116, 147, 173, 190, 229, 261, 306, 324.

554: 120, 139, 190, 202, 229, 283, (306), 442.

555: 36, 48, 50, 121, 141, 173, 190, 220, 229, 261, 391.

556: 139, 190, 191, 193, 229, (306), (332), 340, 442.

557: 120, 188, 190, 191, 256, 343.

558: 91, 120, 160, (190), 259, 330, 343.

559: 105, 116, 141, 147, 190, 229, 254, 261, 264, 328, (332), 347, 358, 391, 404, 430.

560: 89, 120, 172, 187, 188, 321.

561: 48, 105, 141, 147, 173, 191, 254, 264, 347, 358, 391, 404, 430.

562: 26, 106, 136, 200, 228, 263, 264, 281, 405.

563: 41, 55, 109, 141, 160, 190, 191, 206, 211, 261, (306), 377.

564: 191, 228, 284, 309, 310, 370.

565: 27, 160, 190, 220, 270, (306), (332), 430.

566: 69, 160, 190, 191, 261, 263, (306), 397, 410.

567: 24, 53, 56, (99), 152, 190, 213, 255, 294, 295, 325, 355, 371.

568: 48, 57, 103, 121, 160, 173, 179, 190, 229, 241, 257, 261, 263, (306), 312, 324, (332), 337, 350, 391.

569: 58, 190, 229, 241, 263, (306).

570: 5, 48, 105, 160, 173, 191, 253, 263, 391.

571: 45, 48, 99, 121, 147, 150, 173, 190, 215, (306), 321, 399.

572: 40, 46, 47 (99), 148, 150, 160, 190, 220, 296, 346, 387.

573: 32, 121, 138, 147, 176, 190, 229, 260, 261, 262, 263, 325, (332), 335, 337, 391.

574: 5, 32, 48, 173, 191, 263, 284, 301.

575: 5, 48, 160, 173, 191, 253, 263, 391, 392.

576: 164, 173, 190, 191, 223, 251, 392.

577: 43, 46, 164, 190, 191, 253, 391, 392.

578: 58, 190, 191, 193, 303, (306), 324.

579: 96, 173, 190, 191, 253, 301, 391.

580: 17, 142, 144, 182, 198, 284, 313, 321, 324, 337.

581: 28, 190, 191, 220, 247, 253, 263, 391.

582: 64, 160, 173, 191, 229, 253, 301, (332).

583: 43, 46, 190, 191, 253, 263, 392, 400.

584: 94, 190, 191, 229, 261, 336, 337.

585: 48, 121, 147, 168, 173, 190, 191, 261, 262.

586: 48, 64, 124, 173, 190, 191, 229, 253, (306), 332, 392, ·397, 430.

587: 6, 82, 190, 191, 199, 224, 232, 316, 375, 405, 415.

588: 27, 127, 190, 191, 247, 361, 376, 402.

589: 48, 121, 173, 191, 253, 261, 293, 321.

590: 14, 26, 58, 190, 191, 313.

591: 190, 191, 229, (306), 381, 429.

592: 58, 139, 190, 191, 289, (387), 414, 422, 442.

593: 153, 199, 224, 297, 327, 387.

594: 106, 136, 158, 263, 284, 384.

595: 160, 173, 190, 191, 224, 378, 387.

596: 21, 190, 223, 253, 313, 391.

597: 27, 141, 190, 229, 280, 394, 405, 435.

598: 159, 164, 190, 191, 391, 392.

599: 28, 30, 43, 158, 284, 391.

600: 164, 190, 191, 229, 253, 391, 397, 410.

601: 28, 78, 190, 191, 220, 392.

602: 43, 48, 191, 201, 391, 392.

603: 43, 46, 190, 199, 224, 392, 405.

604: 121, 147, 160, (190), 221, 387.

605: (191), 220, 321, 360, 391, 408.

606: 160, 173, 263, 301, 321, (332).

607: 28, 158, 160, 263, 284, (332), 431.

608: 58, 128, 190, 263, 376, 402, 409, 435.

609: 75, 160, 190, 229, 263, (306), 402, 409.

610: 160, 191, 261, 299, 337, 391.

611: 160, 186, 191, 250, 261, 292.

612: 120, 188, 190, 212, 374, 402, 409, 424.

613: 90, 160, 330, 391, 392, 405.

614: 141, 190, 198, 199, 232, (405).

615: 63, (99), (240), 373, 387, 398.

616: 4, 17, 80, 105, 395, 400, 401, 436.

617: 43, 46, 191, 376, 392, 400, 418.

618: 190, 253, 376, 391, 392, 418.

619: 59, 190, 199, 232, 246, 428.

620: 139, 190, 241, 372, 389, 415, 422.

621: 58, 190, 191, (229), 372, 413, 442.

622: 164, 173, 190, 401, 427, 429.
623: 160, 191, 261, 301, 391, 430.
624: 48, 173, 191, 264, 301, 430.
625: 147, 190, 292, 298, 387, 431.
626: (99), 158, 173, 284, 345, 431.
627: 43, 46, 191, 398, 400, 431.
628: 46, 158, 284, 384, 400, 431.

629: 43, 46, 190, 191, 374, 402, 435, 439.
630: (240), 284, 329, 351, 396, 438.
631: 153, 160, 173, 387, 431, 438.
632: 99, 158, 224, 284, 387, 438.
633: (141), 190, 191, 229, (306), 442.
634: (43), (46), 204, 284, 321, 402.

REFERENCES B. General References

Bucknell, M. J., and Peach, J. V. 1976, *Observatory 96*, 61.

Burstein, D., and Heiles, C. 1978, *Ap. J. 225*, 40.

Colomb, F. R., Poppel, W. G. L., and Heiles, C. 1977, *Astronomy and Astrophysics Suppl. 29*, 89.

Corwin, H. G. 1979, private communication.

Curtis, H. D. 1918, *Lick Obs. Pub. Vol. 13*.

de Vaucouleurs, G. 1959, *Handbuch der Physik 53*, 275.

de Vaucouleurs, G. 1977, *Ap. J. Suppl. 33*, 211.

de Vaucouleurs, G., and Bollinger, G. 1977a, *Ap. J. Suppl. 33*, 241.

de Vaucouleurs, G., and Bollinger, G. 1977b, *Ap. J. Suppl. 33*, 247.

de Vaucouleurs, G., and Bollinger, G. 1978, preprint.

de Vaucouleurs, G., and Corwin, H. G., Jr. 1977, *Ap. J. Suppl. 33*, 229.

de Vaucouleurs, G., Corwin, H. G., Jr., and Bollinger, G. 1977, *Ap. J. Suppl. 33*, 229.

de Vaucouleurs, G., and de Vaucouleurs, A. 1964, *Reference Catalog of Bright Galaxies*, Austin: University of Texas Press (*RC1*).

de Vaucouleurs, G., de Vaucouleurs, A., and Corwin, H. G. 1977, *Reference Catalog of Bright Galaxies*, 2nd ed., Austin: University of Texas Press (*RC2*).

de Vaucouleurs, G., and Pence, W. D. 1979, *Ap. J. Suppl. 40*, 425.

Dressler, A., and Sandage, A. 1978, *Pub. A.S.P. 90*, 5.

Dreyer, J. L. E. 1888, *New General Catalogue (NGC)*, *Memoirs Royal Astronomical Society, 49*.

Dreyer, J. L. E. 1895, *First Index Catalogue (IC)*, *Memoirs Royal Astronomical Society, 51*.

Dreyer, J. L. E. 1908, *Second Index Catalogue (IC)*, *Memoirs Royal Astronomical Society, 59*.

Fath, E. A. 1914, *A. J. 28*, 75.

Fisher, J. R., and Tully, R. B. 1975, *Astron. Astrophys. 44*, 151.

Godwin, J. G., Bucknell, M. J., Dijon, K. L., Green, M. R., Peach, J. V., and Wallis, R. E. 1977, *Observatory 97*, 238.

Graham, J. 1979, private communication on distance to NGC 300.

Hanson, R. B. 1980, *Star Clusters*, J. E. Hesser, ed., Dordrecht: D. Reidel (I.A.U. Symp. No. 85), p. 71.

Hardcastle, J. A. 1914, *M.N.R.A.S. 74*, 699.

Heidmann, J., Heidmann, N., and de Vaucouleurs, G. 1972, *Mem. R. Astr. Soc. 75*, 121.

Herzog, E. 1967, *Pub. A.S.P. 79*, 627.

Holmberg, E. 1958, *Medd Lund Obs. Ser. II, No. 136*.

Holmberg, E. 1964, *Ark. for Astron. 3*, 387.

Holmberg, E. B., Lauberts, A., Schuster, H.-E., and West, R. M. 1974, *Astron. Astrophys. Suppl. 18*, 463.

Holmberg, E. B., Lauberts, A., Schuster, H.-E., and West, R. M. 1975, *Astron. Astrophys. Suppl. 22*, 327.

Holmberg, E. B., Lauberts, A., Schuster, H.-E., and West, R. M. 1977, *Astron. Astrophys. Suppl. 27*, 295.

Holmberg, E. B., Lauberts, A., Schuster, H.-E., and West, R. M. 1978a, *Astron. Astrophys. Suppl. 31*, 15.

Holmberg, E. B., Lauberts, A., Schuster, H.-E., and West, R. M. 1978b, *Astron. Astrophys. Suppl. 34*, 285.

Holmberg, E. B., Lauberts, A., Schuster, H.-E., and West, R. M. 1979, *ESO Sci. Preprint No. 60*.

Hubble, E. 1922, *Ap. J. 56*, 162.

Hubble, E. 1926, *Ap. J. 64*, 321.

Humason, M. L., Mayall, N. U., and Sandage, A. 1956, *A. J. 61*, 97.

Keeler, J. E. 1900, *Ap. J. 11*, 325.

Kraan-Korteweg, R. C., and Tammann, G. A. 1979, *Astron. Nach 300*, 181.

Lewis, B. M. 1975, *Mem. Roy. Astron. Soc. 78*, 75.

Lewis, B. M. 1977, *I. A. U. Coll. No. 37*, p. 173.

Lundmark, K. 1927, *Medd. Astr. Obs. Uppsala No. 3*.

Melnick, J. 1978, *Astron. Astrophys. 70*, 157.

Nilson, P. 1973, *Uppsala General Catalogue of Galaxies*, Uppsala: Royal Society of Sciences of Uppsala.

Pease, F. G. 1917, *Ap. J. 46*, 24.

Pease, F. G. 1920, *Ap. J. 51*, 276.

Perrine, C. D. 1904, *Lick Obs. Bull. No. 64*.

Roberts, M. S. 1972, *I. A. U. Symp. 44*, 12.

Rubin, V. C., Ford, W. K., Thonnard, N., Roberts, M. S., and Graham, J. A. 1976, *A. J. 81*, 687.

Sandage, A. 1961, *Hubble Atlas of Galaxies*, Carnegie Institution of Washington Publication 618.

Sandage, A. 1973, *Ap. J. 183*, 711.

Sandage, A. 1975a, in *Galaxies and the Universe*, Sandage, A., Sandage, M., and Kristian J., eds., University of Chicago Press, Chapter 1.

Sandage, A. 1975b, *Ap. J. 202*, 563.

Sandage, A. 1978, *A. J. 83*, 904.

Sandage, A. 1981, in preparation.

Sandage, A., and Brucato, R. 1979, *A. J. 84*, 472.

Sandage, A., and Brucato, R. 1981, *A. J.*, in press.

Sandage, A., and Tammann, G. A. 1971, *Ap. J. 167*, 293.

Sandage, A., and Tammann, G. A., 1974a, *Ap. J. 190*, 525.

Sandage, A., and Tammann, G. A. 1974b, *Ap. J. 191*, 603.

Sandage, A., and Tammann, G. A. 1974c, *Ap. J. 194*, 223.

Sandage, A., and Tammann, G. A. 1975, *Ap. J. 196*, 313.

Sandage, A., and Tammann, G. A. 1976, *Ap. J. 210*, 7.

Sandage, A., Tammann, G. A., and Hardy, E. 1972, *Ap. J. 172*, 253.

Sandage, A., Tammann, G. A., and Yahil, A. 1979, *Ap. J. 232*, 352 (Paper I).

Sandage, A., and Visvanathan, N. 1978, *Ap. J. 223*, 707.

Seyfert, C. K. 1937, *H. A. 105*, 219.

Shapley, H., and Ames, A. 1932, *Annals of the Harvard College Observatory 88, No. 2*.

Stebbins, J., and Whitford, A. E. 1952, *Ap. J. 115*, 284.

Tammann, G. A. 1977, *Mitt. Astron. Ges. No. 42*.

Tammann, G. A., Sandage, A., and Yahil, A. 1980, *Physica Scripta 21*, 630.

Tammann, G. A., and Sandage, A. 1968, *Ap. J. 151*, 825.

Tammann, G. A., Yahil, A., and Sandage, A. 1979, *Ap. J. 234*, 775 (Paper II).

Tammann, G. A., Yahil, A., and Sandage, A. 1981, *Ap. J.* in preparation (Paper V).

van Altena, W. F. 1974, *Pub. A. S. P. 86*, 217.

van den Bergh, S. 1960a, *Ap. J. 131*, 215.

van den Bergh, S. 1960b, *Ap. J. 131*, 558.

van den Bergh, S. 1960c, *Pub. David Dunlap Observatory 2*, 159.

Véron, M. P., and Véron, P. 1974, *Astron. Astrophys. Suppl. 18*, 309.

Véron, M. P., and Véron, P. 1978, unpublished.

Wegner, G. 1979, *Astrophys. Space Sci. 60*, 15.

Yahil, A., Tammann, G. A., and Sandage, A. 1977, *Ap. J. 217*, 903.

Yahil, A., Sandage, A., and Tammann, G. A. 1980, *Ap. J. 242*, in press (Paper III).